COMPANY LAW AND ECONOMIC PROTECTIONISM

Company Law and Economic Protectionism

New Challenges to European Integration

Edited by
ULF BERNITZ
and
WOLF-GEORG RINGE

OXFORD
UNIVERSITY PRESS

OXFORD
UNIVERSITY PRESS

Great Clarendon Street, Oxford OX2 6DP

Oxford University Press is a department of the University of Oxford.
It furthers the University's objective of excellence in research, scholarship,
and education by publishing worldwide in

Oxford New York

Auckland Cape Town Dar es Salaam Hong Kong Karachi
Kuala Lumpur Madrid Melbourne Mexico City Nairobi
New Delhi Shanghai Taipei Toronto

With offices in

Argentina Austria Brazil Chile Czech Republic France Greece
Guatemala Hungary Italy Japan Poland Portugal Singapore
South Korea Switzerland Thailand Turkey Ukraine Vietnam

Oxford is a registered trade mark of Oxford University Press
in the UK and in certain other countries

Published in the United States
by Oxford University Press Inc., New York

First Edition 2010

British Library Cataloguing-in-Publication Data
Data available

Library of Congress Cataloging in Publication Data
Data available

Typeset by Newgen Imaging Systems (P) Ltd., Chennai, India
Printed in Great Britain
on acid-free paper by
CPI Antony Rowe,
Chippenham, Wiltshire

ISBN HB 978–0–19–959145–9

1 3 5 7 9 10 8 6 4 2

Preface

This book offers a perspective on the interaction of company law and states' protectionist attitudes, two areas which at first sight do not seem to be very strongly connected. We hope to show, however, that—beyond the obvious area of trade policy—economic protectionism plays a role in the design of company laws: takeovers, restructurings, golden shares, and Sovereign Wealth Funds are just a few examples of the rich arsenal potentially at hand for regulators wishing to protect national markets.

The topic has become even more relevant since the global financial crisis of 2007/08. In their reaction to that crisis, European leaders have been making a virtue of big government and state intervention. Bail outs were among the first responses to the economic contraction and Sovereign Wealth Funds have gained unprecedented influence. The crisis has truly awoken the old steering tool of protectionism, which the European Union was supposed to overcome.

The contributions in this volume represent the fruit of an academic conference held at Christ Church, Oxford, on 1 October 2009, which brought together a group of leading experts in European company law to discuss these recent developments and possible regulatory or policy responses. Amongst others, the contributions particularly focused on takeovers and restructurings, free movement of capital, Sovereign Wealth Funds, and the internal market.

The conference was held under the auspices of the Institute of European and Comparative Law and was generously funded by the Wallenberg Foundation Oxford/Stockholm Association in European Law.

Special thanks are due to Jenny Dix for her great support in organizing the conference and to James Morrison for excellent editing assistance.

Ulf Bernitz
Wolf-Georg Ringe

Oxford, May 2010

Summary Contents

Detailed Contents

IV. HOW TO OVERCOME ECONOMIC PROTECTIONISM?

Contributors

Ulf Bernitz is Professor of European Law at Stockholm University, Visiting Professor of Örebro University, as well as Senior Research Fellow at St Hilda's College, University of Oxford. He is also Director for the Wallenberg Foundation Oxford/Stockholm Association in European Law, based at the Institute of European and Comparative Law, University of Oxford. His research interests are in the field of European law and private law (especially consumer law, market law, and intellectual property law).

Andrea Biondi is Professor of European Union Law and the Co-Director of the Centre for European Law at King's College, London. He is a Visiting Professor at the College of Europe in Warsaw and at Georgetown University. He is a member of the Bar of Florence as well as being an Academic Member of Francis Taylor Buildings Chambers in London. Professor Biondi is on the International Advisory Board of *European Public Law, King's College Law Journal, London Law Review, the European Public Private Partnership Law Review* and he is the General Editor of the *Kluwer European Law Collection*.

Paul Davies is the Allen & Overy Professor of Corporate Law at the University of Oxford and Professorial Fellow of Jesus College. He was educated at the Universities of Oxford (MA), London (LLM), and Yale (LLM). He was elected a Fellow of the British Academy in 2000, an honorary Queen's Counsel in 2006, and an honorary Bencher of Gray's Inn in 2007. He is a deputy chairman of the Central Arbitration Committee. His first teaching job was as Lecturer in Law at the University of Warwick (1969–1973). He was then elected Fellow and Tutor in Law at Balliol College, Oxford and successively CUF Lecturer, Reader, and Professor in the Faculty. Between 1998 and 2009 he was the Cassel Professor of Commercial Law at the London School of Economics and Political Science.

Horst Eidenmüller is the Professor and Chair of Private Law, German, European, and International Company Law at the University of Munich. He joined the Faculty of Law at the University of Oxford as a Visiting Professor in October 2009. A graduate of Cambridge and Munich University, Eidenmüller has held a research professorship at Munich University since 2003. The focus of his work is on company and insolvency law and on dispute resolution. Eidenmüller is a member of the Berlin-Brandenburg Academy of Sciences and Humanities and a Research Associate of the European Corporate Governance Institute (ECGI).

Andreas Engert is a Professor of Private Law, Company Law, and Law & Economics at the University of Cologne. He obtained his First State Exam at the University of Tübingen in 1997 and his Second State Exam (bar exam equivalent) at the Higher Regional Court of Stuttgart in 1999. He earned an LLM degree from the University of Chicago School of Law in 2000 and a Dr jur from the University of Munich in 2003. Andreas Engert has published on lender liability, corporate finance law, tax law, and the theory of social norms. His main research interests include corporate law, securities law, and law and economics.

Klaus J Hopt is Emeritus Professor at the Max Planck Institute of Foreign Private and Private International Law, Hamburg, Germany. His university experience records professorships of law in Tübingen (1974–78, 1980–85), at the European University Institute, Florence, Italy (1978–80), in Bern, Switzerland (1985–87), in Munich (1987–95) and various visiting professorships in Belgium, France, Italy, Japan, The Netherlands, Switzerland, and the USA. His professional career includes: judge at the State Court of Appeals of Stuttgart/senate for commercial law and trade regulation (1981–85), member of the High Level Group of Company Law Experts, European Commission, Brussels (2001–02), vice president of the German Research Foundation (2003–08), expert for the German Parliament, the German Federal Constitutional Court, various German ministries, the German Central Bank, the European Commission, Bulgaria, and the World Bank. He is author, editor, and co-editor of publications in the field of corporate and commercial law, particularly on corporate governance and takeover law.

Lars Hornuf is currently Visiting Scholar at UC Berkeley. He obtained his MA in Political Economy from the University of Essex in 2005. After working for Deutsche bank and the Ifo Institute for Economic Research he took up his current position as research Associate at the chair for civil law, German, European, and International Business law at the University of Munich. His current research interest is in the empirical analysis of corporate and capital market laws.

Andrew Johnston is a Senior Lecturer at the TC Beirne School of Law, The University of Queensland. He obtained his MA in Law from Cambridge in 1993 and after gaining a Diploma in Legal Practice from the College of Law he qualified and practised as a solicitor with Herbert Smith in London, before moving to the Treasury Solicitor. Between 1998 and 2000 he taught English and European Law at the University of Warsaw. Between 2000 and 2003 he wrote a doctoral thesis at the European University Institute in Florence, Italy, entitled 'Theories of the company, employees and takeover regulation'. Since then he has been a lecturer at the University of Sheffield, a fellow and college lecturer in law at Jesus College, Cambridge, and a Newton Trust Lecturer in the Faculty of Law, University of Cambridge, where he lectured in Company Law and Law and Economics. He is also a Research Associate at the Centre for Business Research at the University of Cambridge and has acted as an external examiner for the LLM at the University of London and King's College, London. Andrew Johnston teaches and researches company law, corporate governance, and law and economics, and has a particular interest in economic and sociological theories of regulation.

Jodie A Kirshner is is a University Lecturer in Corporate Law at Cambridge University, a fellow of Peterhouse College, Cambridge and the Assistant Director of the Cambridge Centre for Corporate and Commercial Law. She is also affiliated with the Cambridge Centre for Business Research and has visiting relationships with US based law schools. She has completed research fellowships at the Oxford Centre for Socio-Legal Studies and the Cambridge Centre for Business Research as a Fulbright Scholar, the London Business School Centre for Corporate Governance, and the Max Planck Institute for Comparative and International Private Law. She received her undergraduate degree from Harvard University and graduate degrees from Columbia S University in New York. As a practising lawyer, she served as a federal judicial clerk on the US Court of Appeals for the Third Circuit and worked as a litigator at Davis Polk & Wardwell LLP and Cravath Swaine & Moore LLP in New York. She is also a Term Member of the Council on Foreign Relations.

Paul Krüger Andersen has been a Full Professor at the Department of Business Law, University of Aarhus since 1991. His research interests are company law, securities law, and market law. He became a solicitor in 1971, joining the staff at ASB in the same year. Currently Head of Company Law Group and Member of Corporate Governance group, he also sits on the board of the Danish Corporate Governance Association and of the Nordic network for company law. Alongside these roles he is a PhD co-ordinator and a Member of Ministry of Trade Working Group on a Corporate Governance Code of Conduct and a Member and co-founder of L'Association Européenne du droit de la publicité, as well as being the Editor of *Nordisk Tidsskrift for selskabsret* (Nordic Journal of Company Law).

Jesper Lau Hansen is the Professor of Financial Markets Law in the Faculty of Law, University of Copenhagen and head of the Research centre FOCOFIMA. Educated in Copenhagen and Cambridge, he worked for six years with a law firm before joining the University of Copenhagen. Currently working with the regulation of public limited companies in the Nordic countries, he also has research interests in financial markets law, corporate law, corporate finance, corporate governance, competition and marketing law, and EU law.

Jennifer Payne is a Reader in Corporate Finance Law at the University of Oxford. She joined the Faculty of Law in October 1998, having previously been at Robinson College, Cambridge. A Fellow of Merton College, Oxford, her main research interests are company law, corporate finance law, and trusts law with particular reference to fiduciary duties. She currently holds the Travers Smith Lectureship in Corporate Finance Law. Jennifer Payne teaches company law and trusts at undergraduate level and a number of corporate options on the BCL/MJur course, principally corporate finance law and corporate insolvency law.

Katharina Pistor is Michael I. Sovern Professor of Law at Columbia Law School, New York, teaching courses on corporate law, European and comparative private law, and law and development. Previously she held appointments as Assistant Professor for Public Policy from 2000–2001 at the Kennedy School of Government, Harvard University. Between 1998–99, she was a Research Associate at the Max Planck Institute for Comparative and International Private Law, Hamburg, where she was in charge of section on East European and Russian Law. With her main areas of research being company law and corporate governance, regulation of institutional investors, capital market development, and contract enforcement in transition economies, she has also held positions as Lecturer at Harvard Law School, Research Associate at the Harvard Institute for International Development, and Senior Research Fellow, Central European University Privatization Project.

Arad Reisberg is currently a Reader in Corporate and Financial Law and Vice Dean for Research at the Faculty of Laws, University College London (UCL). He is also the Director of the Centre for Commercial Law and Co-Director of the Centre for Law and Economics. He has been teaching at UCL since September 2003, and joined full-time in September 2006. He was formerly a Senior Arts Scholar (2001–2003) and a Tutor at Pembroke College, Oxford, where he taught law at six colleges at Oxford University between 2001–2005. He has also been a Visiting Lecturer at Oxford University (2005) and most recently a Lecturer at Warwick Law School (2005–2006). He is the recipient of numerous academic scholarships and awards and has written widely on shareholder remedies and directors' duties. He is an Academic Member of ECGI (European Corporate Governance Institute), a co-editor of *Pettet's Company Law*, sits on the editorial boards of the journal *International Corporate Rescue* and the journal *Corporate Ownership and Control*, and is a contributing author to *Annotated Companies Acts* (Oxford University Press, looseleaf).

Jonathan Rickford is a Visiting Professor in Corporate law at the London School of Economics. He holds Masters and BCL degrees from Oxford University and was a barrister from 1971 to 1985 and is now a solicitor. He was the Project Director of the UK Government's independent Review of Company Law from 1998 to 2001 (the 'Company Law Review') and a member of the Review Steering Group. He was also a member of the European Commission's High Level Group (the 'Winter' Group) on company law (2001–2002). He was in the Government legal service from 1972 to 1987, serving in Trade and Industry departments and in the Attorney General's Office. His main concerns were in company law, European commercial law and its harmonization, economic regulation, counter-inflation, competition, and industrial policy and privatization. He was the Solicitor to the Department of Trade and Industry from 1984 to 1987. At BT plc, he was Solicitor and Chief Legal Adviser from 1987–1989, Director of Government Relations from 1989–1993, and Director of Corporate Strategy from 1993–1996. He was a Competition Commissioner (member of the senior competition policy tribunal) from 1997 to 2005. He was also the Director of the Company Law Centre at the British Institute of International and Comparative Law from 2002 to 2005. In 2001 he was made a Commander of the British Empire.

Wolf-Georg Ringe is a Lecturer in Law at the University of Oxford, Deputy Director of the Institute of European and Comparative Law, and Fellow of Christ Church. He is an associate member of the Oxford-Man Institute of Quantitative Finance. In spring 2010, he was a Visiting Professor of Law at Columbia Law School, New York. He came to Oxford in 2007 after having worked at the Max Planck Institute for Comparative and International Private Law in Hamburg, Germany, having received his legal education in Passau, Lausanne, Bonn (PhD 2006), Oxford (Christ Church, MJur 2004), and Hamburg where he qualified as a German barrister ('Rechtsanwalt'). Georg Ringe teaches comparative and European corporate law, European business regulation, company law, European Union law, and German law. His current research interests are in the general area of law and finance, company law, conflict of laws, and European law.

Edmund-Philip Schuster is a Lecturer in Law at the London School of Economics. Previously, he practised corporate law with Baker & McKenzie LLP in London and Vienna. From 2004 through 2009 he worked for the Austrian Takeover Commission, serving as head of office (2006–2008) and legal consultant (2008–2009). He also taught company and commercial law as an external lecturer at the Vienna University of Economics and Business Administration. He holds law degrees from the University of Vienna and the London School of Economics.

Heike Schweitzer is Professor at the European University Institute in Florence, Italy. Her major research interests are in the fields of European and comparative company and contract law, with a focus on mergers & acquisitions, in corporate governance, and in comparative and European competition law, including competition law in regulated industries (telecommunications, media, energy), state aid law, and public procurement law. Before joining the EUI, she was a Senior Research Fellow at the Max Planck Institute for Comparative and International Private Law (2000–2004), a Junior Professor in the Erasmus Mundus Programme for Law and Economics at Hamburg University (2004–2006), and a Research Fellow at the Center for Law and Economic Studies at Columbia Law School (2005–2006). Her PhD dealt with the liberalization of telecommunications, energy, and postal services in Europe and the concept of 'universal service' and 'service public'. For her thesis, she was awarded the Otto-Hahn-Medal of the Max Planck Society. In 2000, she received the LLM degree from Yale Law School.

Emilie Van De Walle De Ghelcke is an associate at Freshfields Bruckhaus Deringer LLP and a member of the Brussels bar. She is a former research assistant at the London School of Economics. She received her legal education in Louvain (*Licence en droit,* 2004), Brussels (Master in Economic Law, 2005) and at the London Schoo of Economics (LLM, 2009).

Crispin Waymouth has been a Policy Advisor in the Regulatory Affairs Department of the Institute of International Finance in Washington DC since May 2010, covering international securities, supervision and market infrastructure issues. At the time of writing the paper, he was working in the Free Movement of Capital and Financial Integration Unit of the European Commission in Brussels as part of a ten-and-a-half-year period working for the Commission on financial market regulation, including a stint in Washington DC from 2004–2008 as First Secretary (Financial) at the Commission's Delegation to the United States. Prior to the Commission, he spent five years in HM Treasury, London, working on European and public spending issues. He holds a bachelor's degree in Philosophy, Politics, and Economics from Exeter College, Oxford and a master's degree in European studies from the College of Europe.

Table of Cases

EUROPEAN UNION

Case

Germany

United Kingdom

USA

Table of Legislation

EUROPEAN UNION

Treaties

Directives and regulations (in chronological order)

Non-binding (in chronological order)

Danmark

USA

1

Company Law and Economic Protectionism—an Introduction

Wolf-Georg Ringe and Ulf Bernitz

I.

Protectionism is a phenomenon as old as mankind. When we think of protectionism, we remember statesmen like Jean-Baptiste Colbert, the French finance minister under King Louis XIV, whose policies included increasing tariffs and instituting other protectionist policies for French manufacturers. Mercantilist economic theory dominated Western European economic policies from the sixteenth to the late eighteenth century.

And yet, its ghost has and is still coming back from time to time.[1] The most recent example is the worldwide reaction to the 2007/08 financial crisis. Of course, heads of state of the G20 group of nations at their Washington summit in November 2008 strongly pledged to abstain from imposing any trade protectionist measures.[2] Despite insisting that they would refrain from raising protectionist instruments, 17 of these 20 countries were reported by the World Bank as having imposed trade restrictive measures since then.[3] In its report from 2009, the World Bank stated that most of the world's major economies were resorting to protectionist measures as the global economic slowdown began to bite.

The World Bank's observations do not come alone. Many institutions, watchdogs, and governments have uttered concern that countries hit by the financial

[1] See J Bhagwati, 'Protectionism' in D R Henderson (ed), *The Concise Encyclopedia of Economics* (2nd edn, Liberty Fund, 2007).

[2] Statement from G20 Summit, *New York Times* (16 November 2008). Cf the reiteration at the London Summit—Leaders' Statement, 2 April 2009, <http://www.londonsummit.gov.uk/resources/en/PDF/final-communique>.

[3] E Gamberoni and R Newfarmer, 'Trade Protection: Incipient but Worrisome Trends'; World Bank Trade Notes 37/2009, <http://siteresources.worldbank.org/NEWS/Resources/Trade_Note_37.pdf> (last accessed 8 July 2010).

meltdown may resort to protectionist measures. Crises can turn even the closest allies into competitors.

We have observed this behaviour in many areas of public life and activity. Apart from direct trade measures, a number of countries introduced sector-specific bail out packages targeted to support crisis-hit companies, such as automobile firms.[4] The most blatant move was the German Government's hypocritical decision to label the national car scrappage scheme as an 'environmental bonus'. These programmes distort resource allocation, and prove disadvantageous for other sectors and competitors in other countries—thereby effectively becoming trade barriers. Discriminatory procurement actions such as the 'Buy American' clause included in stimulus packages are clearly not right since they run the risk of encouraging retaliation and severely constrain supply chains that use imported inputs.

Also, governments across the world ran into very high fiscal deficits in the process of rescuing their economies. Remaining un-protectionist is necessary, yet not sufficient. It is vital to intensify the process of trade facilitation and removal of the persistent non-tariff border barriers to trade. Diverting resources to trade-creating investment is vital. The G20's commitment of US $250 billion for trade finance is noteworthy in this context, as the decline in trade credit contributed significantly to the fall in trade flows. It is also clear that this needs to be done in a politically palatable manner. The governments will have to tread cleverly the thin line between protectionist measures that help the domestic economy while taking action to accelerate global trade.

It is important to note that protectionism is not only a problem at the national level. Even trade blocks like the European Union, which were set up to overcome trade barriers, are also tempted to use the opportunity to regulate particular issues in a protectionist way. An example is the Draft EU Directive on Alternative Investment Fund Managers:[5] The proposed 'European passport' for EU Hedge Funds entails conditions for marketing of non-EU alternative investment funds (AIFs) and for the marketing of non-EU AIFs by third-country managers in the EU. The conditions imposed would make it harder for non-EU funds and managers to obtain the passport to operate in the EU. This attempt, while laudable in principle, has been criticized as disguised protectionism and the creation of a 'fortress Europe', which will ultimately not benefit European investors.[6] Commentators pointed out that other countries like the US or Australia could even retaliate and prevent European funds from being sold in their respective jurisdictions.

[4] 'Subsidies to stimulate car sales' *The Economist* (4 August 2009).

[5] European Commission, Proposal of 30 April 2009 for a Directive of the European Parliament and of the Council on Alternative Investment Fund Managers and amending Directives 2004/39/EC and 2009/.../EC, COM(2009) 207 final.

[6] House of Lords, European Union Committee, Directive on Alternative Investment Fund Managers, 3rd report of session 2009–10, February 2010.

II.

Far beyond from these well-discussed instances of protectionism, there is and has long been a different type of economic patriotism that rarely makes it to the headlines of the press. We refer to a more refined and subtle kind of protectionist tendency that we witness in the field of company law.

Admittedly, there has long been a basic conflict between the aims of the European Union to establish a well-functioning and integrated internal market and the ambitions of (certain) Member States to boost national champions or maintain national economic control in formerly publicly owned companies. But even seemingly liberal, free-market countries have recently taken a different attitude towards their 'open borders': the United Kingdom, for instance, is reconsidering its liberal takeover regime, following the recent successful takeover of Cadbury by the American food giant Kraft. British politicians even urged the Takeover Panel to reconsider parts of the regulatory framework known as the City Code in order to make takeovers more difficult.[7] Some pressure groups even called for the adoption of a specific 'Cadbury's Law', to 'prevent hostile takeovers of British companies which are not in the public interest'.[8]

In the field of company law, the revival of protectionism can be seen in a wide range of legislative and regulatory measures. Problems were mostly related to companies of general economic interest, which had been privatized over the 1990s. State measures preventing foreign takeovers included the grant of state aid or special rights in privatized companies, often referred to as 'golden shares', which have been found to restrict the European market for corporate control and direct investment. Furthermore, more recent times have seen an enormous increase in the number and the assets of Sovereign Wealth Funds, mainly from Russia, East Asia, or the Gulf States. To their most severe critics, Sovereign Wealth Funds are a threat to the sovereignty of the nations in whose companies they invest. Company law rules are one of the instruments frequently used to enhance or to discourage integration or to deter foreign investment altogether. Furthermore, European leaders now advocate creating their own European Sovereign Wealth Funds to save companies that are vulnerable to takeover by non-European predators.

[7] J Eaglesham and L Saigol, 'Mandelson calls for radical reform of takeover rules for hostile bids' *Financial Times* (London, 2 March 2010) 19. The Labour Party's manifesto for the general election 2010 included a call for the restoration of a 'public interest test' in corporate takeovers (at least for utility or infrastructure companies), an amendment to the City Code so that two-thirds of shareholders must approve the transaction, as opposed to the simple majority required at the moment. See Labour Party, *The Labour Party Manifesto 2010—A future fair to all* (12 April 2010) 1:7, 1:9 (available at <http://www.labour.org.uk/manifesto>).

[8] A Hill, 'Protectionist "Cadbury's Law" is last thing UK needs' *Financial Times* (London, 16 March 2010) 18.

III.

It is the aim of this book to contribute to an understanding of the legal problems associated with this phenomenon. The contributors to this volume discuss recent developments and possible regulatory or policy responses in this field of the law. Amongst others, they particularly focus on takeovers and restructurings, free movement of capital, Sovereign Wealth Funds, and the internal market. The book is divided into four parts, each of them analysing a different aspect of the role of company law in economic protectionism. Each paper is followed by a discussant paper, commenting on the contribution and developing a new perspective on the preceding chapter.

The introductory part offers a general perspective on economic protectionism from EU law. *Klaus J Hopt* paints an overall picture of the state of the art of European company law after the 2007/08 financial crisis.[9] Citing a number of examples, he warns that the crisis has brought up a temptation for many Member States to lock up their markets. The most obvious example, according to Hopt, is the regulation of third-country Sovereign Wealth Funds; but also that states may link bail out payments and subsidies to policies of the failing companies to save jobs at home and give preference to national contract partners.[10] This perspective makes for a nice contrast with the account provided by *Crispin Waymouth*.[11] He is convinced that the term 'protectionism' is not helpful in the context of company law and foreign investment policy, because it is a very broad concept and needs to be replaced with a more balanced approach, taking into account the individual issues of each separate policy problem. His assessment concludes that the record of the EU and Member States is a mixed one: On the one hand, negative integration—ie the application of the provisions on the free movement of capital and services by the Commission and Court of Justice—have prevented Member States from many of the more populist impulses and pressures. On the other hand, positive integration—the adoption of new EU legislation—has been very difficult in recent years and has been prone to encompass populist elements.

Jonathan Rickford helps us understand how the fundamental freedoms—in our context most notably establishment[12] and capital[13]—can overcome protectionist measures by Member States.[14] Discussing the recent golden shares cases, he notes that Member States, in retaining or taking power over companies, whether

[9] K J Hopt, 'European Company and Financial Law: Observations on European Politics, Protectionism, and the Financial Crisis' ch 2 below, p 13.

[10] Cf eg the contentious 'Buy American' clause in the United States. See S O'Connor, 'Buy American regulations debate develops into tug-of-war' *Financial Times* (London, 24 June 2009) 19.

[11] C Waymouth, 'Is "Protectionism" a Useful Concept for Company Law and Foreign Investment Policy? An EU Perspective' ch 3 below, p 32.

[12] Now Article 49 TFEU.

[13] Now Article 63 TFEU.

[14] J Rickford, 'Protectionism, Capital Freedom, and the Internal Market' ch 4 below, p 54.

by public law or private law and whether by special provision or by acquisition of shares in the market place, often intend to use those powers in pursuit of their industrial policies, frequently for protectionist or other purposes conflicting with EU law principles. According to Rickford, both market freedoms mentioned above can and should be adequately used to overcome obstacles in company law. It is settled case law now that the very existence of 'special rights' or 'golden shares' favouring the state carries the risk of abuse; hence the rule that discretionary state powers must be transparent in order to not deter foreign investors. Of course, recent developments in this field have broadened the scope of the capital freedom and might—if no adequate 'filter' is employed—eventually encompass any domestic company law rule.[15] This latter point is picked up in the comment by *Andrea Biondi*.[16] He takes the view that the golden shares case law still reflects exclusively the desire to reduce state prerogatives in companies. However, even here, the Court of Justice might exaggerate it: as always, the risk is that every action attributable to the state might be caught by its scrutiny, leaving the Member States not enough leeway to act. Biondi suggests that one should get inspiration from the law on state aids, in particular with reference to the test known as the 'market investor principle': the Court will not qualify a loan or an acquisition of equity as 'aid' when a private market participant would have acted similarly.[17]

The second part of the book picks one topic which is very prone to protectionist sentiments: takeovers and mergers. *Paul Davies, Edmund-Philip Schuster,* and *Emilie van de Walle de Ghelcke* analyse to what extent the Takeover Directive or its implementation in the Member States was subject to protectionist elements.[18] As a concrete example, they look at the implementation of the 'board neutrality rule' (Article 9 of the Directive), according to which the management of a target company is prevented from frustrating the bid—however, this rule is optional for Member States (Article 12). Their finding is that after the implementation of the Directive, overall more Member States moved to a less 'bidder friendly' takeover regime than there had been before. It seems as if the introduction of an 'optional' rule reminded the lawmakers of the different options that are available to them and that seem to be acceptable from an EU law point of view. One explanation might indeed be that Member States who had previously

[15] See See WG Ringe, 'Company Law and Free Movement of Capital' (2010) 69 Cambridge LJ 378.

[16] A Biondi, 'When the State is the Owner: Some Further Comments on the Court of Justice "Golden Shares" Strategy' ch 5 below, pp 95.

[17] Case 40/85 *Belgium v Commission* [1986] ECR 2321; Joined Cases 296 and 318/82 *The Netherlands and Leeuwarder Papierwarenfabriek BV v Commission* [1985] ECR 809; Joined Cases C-278 to C-280/92 *Spain v Commission* [1994] ECR I-4103; Case C-56/93 *Belgium v Commission* [1996] ECR I-723; Case C-39/94 *SFEI and others v La Poste and others* [1996] ECR I-3547; Case C-342/96 *Spain v Commission* [1999] ECR I-2459; Case C-256/97 *DM Transport* [1999] ECR I-3913; Case T-46/97 *SIC v Commission* [2000] ECR II-2125.

[18] P Davies and others, 'The Takeover Directive as a Protectionist Tool?' ch 6 below, pp 105.

been sceptical about a conflict between EU law principles and a possible national law allowing management to take defensive measures now had a guarantee that such a national law would be compatible with EU law.[19] In any case, the finding sheds light on the value of 'optional law' in the European context, which has been criticized by some as an 'ugly' political compromise but hailed by others as giving Member States enough flexibility to adapt the implementation measures to their specific needs.[20] Optionality might offer flexibility to Member States, but the Commission's goal of establishing a level playing field has clearly not been reached. Worse: the optionality of Article 9 has had the opposite effect for the law of some Member States. This is, of course, the Commission's perspective. Whether the board neutrality rule is indeed necessary or desirable for each individual Member State is another question. In his comment, *Andrew Johnston* picks up the issue of optional or reflexive regulation.[21] He compares the optionality of the Takeover Directive to existing EU legislation like the European Company Statute,[22] which arguably represents a reflexive regulatory tool in that it leaves the question of employee participation to the national political process and bargaining powers of the social partners. Both instances can be described as 'pragmatic political solutions' or 'workable balances' between integration and national diversity, and both examples have clear advantages. As Johnston points out, however, the very existence of optionality comes at the price of an increased risk that the various options will be used in a 'strategic', maybe even protectionist way by the Member State implementing the Directive.

Jesper Lau Hansen in his contribution[23] builds the bridge between the takeover/merger chapter and the introductory chapter 1. He shows that Member States may protect their markets and their companies by (legally) attributing enhanced voting power to specific shareholders. One of the strongest forms of these 'control-enhancing mechanisms' is surely a golden share, ie a special right for the state, disproportionate to the size of its shareholding. But other control-enhancing mechanisms (CEMs) of a less dramatic scale can sometimes have an equally strong impact and interfere with and possibly obstruct cross-border restructuring. Lau Hansen shows a more nuanced understanding of what he would term 'protectionist'. Consequently and unlike the paper by Davies and others,[24] he welcomes the optionality in the Takeover Directive, and unlike the

[19] This presupposes, of course, that the Takeover Directive complies with primary EU law. See on this question Rickford (n 14) footnote 95.

[20] G Hertig and J A McCahery, 'Optional rather than Mandatory EU Company Law: Framework and Specific Proposals' (2006) 3 Eur Company and Financial L Rev 341.

[21] A Johnston, 'Varieties of Corporate Governance and Reflexive Takeover Regulation' ch 7 below, pp 161.

[22] Council Regulation (EC) 2157/2001 on the Statute for a European Company (SE) [2001] OJ L294/1 and Council Directive 2001/86/EC supplementing the Statute for a European company with regard to the involvement of employees [2001] OJ L294/22.

[23] J Lau Hansen, 'Cross-Border Restructuring—Company Law between Treaty Freedom and State Protectionism' ch 8 below, pp 176.

[24] Davies and others (n 18).

Commission,[25] he does not characterize the implementation measures by some Member States as protectionist. In conclusion then, his view is that the term 'protectionism' should only be used where states grant themselves disproportionate influence in companies, however not where they allocate power between private parties. *Ulf Bernitz* subsequently expands on the role CEMs play in a takeover market.[26] He cites features of Swedish company law to illustrate that a well-functioning takeover market can exist in spite of the availability of CEMs.

The third part of the volume is dedicated to the question how company law may be used to foreclose markets. As one example, *Wolf-Georg Ringe* revisits the debate on 'one share/one vote' (OSOV) after the financial crisis.[27] Recently, policy makers have re-advocated the introduction of multiple voting rights or other CEMs to reward long-term shareholders in an attempt to curb the short-termism that is perceived by many to have provided the prevalent business incentive prior to the financial crisis. The European Commission abandoned its project to make OSOV mandatory across the EU in 2007. Ringe explains the pros and cons of a OSOV rule and historically explores where and when such a rule was promoted in various jurisdictions. He concludes that much of the usefulness of OSOV depends on the shareholder environment in which it operates. There is, however, no case for making such a rule mandatory; even less so in a concentrated shareholding environment. In his comment,[28] *Arad Reisberg* adds a social element to the historical observations: corporate law may need to evolve in response to changing social and environmental realities in which they operate. To be sure, this is not entirely novel territory for corporate law. In reality, corporate law has long faced multi-challenges and changing business realities, especially in the last few decades with the growth of diverse and complex investment mechanisms. He takes the view that a historical perspective reveals not 'change' but rather 'trends' towards OSOV, and this will probably hold true for the current, post-crisis debate as well.

Heike Schweitzer discusses a very timely topic and explores European attitudes towards Sovereign Wealth Funds.[29] This is yet another example to illustrate how company law may be used to close the domestic market against foreign 'intruders'. Finding a common European stance against allegedly strategic investment will be a major challenge—the European Commission has so far only published

[25] European Commission, *Report on the implementation of the Directive on Takeover Bids*, 21 February 2007, SEC (2007) 268.

[26] U Bernitz, 'Mechanisms of Ownership Control and the Issue of Disproportionate Distribution of Power' ch 9 below, pp 191.

[27] WG Ringe, 'Deviations from Ownership-Control Proportionality—Economic Protectionism Revisited' ch 10 below, p 209.

[28] A Reisberg, 'Deviations from Ownership-Control Proportionality—Private Benefits and the Bigger Picture' ch 11 below, p 241.

[29] H Schweitzer, 'Sovereign Wealth Funds—Market Investors or 'Imperialist Capitalists'? The European Response to Direct Investments by Non-EU State-Controlled Entities' ch 12 below, p 250.

a communication on the SWF problem.[30] The legal situation is unclear and full of questions: do third-country SWFs benefit from the European free movement of capital[31] rules? How is the relationship to establishment? Does it make a difference whether the SWF originates in a third country or in the EU (like the newly created French fund)[32]? Ultimately, the question is—should Member States intervene? Schweitzer answers this ultimately in the affirmative, however limited to sensitive industries and insisting on careful law-drafting, respecting proportionality, legal certainty, and predictability. Interestingly, *Katharina Pistor* takes a different stance:[33] She argues that SWFs are *neither* pure 'market investors' nor 'imperialist capitalists', but rather operate under mechanisms that escape a traditional classification under Western typology. They are deeply interwoven with the political system they serve and show patterns both of market and political strategy. Overall, she comes to the conclusion that the West does not have to fear most of the SWFs.

The fourth and last part presents European attempts to overcome protectionist tendencies. The focus is thereby not on traditional harmonization attempts, but rather on new, innovative ways to advance European integration in the field of company law. Two of them are presented here: a 'Model Act' for companies, and the creation of European legal forms. First, *Paul Krüger Andersen* gives an update on the state of play of the 'European Model Company Act'.[34] In a way, this project fits into the discussion around 'optionality' in company law.[35] If 'hard-core' harmonization is no longer desirable—or politically feasible—other ways of integration have to be explored. However, as we have seen above, optionality does not always have the desired effect and can even sometimes be counterproductive.[36] Moreover, as *Jennifer Payne* predicts,[37] a model acts project will 'have to tackle just the same issues and will face just these same difficulties' as mandatory harmonization. She points out that the project might be well placed to offer guidance to emerging Member States in helping them to develop their company law regimes, whereas established Member States may not necessarily need additional drafting guidance for their advanced company laws.

An alternative path might be to develop further the concept of European legal entities. The prime example for this is the *Societas Europaea* (SE). In a way, this also represents a variant of 'optional' EU law: Supranational legal forms do not harmonize the domestic law, but rather serve as an option for businesses to

[30] European Commission, 'A common European approach to Sovereign Wealth Funds' COM(2008)115 final.

[31] Now Article 63 TFEU.

[32] *Fonds stratégique d'investissement.*

[33] K Pistor, 'Sovereign Wealth Funds: Neither Market Investors Nor "Imperialist Capitalists"—A Response to Heike Schweitzer' ch 13 below, p 290.

[34] P Krüger Andersen, 'The European Model Company Act (EMCA)—A new way forward' ch 14 below, p 303.

[35] See above nn 20–22 and accompanying text.

[36] Cf Davies and others (n 18).

[37] J Payne, 'The Role of European Regulation and Model Acts in Company Law' ch 15 below, p 326.

choose deliberately this set of rules. *Horst Eidenmüller*, *Andreas Engert*, and *Lars Hornuf* explore, a few years after its introduction, how the market accepts the new European Company and draw important policy conclusions.[38] In contrast to an earlier working paper version of their study,[39] the positive abnormal returns on and after the event day cease to be statistically significant in a new and extended sample. This can be deplored, but also simply accepted as a fact—and stands itself as an interesting finding: if the finding in the extended sample is correct, it simply means that the market does *not* honour that firms change their legal form to become a European Company. This could be interpreted as reflecting the fact that the SE offers little additional benefit over the national legal forms and employs many references to domestic law. *Jodie Kirshner* adds to these concerns[40] by asking to what extent the data shows an attitude towards the specific issue of co-determination? And can conclusions be drawn on possible benefits for other stakeholders, not only the shareholders that are represented in this study? In any event, the empirical study on the SE is pioneering work and a great first step to understand the value of this legal form and optional legal forms altogether.

IV.

Drawing these issues together, we see a rich menu of instances that are relevant for the topic of enquiry. Protectionism is not only big trade policy, but rather comes in more subtle forms of law-making: protection against foreign take-overs, government control of privatized companies, legislation against Sovereign Wealth Funds, to name only the most obvious ones in the field of company law. Law is not only law, but also politics: Both legislation and case law may involve a political statement. Law can be and is used for political purposes: It defines the cornerstones for our capitalist societies, but it may also be used to shield them against influence from other nations or against each other. Company law is only seemingly value-neutral. Upon closer inspection we discover the many ways in which it can be exploited for political objectives.

The European Union has gone a long way to overcome these problems. Positive integration through active law-making and harmonization of company laws was accompanied by negative integration through radical decisions by the Court of Justice, whereby the latter element seems to have had prevalence over the last years. New challenges are waiting. This volume covers a number of them and hopes to contribute to a better understanding of the underlying policy reasons and their implications.

[38] H Eidenmüller, A Engert, and L Hornuf, 'How Does the Market React to the Societas Europaea?' ch 16 below, p 334.

[39] H Eidenmüller, A Engert, and L Hornuf, 'The Societas Europaea: Good News for European Firms' Law Working Paper no 127 (European Corporate Governance Institute 2009).

[40] J Kirshner 'Empirical Notes on the Scietas Europaea' ch 17 below, p 349.

PART I

EU LAW AND ECONOMIC PROTECTIONISM

2

European Company and Financial Law: Observations on European Politics, Protectionism, and the Financial Crisis

Klaus J Hopt

European company and financial law and economic protectionism is one of the most timely, controversial, and challenging topics in these days of financial crisis. To be sure, economic protectionism[1] is anything but new. We find it with periodic ups and downs from the early days of modern company law in the first half of the nineteenth century. But it is only the European Community in the second half of the twentieth century which opened a new era of trying to cope with economic protectionism through the freedoms of the EC Treaty and through company and financial law harmonization. The aim to build a truly internal market was clear, but the way to that goal turned out to be winding and thorny owing to state egoism and lobby influence. More and more often, less satisfactory regulatory compromises were the result. Two striking examples are the development of the SE from the first ideas in 1959 to the enactment of the statute in 2001 and the 'long march' of the Takeover Directive from the Pennington draft of 1974 to the horse trading involving agriculture, terrorism, and Gibraltar until the opt-out compromise which led to the final enactment in 2004. Still, the overall direction of the development was clear: more European law, either secondary as developed by the European Commission (sometimes called positive harmonization), or primary—ie treaty provisions—as interpreted by the European Court of Justice in its path-

[1] Cf R E Baldwin, 'The Political Economy of Protectionism' in J N Bhagwati (ed), *Import Competition and Response* (Chicago: National Bureau of Economic Research, 1982) 263–92; K J Hopt, 'Obstacles to Corporate Restructuring: Observations from a European and German Perspective' in M Tison, H de Wulf, C van der Elst, R Steennot (eds), *Perspectives in Company Law and Financial Regulation. Essays in Honour of Eddy Wymeersch* (Cambridge: Cambridge University Press, 2009) 373–96; WG Ringe, 'Deviations of Ownership-Control Proportionality—Economic Protectionism Revisited' ch 10 in this volume who rightly criticizes the 'clear protectionist aspect of deviations from OSOV'.

breaking decisions on the freedoms of establishment and capital: *Überseering*, *Inspire Art*, and *Cartesio* as well as *Volkswagen* and the numerous golden share decisions (negative harmonization). There are some who explain this development by attributing it to the market forces of convergence. Others point to the many influences that US law has exercised and still exercises on European company and financial law, though upon closer inspection considerable path dependencies appear.

Most recently, two counter-developments seem to be running against the free market idea: one marked by the rise of state funds[2] and the second by the financial crisis.[3] Both phenomena have inspired fear and led to protectionist reactions, the first still directed toward non-Member States, in particular Arab countries and China, and the second more or less hidden also within the EU. In this light it seems appropriate to rethink, not necessarily to reshape and rebuild,[4] harmonization of European company and financial law. This article is meant to add to this emerging discussion some observations on European politics, protectionism, and the financial crisis.

[2] See most recently K Pistor, 'Sovereign Wealth Funds, Banks and Governments in the Global Crisis: Towards a New Governance of Global Finance?' (2009) 10 Eur Business Organization L Rev (EBOR) 333–52; H Schweitzer, 'Sovereign Wealth Funds—Market Investors or 'Imperialistic Capitalists'? The European Response to Direct Investments by Non-EU State-Controlled Entities' ch 12 of this volume. For further references, see n 59.

[3] There is already a host of reports and literature on the subject. Cf only the following major reports: Basel Committee on Banking Supervision, *Consultative Document, Report and Recommendations of the Cross-border Bank Resolution Group* (September 2009); *de Larosière-Report: The High Level Group on Financial Supervision in the EU, Report* (Brussels, 25 February 2009); Department of the Treasury, *Financial Regulatory Reform, A New Foundation: Rebuilding Financial Supervision and Regulation* (New York, 17 June 2009); Financial Services Authority (FSA), *A Regulatory Response to the Global Banking Crisis (Turner-Review)* (London, 18 March 2009); Financial Stability Board (FSB), *Improving Financial Regulation, Report to G20 Leaders* (25 September 2009); Financial Stability Board (FSB), *Overview of Progress in Implementing the London Summit Recommendations for Strengthening Financial Stability, Report to G20 Leaders* (25 September 2009); Financial Stability Forum (FSF), *Enhancing Market and Institutional Resilience (Draghi-Report)* (7 April 2008); Group of Twenty (G20), *Declaration on Strengthening the Financial System* (Washington, 2 April 2009); Group of Thirty (G30) *Report: Financial Reform: A Framework for Financial Stability (Volcker-Report)* (15 January 2009); IIF Report: *Final Report of the Institute of International Finance, Committee on Market Best Practices, Principles of Conduct and Best Practice Recommendations* (17 July 2008); Ricol Report: *Report on the Financial Crisis* (Paris, 2 September 2008); *Sachverständigenrat zur Begutachtung der Gesamtwirtschaftlichen Entwicklung, Die Finanzkrise meistern—Wachstumskräfte stärken, Jahresgutachten 2008/09* (Paderborn 2008, under IV).

[4] 'Rethink, rebuild, and reshape' was the general topic of the World Economic Forum in Davos on 28 January 2010.

I. The right balance between negative and positive harmonization in the European Union

1. Positive and negative harmonization

The overall question to start with is this: Has the European Union struck the right balance between positive and negative harmonization up to now, and is this changing under the influence of the financial crisis? In my view, this question can be answered only for specific fields and rules set or initiated by the European Commission and the relevant decisions of the Court of Justice. The answer may well be different, say, for competition law, state subsidies, and state enterprises than for harmonization of company and financial law, and even between company law and financial law the evaluation may differ. The general answer of those who are in favour of more unity, or at least more centralization, and of those who stand for more competition, diversity, and decentralization is therefore too simplistic. What would be needed is an in-depth analysis of each rule in its specific legal and economic context.

As to harmonization, usually a distinction is made between negative harmonization and positive harmonization. Harmonization can be promoted positively by regulations, directives, and recommendations. There the European Commission is in the driving seat.[5] In contrast, negative harmonization refers to the cutting down of impediments to free trade in an internal market. This is how the Court of Justice proceeds by declaring illegal under the Treaty national laws and impediments that are incompatible with the freedoms of the Treaty. While the distinction between negative and positive harmonization is conceptually tempting and leads to two different but parallel ways of marching toward a truly internal market, there remain major legal and functional differences between these two forms, not only in how and by which players such harmonization is reached, but also as far as its legal and economic content is concerned. Yet if one keeps these differences in mind, speaking of negative and positive harmonization does make sense.

[5] Most recently the European Commission has conceded to the European Parliament to start legislative proceedings via the Commission: the Commission promised to present a draft within three months or to explain why it did not ('comply or explain'). The Member States, among them Germany, criticized the Commission strongly because they fear that even more matters will be taken up on the European level.

2. Pros and cons of harmonization by the Court of Justice

With negative harmonization, the role of the Court of Justice as the promoter of European unity is at stake. There is a vast body of literature on this,[6] as on any other supreme court.[7] Most prominent is the jurisprudence of the Court of Justice regarding the full recognition of all companies within the European Union and the incompatibility of the seat theory and other national obstacles to prevent companies created in one Member State from freely moving into others. This jurisprudence, in which *Centros* (1999), *Überseering* (2002), *Inspire Art* (2003), *Hughes de Lasteyrie du Saillant* (2004), and *Cartesio* (2009) stand out, is well known[8] and has been generally accepted, even though a number of demarcation questions remain, in particular as far as *Cartesio* and the freedom of exit of companies is concerned. Overall, its case law has reached reasonable results, though it is true that the decisions lack consistency and the rules should definitely be more predictable.[9] *Cartesio*[10] in particular seems too cautious in moving away from *Daily Mail* (1989). The Court would have done better to follow, as it most often does and as most of the observers had expected, the Attorney General's proposal.

There are, of course, also those who criticize the Court for having opened the floodgates for the free entry of thinly capitalized and badly regulated foreign companies. The very aim of the real seat theory was to prevent this and to preserve high national company law standards such as creditor protection and labour co-determination. Indeed, this jurisprudence led to a multitude of mainly British private limited companies in Germany, and motivated German legislators in reaction to this to deregulate the German limited liability company (GmbH) considerably and to create a new form of company (*Unternehmergesellschaft*)[11] with a minimum capital of only €1 as in France and other Member States. Some call it deprecatorily 'GmbH light', and indeed the failure and insolvency rate of these new companies is far higher than for other company forms apart from the 'German' English private company. On the other hand, the number of new

[6] Cf with many, eg L N Brown and T Kennedy, *The Court of Justice of the European Communities* (5th edn, London: Sweet & Maxwell, 2000); G de Burca and J Weiler, *The European Court of Justice* (Oxford: Oxford University Press, 2001); D F Waelbroeck and H G Schermers, *Judicial protection in the EU* (6th edn, The Hague: Kluwer Law International, 2001).

[7] For the US Supreme Court, see recently J Toobin, *The Nine: Inside the Secret World of the Supreme Court* (New York: Doubleday, 2007).

[8] Cf most recently G H Roth, *Vorgaben der Niederlassungsfreiheit für das Kapitalgesellschaftsrecht / Exigences de la liberté d'établissement pour le droit des sociétés de capitaux* (Munich: CH Beck, 2009).

[9] Concurring J Rickford, ch 4 in this volume.

[10] Cf D Zimmer and C Naendrup, 'Das Cartesio-Urteil des EuGH: Rück- oder Fortschritt für das internationale Gesellschaftsrecht?' (2009) 62 Neue Juristische Wochenschrift 545; S Leible and J Hoffmann, 'Cartesio—fortgeltende Sitztheorie, grenzüberschreitender Formwechsel und Verbot materiellrechtlicher Wegzugsbeschränkungen' (2009) 64 Betriebs-Berater 58.

[11] Section 5a of the German Limited Liability Act (GmbHG) as introduced by the MoMiG-Reform Act of 23 October 2008, [2008] Bundesgesetzblatt (*German Federal Gazette*) I 2026.

English companies in Germany has drastically declined since the introduction of the new company form, and it seems there was a need for it. In any case, the logic of the internal market is with the Court, and a certain amount of competition between the legislators, as evidenced in the aftermath of the Court's jurisprudence, is healthy.

Other examples of pro-European case law of the Court could be given, most prominently the golden share jurisprudence which began in 2002 with a series of judgments against Portugal, France, and Belgium and continued afterwards with judgments against Spain, the UK, Italy, the Netherlands, and Germany.[12] In Germany, the judgment that declared the Volkswagen Act of 1960 (with amendments in 1966 and 1970) to violate the freedom of establishment is most prominent.[13] Again the evaluations differ fundamentally. Unsurprisingly, the Member States whose acts were held in violation of the Treaty and many of their academics and practitioners were critical, and Germany even defied the Commission (and the Court) in enacting a reform act that eliminated only the two obstacles which the Court had expressly mentioned, while upholding the voting cap of 20 per cent and the supermajority of 80 per cent and thereby cementing the veto power of Lower Saxony. Most recently, Volkswagen even changed its statutes by incorporating in them both the voting cap and the supermajority, in the hope that this would remove these obstacles from the reach of the European Court for good. I am among those who would have been in favour of striking down all golden share obstacles in the Volkswagen Act and who also consider the new version of the Volkswagen law to be clearly protectionist and at least arguably in violation of the freedom of establishment, since the new Volkswagen statutes give too much privilege to the state, though in the form of private company law arrangements. In any case, the Court has missed its chance since now the much more difficult question arises, namely whether obstacles inserted—freely and in conformity with the general company act—into the articles of incorporation could still violate the Treaty provisions if they privilege the state as owner. I tend to answer this question in the affirmative,[14] but see of course the danger of the Court entering too very far into national company and private law and the

[12] See S Grundmann and F Möslein, 'The Golden Share—State Control in Privatised Companies: Comparative Law, European Law and Policy Aspects' (2004) 4 Eur Banking and Financial L J (EUREDIA) 623; S Grundmann and F Möslein, 'Die Goldene Aktie, Staatskontrollrechte in Europarecht und wirtschaftspolitischer Bewertung' [2003] Zeitschrift für Unternehmens- und Gesellschaftsrecht (ZGR) 317–66.

[13] Case C-112/05 *Commission v Germany* [2007] ECR I-8995, annotation by WG Ringe, 'Case C-112/05, *Commission v. Germany* ("VW Law"), Judgment of the Grand Chamber of 23 October 2007' (2008) 45 Common Market L Rev 537. Cf also J van Bekkum, J Kloosterman, and J Winter, 'Golden Shares and European Company Law: The Implications of Volkswagen' (2008) 5 Eur Company L 6–12.

[14] Cf P H Holle, 'Der "Fall VW"—ein gemeinschaftsrechtlicher Dauerbrenner' (2010) 55 Die Aktiengesellschaft 14 with further references; F Möslein, 'Aufsichtsratsverfassung und Kapitalverkehrsfreiheit' (2008) 5 Der Aufsichtsrat 72.

difficulties of distinguishing this case from merely private impediments.[15] Yet irrespective of how one answers this legal question, what is undeniable is the protectionist character of the reformed Volkswagen Act due to an unholy alliance of top management, block owners, trade unions, and the state of Lower Saxony in getting this legislation enacted.

3. Pros and cons of harmonization by the European Commission

The answer to the overall question posed above is even more controversial as far as positive harmonization is concerned, both as to the fundamental question of regulatory competition versus harmonization as well as to the need for and content of the harmonization of company and financial law in particular. Economists and proponents of the law and economics movement are in general against harmonization,[16] while European law specialists are usually in favour of it. The truth, as often, is probably in between. Neither the whole of company law should be harmonized nor is regulatory competition always the best of all worlds. Nor is it particularly useful to enumerate in theory one by one the supposed (and well-known) pros and cons of harmonization. What is needed rather is to find out how to build a truly internal market and how company and financial law can help in creating it. In this context it has rightly been remarked that '(i)t is not unlikely that harmonization will facilitate cross-border activities and therefore regulatory competition'.[17] The question, therefore, cannot be answered by a general credo for or against European harmonization, and even less so by just invoking the subsidiarity principle or the general freedom of contract. This would be too legalistic and far from the reality of the markets. The answer can only be given for the various regulatory problems on the background of the economic and legal system involved. The Takeover Directive may be a good candidate for this.[18]

As far as the need for and content of harmonization of company and financial law in particular, the record of the Commission is mixed. Concerning financial law and, more specifically, securities regulation—or, to use the European term, capital market law—a European 'insider' stated in 2005 that financial regulation was already at that time largely co-ordinated at the EU level despite the fact that

[15] F Möslein, 'Kapitalverkehrsfreiheit und Gesellschaftsrecht' [2007] Zeitschrift für Wirtschaftsrecht (ZIP) 208, 213 ff.

[16] Cf for example L Enriques and M Gatti, 'The Uneasy Case for Top-Down Corporate Law Harmonization in the European Union' (2006) 27 U of Pennsylvania J of Intl Economic L 939; J Armour, 'Who Should Make Corporate Law? EC Legislation versus Regulatory Competition' (2005) 58 Current Legal Problems 369. As to the proponents of subsidiarity, cf R Herzog, F Bolkestein, and L Gerken, 'Die EU schadet der Europa-Idee' *Frankfurter Allgemeine Zeitung* (Frankfurt, 15 January 2010) 14.

[17] G Hertig, 'Regulatory Competition for EU Financial Services' (2000) 3 J of Intl Economic L 349, 374.

[18] P Davies and others, 'The Takeover Directive as a Protectionist Tool?' ch 6 in this volume, have given an excellent example of how to go ahead with this in evaluating European takeover regulation. See also K J Hopt (n 1) 375 ff.

differences still existed in the transformation process.[19] The real breakthrough was the voluminous and highly detailed MiFID[20] that later was further considerably refined by Commission instruments, the Lamfalussy rule-making process, and the work of the Committee of European Securities Regulators (CESR). For the Member States this was a real revolution. Yet today the MiFID is considered to be the fundamental law (*Grundgesetz*) of securities regulation and, despite certain needs for reform, full harmonization in this field is taken for granted by practice and academia. As has been rightly remarked, harmonization in this field has become 'the device through which centralized regulation is imposed on the EC market-place and by which national regulatory instincts to protect national markets are curbed'.[21]

With takeover regulation, to take a more controversial example, the Commission was less successful. The Takeover Directive is a difficult compromise that was made possible only by last-minute opt-out and reciprocity changes. Commissioner Bolkestein was so disappointed that at a certain point he considered withdrawing the Commission proposal of the Directive for good. The evaluation of the implementation of the Thirteenth Directive by the Commission also reflects this disappointment. The report concludes on a pessimistic note: 'The number of Member States implementing the Directive in a seemingly protectionist way is unexpectedly large.'[22] Yet others hold a more positive view:[23] while the experience with the implementation is sobering, the Directive represents progress insofar as it contains uncontested and well-implemented rules on many issues other than the anti-frustration and breakthrough rules in Articles 9 and 11, in particular transparency rules and rules on fair behaviour and procedure in takeovers. This gives companies and shareholders a good part of the much-needed legal certainty in transnational takeovers.

Regarding core company law, some consider European company law to be outright trivial.[24] This is a bold statement that is not tenable in practice. It is common for key areas of company law to have remained national, as the fate of the ex-Fifth Directive on the structure of the company and of the ex-draft of the Ninth Directive on group law show.[25] On the other hand, there are many examples that mark a considerable imprint of European company law, not only on its theory but also on its practice. Just take the Directive of 2005 on

[19] E Wymeersch, 'The Future of Financial Regulation and Supervision in Europe' (2005) 42 Common Market L Rev 987, 993.

[20] Directive 2004/39/EC of 21 April 2004 on markets in financial instruments (MiFID), [2004] OJ L145/1.

[21] N Moloney, *EC Securities Regulation* (2nd edn, Oxford: Oxford University Press, 2008) 33.

[22] European Commission Staff Working Document, *Report on the implementation of the Directive on Takeover Bids* (21 February 2007), SEC(2007) 268, 10. Cf P Davies and others (n 18).

[23] Hopt (n 1) 378 ff.

[24] L Enriques, 'EC Company Law Directives and Regulations: How Trivial Are They?' (2006) 27 U of Pennsylvania J of Intl Economic L 1086.

[25] Cf S Grundmann, *European Company Law, Organization, Finance and Capital Markets* (Antwerp, Oxford: Intersentia 2007) 217 ff, 623 ff.

cross-border mergers, the 2006 Directive on statutory audits of annual accounts and consolidated accounts, European accounting law in particular after the shift to IAS/IFRS, and even the unexpected rise of the European Company. Even as far as European group law is concerned, an area in which it is generally said that European harmonization failed completely, the picture changes if one looks at European group law of banks, insurance companies, and financial conglomerates,[26] and it will change further and considerably as a consequence of the financial crisis. Yet it is also true that in order to arrive at a truly internal market more could be done on a European level. The original plans of the European Commission as laid down in its Action Plan of 2003[27] and spelled out in more detail in the second report of the High Level Group[28] show the direction.[29]

II. Different patterns of harmonization of company and financial law: Evolution and European politics

1. State egoism, lobby interests, and compromise solutions: The examples of the Takeover Directive and the new European financial architecture

What are the political forces that shape the balance between negative and positive harmonization in European company and financial law and how has it evolved over time? This is a touchy question since much of European law, including European company law, is the result of lobby work, state resistance to any departure of their beloved idiosyncrasies, and outright political horse trading. The Commission tries to do its best, and the new way of mandating feasibility studies and studies which may prepare the economic and legal ground for reform and further harmonization is excellent. But again, the answers to the question posed are meaningful only if one looks at specific regulatory problems and how they are dealt with on the European level.

[26] Cf K J Hopt, 'Konzernrecht: Die europäische Perspektive' (2007) 171 Zeitschrift für das gesamte Handelsrecht und Wirtschaftsrecht (ZHR) 199–240.

[27] Communication from the Commission to the Council and the European Parliament, *Modernising Company Law and Enhancing Corporate Governance in the European Union—A Plan to Move Forward* (21 May 2003), COM(2003) 284 final.

[28] High Level Group of Company Law Experts (J Winter, J Schans Christensen, J M Garrido Garcia, K J Hopt, J Rickford, G Rossi, J Simon), *A Modern Regulatory Framework for Company Law in Europe* (Brussels: European Commission, 4 November 2002); also in G Ferrarini, K J Hopt, J Winter, and E Wymeersch (eds), *Reforming Company and Takeover Law in Europe* (Oxford: Oxford University Press, 2004) annex 3, 925–1086.

[29] Cf K Geens and K J Hopt (eds), *The European Company Law Action Plan Revisited, Reassessment of the 2003 Priorities of the European Commission* (Leuven: Leuven University Press, 2010) and therein K J Hopt, 'The European Company Law Action Plan Revisited: An Introduction' 9–23.

The Takeover Directive is a perfect example of the worst horse trading between the Member States—in particular Spain, Sweden, Germany, and the UK and in the end Portugal as a mediator—even involving policy matters completely outside of company law and securities regulation, namely agriculture, terrorism, and Gibraltar. The volte face of former Chancellor Schröder in April 2001 when he withdrew his original consent to the unanimous Common Position of the Council of 19 June 2000 was revealing.[30] Representatives of car maker Volkswagen had met with Schröder just before and convinced him of the threat to Volkswagen by the draft directive. Why did Schröder give in so easily, though he must have anticipated the anger and disappointment of his fellow council members who would feel duped by his change of mind? Well, before becoming Chancellor, Schröder was the prime minister of Lower Saxony where Volkswagen has its seat. As such, he had been one of the two representatives of Lower Saxony on the supervisory board of Volkswagen. It is telling that Schröder was nicknamed the 'automobile chancellor'.

An example from European financial law is the resistance of the Member States to the attempts of the European Commission to develop a European financial architecture in Europe. Leaving financial supervision exclusively to national supervisors and to the colleges of supervisors formed by them (and by supervisors from other interested non-Member States) has proven to reach too short in the financial crisis. Regulation and supervision must follow the markets and the actors at the markets; otherwise it cannot but lag behind.[31] More concretely, with insolvency law, it is absurd that banks today act globally but die nationally. In times of crisis, the temptation of the states and of national supervisors to keep an eye primarily on saving their own banks is just too great, in particular if national rescue money is needed. The European Commission has therefore made proposals for establishing a European Systemic Risk Board (ESRB) and for transforming the three Lamfalussy Committees—the CEBS for bank supervision, the CEIOPS for the supervision of insurance companies, and the CESR for capital market supervision—into three European supervisory agencies: the EBA, EIOPA, and ESMA.[32] The ESRB is meant to deal with macro-supervision, while the three other authorities are to be responsible for micro-supervisory tasks. As was foreseeable, the creation of the ESRB was accepted by the Economic and

[30] Cf K J Hopt, 'La treizième directive sur les OPA-OPE et le droit allemand' in *Aspects actuels du droit des affaires, Mélanges en l'honneur de Yves Guyon* (Paris: Dalloz, 2003) 529, 537 ff; R Skog, 'The Takeover Directive: An Endless Saga?' (2002) 13 Eur Business L Rev 301.

[31] E Hüpkes, "Form Follows Function'—A New Architecture for Regulating and Resolving Global Financial Institutions' (2009) 10 Eur Business Organization L Rev 369 ff.

[32] The European Banking Authority, the European Insurance and Occupational Pensions Authority, and the European Securities and Markets Authority. On the institutional structure of EC securities regulation up to now and on a critique, see Moloney (n 21) part VII, 1007 ff, 1086 ff. See also E Wymeersch, 'The Structure of Financial Supervision in Europe: About Single Financial Supervisors, Twin Peaks and Multiple Financial Supervisors' (2007) 8 Eur Business Organization L Rev 237 ff.

Financial Affairs Council (ECOFIN) without much ado. So was the creation of the three authorities, yet—and this is the decisive point—without granting them even the only few and very modest direct intervention powers the European Commission had proposed in its draft. The result, according to the compromise draft to be brought before the European Parliament in the spring, is that the ESRB has only the task of collecting and exchanging information and of issuing warnings and recommendations. Where a recommendation is not followed, the addressee shall (merely) provide an adequate justification ('act or explain'). As to the three European authorities, national supervision remains fully untouched; this is acceptable and is said to concern about 90 per cent of the bank business. However, international supervision is also reserved to the co-operation of the national supervisory bodies that are supposed to work together in the so-called colleges of supervisors. It is telling that in these colleges the newly created European authorities will merely have the status of an observer.[33] The large internationally operating financial institutions that will continue to have to deal with 27 supervisory agencies consider this most disappointing.[34] Even further, any kind of direct intervention competence foreseen in particular for financial crises has been turned down by the UK, Germany, and other Member States. There is one exception, though, namely the direct supervision of rating agencies by the ESMA. Yet this exception is a rather obvious case since the rating agencies' market is global and forms a close oligopoly with Standard & Poors, Moody's, and Fitch being the protagonists on which national regulators just do not have any bearing.

2. Different patterns of harmonization in company and financial law

What is surprising at first glance is that company law and financial law show rather different patterns of harmonization. Financial law, in particular banking, insurance, and capital markets law, is much more developed on the EU level than company law. Even before the present financial crisis, the credit institutions directive of 2000, the corresponding directives for insurance undertakings, and the 2004 MiFID for capital markets amounted more or less to full or maximum harmonization,[35] at least as far as they reach. And they reach very far. The proposals of the European Commission of 23 September 2009 on a

[33] Cf for example Article 12 of the draft EBA Regulation.

[34] K J Hopt, 'Auf dem Weg zu einer neuen europäischen und internationalen Finanzmarktarchitektur' (2009) 12 Neue Zeitschrift für Gesellschaftsrecht (NZG) 1401, 1405 ff. Cf already M Lamandini, 'When More is Needed ...' (2009) 6 Eur Company L 197, 202.

[35] On maximum harmonization, see B Gsell and C Herresthal (eds), *Vollharmonisierung im Privatrecht, Die Konzeption der Richtlinie am Scheideweg?* (Tübingen: Mohr Siebeck, 2009) and, specifically regarding company law, J Schürnbrand, 'Vollharmonisierung im Gesellschaftsrecht' ibid 273 ff.

European System of Financial Supervisors (ESFS) which comprise the above-mentioned macro- and micro-supervision would, if adopted, complement this quasi-full substantive harmonization by procedural reforms for supervision and enforcement. Though these do not go far enough, they are nevertheless an important step toward what is needed for regulating and supervising international financial players.

In addition to the work on the supervisory framework, the financial crisis has led to many other regulatory reform plans concerning a framework for crisis prevention, management, and resolution (inter alia: bank resolution framework, guarantee schemes, an EU-wide framework for policy co-ordination on financial stability); the regulatory framework (inter alia: valuation and accounting standards, capital requirements for banks, pro-cyclicality of accounting rules like the mark-to-the-market rule and Basel capital requirements, OTC derivatives); and promoting integrity of financial markets (including remuneration policies and governance as well as corporate governance principles for financial institutions).[36] The reason for these many and far-reaching harmonization measures and reform plans is that the financial markets need uniformity, previsibility, and control; otherwise their operation in the internal market is unduly hampered and the systemic risks arising from the financial sector threaten each Member State.

In the company law field, much less European activity is going on (apart from the politically driven remuneration question). The great design of the European Commission under Commissioner Frits Bolkestein to move forward as set out in the Action Plan of 25 May 2003[37] has not been pursued under his passive and unlucky successor. There are primarily two exceptions: the Directive of 26 October 2005 on Cross-border Mergers of Limited Liability Companies, and the Directive of 11 July 2007 on the Exercise of Certain Rights of Shareholders in Listed Companies. The former was pressed very hard by the practice that needed a framework for cross-border mergers. The latter corresponded to the popular movement of shareholder protection and participation. With regard to board reform and corporate governance, the Commission confined itself to several recommendations. Far-reaching convergence as has been claimed by some American corporate law scholars—the end of history for corporate law[38]—is not in sight, at least for Europe.

[36] Cf ECOFIN, *Council conclusions on strengthening EU financial stability arrangements* (Luxembourg, 20 October 2009). See also Financial Stability Board (FSB), *Improving Financial Regulation* (25 September 2009).

[37] See n 27.

[38] H Hansmann and R Kraakman, 'The End of History for Corporate Law' (2001) 89 Georgetown L J 439. As to the discussion, see J N Gordon and M J Roe (eds), *Convergence and Persistence in Corporate Governance,* (Cambridge: Cambridge University Press, 2004).

3. Interaction of European company and financial law harmonization

While it is true that the harmonization of company law and financial law have followed different patterns, there are also signs of interaction between European company and financial law harmonization as some examples may illustrate.

Excessive remuneration has been a topic in Europe for quite a while as well. The European Commission issued a recommendation on this in 2004.[39] This recommendation was received rather well by the Member States, apart from the say on pay of the shareholders' general assembly, which the Commission had suggested introducing into national company law. Yet during the crisis the remuneration issue came up even more vividly in many Member States, and the European Commission jumped on the bandwagon by issuing two more recommendations, one on the remuneration of directors of listed companies[40] and another on remuneration in the financial services sector.[41] It is certainly true that inappropriate incentives for engaging in highly profitable but risky transactions and forgetting the long-term perspective in favour of short-time results have contributed to the financial crisis. Yet the fact is that this was only one of a whole bundle of reasons, and certainly not the major ones, which were the lack of transparency and the lack of sufficient equity capital of banks.[42]

Impacts on company law also come more indirectly from auditing law and from banking and insurance law. The Directive of 2006 on statutory audits[43] is not at all confined to auditors and auditing, but contains requirements on core company law, namely the audit committee of public-interest entities. For the formation and composition of the audit committee, Article 41 of the Directive requires that each public-interest entity shall have an audit committee and that at least one member of the audit committee shall be independent and shall have competence in accounting and/or auditing. As to its tasks, the Directive enumerates: (a) monitoring of the financial reporting process; (b) monitoring of the effectiveness of the company's internal control, internal audit where applicable, and risk management systems; (c) monitoring of the statutory audit of the annual and consolidated accounts; and (d) reviewing and monitoring of the independence of the statutory auditor or audit firm, and in particular the provision of additional services to the audited entity. Regarding the procedure, it is stated that the auditor shall report to the audit committee on key matters arising from the

[39] European Commission, *Recommendation of 14 December 2004 fostering an appropriate regime for the remuneration of directors of listed companies* [2004] OJ L385/55.

[40] European Commission, *Recommendation of 30 April 2009 complementing Recommendations 2004/913/EC and 2005/162/EC as regards the regime for the remuneration of directors of listed companies* [2009] OJ L120/28.

[41] European Commission, *Recommendation of 30 April 2009 on remuneration policies in the financial services sector* [2009] OJ L120/22.

[42] See ECOFIN (n 36).

[43] Directive 2006/43/EC of the European Parliament and the Council of 17 May 2006 on statutory audits of annual accounts and consolidated accounts [2006] OJ L87.

statutory audit, and in particular on material weaknesses in internal control in relation to the financial reporting process.

Further developments following the lead of European financial law are not improbable. Take for example the MiFID and the mandatory rules on loyal behaviour of financial intermediaries. Aren't the directors of capital-market-oriented companies also intermediaries for the shareholders and subject to similar principal–agent conflicts? Are large banks and financial institutions for which risk prevention rules are mandatory by European law so much different from large capital-market-oriented companies? I do not purport to say that the same rules are needed for banks and large companies. Not at all—this would be far too rigid and not compatible with a market economy where there must be a clear distinction between state-authorized and -supervised branches like banks and insurance companies and normal companies that are just under the regime of company and private law. But more recently it can be observed that the rules on establishing a system of internal control and early warning within the banks tend to spill over from banking law to the law of large companies. For the moment this can still be called an infiltration into company law that is silent, inconsistent, and methodologically on unsafe ground.[44] Yet under the influence of the financial crisis this may become an open influence that could be more consistent, though methodologically hard to grasp. And to give a final example: company law could also learn from the experience of capital markets supervisory law, and the supervisory agencies should probably have more say on certain company law issues, as the Belgian and French experiences show.[45] Of course, the latter results from the observation that the traditional deep divide between company and capital market law has proven to be dated, a conviction that at least in Germany seems already to be shared by the majority opinion.

III. US and European company and financial law: Convergence, transplants, and path dependencies

1. Company law

What lessons, if any, can be learned from the US experience? Despite all the differences, quite a lot can be learned, though one has to be very careful when comparing isolated legal rules. Takeover regulation is once more a good example. When the Thirteenth Directive came to its well-known deadlock in the

[44] These problems were treated at the 2010 biannual symposium of the *Zeitschrift für Unternehmens- und Gesellschaftsrecht* (*ZGR*) in Königstein; cf M Dreher, 'Ausstrahlungen des Aufsichtsrechts auf das Aktienrecht' and D Weber-Rey, 'Ausstrahlungen des Aufsichtsrechts auf das Aktienrecht'. The contributions will be published in issue 2/3 of the review.

[45] In Belgium, group law that had not been codified was considerably shaped by the *Commission Bancaire* (now: the *Commission Bancaire, Financière et des Assurances*).

European Parliament, and when in its aftermath the discussion on the British anti-frustration rule as embedded in Article 9 of the draft directive became one of the most controversial topics,[46] there were many who pointed to the US example of the wide discretion of directors to take defensive action without shareholder approval and even to 'just say no'. Among those who invoked this 'example' were understandably companies that might themselves become targets, trade unions that feared restructuring and loss of jobs, and politicians who were keen for votes; however, there were also academics who favoured that view.

The High Level Group, whose members were convinced that the UK-style anti-frustration rule was better because of the inherent self-interest of the target management not to lose their jobs, looked more closely at the environment in which the 'just-say-no' rule is practised in the US.[47] Upon closer inspection, major differences appeared compared with Europe. The US board discretion operates in a widely differing general legal and capital market environment. These include more pressures from non-executive directors on the board, investment banks, and advisors, and in particular from institutional investors; far-reaching legal transparency rules and intense scrutiny by the media; the threat of replacement of the directors in a successful proxy contest; and, last but not least, a very different court system with shareholder derivative action, higher risk of liability for disloyal behaviour, treble damage suits, discovery, etc. Most of this is lacking, at least in continental Europe.

More generally the principal–agent conflicts in the US and the UK on the one side and continental European companies on the other are very different. In the US, the standard principal–agent conflict is between the shareholders and management since companies without controlling shareholders seem to be the rule.[48] In continental European countries, family-owned companies and companies with controlling shareholders or blockholders are frequent; the relevant principal–agent conflict then is between the minority shareholders and the controlling shareholder. This has led to different emphases in the development of American and European company laws.[49] An example of this is the key attention on the board in the US, while in Europe minority protection rules have ever

[46] For a comprehensive functional and comparative law treatment, see F Möslein, *Grenzen unternehmerischer Leitungsmacht im marktoffenen Verband—Aktien- und Übernahmerecht, Rechtsvergleich und europäischer Rahmen* (Berlin: de Gruyter, 2007).

[47] High Level Group of Company Law Experts (see n 28), *Report on Issues Related to Takeover Bids, Report of the High Level Group of Company Law Experts* (European Commission, Brussels, 10 January 2002), ch 1.5, 39; also in Ferrarini and others (n 28) annex 2, 825–924.

[48] Most recently there are signs that in the US as well companies with blockholders and even with controlling shareholders are getting more common. Cf C G Holderness, 'The Myth of Diffuse Ownership in the United States' (2009) 22 Rev of Financial Studies 1377, 1382–5 and Table 1.

[49] K J Hopt, 'Company Law Modernization: Transatlantic Perspectives' (2006) 51 Rivista delle società 906 ff; K J Hopt, 'American Corporate Governance Indices as Seen from a European Perspective' (2009) 158 U of Pennsylvania L Rev PENNumbra 27–38; L Enriques and P Volpin, 'Corporate Governance Reforms in Continental Europe' (2007) 21 J of Economic Perspectives 117.

been a key concern of the legislators.[50] But not only the shareholder structures are different, so is the role of banks and labour among the group of creditors. In the comparative corporate governance discussion, insider and outsider systems are distinguished. Germany and other European countries with heavy influence of banks and other financial institutions[51] belong to the former group. In European company law, the principal–agent conflict between the shareholders as a group and the creditors as a group is much more prominent within company law as well.[52] The picture changes fully if one looks at the role of labour and labour co-determination in company boards.[53] It is true that parity or, more correctly, quasi-parity labour co-determination is a path-dependent singularity of Germany[54] for historical reasons, in particular the two world wars and the need to rebuild Germany twice with the allied forces of capital and labour. But the representation of labour in the board, though only at a third or even less, is common in continental European countries.

2. Financial law

With financial law the observation can be much shorter. There are two main reasons for this. The first concerns securities regulation, which may be classified as part of financial law. It is a commonplace that the United States securities regulation has served as a model for securities regulation all over the world, a development that has been studied extensively. This does not need further elaboration.[55]

On the other hand, financial law in a more narrow sense—in particular the regulation and supervision of banks, insurance companies, and other financial institutions—has been much less in the focus of comparative law scholars comparing US and European law. This is understandable because these sectors of the economy are very specialized and their regulations have long been the nearly exclusive competence of practitioners and a few specialists in academia.

[50] See E Perakis (ed), *Rights of Minority Shareholders: XVIth Congress of the International Academy of Comparative Law* (Brussels: Bruylant, 2004).

[51] This is still true despite the fading away of 'Rhenanian capitalism' in Germany.

[52] Cf J Armour, G Hertig, and H Kanda, 'Transactions with Creditors' in R Kraakman, J Armour, P Davies, L Enriques, H Hansmann, G Hertig, K J Hopt, H Kanda, E Rock, *The Anatomy of Corporate Law, A Comparative and Functional Approach* (2nd edn, Oxford: Oxford University Press, 2009) 115 ff.

[53] See briefly L Enriques, H Hansmann, and R Kraakman, 'The Basic Governance Structure: Minority Shareholders and Non-Shareholder Constituencies' in Kraakman and (n 52) 100 ff.

[54] Cf K Pistor, 'Codetermination in Germany: A Socio-Political Model with Governance Externalities' in M Blair and M Roe (eds), *Employees and Corporate Governance* (Washington DC: Brookings, 1999) 163 ff and most recently K Pistor, 'Corporate Governance durch Mitbestimmung und Arbeitsmärkte' in P Hommelhoff, K J Hopt, and A von Werder (eds), *Handbuch Corporate Governance* (2nd edn, Stuttgart/Cologne: Otto Schmidt/Schaeffer-Poeschel, 2009) 231 ff; C Windbichler, 'Cheers and Boos for Employee Involvement: Co-Determination as Corporate Governance Conundrum' (2005) 6 Eur Business Organization L Rev 507.

[55] See briefly K J Hopt, 'Comparative Company Law' in M Reimann and R Zimmermann (eds), *The Oxford Handbook of Comparative Law* (Oxford: Oxford University Press, 2006) 1161, 1179 ff.

Furthermore, US banking regulation is not only incredibly technical, but it is also split up among many regulators—such as the central bank Federal Reserve (for large bank holding companies), the Office of the Comptroller of the Currency of the Finance Ministry (national banks), the Office of Thrift Supervision (savings institutions), the SEC (investment banks), the CFTC (future markets), the FIDIC (depositor protection), the insurance supervisory bodies and others—all of them developing their own rules and regulation and supervisory practices. As a consequence of the financial crisis there are reform plans in the US to simplify this confusion by creating a new Financial Services Oversight Council, but not only is the fate of this reform unclear, even if it comes through a real consolidation is not in sight.[56] Therefore, US financial law—at least US banking law—has never been very attractive for comparatists. Of course, this may change in the aftermath of the financial crisis.

3. Towards a better and more permanent transatlantic dialogue

In sum, it must not be forgotten that similar regulatory changes or even transplants[57] may have very different effects within different corporate governance systems, and in particular under different shareholder structures. As was stated before, what is needed is to have a careful look at the possible effects of the particular regulation under the specific legal and economic background. As far as the US and Europe are concerned, there is a need for a better and more permanent transatlantic dialogue, not only between high level politicians and academics, but also between legislators and rule makers. This dialogue began quite some time ago in the field of antitrust law and is firmly established there. The growing self-assurance of the European Commission in its role as European cartel commission and the beginning of the extraterritorial application—or more concretely the consideration of the impacts of foreign antitrust practices on internal markets as acknowledged by the Court of Justice of the European Union—have played a major role in this. A similar dialogue began some years ago in the field of corporate governance and auditing between the US SEC and European supervisory authorities under the auspices of the European Commission and with the help of the European Corporate Governance Institute and its annual transatlantic congresses.[58] This sort of dialogue is needed more broadly in financial law, and as a consequence of the financial crisis it is quickly coming.

[56] Cf D Marin, S Saba, and F G Alogna, 'European Responses to the Financial Crisis' [2009] *Forum Financier/Droit Bancaire et Financier* 187, 208 ff.

[57] J von Hein, *Die Rezeption des US-amerikanischen Gesellschaftsrechts in Deutschland* (Tübingen: Mohr Siebeck, 2008), in particular § 8: Conditions for successful adoption in company law.

[58] See the homepage of the ECGI, <http://www.ecgi.org>.

IV. Conclusion: Impacts of the financial crisis and the dangers of protectionism and under- and overregulation

These few observations may be summed up by pointing to three actual or at least very probable impacts of the financial crisis on European company and financial law. They are marked by protectionism, underreactions, and overreactions, three impacts that are not mutually exclusive but rather cumulative.

The most obvious impact consists in growing protectionism. Examples for this have been mentioned throughout this paper. Most obvious has been the reaction of many countries, not only Member States of the European Union, but also the US, toward the growing role of state funds. The rise of these funds, their size and economic importance, and their investment pattern has been described at length elsewhere.[59] The problem reaches well beyond company and financial law. A good example are the attempts of national governments—both in the European Union, for example France, and in the US—to link state rescues and subsidies to policies of the failing companies for saving jobs at home and giving preference, even an exclusive one, to national contract partners.

In the public perception and the political arena there is much talk about underreaction because banks, most prominently Goldman Sachs, have begun again to pay large bonuses. This has even occurred in banks that previously received rescue and subsidy moneys from the state. While the latter is clearly unacceptable, the former is linked to economic recovery and may be a reaction to competition for managers and the imminent need of getting the best management to lead the company out of the trouble area.

Yet overreaction may be more probable and more dangerous. Legislators are always late and tend to exaggerate when facing abuses, as the history of corporate governance amply illustrates,[60] and from case law we know that 'hard cases make bad law'. To give a first example: The heated discussion on remuneration and bonuses has led legislators to intrude considerably into private payment schemes. Fixed maximum ceilings for remuneration, as called for by the French

[59] See the most recent contributions by Pistor and Schweitzer (n 2). Furthermore, eg Germany's State Experts Council for Evaluation of the Economic Development at Large (*Sachverständigenrat zur Begutachtung der gesamtwirtschaftlichen Entwicklung*), *Das Erreichte nicht verspielen: Jahresgutachten 2007/2008 (Annual Expert Opinion 2007/08)* (Wiesbaden, 2007); S Butt, A Shivdasani, C Stendevad, and A Wyman, 'Sovereign Wealth Funds: A Growing Global Force in Corporate Finance' (2007) 19 J of Applied Corporate Finance 73; R J Gilson and C J Milhaupt, 'Sovereign Wealth Funds and Corporate Governance: A Minimalist Response to the New Mercantilism' (2008) 60 Stanford L Rev 1345; M Nettesheim, 'Unternehmensübernahmen durch Staatsfonds: Europarechtliche Vorgaben und Schranken' (2008) 172 ZHR 729, and M Hellwig, 'Zur Problematik staatlicher Beschränkungen der Beteiligung und der Einflussnahme von Investoren bei großen Unternehmen' (2008) 172 ZHR 768; Hopt (n 1) 388 ff.

[60] Cf P Frentrop, *A History of Corporate Governance 1602–2002* (Amsterdam: Deminor Press, 2002/2003), original: *Ondernemingen en hun aandeelhouders sinds de VOC* (Amsterdam: Prometheus, 2002).

President Sarkozy, are certainly wrong; this would be price control by the state and it has long been proven to be ineffective and outright harmful for the market and the economy. But too many strict procedural rules on remuneration are also not advisable. One size does not fit all, and different companies—large or small, capital-market-oriented or closed, globally active companies and domestic ones—may need different rules. In principle, it must remain up to the shareholders how to respond to remuneration abuses. Therefore, a say on pay as in the UK, and most recently German company law—mandatory discussion and decision of the remuneration policy of the company by the general assembly—is helpful, but, as experience shows, not a panacea. Limits are reached when the remuneration reaches levels that call into question the social coherence of a society.

As to rule-making itself, it might have been preferable to leave the details of remuneration regulation to the companies themselves and to the various corporate governance codes. In Germany, for example, the German Corporate Governance Commission was about to tackle the problem prudently when the legislators stepped in and changed the Company Act, quite obviously joining the public bandwagon in hopes of attaining more popularity and votes. As a result, the standing of the German Corporate Governance Commission in particular and of self-regulation in general suffered. But self-regulation in the shadow of the law may often be better than law for itself, and fall-back rules may sometimes be better than mandatory law.

A similar development may occur in the regulation of banks and other financial institutions—though not so much in their supervision, at least not in the direction of a more centralized European supervision, which has been advocated here.[61] The range of envisaged measures is huge.[62] What is needed instead is a sober reflection on the really important causes of the crisis and how to react to them, not misusing this opportunity to lash out on all sides. Less is often more or, as Pliny the Younger said, *multum non multa*. Of course, this does not mean that the appropriate reaction should not bite. Quite the contrary. If equity capital requirements are raised considerably, and if even additional equity reserves are required from systemically relevant financial institutions, ie if limits are set for leverage, this may be the most appropriate remedy.

There are even some who pretend that the financial crisis has reversed the well-established roles of the market and the state. The German trade unions, for example, campaign with the slogan, 'The state instead of the market'. This is sheer economic ignorance. What is needed, of course, are binding rules of the game for all players of, and all products in, the financial markets, ie the banks, the rating agencies, and more generally the financial institutions, their boards, and their

[61] See II.1 above. [62] See II.2 above and ECOFIN (n 36).

staff as far as wrong incentives are concerned. But legislators and rule makers must watch out that the rules needed for coping with the crisis remain exceptions geared toward the crisis and do not become and remain the general rules once the crisis is over. Eastern Germany and the Central European countries should have taught us this lesson: the market knows better than the state, provided that the state sets the appropriate rules of the game.

3

Is 'Protectionism' a Useful Concept for Company Law and Foreign Investment Policy? An EU Perspective

Crispin Waymouth[1]

The term 'protectionism' has been much used recently with fears that countries will respond to the financial crisis with the same mix of trade-restricting measures that they adopted in the aftermath of the 1929 Wall Street Crash. This chapter shall examine the term 'protectionism' and whether it is possible to apply it meaningfully to company law and foreign investment policy.

After looking at the various definitions of 'protectionism', it shall be argued that whilst the word is perhaps useful as a general term for describing an economic 'bad' that should be avoided, it is nearly useless at describing specific actions, particularly in the regulatory field and its employment today often risks doing more harm than good.

Four alternative criteria shall here be set out: the general public interest, non-discrimination, proportionality, and predictability. The second part of the chapter will test EU and Member State behaviour in company law and foreign investment policy against these criteria. It concludes that there is a mixed picture and that more needs to be done to promote open investment, including through international co-operation.

I. Introduction: 'Protectionism' is the new black

In the current economic crisis, a number of economic phrases have come back into fashion: 'Quantitative easing', 'Interconnectedness', 'Pro-cyclicality'... even the Tobin Tax. But the concept of 'protectionism' is the new black. Though it never went entirely out of fashion, it is now back with a vengeance.

[1] The views set out below are solely those of the author and do not necessarily represent those of the European Commission or the Institute of International Finance. I wish to thank Zsófia Kerecsen, Claire Bury, Ariane Demeneix, Tomas Baert, Ludmila Zalik, Jörg Reinbothe, and Ken Lennan for their many helpful comments and contributions in helping me to prepare this paper.

To give just a few examples from the *Financial Times* over the summer months of 2009:

> 'Beijing rejects protectionism charge'[2]
>
> 'Protectionism is coming at us from all directions. [...] the reality, in this financial crisis, is that we have protectionism by the financial backdoor and may soon have it by the front door.'[3]
>
> 'Protectionism has become a growth industry, with numerous nations—including the US—opting for various direct and indirect barriers to trade since the global financial meltdown of September 2008. [...] the government-led global rebound could still be aborted by government-sponsored protectionism.'[4]
>
> 'Regulatory protectionism won't stop shocks'[5]
>
> 'Unfortunately the proposed [Hedge Funds] directive fails to meet any of these requirements. The restrictions on access to the European market that it would place on fund managers in "third countries" that do not adopt equivalent regulation are protectionist.'[6]

Further evidence of the term's vogue is found by comparing the archives of the *Financial Times*, the website of which shows that between 1 September 2008 and 1 September 2009, there were more articles with the word 'protectionism' in them than the two previous years combined: 908 articles in contrast to 460 for 2007–8 and 404 for 2006–7. Indeed, it is suggested that these results may perhaps be regarded as even more indicative of the unusual prevalence of the word when it is remembered that 2006–8 covered a period when the reaction to the proposed Dubai Ports World purchase of P&O, ongoing US concerns about access to Chinese markets, and global concerns about the behaviour of Sovereign Wealth Funds were all front page news. In the first quarter of 2009 alone, there were more articles published that contained the word 'protectionism' than there were in the whole of 2008.

The same is true for the term 'financial protectionism': 769 articles in 2008–9 compared to 647 for the two previous years combined, and 404 articles in the first months of 2009 alone.

This is only natural. In the first three months of 2009, the world was in the throes of the financial crisis and the start of the economic period variously

[2] Jamil Anderlini, 'Beijing rejects protectionism charge' *Financial Times* (London, 24 June 2009).

[3] J Plender, 'Protectionism is coming at us from all directions' *Financial Times* (London, 1 July 2009) 24.

[4] J Quinlan, Chief Market Strategist, Global wealth and investment management, Bank of America, in 'Insight: the perils of de-globalisation' *Financial Times* (London, 21 July 2009).

[5] H Sender, 'Regulatory protectionism won't stop shocks' *Financial Times* (London, 26 August 2009).

[6] P Montagnon, 'Europe must not cut hedge funds at the root' *Financial Times* (London, 1 September 2009).

described as a 'downturn', 'recession', or 'crisis'. Given the parallels that were being drawn to the 1930s, it was only sensible for policy makers to be concerned that countries would react to the crisis by restricting imports and protecting local industries in the way that they had done almost eight decades previously.

So in principle this is an excellent time to discuss protectionism and to ask ourselves whether, either as a result of the financial crisis or even before that, the EU's approach to company law and financial regulation, and that of its Member States, amounts to protectionism.

To a certain extent, if I were to be speaking on behalf of the European Commission, I could reply to the question 'What is the European Commission's position on economic protectionism?'

Very simply, 'We're against it. Thank you.'

Though, as I will suggest below, both the question and the answer have to be rather more detailed and nuanced than it might first seem.

The structure of this chapter is as follows; in the first half, the theoretical approach shall be taken in order to consider the term 'protectionism' and whether it is a useful way of looking at company law and foreign investment policy, or whether an alternative approach might shed more light on state policies and actions. In so doing we shall ask whether there is a universally agreed definition of the term, and if so, whether this term is viable beyond the imposition of tariff barriers. The core issues in the field of investment and company law will then be examined from the angle of the criteria developed by the Court of Justice of the European Union. It is argued that 'protectionism', whilst useful as a general term, may be inadequate to capture the specifics of what is going on in company law and that these more specific and nuanced criteria should instead be used to guide the debate.

In the second half a more practical approach shall be taken in the form of an examination of the current record of the EU and Member States in two areas—investment and company law—to determine whether they meet the approach that is proposed. I look at how the EU needs to go forward in the coming years in these areas in ensuring that its actions and those of Member States meet the criteria that I have proposed.

What I question in this paper is the value of a specific application of the term 'protectionist' to specific policy actions in a specific area and whether alternative terms or criteria would be of more use. What I do not question is the value of the term in a general sense and more importantly the underlying motivation behind its use. The position of the European Commission and the EU is very clearly towards open investment.

I want to make it clear from the start that the approach that I outline in this paper and the language that I use are very consciously not rigorous legal ones. I am not a lawyer but a policy maker, looking at the practical application and improvement of policy within a set legal framework.

Equally, in discussing the notion of 'protectionism' in the following section, I have inevitably been forced to wade into trade theory. I have tried to do this in a way that strikes a balance between explaining the concept and avoiding turning a discussion of company law and regulation into one on trade law. What follows is somewhat 'Trade Theory for Dummies', an attempt to simplify complex trade concepts down to what is strictly necessary. There is always a danger in simplifying and I therefore apologize to trade lawyers for any oversimplifications.

II. What is 'protectionism' and is it a useful concept for company law?

1. What is 'protectionism'?

One of the things that is very striking about the use of the word 'protectionist' or 'protectionism' both in academic articles and in the press is that it is very rarely defined. We are all assumed to know exactly what it means. This is far from the only expression that gets this treatment. You will not find 'globalization', 'financial stability', 'liberalization', or a large number of other concepts defined on a regular basis either. So why nitpick on 'protectionism'?

First, because if we are moving beyond a generalized use of the term as a sin that we should collectively avoid into an academic or specific application, then we need to be absolutely clear and to agree on exactly what it is we are trying to avoid.

At this point, it is worth also being clear about why we are trying to apply the term to the area of company law and the purpose of the discussion that we are having within this work. I would contend that the purpose of discussing whether a particular law or behaviour is or is not 'protectionist' is because we see 'protectionism' as an economic and societal 'bad' especially between countries which have agreed to the creation of a single market and would want to persuade those jurisdictions carrying it out that it is in their interest to abolish or reform any laws or behaviours that constitute it.

Secondly, because linked to this idea of a societal or economic 'bad', the difference between 'protectionism' and a concept such as 'globalization' is that you can easily find people who will openly say 'I am in favour of globalization' and you can easily find people who will openly say 'I am opposed to further globalization', whereas to my knowledge not a single government currently in power has said or would say 'I am in favour of protectionism'.

The overwhelming majority of developed economies are in principle against it and yet we can all see that it exists. Indeed, if you want to be flippant, you can give a very simple definition of the term, inspired by one-time British Deputy

Prime Minister Herbert Morrison's comment that 'Socialism is what a Labour Government does':[7]

Protectionism is what the other bastards are up to

It is my contention that most trade officials in national administrations privately subscribe to this definition. Like 'evil', protectionism is something done by someone else. This creates problems as I will discuss below.

Thirdly, and linked to this, because if we do not define it, it becomes a term that anyone can use about anything that they do not like. It becomes the economic equivalent of the political expression 'fascist'. And if anyone can use it about anything they like, and no one accepts that it is what they do, then what, ultimately, is the benefit in its usage? So how should we define it? Paramithiotti defines it as:

any state policy action which is adopted for the purpose of improving the competitive position of local firms[8]

If you go to Wikipedia, you find a more precise definition from an unnamed contributor:

Protectionism is the economic policy of restraining trade between states, through methods such as tariffs on imported goods, restrictive quotas, and a variety of other restrictive government regulations designed to discourage imports, and prevent foreign take-over of local markets and companies.[9]

Both of these definitions hint at a basic truth that all of us intuitively understand, like Supreme Court Justice Potter Stewart who memorably wrote that he could not give an exact definition of hard-core pornography, but 'I know it when I see it'.[10] There are many examples in history of economic and trade policy that all of us or indeed the vast majority of us would clearly recognize as 'protectionism' not least the behaviour of many advanced countries during the 1930s in raising tariff barriers.

2. Can it be applied meaningfully to company law?

Now we shall look more closely, however, at the two definitions and how we would judge whether a particular government law, rule, or behaviour in the field of company law (or elsewhere) was 'protectionist'. Let us begin with Paramithiotti's

[7] F Beckett, *Clem Attlee* (London: Politico, 2007).

[8] G Paramithiotti, 'Is project 1992 the first towards European protectionism?' in S Sideri and J Sengupta (eds), *The 1992 European Single Market and the Third World* (London: F Cass, 1992).

[9] <http://en.wikipedia.org/wiki/Protectionism>.

[10] *Jacobellis v Ohio*, 378 US 184 (1964).

definition of it as *any* state policy action which is adopted for the purpose of improving the competitive position of local firms. I emphasize the word 'any'. *Anything* that the state does which improves the competitive position of local firms is protectionist.

What if the state increases funding of education, increasing the number of teachers per pupil, or the academic resources? That increase will in due course lead to a better qualified workforce. That in turn enables employers to recruit higher quality employees, which under most economic theory should lead to higher efficiency and output per firm, which in turn should improve the competitive position of local firms. This would be, according to Paramithiotti, 'protectionist'. It can go on: if the state lowers taxes, it should improve the competitive position of local firms. Which is, according to Paramithiotti, 'protectionist'. Improvements to transport networks, national health—healthier and more productive employees—bank lending, national security, all improve the competitive position of local firms. So, in continuing to forbid protectionist action, the application of Paramithiotti's definition could lead us to a set of outcomes that the vast majority and possibly all of us, would recognize as economically and societally undesirable.

Let us turn to our anonymous Wikipedia contributor's definition of 'protectionism' as,

> the economic policy of restraining trade between states, through methods such as tariffs on imported goods, restrictive quotas, and a variety of other restrictive government regulations designed to discourage imports, and prevent foreign take-over of local markets and companies.

This reminds me of a former colleague in the European Commission who once said to his American counterpart:

> I absolutely agree... with parts of what you say.[11]

Like Paramithiotti, at first sight, this is easy and intuitive. Most of us would agree that whatever 'protectionism' means, it ought to cover tariff barriers against imported goods. Equally, we would agree that it ought to cover restrictive quotas. And intuitively we would understand attempts to prevent foreign takeover of local markets and companies as being protectionist. It is true that the push of global trade talks is and has always been, to cut away at tariff barriers and quotas and to open up local markets and companies to foreign investment.

Indeed, turning to the EU, one of the driving ideas behind its creation was, and remains, the elimination of tariff barriers and quotas between Member States and the creation of a single market based on the free movement of goods, people,

[11] Anonymous European Commission official.

services, and capital. On capital movements, Article 63(1) of the Treaty on the Functioning of the European Union states that:

> ... all restrictions on the movement of capital between Member States and between Member States and third countries shall be prohibited[12]

But the problem comes when you look at other parts of the Wikipedia definition and at its potential practical application. Consider the first part:

> the economic policy of restraining trade between states

Is this really the aim of any government except one engaged in a specific embargo? It might well be the effect, but is it the policy? Surely what any government sees itself as trying to do is to reset the terms in its favour—even if necessary by underhand means—from many of the same grounds as it might increase education or transport spending. So this does not work.

What is more, consider 'designed to discourage imports'. At one level this is intuitively true. If 'protectionism' has any meaning, it is surely an attempt to discourage imports. But the problem with it is its practical application. As we have seen, tariff barriers are inherently designed to discourage imports. However, the problem comes when you move beyond tariff barriers to consider other restrictions to trade, or non-tariff barriers. At one level, such barriers clearly exist and are intuitively undesirable. All of us are aware of direct or indirect import restrictions that we would feel satisfied our basic understanding of 'protectionism': dumping, quotas, arbitrary and excessive import requirements.

At another level though, if we attempt to define non-tariff barriers as any government regulation that restricts imports, we run into the problem that there are lots of examples of government regulation that restrict import and yet can be economically or socially desirable.

Let us take an easy example. Most of us would accept that it is reasonable for a government to set standards on products for consumer safety reasons. Few of us would condemn import bans on easily flammable sofas or mattresses. Almost none of us would object to insisting on high safety standards for children's toys. Equally most of us do not object to the ban on sales of ivory. Equally after the financial crisis, only the most extreme libertarians would object to the idea of governments regulating financial markets. Yet, if we look at it at face value, all government regulation restricts trade in some form because it applies restrictions or conditions, and all government product safety standards restrict trade *per se*. So we are caught between the knowledge that regulation, import standards, and other non-tariff barriers can be and indeed are used by governments to restrict trade and discourage imports, and the realization that there are a huge number of cases where direct or indirect non-tariff barriers can be desirable.

[12] Formerly Article 56 of the EC Treaty.

It is tempting to say 'Welcome to the life of the trade lawyer'. But what all this tells us is that the concept of 'protectionism' whilst extremely useful from a distance as a broad term encapsulating a set of behaviours that we intuitively understand, becomes increasingly muddled the closer that we get to specific cases. 'Protectionism' is like a Claude Monet painting: impressive and clear from afar but dissolving into vague strokes of paint once we get up close. How do we know if a government regulation is intended to promote consumer protection or to discourage imports? Or both?

A potential criticism of this is that I have set up straw men to attack, choosing two weak definitions of 'protectionism' to prove my point. The problem is that whichever definition you go for instead will struggle with the same problems. It is notable that WTO rules do not make 'protectionism' *per se* illegal because they cannot define it. They make specific government behaviours or types of rules illegal. Nor indeed do the Treaties establishing the EU. Indeed when the United Nations Conference on Trade and Development (UNCTAD) had an online debate on investment protectionism, it noted that,

> there seems to be agreement on the lack of a specific definition and meaning for 'investment protectionism'. Some of the experts raised questions about the adequacy of the terminology or suggested that there was a definitional misfit.[13]

'Protectionism' therefore becomes a term that can be very useful at capturing a general picture and a number of actions that could potentially be protectionist, but very bad at looking at specific actions.

3. How should we look at company law and regulation instead?

How do we translate all this into EU company law? How do we move from Monet to Monnet? My suggestion is that like trade lawyers, we should abandon the use of the term in anything but the distant and generalized 'Let us avoid protectionism' sense and find some other language to address the societal and economic 'bad' that we are concerned about. The best way to do this is to begin by going back to first principles. At the moment, what lie behind the concern of global leaders and industry about 'protectionism' are, broadly speaking, two things:

- an emotional fear of return to the policies of the 1930s where increases in trade tariffs and the imposition of tight quotas are perceived by most people to have contributed to the Depression and hindered economic recovery and in turn led to political instability which in turn provided the breeding ground for political extremism, and in particular the rise of fascist regimes in Europe, which in turn led to the Second World War

[13] E-mail from UNCTAD Division on Investment and Enterprise to International Investment Agreement experts, 25 May 2009.

- underlying this, the economic theory of comparative advantage. As Paul Krugman put it: 'If there were an Economist's Creed, it would surely contain the affirmations "I understand the Principle of Comparative Advantage" and "I advocate Free Trade"'.[14] Free trade is vital because it is a contributor to economic growth. By extension 'protectionism' is a bad because it goes against free trade.

So the reason why most of us have such an emotional gut reaction to 'protectionism' and why you will not find a single democratically elected government openly espousing it, is because the underlying goal of governments is economic growth and because we all understand that generally speaking, restrictions on free trade are inimical to this.

So what we are looking for is economic growth and prosperity, and in principle, free trade is part of the means to achieve it, not an end in itself, and by extension 'protectionism' threatens this. Indeed this is the founding insight behind the agreements and treaties that led ultimately to the creation of the EU, the World Trade Organization, and most international financial institutions. The more that we trade with each other, the more that we reduce barriers, the more economic growth there will be, the happier our citizens will be, and the less that countries will see their economic and political interests as competing and the less therefore that they will be inclined to seek more radical solutions and ultimately go to war. Article 3 of the Treaty on European Union defines one objective of the EU as being:

> the sustainable development of Europe based on balanced economic growth and price stability, a highly competitive social market economy, aiming at full employment and social progress, and a high level of protection and improvement of the quality of the environment.[15]

The EU's position, then, is the promotion of economic and social progress, a high level of employment, and balanced and sustainable development. Everything else springs from this. Indeed whilst other jurisdictions will have other ways of phrasing their core economic objectives, and might quibble for instance over whether 'sustainable development' and 'balanced economic growth' are core parts of their aim, the EU's position is at least broadly compatible with that of other jurisdictions and with what most of us would agree is the core economic aim of government.

So, the issue for the EU is how investment policies and regulation, including company law, can best contribute to that economic and social progress, and whether specific measures by the EU and national governments contribute to, or impede, that progress. We need to find a way of measuring and evaluating this

[14] P R Krugman, 'Is Free Trade Passé?' (1987) 1 J of Economic Perspectives 131–44.
[15] Cf formerly Article 2 EU Treaty.

that avoids the term 'protectionism'. How do you make this abstract concept any more meaningful and applicable than 'protectionism'?

Going back to EU Treaties, it is clear that the EU aims to do this by, inter alia:

- establishing a common customs area in which customs duties and quantitative restrictions on the import and export of goods and measures having equivalent effect between Member States are prohibited
- having a common commercial or trade policy
- establishing an internal market based on the free movement of goods, persons, services, and capital
- having an EU-wide competition policy that avoids distortions in the internal market.[16]

As such, the importance of company law for the European Union is in the delivery of an internal market based on the free movement of capital and services.

How do you measure whether the concrete application of these policies by the European Union or by Member States contributes to economic and social progress? How do you make this abstract concept of economic and social progress any more meaningful and applicable than 'protectionism'? My answer is that you need to develop a set of informal specific criteria to help you evaluate individual, national, or EU policies in this area. This is easier said than done and would benefit from further analysis, but as a start, I suggest the following non-exhaustive list of criteria to guide any evaluation:

- that state and EU policy actions be in the general public interest
- that any policy or action be non-discriminatory between companies and individuals in one country or Member State and companies and individuals in another except where justified in the interests of national security or public order
- that any regulatory or legal actions aimed to establish consumer or investor protections be strictly proportionate
- that state policy and actions produce outcomes and a business climate that is predictable and produces predictable outcomes.

Let me look at each of these in turn.

I start with potentially the most difficult: the requirement that state and EU actions be in the general public interest. I have argued above that most of us, deep down, accept that there can be legitimate grounds for governments or other state actors to regulate or otherwise intervene in the economy, even if it means imposing restrictions to trade. In a world of imperfect information, we want to be assured of basic minimum standards when we shop for food, household goods, or cars. But equally, at the other extreme, we do not want states to impose arbitrary

[16] This is a simplification. For the full wording, see Articles 3 ff of the Treaty on the Function of the European Union.

restrictions on products from companies from our country under the guise of consumer or investor protection.

This applies equally when looking at financial regulation and company law. We want to be assured that banks are sufficiently regulated so that our money is safe and that insurers will pay up when faced with a legitimate claim, but we do not want to be prevented from accessing financial services from other countries where it is safe to do so. So the first criterion is a deliberately wide one: that the state action be in the public interest. Nevertheless, in the same way as 'protectionism' suffers from being too vague a concept, so 'in the public interest' is clearly also too vague. What is the public interest and how do you define it?

In financial market regulation and company law, it could be in the public interest to act or intervene on matters of:

- investor or creditor protection
- consumer protection
- prudential supervision of financial institutions and linked to this, financial stability
- national or public security or public order.

Nevertheless, relying on this criterion alone allows for a big leeway of action and plenty of room for actions that would restrict trade in a way that would favour uncompetitive local companies or service providers, so it needs to be limited by other criteria.

The next criterion is therefore that any policy or action be non-discriminatory between companies, goods, services, and individuals from one country or Member State and companies and individuals from another. This is in principle a rather basic and uncontroversial criterion. Countries should not treat equally those that are unequal, or treat unequally those that are equal. WTO rules already require such 'national treatment' between members. Nevertheless, it is an absolutely necessary criterion. This is not, it must be said, a very ambitious criterion and should be considered a minimum requirement for policy. As we will see in the final section, the EU's policy in company law and financial services is to be much more ambitious than this wherever possible.

The requirement for non-discrimination should, however, have very limited exceptions in the interests of national security or public order. Most of us would accept that there are cases where it is legitimate for a state to make a distinction between actors in its own jurisdiction and actors in another. To take an extreme example, supposing that an EU Member State was at war with a third country, would we really allow an arms manufacturer from that third country to take over a defence company in the Member State? Nevertheless these exceptions need to be very tightly drawn, and in any case, as WTO rules stipulate, for example, exceptions cannot lead to arbitrary, unjustifiable discrimination or disguised restrictions.

The next criterion is that any regulatory or legal actions be strictly proportionate to the objective or public interest being pursued. The measure or action should be necessary and should be the least restrictive way to achieve the objective pursued. Anything that goes beyond this is economically inefficient and thus detrimental to economic and social progress.

Linked to this is the criterion that state policy and actions produce outcomes and a business climate that is predictable and produces predictable outcomes. Any company or investor subject to regulation or requirements should know what is required of them ahead of time and be able to predict that if they behave in a certain way or follow a certain procedure, the government or regulator will in turn behave in a certain way. For instance, if a government requires that a potential foreign bidder for a domestic company with potential national security implications undergo an approval process, it should be broadly clear to that foreign bidder what the process will be and what their likelihood of success will be.

If you look closely at the criteria, you see that they are describing in non-legal terms either what the Treaty on the Functioning of the European Union (TFEU) already requires (at least for commerce between Member States and in some cases for commerce between Member States and third countries) or in the case of predictability what the European Union is already broadly doing.

Take the public interest. Articles 34 and 35 TFEU provide that quantitative restrictions on imports and exports and all measures having equivalent effect shall be prohibited between Member States, but Article 36 states that:

> The provisions of Articles 34 and 35 shall not preclude prohibitions or restrictions on imports, exports or goods in transit justified on grounds of public morality, public policy or public security; the protection of health and life of humans, animals or plants; the protection of national treasures possessing artistic, historic or archaeological value; or the protection of industrial and commercial property. Such prohibitions or restrictions shall not, however, constitute a means of arbitrary discrimination or a disguised restriction on trade between Member States.[17]

Equally, on establishment, Article 52(1) TFEU states that:

> The provisions of this Chapter [...] shall not prejudice the applicability of provisions laid down by law, regulation or administrative action providing for special treatment for foreign nationals on grounds of public policy, public security or public health.[18]

And on capital, Article 65(1) TFEU states that:

> The provisions of Article 63 shall be without prejudice to the right of Member States:
>
> (a) to apply the relevant provisions of their tax law which distinguish between taxpayers who are not in the same situation with regard to their place of residence or with regard to the place where their capital is invested;

[17] Formerly Article 30 of the EC Treaty.

[18] Formerly Article 46 of the EC Treaty.

(b) to take all requisite measures to prevent infringements of national law and regulations, in particular in the field of taxation and the prudential supervision of financial institutions, or to lay down procedures for the declaration of capital movements for purposes of administrative or statistical information, or to take measures which are justified on grounds of public policy or public security.[19]

The same is true for non-discrimination. The first paragraph of Article 18 TFEU reads:

Within the scope of application of the Treaties, and without prejudice to any special provisions contained therein, any discrimination on grounds of nationality shall be prohibited.[20]

The proportionality of individual Member State rules or measures is not covered by the Treaties, but the fourth paragraph of Article 5 TEU states that:

Under the principle of proportionality, the content and form of Union action shall not exceed what is necessary to achieve the objectives of the Treaties.[21]

Furthermore proportionality is a fundamental principle of EU law. Predictability is not explicitly covered in the Treaties but the principle of legal certainty is one of the fundamental principles of all law. The only difference is that the Treaties do not group all these criteria into one place as a means of evaluating individual measures. The question though is whether the European Union is actually doing this in practice or whether it needs to do more, and this is what I turn to in the second half of this paper.

III. How do the EU and its Member States measure up?

Given that the subject of this publication is company law, I intend to focus on the record of the EU and Member States there. Nevertheless, I think that it is useful to begin by looking at policies on investment. I then look at the kind of changes that could be made going forward in company law and foreign investment policy.

1. Do policies on investment meet the above criteria?

On investment, there are three areas of potential interest: the record of Member States on sectoral interests, on general third-country investment policy, and the EU's approach to Sovereign Wealth Funds.

Let us not be naïve about this. No matter where we look in the world today, there is domestic political pressure on governments to intervene to protect local companies and assets from foreign takeover or acquisition. There is pressure for

[19] Formerly Article 58(1) of the EC Treaty.
[20] Formerly Article 12 of the EC Treaty.
[21] Formerly Article 5(3) of the EC Treaty.

subsidies to protect industries. There remains a lot of suspicion of foreign direct investment (FDI), foreign takeovers, and foreign acquisition of real estate or other assets, especially when this involves brand name companies. People do not like their brewers or their yogurt manufacturers taken over!

This pressure is as old as the stones.

There have been several examples where governments have succumbed to those pressures and have introduced measures that have not been justified by the interests of public order or security; of financial stability; or of consumer or investor protection. There have been examples where even if there have been reasonable investor protection reasons for intervening, governments have gone far beyond what is necessary or proportionate.

And let us not be naïve about the fact that despite Articles 49 and 63 of the TFEU, these pressures have been felt by EU Member States. As noted in the introduction, this pressure was rising globally even before the financial crisis. In the last five years, the European Commission has launched infringement procedures over aborted takeovers of Italian banks, Spanish energy companies, and part-owned steel conglomerates. At any given moment, both the competition authorities and internal market officials of the Commission are monitoring and investigating a number of suspected or alleged breaches of Treaty rules that could potentially protect local industries from foreign competitors.

At the time of writing, in autumn 2009, the pressures are being felt particularly in the banking sector. The Commission accepted the need for state intervention to rescue banks during the red heat of the financial crisis as a means of ensuring financial stability (and effectively public order), but has made it clear that such intervention should be purely temporary and should be accompanied as soon as possible by financial restructuring.

On 22 July 2009, the Commission adopted a communication on restructuring aid for individual financial institutions, with guidance setting out the conditions banks should meet for the Commission to authorize restructuring aid to them. It aims at transparency, predictability, and equality of treatment between Member States and the different financial institutions. In a recent speech, former EU Competition Commissioner Neelie Kroes stated that:

> ...there is no trade-off between competition policy and financial stability. This Communication is about competition policy supporting financial stability and being a tool to manage orderly the return to normal market functioning. [...] we don't want restructuring to be a band-aid, it must work in the long-term. [...] One element we pay attention to is notably the remuneration incentive structure, in accordance with Commission Recommendation of 30 April 2009 on remuneration policies in the financial services sector, to verify whether it promotes the beneficiary's long-term profitability. [...] competition distortions created by the aid need to be addressed in order to restore conditions which foster the development of competitive markets after the crisis.[22]

[22] N Kroes 'Competition law in an economic crisis', Opening address at 13th Annual Competition Conference of the International Bar Association (Fiesole, 11 September 2009).

In addition to these sectoral pressures, there have been more generalized pressures over the last years. As noted in the introduction, there was huge domestic resistance in the United States to the proposed acquisition of P&O by Dubai Ports World, and with it six American port facilities. The US response to this was the Foreign Investment and National Security Act of 2007 (FINSA), tightening up rules on national security screening of proposed acquisitions of US companies by companies from third countries. This in turn fed pressure in the EU and other jurisdictions for tighter rules on foreign investment in general.

It is no secret that there have been draft laws that would inherently have been discriminatory without the justification of a strict definition of public order or security, that could potentially have been disproportionate in their treatment of proposed foreign takeovers, that would have had difficulty in establishing a predictable foreign investment climate, and that by restricting beneficial foreign investment would have been counter to the creation of a sustainable economy. Nevertheless, so far at least, the battle has been broadly won. The European Commission has engaged with Member State governments in the drafting of laws to ensure that they comply with Article 63 TFEU, which as noted earlier, states that:

> Within the framework of the provisions set out in this chapter, all restrictions on the movement of capital between Member States *and* between Member States and *third* countries shall be prohibited[23]

This is a big stick to wield, and the early signs are that it has been a successful deterrent to measures that would undercut foreign investment in a way not consistent with public order or security. In particular, the Commission was active in opposing the principle of economic security and in persuading Member States to limit the burden of regulations. And what is more, Article 63 goes further than other parts of the Treaties and indeed further than any foreign investment law in any third country by specifying not only that restrictions between Member States be prohibited, but restrictions between Member States and third countries be prohibited.

Nevertheless, most general foreign investment laws that might have raised concern in Member States have only been adopted relatively recently, and the Commission will need to monitor the way in which they are applied in practice. The battle in this area has been won so far but the war is a never-ending one.

In contrast to sectoral pressures though, the short-term effect of the financial crisis has actually been to make most countries more open to foreign investment. As shown with the efforts of the German Government to secure a buyer for Opel and the European arm of GM, when the choice is between bankruptcy and job losses, and foreign investment, Member States and their voters become a lot less selective. The emerging evidence is that countries are looking to suck in as much

[23] Formerly Article 56 of the EC Treaty.

foreign investment as possible to fill the gaps left by the financial crisis and economic downturn. So in many ways, the crisis has had a salutary effect in reminding policy makers of the benefits of inward investment, although it would be foolish to think that domestic fears of foreign takeovers have retreated forever.

This has extended to the way in which countries see Sovereign Wealth Funds (SWFs). Just half a year before the financial crisis, the activities and purchases of SWFs were of major political concern. Anecdotal evidence suggests that a number of countries and private companies have approached and are approaching SWFs looking for investment. Nevertheless, one needs to be cautious here about what has happened and what will happen. There are very real and legitimate underlying concerns about the behaviour of SWFs. In its February 2008 communication on SWFs, the European Commission noted that whilst SWFs benefited the global capital market and provided funding for global investment and could contribute to financial stability, they also raise concerns in terms of accumulated current account imbalances, the ultimate aim, and transparency, so:

> A more specific concern raised by SWF investment in equities relates to the opaque way in which some SWFs function and their possible use as an instrument to gain strategic control. [...] SWF investment in certain sectors could be used for ends other than for maximising return.[24]

The Commission argued that no further legislation was required for the time being and called for a common EU approach based on the following principles:

- commitment to an open investment environment
- support of multilateral work
- use of existing instruments
- respect of Treaty obligations and international commitments
- proportionality and transparency.

In addition, it argued that:

> the right approach is to promote a cooperative effort between recipient countries and SWFs and their sponsor countries to establish a set of principles ensuring the transparency, predictability and accountability of SWFs investments. It is essential that all relevant actors are actively involved in the creation of a balanced and stable framework covering SWF investments.[25]

The reason why SWFs have gone down the political agenda is not just because of the financial crisis, but because this co-operative effort has and is taking place. In October 2008, the International Working Group of Sovereign Wealth Funds (IWG) composed of SWFs and government representatives of

[24] 'A common European approach to Sovereign Wealth Funds', Communication from the Commission to the European Parliament, the Council, the European Economic and Social Committee, and the Committee of the Regions, 27 February 2008, 4.

[25] Ibid, 7.

23 countries with SWFs and assisted by the International Monetary Fund (IMF) agreed a set of 24 'Generally Accepted Principles and Practices' (GAPP), known as the 'Santiago Principles',[26] covering, broadly speaking, transparency and governance arrangements. Whilst the principles are being implemented, this agreement has gone a long way to assuaging the concerns of recipient countries. The EU will continue to review the situation and the implementation of the principles. As Member States return to economic health and if the principles are not properly implemented or not implemented by all SWFs, the tensions could well return.

How does the EU's approach on SWFs measure up against the criteria I set out earlier? Given the concern that SWFs could act for non-economic reasons, could be used as an instrument to gain strategic control, and could impact on current account imbalances, which in turn would threaten financial stability, there is a valid public interest and public security interest to monitor their behaviour. The EU's approach is also non-discriminatory in the sense that it makes no distinction between SWFs based in EU and non-EU countries. It is also explicitly proportionate and predictable. The communication argues that:

> Measures taken for public interest reasons on investment should not go beyond what is necessary to achieve the justified goal, in line with the principle of proportionality, and the legal framework should be predictable and transparent.[24]

So in general, on investment issues, the battle to meet the criteria has so far been won. As the economic situation improves, so parts of the battle will get easier—sectoral pressures for action—but other parts could get harder.

2. Do policies on company law meet the criteria?

Takeover regulation is an area where countries often face criticism of being protectionist.

Although a few takeovers may be outright harmful, evidence shows that an open takeover market leads to efficiencies and has an overall beneficial effect on the economy. The European Commission has been promoting an open market for corporate control in the EU for a long time. Apart from publicly 'naming and shaming' national governments who exercised political pressure over the bidder or the target during the takeover process, the Commission has proposed ambitious regulation for the takeover process.

The Takeover Directive originally aimed at introducing high corporate governance standards which would have facilitated takeovers to a large extent. It would have given a final say for shareholders in the takeover debate and aimed to neutralize the effect of certain mechanisms that provided disproportionate

[26] International Working Group of Sovereign Wealth Funds, *Sovereign Wealth Funds: Generally Accepted Principles and Practices* (Santiago Principles) (October 2008).

control over the company for certain shareholders or the management during the takeover. Such rules would have helped to eliminate numerous mechanisms which can prevent a successful change of control.

The Directive, however, met opposition from certain EU Member States on the grounds that the EU rules would set very high standards as to the ways in which companies can defend themselves compared to the rest of the world. As capital flows freely between the EU and third countries, fear of an uneven playing field with third countries—or the allegation of it—has prevented any meaningful market opening within the EU. The Directive's core rules have been made optional and very few Member States have improved their legislation when transposing the Directive. The way these options have been implemented could even have contributed to making takeovers more difficult in some Member States.

The Takeover Directive clearly shows the perceived limits of any individual action within a global market. There is no willingness to give more than what one can expect in return. The fundamental problem is that the application of such a 'mercantilist approach' could be considered as reasonable and legitimate in international trade negotiations, but may not necessarily be in the interest of the shareholders of companies and their employees, and ultimately of the European economy.

Takeover barriers have wide-ranging effects, but most of them are designed to ring-fence weak and inefficient management to the detriment of shareholders and/or to protect a lucky few shareholders to the detriment of the rest. It is sobering to see that in some Member States shareholders who had the final word on any 'poison pill' launched by the management to frustrate a takeover bid before the implementation of the Directive might no longer have such a right in all circumstances. Some Member States do not even consider it necessary to give shareholders such an approval right.

Who is protected by such rules? Are they in the general interest? Definitely not.

Another distinctive feature of the Directive is the so called 'reciprocity rule'. Under its terms, if a company that does not apply the Directive's aforementioned takeover-facilitating rules and can therefore be considered as a 'protected company' launches a takeover bid for a 'non-protected company', the non-protected company can easily switch to a 'protected' status. Thus, it will be easier for it to thwart the bid.

Is such a rule in the general interest? Does it protect the shareholders of the target company? Not necessarily. One may argue that the corporate governance system—including whether shareholders have a say over a bid—of the bidder company is indeed important for those shareholders who may want to stay within the company but what about those who want to sell their shares? It is simply not relevant for them whether or not the target's shareholders have the approval right.

Does it protect the employees of the company? Not necessarily either, as the bidder's management may be more efficient and offer better employment conditions.

Are the Directives' rules or the way it has been implemented at national level discriminatory? In principle, no. The Directive applies the same way to EU companies and to third-country companies. As some of the Directive's rules have not been applied in practice (eg reciprocity), we do not yet know what practical difficulties it might create for EU and third-country bidders.

Are the Directive's rules as applied by Member States proportional? In other words, for example, is preventing shareholders from a final say over the takeover the only means to achieve certain legitimate goals, such as giving the target companies' management a chance to respond to the takeover offer and provide an alternative? Probably not.

Another alleged example of 'protectionism' in the company law context is the unfavourable treatment of the mobility of companies. In principle, the EU Treaty offers companies freedom to move. However, Member States make this very costly or prohibit it altogether. Therefore, it is almost impossible for companies to deregister from one Member State and continue their business under another Member State's company law regime.

Although mobility and freedom establishment is one of the fundamental rights in the Internal Market, it does not work in practice for companies. What general interest reasons could justify such artificial safeguards against company mobility? The Court of Justice of the European Union has repeatedly said that economic, including fiscal, considerations can never justify restrictions on the fundamental freedoms. So the current behaviour of such Member States cannot be said to meet the public interest criterion.

It is also clear that such behaviour effectively discriminates against companies, but in this case, against companies from the home jurisdiction.

Some Member States argue that it would be difficult to supervise companies if they were able to maintain their registration in their territory but could move their activities to another Member State. Would such a consideration be proportionate? Certain Member States allow companies to move despite such hurdles. But in general, this problem could be resolved with improvement to the ways in which company registries co-operate with each other. Work has already been started on this matter. So once again, the behaviour is disproportionate to what is needed. The behaviour does at least create a predictable business climate in those Member States, but predictable only in the sense of producing predictably sub-optimal outcomes.

Both company law examples underline the same problem: Member States' governments might believe in principle in an 'EU of opportunities' and its wide-ranging beneficial effects for their own companies and economy, but when it comes to practice, they continue to stick to the status quo or, at worst, even restrict the opportunities of their own firms.

3. How do we need to go forward?

The record then of the EU and Member States is a mixed one. On the one hand, the provisions of the Treaty on the free movement of capital and services, together with the rigorous enforcement policy of the European Commission have steered Member States away from many of the more populist impulses and pressures. On the other, on proposing new EU legislation, the way forward has been very difficult.

How can the EU and its Member States improve?

The first way is for the EU (and the academic and business community) to be much more vocal and persuasive about the benefits of open investment. In general, Member States should avoid restrictions and potential distortions. Countries with more open investment regimes tend to be better placed to benefit from sustainable economic growth. As we have seen, foreign investment has actually put many countries in a better position to withstand the shocks of the financial crisis, not worse. This message is obvious to economists but needs to be repeated and repeated.

The second way though is to accept that there can be valid reasons for economic intervention or regulation. Indeed, well-judged, proportionate, and predictable regulation can stabilize the economy and lay the grounds for sustainable economic and social progress. This is particularly true in the light of the financial crisis. European investors and companies need complete confidence in the integrity of the financial system and in its regulation and supervision. In other words, it is all about a delicate balance rather than black and white terms of 'protectionism' or 'economic nationalism' that serve only to divide people and entrench views. The criteria that I have set out could easily be improved, for instance to look more at the effect of competition and competitiveness, but hopefully at least suggest a route forward.

Third, and more concretely, the European Commission will need to remain vigorous in its enforcement of the Treaty and rules on competition, state aids, the free movement of capital, and other internal market rules. In particular, in the coming years, the Commission will need to be vigilant in ensuring that Member States implement a co-ordinated exit strategy from bank rescue schemes and other forms of economic intervention introduced during the crisis.

Fourth, as regards the Takeover Directive, it is likely that any improvement to the Directive would meet resistance as long as third-country standards do not improve.

The financial crisis has shed more light on certain key corporate governance failures, (eg lack of accountability of management, absence of shareholders in the governance of companies, etc) which have prompted a new debate on the need to strengthen corporate governance standards. This debate is highly relevant in the takeover context. There is a need for a deep analysis of the actual functioning and any possible meaningful improvements of the Directive. This analysis will also take into account any lessons to be drawn from the current corporate governance debate and the effect of possible measures which could be introduced to improve corporate governance.

Work will start on the examination of the Takeover Directive in 2010/2011 in order to produce a report that the Commission is required to issue on the Directive's operation in 2011. Finally, whilst the focus of this paper has been the EU and the actions of Member States, there is a clear danger in a 'Euro-centric' approach to regulation. The financial crisis has highlighted the extent to which regulatory and financial actions and behaviours in one part of the global economy inevitably impact on other parts and thus require co-ordinated international responses.

In fairness, these did not begin with the financial crisis. There are many forms of international co-operation which have been going for decades, and even before the crisis, there had been a marked stepping up of international regulatory co-operation, particularly between the EU and the United States. To give one example, in the last decade, the EU and US have moved to a point where they have effectively mutually recognized the accounting standards used in the other, with the US Securities and Exchange Commission (SEC) accepting the use of International Financial Reporting Standards (IFRS) by non-US companies listed on a US exchange, and the EU finding the use of US Generally Accepted Accounting Principles (US GAAP) by US issuers. The EU in particular has been pioneering the usage of 'equivalence' clauses in which a firm from a non-EU country can access EU markets if it is regulated in a way that is deemed to be equivalent—but not necessarily identical—to the standards set out in the relevant EU Directive.

This international co-operation needs to be stepped up. The European Commission and EU Member States have actively supported the work of the G20 over the last year and the new Financial Stability Board, but a lot more will need to be done. Equally, and in complement to this, the EU will need to continue to build up its bilateral relationships on company law, most notably with the US in the Financial Markets Regulatory Dialogue but also with China, Japan, India, and other commercial partners.

IV. Conclusion

Without getting into a rather sterile, clichéd, and pointless debate about whether we are passing through the worst economic crisis since the Second World War, the Great Depression, or the Ice Age and the end of the dinosaurs, it is clear that the world is going through an exceptionally difficult economic period and that there is little prospect of an early exit.

From the moment that the financial crisis erupted over a year ago, there has been a real danger that countries would react to it by turning in on themselves and succumbing to political pressures from national sectoral interests, rather than co-operating to resolve the crisis and ensure economic recovery.

Whilst the most critical point seems to have passed, the danger remains acute, and will likely do so for a considerable time to come. There is a very real possibility that trade restrictions that are unjustified by any sensible reading of the public interest will be introduced and that countries could get into a spiral of retaliation. As this paper was being written, a trade dispute was breaking between the United States and China over the Obama Administration's decision to impose tariffs on the import of Chinese tyres, with both sides accusing each other of protectionism.

It is vital that the EU guards against this by continually reminding itself and partners of the dangers, and being ready to act. But at the same time, industry and others will get nowhere by crying wolf every time a financial regulation is introduced. We need to recognize that not all regulations and restrictions on trade or measures to support local industry are motivated by base nationalistic motives or would produce negative outcomes. We should guard against attempting to tar all measures with the same brush of 'protectionism' if we are not to get into a totally meaningless debate in which we convince no one and instead succeed in promoting division and entrenching positions.

Economic growth and social progress should be the focus of policy. Well-designed regulation and company law can actually sustain economic growth rather than inhibit it. All policies and actions should be judged against whether they contribute to that growth and do so in a way that is in the public interest, non-discriminatory except for reasons of public order or security, proportionate, and predictable.

Whilst the term 'protectionist' has its uses at a general level, it is these other terms that are much more useful in judging specific measures in company law and foreign investment policy. Whilst they have been part of EU law for decades, they are of special relevance now. Such terms better enable policy makers to focus on good regulation which will in turn produce better outcomes and will in turn promote better policy and outcomes by commercial partners.

The EU has been a tremendous force for good on these issues and on the promotion of a single market in general. Indeed, the early signs from the crisis have been that Treaty rules and the introduction of the euro played a vital stabilizing role. But more needs to be done and there are huge challenges over the coming years: ensuring a successful exit from the crisis, reforming financial markets, defending the EU's Single Market and, within this, promoting a sustainable and open business environment through improvements to company law.

Much has been done and yet there is still so much more left to do.

4

Protectionism, Capital Freedom, and the Internal Market

Jonathan Rickford[1]

Protectionism in the company law field takes two main forms: action by governments to insulate national markets from foreign competition, mainly in markets for capital and corporate control (often dressed up as social policy) and action by company controllers to protect themselves (sometimes dressed up as the corporate interest) from competitive forces (particularly foreign ones) in the same markets. There thus emerges an arena for the interplay of national (governmental) and corporate (managerial) self-interest, social policy, and internal market freedoms.

The Treaty provisions on free movement of capital, for long the orphan child of the internal market, have more recently been recognized as an important tool in addressing the tensions involved. Even more recently their relevance has been thrown into doubt.

This chapter explores the special problems of the capital freedom and examines its current and expected direction of development, taking account of the implications of developments in other fields of internal market law, notably horizontal application of freedoms of establishment and services and recent rapid developments in the complex field of corporate taxation. These have led to the most recent Court decisions on the boundary between capital and establishment, which are finally critically examined.

[1] This chapter explores thoughts first uttered at the Finnish EU presidency conference in Stockholm in October 2006 and developed in 'Free Movement of Capital and Protectionism—an Essay in Honour of Eddy Wymeersch', in M Tison and others (eds), *Perspectives in Company Law and Financial Regulation* (Cambridge: Cambridge University Press, 2009).

I. Protectionism defined and located

1. 'Economic protectionism'

As it has been dealt with elsewhere in this book, little time needs to be spent achieving a common understanding of what we mean by protectionism. Its essence is the assertion of selfish interests in defiance of market forces, by those in a position to influence the outcome to that end by legal means. The two main players in the game are governments exercising public powers and private individuals (whether or not clothed in corporate form) exercising private powers to the same effect. Sometimes governments also seek to achieve their objective under the guise of private powers. The target of such activity is usually foreign claims, which are usually regarded as a greater threat to the national or managerial self-interests concerned.

This volume is concerned with Company Law and Protectionism and thus the particular arena with which we are concerned is the use of powers of corporate control and governance. The context is of course the internal market, with its philosophy of achieving welfare aims by the operation of economic freedoms throughout Europe based on an economic policy founded on 'the principle of an open market economy with free competition'.[2] The key internal market freedoms for our purposes are:

- free movement of capital (Article 63 Treaty on the Functioning of the European Union [TFEU])—ie that:

> all restrictions on the movement of capital between Member States and third countries shall be prohibited

(we may note in passing at the outset that this freedom is not in fact 'internal' purporting to regulate aspects of third-country markets as well) and

- freedom of establishment (Articles 49 and 54 TFEU)—ie (condensing these Articles to bring out their effect on companies) that:

> restrictions on the freedom of establishment of... [inter...alia] companies formed in accordance with the law of a Member State[3]... in the territory of another Member State shall be prohibited... Freedom of establishment shall include the right... to set up and manage [such] companies under the conditions laid down for its own... com-

[2] Formerly Article 4 EC Treaty, now re-enacted, arguably in slightly stronger form, in Treaty on the Functioning of the European Union (TFEU) Article 119. Note, however, that Article 119 serves the purposes of Article 3 Treaty on European Union which as well as the internal market cites 'a highly competitive social market economy'.

[3] The additional conditions in Article 54 having to do with the 'real seat' qualification of such companies are omitted here as irrelevant for the purposes of this paper.

panies by the law of the country where such establishment is effected, subject to the provisions of the Chapter relating to capital.

The pressures on governments to interfere with and distort the operation of these freedoms for reasons of national or electoral self-interest are notorious. During the period of the preparation of this chapter, for example, President Sarkozy has announced the establishment of a fund of €20 billion to be vested in the *Caisse des Dépots* and designed to fund and safeguard the capital of 'strategic businesses'.[4] On the same day, in the context of banking failures in Germany, Chancellor Merkel announced that a 'German solution' needed to be found. The powers conferred on company boards by and under the Directive on Takeover Bids[5] to frustrate the operation of such bids without doubt reflect the wish of some Member States to allow similar measures to be adopted in the private law domain.

2. Location

This contribution sets out to identify the principles which the Court of Justice of the European Union has developed to deal with this problem and, tentatively, to elucidate the possible directions of future development. The story begins with the aggressive privatization programmes adopted in many Member States to fund national deficits in the run-up to the final stage of economic and monetary union and the desire manifested at the same time to retain control of the privatized entities for reasons of national policy, including security of supply in the public utilities but also in many (perhaps all) cases to achieve industrial policy and market management objectives.[6] The powers (collectively known as 'golden shares' although in many cases no special share was issued and the powers were based entirely on public law) were also capable of being used to frustrate foreign ownership and takeovers generally.[7] The Commission rightly saw a major threat to the internal market in these measures and mounted a campaign of pressure and litigation, based on arguments that the provisions infringed both (what is now) Articles 49 and 63 TFEU, but, for reasons which may be no more than accidental, until very recently the law which has developed as a result has been based on Article 63.

[4] B Hall, 'Sarkozy acts to protect industry' *Financial Times* (London, 21 November 2008) 7.

[5] Directive 2004/25/EC of the European Parliament and of the Council of 21 April 2004 on Takeover Bids, [2004] OJ L142/12 Articles 9–12.

[6] Quite explicit in Case C-367/98 *Commission v Portugal* [2002] ECR I-4731 (structure of the economy), Case C-174/04 *Commission v Italy* [2005] ECR I-4933, and Cases C-463 and 464/04 *Federconsumatori v Milano* [2007] ECR I-10419 (competitive structure, foreign state control).

[7] Quite explicit in Case C-112/05 *Commission v Germany* [2007] ECR I-8995 (*Volkswagen* ('*VW*') case).

II. Golden shares and Article 63 TFEU

What is the connection between such golden share-type powers and the prohibition on restricting free movement of capital in Article 63? This depends on the scope of the Article and the meaning of 'capital movement'.

1. The scope of capital

It has been established since 1999[8] that the nomenclature in Annex I (including important clarifications in its explanatory notes) to the Capital Directive of 1988[9] is 'indicative'[10] as to the meaning of capital movement. This, in brief, makes it clear that any participation in companies, whether by 'direct' investment (ie 'to establish or maintain lasting economic links'), or portfolio (ie broadly speaking passive) (listed or unlisted), is covered. 'Direct' investment includes 'establishment and extension of branches or new undertakings' wholly owned by the provider of the capital (whether by foundation *ab initio* or acquisition) and the acquisition, establishment, and extension of existing branches of such undertakings is also covered. 'Direct' investment also includes participation in a company through a 'block of shares' which enables the shareholder 'to participate effectively in the management of the company or in its control'.[11] So capital rights are exercised on acquisition or disposal or enjoyment[12] of complete or partial ownership of a company, with or without control rights. This at least seems to be the clear effect of the Directive and the case law until very recently.[13]

[8] Case C-22/97 *Trummer and Mayer* [1999] ECR I-1661 at [20], [21]. Repeated in all the golden share cases (see below) most recently in the *Volkswagen* case (n 7) at [18].

[9] Council Directive 88/361/EEC, [1988] OJ L178/5, providing direct implementation of the original indirectly effective Article 67 EC (the pre-predecessor to Article 63 TFEU). Use of secondary legislation to interpret the Treaty is questionable: old Article 67 was materially different from Article 63 (enacted by the Treaty of Amsterdam as Article 56 EC); it applied only to 'movements of capital belonging to persons resident in Member States'—repeated in its Article 1. Also how can secondary legislation define primary, on which it depends? But this is now very well established.

[10] 'Indicative' is obscure. In practice the Court follows the annex list, interpreting it broadly.

[11] Rigid distinction between direct and portfolio investment in shares is unsatisfactory—any share carries rights of control and influence and may at any time become an active investment, for example in a public offer—a good reason for rejecting (as the Court did) the arguments of AG Colomer in Case C-98/01 *Commission v United Kingdom* [2003] ECR I-4641 ('*BAA*'), that direct investment issues be resolved solely under the establishment chapter. This is important in restructuring—portfolio investment often becomes direct, when mergers or takeovers are proposed.

[12] As with the other freedoms the protection from restriction extends to all the incidents of enjoyment—see here the Capital Directive (n 9) Annex I, preamble.

[13] But Case C-326/07 *Commission v Italy* [2009] ECR I-2291 seems clearly to imply a curtailing of this definition.

2. The prohibition

Having characterized a capital movement for Treaty purposes as including such investment in companies, it seems easy enough to identify the obligation of Member States—surely any state measure, legislative or administrative, which has the potential, object, or effect of restricting the enjoyment of the freedom should be prohibited, subject to general interest justification, on the analogy of the other freedoms?[14]

Matters are, however, not so simple.[15] The cases on Member States' reservations of control powers over companies on privatization by means of so-called 'golden shares' powers show a quite complex picture.[16]

Typically these powers enable Member States to veto certain strategic transactions, such as disposals of core assets or subsidiaries (strategic consent powers), or to veto the acquisition of blocks of shares and/or of voting powers by persons, or associates, above a percentage ceiling (voting or shareholding caps). In some cases they also include powers to nominate board members, so as to secure influence over ongoing operations, or at least to secure sources of information so that other powers can be exercised (board nomination powers). In such cases Member States or their public authorities may have *special* powers in the sense that the powers in question are not available to other shareholders. However, it is also possible for Member States to acquire shares (whether as a result of a new issue or in the market[17]) giving general powers of control under the articles of association—ie which are available also to other shareholders should they choose to acquire the shares necessary for the purpose. For example a voting cap or nomination power may apply generally, but the state may take a shareholding sufficient to exploit (or control) this general provision under the company's constitution.[18]

[14] Cf the familiar jurisprudence on goods based on Case 8/74 *Procureur du Roi v Benoît and Gustave Dassonville* [1974] ECR 837 at [5] 'all rules . . . which are capable of hindering, directly or indirectly, actually or potentially, intra community trade'.

[15] The following part of this chapter essentially follows the essay in Honour of Eddy Wymeersch (n 1). See too for further analysis WG Ringe, 'Company law and free movement of capital' (2010) 69 Cambridge L J, forthcoming, available at <http:ssrn.com/abstract=1295905> (last accessed 20 January 2010).

[16] The key cases fall into three groups, represented selectively in this paper by: (1) Case C-367/98 *Commission v Portugal* (n 6) (privatization of a wide range of enterprises); Case C-483/99 *Commission v France* [2002] ECR I-4781 (*Elf Aquitaine*); Case C-503/99 *Commission v Belgium* [2002] ECR I-4809 (*Distrigas*); similar is Case C-463/00, *Commission v Spain* [2003] ECR I-4581 (petroleum, telecommunications, banking, tobacco, and electricity); (public law cases); (2) C-98/01 *Commission v United Kingdom* (*BAA* case, n 11), C-463/00, and C-282/04, and C-283/04 *Commission v Netherlands* [2006] ECR I-9141 (*KPN/TPG* cases) (private law cases); and more recently (3) C-112/05 *Commission v Germany* (*Volkswagen* case, n 7).

[17] The typical golden share is issued on or before privatization. The shares in the *KPN* case were issued after incorporation as a company but before the IPO. The Lower Saxony shares in the *Volkswagen* case were acquired in the market—see *Commission v Germany* (*Volkswagen*) (n 7) at [37].

[18] *Volkswagen* is the only such decided case so far.

Such powers may thus be acquired under purely public law provisions, or under public law provisions authorizing or requiring issue to Member States of shares conferring ostensibly private law powers to the same effect (ie a mixture of public and private law), or through issue to, or acquisition by, the state of such shares under private law processes and procedures[19] (ie purely private law provision). The variation between the public or private source of the state powers concerned and between special and general powers has been argued to have different legal effects under the Treaty.

In 1997 the Commission, viewing such measures as liable to infringe EU law, issued a communication[20] and began a series of legal proceedings. The subsequent cases can be conveniently dealt with in three groups:

- those involving public law powers reserved to the state
- those involving private law powers—ie powers which could have been conferred on any shareholder under applicable company law—also reserved to the state
- one case also involving state exercise of three powers conferred by the Articles, (themselves, however, enacted by public legislation), one reserved to the state but the other two available to all shareholders—the *Volkswagen* case.[21]

The position is complicated by the recent decision in a case involving private law powers that has been decided under the establishment as well as the capital Treaty provisions.[22] The implications of this are reserved to the end of the chapter.

III. First group of cases—powers reserved to the state under public law

The first three cases, against *Portugal, France,* and *Belgium*,[23] all involved special powers conferred on the state by or under[24] public law provision, either to intervene in strategic decisions or to cap participation rights or to nominate board members, or some combination of these. The powers in question were conceded

[19] eg via issue by the company of shares for subscription, or via purchase in the market.

[20] On Certain Legal Aspects concerning Intra-EU investment of 19 July 1997, [1997] OJ C220/15.

[21] In *Volkswagen* there were three restrictions, of which two were of this general character but the third, a special board nomination power, was special to the state bodies concerned and not available under general company law and therefore falls into the first category. See in detail below.

[22] *Commission v Italy* (n 13), see below. [23] n 16 above.

[24] In all three cases the powers were conferred under special public legislation—in *Commission v Belgium* (n 16) and *Commission v France* (n 16) this operated by conferring special shares, but in *Commission v Portugal* (n 6) the legislation conferred powers directly on the state. The distinction was not raised in the Court.

to amount to restrictions on capital. France and Portugal[25] did argue that the provisions were not discriminatory and did not involve any particularly restrictive treatment of nationals of other Member States;[26] but the court ruled that they were 'liable to impede the acquisition of shares in the enterprises concerned and to dissuade investors in other Member States from investing in their capital' and 'as a result to render free movement of capital illusory' thus restricting the right to make direct investments as defined by the Capital Directive.[27] The Court thus, implicitly at least,[28] refused to accept the argument that the provisions were not prohibited restrictions because they did not bear differentially on investors from outside the home Member State, ie inhibit 'access' to the state market.[29] The Court focused on the impact on investors generally, and saw no need for a finding that investors from other states would be more 'impeded' than domestic ones.

The effect of this first set of cases was that where special powers to intervene in strategic decision-making or to disallow acquisition of strategic stakes were conferred by or under public law on Member States then if the effect was to render investment from other Member States less attractive (inevitably so, given the operational constraints and limits on realization of investment, eg in takeovers) the provisions would be prohibited restrictions. (They might of course nevertheless have been justified, the grounds for which are discussed separately below.) Actual impediment to investors was not required to be proved; the fact that foreign investors were 'liable' to be impeded was sufficient and the court had no hesitation in inferring this from the facts.

IV. Second group of cases—powers under private law

The powers in these cases were conferred by or under private law provisions which made special exceptions in favour of the state from the normal rules of company governance.

In the following two cases the powers were conferred by or under the company's articles of association. The result was achieved by vesting a special share bearing the relevant powers in a government official under private law. These powers were consistent with the general company law—ie their legal source was

[25] Portugal argued that insofar as some of the powers were discriminatory on their face there was a policy of not applying them in that way. The Court rejected this argument applying well-established case law to the effect that legislation must be 'cleaned' of discriminatory provisions—*Commission v Portugal* (n 6) at [41].

[26] *Commission v Portugal* (n 6) at [43]; *Commission v France* (n 16) at [39].

[27] *Commission v Portugal* (n 6) at [30] and [45]–[46]; *Commission v France* (n 16) at [37]–[42].

[28] In *Commission v France* (n 16) at [40] the Court ruled that the prohibition 'goes beyond the mere elimination of unequal treatment on grounds of nationality' but this arguably refers only to discrimination.

[29] See the discussion in P Oliver and W Roth, 'The Internal Market and the Four Freedoms' (2004) 41 CML Rev 407.

the company's (private law) constitution and they could lawfully have been conferred on any shareholder.

1. *BAA* case

The first of these was the *BAA* case, concerning a golden share in the company owning the major UK airports.[30] Issue of this share was authorized by the privatization legislation. The UK Government made two important arguments:

The first argument was that the constraints in question (which conferred a prior approval power on government for disposals of major airports and for acquisitions of more than a 15 per cent voting stake) could not amount to restrictions because they bore equally on all shareholders and thus did not constrain access to the market.[31] The Court responded, following the Commission, that the restrictions 'affected the position of a person acquiring a shareholding as such and are thus liable to deter investors from other Member States and, *consequently, affect access* to the market'[32] [emphasis added]. The Court seems to have regarded it as obvious that these special powers made investment in the company less attractive to other investors and ruled that that in itself affected access. This confirmed the less explicit rulings in the first group of cases; it amounts to an assertion that *the likelihood ('liability') of deterrence of other Member States investors* amounts to an effect on access and therefore restricts the freedom, regardless of whether it is greater than the effect on domestic investors.

This conclusion about access was not a surprise.[33] Although the issue had been obscured in the previous cases by the concessions by the Member States the Court had found a restriction in each case in spite of equal applicability.[34]

It is nevertheless difficult to follow and open to challenge.[35] Internal market law is concerned with effects on inter-state trade. There are also apparently wide implications: if provisions which bear equally on domestic and foreign

[30] *Commission v UK* (n 11).

[31] At [24]–[27], citing the well-known cases on goods, Cases C-267/91 and 268/91 *Criminal Proceedings against Keck and Mithouard* [1993] ECR I-6097.

[32] Ibid at [46].

[33] Although AG Colomer protested, arguing that in the interests of uniformity of application of all the freedoms the Court 'should temper the rigour with which it applied its principles on restrictions applicable without distinction . . . as it did . . . in *Keck*', opinion at [36] footnote 10.

[34] There is also a formidable objection, based on Article 345 TFEU (formerly Article 295 EC) (property rights unaffected by the Treaty), and indeed on logic (the greater includes the less), that since it was lawful for the state to reserve the whole of the property rights in BAA to itself by not privatizing at all (thus totally stifling any private capital investment in the enterprise), it must have been lawful to reserve part, while privatizing the rest, allowing some such investment subject to such powers. In the *UK (BAA)* case (n 11), AG Colomer adopted this reasoning at [37], but the Court has consistently rejected it on the ground that the freedoms trump Article 345 TFEU—see eg *BAA* case at [67]. Colomer returned to the point in *Commission v Italy* (n 13) but did not carry it through—see below. Compare the approach of AG Maduro in *Commission v Netherlands,* the *KPN* case (n 16) at [28] (once the state puts an enterprise into the market it is bound by market norms).

[35] In *Commission v Netherlands* (n 16), AG Maduro at [24] suggested that where any shares confer special rights they are likely to inhibit access because those rights are likely to be vested

shareholders are subject to the Treaty then any general provision of mandatory company law—eg one which requires directors to be removable by a particular majority—or indeed any such provision of a company's constitution—eg a limitation on the objects, or a provision which restricts constitutional change—may deter an investor and therefore apparently amount to a restriction. If the provision is there for private purposes then *ex hypothesi* there will be no general interest to be invoked by way of justification. If it is there for public purposes it will also require justification; but does all mandatory company law require justification? As we shall see below, these lines of argument suggested that the breadth of the ruling required qualification, at least in cases not involving the exercise of powers by states and/or not involving special powers reserved to states.

On the other hand, there is a considerable likelihood in practice that foreign investors will be deterred more than domestic ones by powers if vested in public authorities, because of the risk, and sometimes even explicit threat, that they will be used to achieve national policies which damage non-nationals, or even for purposes which are covertly, or even overtly, discriminatory. The very existence of the powers in such hands may be sufficient to deter foreign investors and thus to make it unnecessary ever actually to exploit the powers in this anti-market way. The reality is that such equally applicable restrictions in such hands do in fact bear unequally on access as a matter of fact. It is submitted that this justifies the Court's position.

The second argument made by the UK Government in the *BAA* case was that the powers were private law powers, compatible with UK company law (albeit unusual) and thus not 'repugnant to company law'. The Commission responded that this made no difference, because the powers were exercisable exclusively by the UK Government *qua* state. The Court rejected the UK argument on somewhat different grounds: that the articles 'do not arise as the result of the normal operation of company law' but had to be approved under the privatization Act; the UK therefore acted 'in its capacity as a public authority'.[36]

On this point the decision thus appears to have turned on whether there was a state measure.[37] (The Court appears implicitly to have conceded that a provision compatible with company law that was not such a measure would have been lawful.) The statutory authorization was deemed to constitute such a measure. But that was essentially an accident: the same result could have been achieved by

in nationals, thus deterring investment by non-nationals. This point (not adopted by the Court) clearly applies *a fortiori* to cases where the shares are vested in national governments.

36 Ibid at [47]. The Commission itself suggested a 'derogation from company law' test in 1999, n 35 above. The Court's reference to normal company law may have been a reference to the substance of the provision rather than (or as well as?) the process for its adoption. In other words this may have also been a 'disproportionality' ruling. But the issue scarcely matters as the Court has exposed the point elsewhere—see below.

37 The restriction at 15% on voting rights was not 'special'—it bore equally on all shareholders (except the Government which had powers to disapply it) but nothing was made of this in the case. Compare the *Volkswagen* case (n 7), discussed below.

the UK as shareholder adopting the relevant Articles before privatization, exercising normal shareholder powers. While the method of restriction would have been different, the purpose and effect would have been the same.

2. The *KPN* case—state measure, disproportionality, and risk

This issue presented itself in the second of the cases about the use of private law powers, *Commission v Netherlands*.[38] Shortly before their privatization the Netherlands postal and telecommunications companies resolved[39] to issue to the Dutch Government special shares which enabled it to require prior approval of a wide variety of transactions, including share issues and repurchases, distributions, mergers and demergers, and Articles changes, but not acquisition of shares; the Government also agreed that it would not use its powers to defeat a hostile takeover. It argued that these provisions did not result from exercise of public power but from its powers as a shareholder, acquired as a market operation, and did not therefore fall within Article 63.[40]

The Court had no difficulty, following established jurisprudence, in finding that the provisions constituted restrictions on capital, as 'likely to prevent or limit the acquisition of shares . . . or to deter investors of other Member States'.[41] To the argument that they were not public measures, it responded that they were 'state measures', because they were 'the result of decisions taken by the Netherlands state in the course of the privatization of the two companies with a view to reserving a certain number of special rights under the companies' statutes'.[42] But, unlike the UK case, the Court found it necessary to go on to add two points: that the special shares conferred on the state important powers and a *disproportionate influence*—ie one 'not justified by the size of its investment and greater than that which an ordinary shareholding would normally allow it to obtain'[43] and thus 'limited the influence of other shareholders in relation to the size of their holding'; and that they created *a risk* that the Netherlands might 'pursue interests which do not coincide with the economic interests of the company', thus discouraging direct (and portfolio) investors.[44]

Thus the ruling turned on three points, apart from the familiar point that the powers attached to the shares were liable to deter investors (albeit equally applicable)—ie that they:

- constituted a '*state measure*' because taken for privatization purposes (and reserving special rights)
- conferred *disproportionate powers* at the expense of other shareholders

[38] n 16.

[39] The resolution was carried by the Dutch Government as shareholder—see the following footnote.

[40] See opinion of AG Maduro at [19]; cf the ruling at [16], characterizing the argument as that the powers were 'not State measures'.

[41] *Commission v Netherlands* (n 16), at [20], [21].

[42] *Commission v Netherlands* (n 16), at [22].

[43] Ibid at [24]

[44] Ibid at [28].

- created *a risk* of state interference with operation of the company, with effects contrary to the latter's best economic interests.

(i) 'State measure'

The state measure argument is in substance that use by a state of private law powers is to be regarded as such a measure where the purpose for their adoption is a public purpose of a certain kind—*in casu* a privatization policy. Such a 'public purpose' test is arguably likely to be satisfied whenever a state takes a shareholding with a view to exercising influence on the governance of a company. Only where the state is investing as a pure[45] portfolio investor is it likely that it is not exercising some industrial or other public policy objective. So the state measure requirement looks weak—it is likely always to be satisfied at least in the context with which we are concerned—state interference in company control.

(ii) 'Disproportionality'

The nature of the disproportionality test is obscure.[46] It may refer to some idealized vision of what level of shareholding entitles a company member to any particular level of influence. But, as the UK Government pointed out in *BAA*, national company law often allows shareholders autonomously to determine the allocation of powers between them, independently of the weight of their holdings, a freedom allowed by the EU legislators to continue in the context of the Takeover Bids Directive. Furthermore a subsequent Commission study led to the conclusion that departures from proportionality could not on the evidence be regarded as contrary to the general interest and that no further work should be done on the issue.[47] So the idealized view of proportionality is neither defined, nor agreed, but indeed explicitly as a matter of EU policy regarded as open. It would not appear to be a reliable, or predictable, or desirable basis for disallowing state powers.

An alternative view of proportionality, not open to these objections and perhaps more likely to be what the Court had in mind, would be by reference to the default rules of the national company law applicable; a departure from these being not 'normal'.[48] It is true that default rules in all Member States seem

[45] But even a purely passive holding may have defensive purposes.

[46] It is probably not the same as the test of 'normality' adopted in *BAA* which is tied in with whether the measure was a state measure—see the *BAA* case (n 11) at [47].

[47] Commission announcement of October 2007 referring to a report by KPMG.

[48] Cf *Commission v Netherlands* (n 16), at [24]. Compare the Commission assertion in its communication of 1999 that even provisions of general application allowing state veto of certain operational decisions and state board nominations for that purpose are offensive as 'in derogation of company law'. This, however, seems to posit some single Platonic ideal, so to speak, of company law, rather than one that varies between Member States. No such ideal model exists and special veto or nomination rights for particular shareholders or others are quite lawful under general law in many states. For an example see the law of Germany as explained in *Volkswagen*, below.

to provide for a 'one share/one vote'[49] rule and a standard level of minority blocking power in relation to decisions of major importance. However, the decisions that require special majority approval (and thus confer a disproportionate blocking power on dissentients) are by no means uniform in their nature as between Member States, nor are the majorities required the same. Moreover, ordinary default rules are by no means uniform as between Member States. So reference to departure from such rules would produce different results in different Member States, which seems an undesirable basis for application of a fundamental Treaty principle. Again, it by no means follows from the existence of a default rule that it is 'normally' followed even within the Member State in question—a conclusion that would require a statistical examination of national practice (based on an appropriate sample—one wonders what that would be). So this 'non-idealized' version of the proportionality rule would have a subjective effect as between Member States, producing an absence of uniformity in the measures permitted to deter capital movement as between different states[50] and would not even ensure that states took powers which conformed to national best practice. It is not evident why company law rules should have this differential effect as between Member States on the operation of a fundamental freedom, nor what principle underlies a test which has so diverse an effect, nor why national rules or practice should determine whether capital movement is restricted.

In short, a test of proportionality by reference to compliance with national default rules has little or no objective justification and would produce widely diverging results. Moreover, the criterion bears no relation to the interest under threat—the risk that the provision may deter investors. It must nonetheless be admitted that the Court has continued to attach importance to this proportionality/normality criterion in subsequent cases.

(iii) 'Risk of departure from corporate economic interest'

The third test, relating to risk of abuse, appears to be closer to the heart of the policy concern, which is, I would argue, the risk that powers may be exercised for purposes contrary to EU principles, particularly in pursuit of economic policies designed to achieve nationalist industrial policies and protectionism, or that their existence creates an effective threat of this.

The Court expresses its concern in rather different terms, however—ie of the risk that the state will depart from *the economic interests of the company*—following the Advocate General, who suggested that the principle should be that once the state places an enterprise in the market place it must live by the laws

[49] See WG Ringe 'Deviations from Ownership-Control Proportionality—Economic Protectionism Revisited' ch 10 of this volume.

[50] The same can be said of reference to departures from mandatory, as opposed to default, company law rules, not in issue in the *BAA* or *KPN* cases, but which may be implicit in the first generation cases and as we shall see below were relevant in *Volkswagen*.

of the market place and in consequence must respect the company's economic autonomy, justifications by reference to security of public services apart.[51] But this is too wide—it is not in fact a universal principle of states' company laws that shareholders' powers must be exercised in the economic interest of the company (whatever that means[52]) and even when such a principle operates it is not part of the competence of the European Union to ensure that it is upheld. On the other hand, exercise of discretionary powers *to impede the common market* is of course highly offensive to European Union principle and this is, I would argue, the risk of abuse which should be considered here.

Two further comments can be made about this risk test (whether or not this narrower scope is accepted). First, it will be satisfied in all cases where a Member State holds powers to determine or influence a company's operations, whether conferred by a company constitution or by public law. Thus, while vital, it does not provide a useful criterion for determining which powers amount to a restriction—it suggests that all do.

Second, the essence of the matter is the risk, or potential, for abuse. This suggests that, short of outlawing all such powers, the appropriate response is to outlaw those that conflict with Union principles on their face and to ensure that the remainder are not abused so as to conflict. This suggestion is followed up in the proposal for a way forward below.[53] Further questions arise from the *Netherlands (KPN)* case:

- To what extent are the three grounds in the case independent?
- Would it have been decided the same way on the basis of any one of them, or are two, or even all three required, at least in cases where private law powers are in play?
- Is it enough that investment is deterred either by a state measure, or by 'disproportionate' powers conferred on a state, or by powers which create a risk (whether to the company as the Court asserts or to the common market, as is argued here)?

[51] *Commission v Netherlands* (n 16) at [27]–[28], Opinion by AG Maduro at [27]–[30]. Cf D Wyatt, A Dashwood, and others, *European Union Law* (5th edn, London: Sweet and Maxwell, 2005) 860–1, suggesting that this is the meaning to be attached to the Commission's 'derogation from company law' test.

[52] The reader is reminded that in the UK at least the company is not regarded as having an interest distinct from that of its shareholders as such—ie subject to the company constitution; 'stakeholder' jurisdictions are different—the interest of the company appears to embrace certain public interest purposes.

[53] With this in mind the High Level Group on Company Law and Corporate Governance ('Winter Group') in its first report, recommended golden shares should be subjected to public law due process principles—ie transparency and judicial review—cf the approach to discretionary powers conferred by public law and the concern about the assertion of Member States' 'economic policy', considered by the Court at the level of justification in the first group of cases, discussed below. The Court there required that discretionary powers be subject to due process and seems to have rejected economic policies contrary to the market. The scope of the Court's economic policy objection is vague. For a similar suggestion as to its scope see Wyatt and Dashwood, ibid. Compare Case C-174/04, *Commission v Italy* (n 6) ('golden share' to achieve interstate competition policy).

- Are the state measure and risk considerations aspects of the same concern—anti-market state activity?
- Is disproportionality perhaps merely an indicator of the same concern?
- Indeed, does this concern provide an underlying and unifying rationale for all three criteria?

These questions are best examined after considering *Volkswagen*.

V. Recent jurisprudence—*Volkswagen*[54]

This famous case epitomizes the conflict between internal market and social objectives. But there can (perhaps) be little doubt that a foreign takeover of Volkswagen would be quite widely regarded as a national disaster in Germany and that the function of the VW law is as much nationalist and political as it is social. The factual background is certainly important and the account given of it in the case was surely intended to influence the Court.

Volkswagen AG was founded in the 1930s. After the 1939–45 war the German Government had to determine how the enterprise (*bona vacantia* but subject to various moral claims) was to be owned and controlled. Under a historic compromise, after long debate between the Federal Government, the Land of Lower Saxony (where the enterprise was based), the trades unions, and others, the matter was settled by federal legislation privatizing Volkswagen, in 1960. This Act incorporated the statutes of the new Volkswagen AG, and enabled 60 per cent of the shares to be sold to the public with 20 per cent each held by the Federal Government (since sold) and Lower Saxony.[55]

The Articles included three provisions that the Commission argued were unlawful restrictions on free movement of capital and freedom of establishment:[56]

(1) a voting rights cap of 20 per cent—ie provision that any holding in excess of 20 per cent was disenfranchised to that extent;

(2) special board nomination powers—ie power for the Federal Government and the Land of Lower Saxony each to appoint two members of the supervisory board; and

(3) a 20 per cent enhanced blocking minority power—ie special company resolutions normally requiring a 75 per cent majority were to require 80 per cent.

[54] *Commission v Germany* (n 7).

[55] This settlement has been widely regarded in Germany as epitomizing the German post-war 'economic miracle' and its 'social market' model. For a fuller account see AG Colomer, ibid.

[56] The Commission failed to pursue the establishment charge which was on that ground dismissed by the Court, ibid at [13]–[16].

Two general arguments were dealt with by the court for all three restrictions:

(1) Germany argued this was not a state measure as required by previous cases. The Court assumed such a measure was needed but had no difficulty in concluding the restrictions, as imposed by legislation, were 'a manifestation par excellence of State power';[57] and

(2) the Court concluded the provisions deterred investors from other Member States by restricting their ability to participate effectively in management. This conclusion was reached for the board appointment power independently,[58] but for the enhanced minority and voting cap provisions in combination—ie the two provisions *taken together* had this effect.[59]

However, apparently these two conclusions were not enough to settle the case. On the board appointment provisions, the Court noted that these enabled the Land and Federal Government to appoint more members by such special powers than was permitted under general law (which limited such rights to one-third of shareholders' representatives).[60] This was thus a specific right which derogated from general company law, enabling the two governments 'to participate in a more significant manner in the... supervisory board than their status of shareholders would normally allow'. This possibility would continue even if they held only one share each. So the provision gave these authorities 'the possibility of exercising influence which exceeds their levels of investment'.[61]

It is not clear whether the two points—that the appointment powers (i) were greater than normally allowed (ie conflicted with general mandatory company law); and (ii) 'exceeded the level of their investment' (ie were disproportionate to the potential level of shareholding which conferred them), were separate points. If the Land had only been entitled to appoint one of the ten shareholder members would this have been disproportionate, albeit that German company law would have allowed it, or would the provision have needed to require that the Land should for this purpose retain 10 per cent of the share capital (corresponding to 10 per cent of the shareholder members) to satisfy the proportionality criterion? The decision indeed reads on first impression as if the Court regarded a level of representation corresponding to shareholding ('proportionate') as both necessary and sufficient[62] but this is by no means a principle of the generality of EU law. In

[57] at [27]. [58] at [66]. [59] Ibid at [51]–[55].

[60] § 101(2) *Aktiengesetz* (*AktG*), with an exception for Volkswagen. German law sets the size of the supervisory board (which appoints and dismisses the management board and thus ultimately controls both strategy and operations) for companies of this size at 20, with 10 to be appointed by or on behalf of employees (§ 7 Mitbestimmungsgesetz). The maximum number of shareholder representatives allowed to be appointed by such special appointment powers was therefore three. The effect of the power even when exercised only by Lower Saxony was to confer a blocking majority on a combination of Lower Saxony and the employee representatives thus creating an effective veto on takeovers for Lower Saxony.

[61] Ibid at [61]–[64].

[62] A position adopted by AG Colomer at [72] 'this exclusive power is totally detached from the importance of their respective shareholdings... and *ruptures the symmetry between the power of capital and the possibilities of management*' (author's translation, emphasis added).

many EU states, including the UK and Ireland (and I believe France and Belgium), directors can only be securely maintained in office by an ordinary majority.[63] It is also unclear whether if the power had been proportionate but had conflicted with mandatory company law it would have been acceptable. For example, in the UK, would it have been acceptable to have a power of appointment proportionate to the holding, even though this would have conflicted with the normal UK mandatory provision allowing a bare majority to dismiss *ad nutum*?

It may be argued that this ruling creates an EU proportionality principle, in the generally recognized sense, for shareholder powers exercisable by states by virtue of state measures.[64] This seems doubtful in view of the above points. Nor does the test seem apt to address the mischief in hand. The proportionality of the powers held by a state by reference to the size of its holding bears no relation to the risk that the powers held will (be used to) deter investors. The mere fact that a holding is proportional to the powers of a state can hardly be regarded as allowing those powers to be exercised in a discriminatory fashion. Why should such proportionality allow powers to be used to impede access by investors from other Member States? Yet if satisfaction of this test renders a power no longer a restriction its potential or actual use to hinder access to the state market is presumably not open to challenge.

The Court considered the remaining two provisions in question, the voting cap and the enhanced minority provision, together, like the Advocate General. Germany argued these provisions could not amount to restrictions because, unlike all the earlier cases, they bore equally on all shareholders, conferring burdens and (allegedly) benefits on all, rather than conferring special privileges on the state authorities. While the voting cap was contrary to mandatory German law (which generally imposes OSOV [one share/one vote] for listed companies)[65] nothing in EU law prevented Germany varying this rule for particular companies.

This was a strong line of argument. If provisions which bear equally on all shareholders are objectionable where is the limit to the powers exercisable by Member States as shareholders which are objectionable? Any normal company law power could be so if its existence in the hands of the state was liable to deter investors, as it very likely would.

The Advocate General considered the two provisions together, maintaining their combined effect must be considered (without explaining what special effect the combination achieved) and relied on two points (apart from the general deterrent effect of the provisions on investors seeking to exercise management control): that the provisions were imposed by a special law by the Government itself and that the special minority position entrenched the Land, because its 20 per cent shareholding conferred the very blocking minority required.

[63] Companies Act 2006, ss 168, 169.

[64] As argued by J van Bekkum, J Kloosterman, and J Winter, 'Golden Shares and European Company Law—the Implications of Volkswagen' (2008) 5 Eur Company L 8.

[65] § 134(1) Aktiengesetz.

The Court accepted the German assertion that the cap provision was applicable without distinction to all shareholders and was a 'recognized instrument of company law',[66] but noted it was an infringement of German mandatory company law for listed companies like Volkswagen. However, it clearly did not regard this as sufficient to outlaw it. So it turned, like the Advocate General, to consider the cap and enhanced minority together.

The relevant German special resolution provisions to which the special minority rule applied were those on various key strategic issues including amendment of the statutes and certain decisions relating to capital and financial structures.[67] While the 75 per cent majority was the default rule nothing prevented companies from adopting articles with a higher requirement. However, the Court noted that for Volkswagen the provision had been made mandatory by legislation and could not be revoked by the shareholders.[68] The provision was thus an exception to mandatory German company law in that sense (ie such law requires such provisions to be autonomous and reversible); however, the Court did not explicitly rely on that point.

But the critical aspect in this connection seems to have been that at the time of the enactment both state authorities, and still at the time of judgment the Land, held an approximately 20 per cent holding—ie perfectly fitted to take advantage of the blocking minority provision—and were thus able to ensure, once the legislation was enacted, that no structural changes of the relevant kind could ever take place without the consent of each of them—a position which was bound to deter direct investors and particularly takeover bidders.[69] This enabled the court to hold that the provision thus enabled the Federal and state authorities 'to procure for themselves a blocking minority on the basis of a lower level of investment than would be required under general company law'.[70] In other words *on the facts* the effect of the provision was to confer *a special right* on Lower Saxony (and allegedly on the Federal Government, which was true at the time of the legislation but was, however, no longer true). While the court did not say so, and perhaps implies otherwise,[71] a further shareholder could take a 20 per cent holding (or less but sufficient for the necessary blocking minority *de facto*) and would be able to exercise the same right of veto; but in practice such a second

[66] Ibid at [42], [38]. German law allows voting caps for unlisted companies and they are common in certain other European states: see the *Report of Institutional Shareholder Services on Proportionality between Ownership and Control in the EU* (April 2007) 31. Note that the Court accepted this argument although the cap infringes any 'ideal' notion of proportionality of holding to voting power.

[67] This is all that is mentioned by the Court but a 75% majority is, I understand, required for a number of other matters, including mergers and voluntary dissolution.

[68] Ibid at [45].

[69] The Court noted that takeover bids were in issue, though somewhat curiously, it mentions this in the context of the establishment issue, at [14], [15]. (For Porsche SE's contemporaneous attempts to acquire control, see G J Vossestein, 'Volkswagen, The State of Affairs of Golden Shares' (2008) 5 Eur Company and Financial L Rev 115, 132.)

[70] Ibid at [50].

[71] 'enabling the authorities to procure for themselves'—ibid.

veto would, perhaps, be of little value given the Land's first mover advantage and would depress the share value.

What of the voting cap? The Court held that this, 'by capping voting rights at the same level of 20% supplements a legal framework which enables [these] authorities to exercise considerable influence on the basis of such a reduced investment (ie 20%)' and this situation (the combination of powers) was likely to deter investors. This combined ruling is problematic. It implies each of the two powers would have been lawful without the other, and there was some synergy which rendered them unlawful.

So apparently the Court did not believe that either provision, the cap or the enhanced blocking power, were sufficient in themselves to constitute a restriction. This was so although the former was contrary to German mandatory law (and clearly made the company a less attractive target for direct investors seeking to exercise control or influence) and the latter was contrary to default law (and excluded a mandatory consensual power, though it would have been lawful as a consensual provision), and also conferred on Lower Saxony *de facto* a special blocking power over constitutional change and other strategic decisions based on a lower than normal level of investment. The reason why the Court felt unable to find against the cap seems to have been that it conferred no special right on the authorities. The enhanced blocking power did do so *de facto*. Why did the Court not regard this as sufficient to find against this enhanced blocking power in isolation? Perhaps the Court believed or assumed that a special *legal* power was needed; but the factual result was to confer a special right, which would be a wholly effective deterrent for strategic investors, as it recognized. That is the concern of European law.

In order to understand the Court's objection to the two powers in combination (and its failure to object to each one taken separately), we need to identify the objectionable synergy between them (and what was lacking in each case to render each alone unobjectionable). In what way was the operation of the two powers in combination, but only in combination, offensive? Each provision deters direct investors, but separately—the cap, because it makes it difficult for them to exercise influence *outside* the field of the special minority decision—the special minority provision, because it makes influence impossible (without state consent) *within* that field. The Court drew attention to the fact that the cap and the minority provision both applied at 20 per cent[72] but that seems merely incidental. There therefore seems to have been no legal synergy between the two provisions. One conferred a veto on certain strategic decisions; the other made investment less attractive in relation to the remaining, mainly operational, decisions because it made collective action more difficult—a difficulty increased by the Lower Saxony 20 per cent holding, but there was no magic in that context in the 20 per cent. If there was no legal synergy we are

[72] 'at the same level'—at [51].

driven to consider synergy on the facts. The two provisions taken together did deter investors more than each provision separately. Perhaps this point about the degree of deterrence by the two restrictions taken together founded the Court's conclusion.

But this rationale is unsatisfactory. If the fact that provisions confer no special powers on Member States excludes them as a matter of law, even if contrary to mandatory law and even if disproportionate, then how can two such provisions be objectionable taken together? If on the other hand the *de facto* special benefit of the enhanced minority provision rendered it objectionable (as is strongly arguable if we accept the general rationale, although an alternative approach will be suggested below) then why was that provision (which absolutely barred direct investors from power to change the constitution without Lower Saxony's consent, for example) not objectionable in isolation? Why was it necessary that there should have been a voting cap as well? Finally, if the objection to a power depends on the degree of deterrence *de facto*, then how is the objectionable degree to be calibrated?

Very arguably the Court should have had little difficulty in finding against the enhanced minority in isolation, as a *de facto* special veto power conferred on the basis of a lower shareholding than normal. It clearly felt the need to find against the cap as well. But what was the real objection to the cap?—Surely that, although it applied equally to all shareholders, in practice it made direct investment less attractive, thus enhancing the control powers of Lower Saxony[73] and creating a threat which would be liable to deter investors. But this is an objection to the cap in isolation.

There are thus considerable problems in reconciling and making sense of the various criteria applied by the Court in this field. The position has become very complex and a rationale is required. Table 4.1 below sets out for ease of reference the criteria which were held to be operative in relation to each of the three restrictions in *VW*. In the light of this a quick conspectus of the impact of the various criteria in the *VW* case may be useful.

1. Impact

(i) 'State measure' and 'special' powers in VW

The Court's identification of the use of primary legislation to achieve the VW governance framework as a state measure looks obvious. But it bears deeper scrutiny.

[73] The enhanced blocking minority looks particularly objectionable *per se*. I understand the German Government, relying on the combined nature of the ruling, has now amended the VW law to leave this in place, repealing the cap and appointment power, retaining a discretionary block to Porsche control. However, an agreed merger is now planned.

What is the rationale of the state measure requirement? Is the requirement for a state measure merely a reflection of the traditional view that the freedoms bind only states? Clearly any mandatory (as opposed to autonomous) governance structure depends on legislation of some kind for its legal effectiveness and that is sufficient to satisfy that (arguably outmoded—see below) requirement. For the nature of that legislation to be material in the freedom of capital context its character needs to have some ongoing influence on access to the market by investors. It is not clear that the German legislation as such had any such impact. What gave VW its state character was in fact two things—the 20 per cent approximately holding by Lower Saxony, leveraged by the special restrictions, and the fact that the articles could not be changed without primary legislation. It was the ongoing involvement of the state in these two respects which presented a threat or deterrent for investors. In this connection the argument that the cap and enhanced blocking power were not 'special' to the state deserves reflection. Both were special in the sense that only the state could revoke them and that position in fact enhanced the position of Lower Saxony. Both were also special in the sense that they were likely, indeed designed, to be exploited by Saxony in a non-market way. In this sense the state component is another aspect of the other components.

(ii) Deterring investors in VW

There can be little doubt each of the three restrictions in fact deterred investors and the Court was convinced of this. Each in a different way rendered ineffective any takeover bid.

(iii) Disproportionality in VW

Each of the three restrictions was disproportionate in all the possible senses of the term proposed above. Each was inconsistent with mandatory German company law. Each conferred a power on Saxony that was greater than 'normal' in German law and practice. Each was thus 'inconsistent with company law'. Each was also inconsistent with an abstract proportionate power-for-capital rule.

But the cap and blocking majority did not confer any greater power on the state in proportion to its holding than it conferred on any other shareholder; so it is not clear what the mischief was on abstract proportionality grounds.

(iv) Risk of departure from corporate economic interest in VW

The existence of this risk is evident from the arguments put by Germany. The measures were part of an industrial, regional, and social policy. Their very purpose was to frustrate the usual economic process of governance at the expense of investors' interests. Yet the Court while addressing the arguments in the context of German claims of justification does not invoke them in the context of determining the criteria applicable for identifying the restrictions.

A convincing rationale is badly needed. But before proposing one it is desirable to complete the picture by considering the law on justification of restrictions in this field, and the trends on 'horizontal effect'—the binding effect of the freedoms on non-state parties.

2. Justifying state intervention

It is well established that the well-known 'rule of reason'/'public interest'/'mandatory requirements'/*Gebhard* principle of justification[74] is generally available to justify restricting the freedoms, including in capital cases. But the special nature of golden share cases has led to important developments on justification in that field which are arguably relevant to any possible overall rationale of the capital jurisprudence.

In the first group of golden share cases mentioned above (*France, Belgium*, and *Portugal*), breach of the prohibition was largely admitted and the main discussion turned on whether the restrictions established were justifiable. The Court made three important rulings on legitimate general interests, and proportionate protection thereof, in this context.

First, such interests would include protection of the national petroleum and gas supply or other vital public services, such as telecommunications and electricity, but not retention of state controls over other kinds of enterprises such as banking, or tobacco.[75]

Second, 'national economic policy' could not be invoked as a general interest; so that an attempt to uphold restrictions as necessary to secure that national industry was restructured satisfactorily after the mass privatizations, could not be sustained;[76] (this ruling requires qualification—as we have noted, all golden share-type provisions are likely to have been imposed for economic policy reasons; it seems that policies are objectionable which compete with, or cut across, common market or other Treaty principles).

Third, where the powers were discretionary, procedural safeguards were required to ensure transparency of the grounds (which must of course conform

[74] Case C-55/94 *Gebhard v Consiglio dell' Ordine degli Avvocati e Procuratori di Milano* [1995] ECR I-4165, restrictions to be justifiable must be imposed in order to serve a (legitimate) general interest, must be non-discriminatory, must be appropriate for the purpose, and must impose no greater restriction than is necessary to achieve the objective. In *Gebhard* itself the Court ruled that the doctrine applied to all the freedoms. It has been applied in all the capital cases cited below.

[75] *Commission v Spain* (n 16) at [70]; but in *Volkswagen* (n 7), the Court failed to object to invocation of a general interest in the context of a particular manufacturing company—see below.

[76] *Commission v Portugal* (n 6) at [52], [53]. 'It is settled case law that economic grounds can never serve as justification for obstacles prohibited by the Treaty'. Portugal claimed the powers were necessary to enable it to ensure appropriate strategic partners, to strengthen the competitive market, and to modernize and increase efficiency of production. Similarly in *Commission v Italy* (n 6), the Court ruled that restrictions on investment by state bodies could not be justified as necessary for 'generally strengthening the competitive structure of the market', at [36]. See also case C-35/98 *Staatssecretaris van Financiën v Verkooijen* [2000] ECR I-4071 (inward investment policy).

to the *Gebhard* test) on which the powers were to be exercised, together with available recourse to legal challenge to secure this. This was an application of the proportionality principle: otherwise the powers would intrude further into the freedom than was necessary to secure the relevant general interest, leaving investors unnecessarily exposed to risk. This is an important point—even where such powers constraining or encumbering investment are exercisable on legitimate grounds they may in fact be abused. Transparent grounds and legal recourse must be available to meet this risk.[77] It is also the case that such provisions, if convincing, should give comfort to potential investors against the risk of abuse—in other words they reduce the deterrent effect to the minimum necessary and prevent powers having a *de facto* deterrent and discriminatory effect.

The main feature of the remainder of the case law on justification seems to be the strong disinclination of the court to find justifications convincing. The most significant example is perhaps *Volkswagen*, where Germany invoked a broad social policy justification. In the forefront was the need to protect employees (and, allegedly, minority shareholders) against threats from 'large' shareholders (allegedly by establishing an 'equitable balance of power' to achieve 'a socio-political and regional' and economic and industrial policy).[78] The Court ruled that Germany had failed to explain why the 'strengthened and irremovable position' of the German authorities in the company's capital was necessary for such protection of employees.[79] The Court also dismissed the German claim of justification based on the need of shareholders for minority protection, where the disproportionality of the authorities' position was regarded as particularly relevant.[80] It also drew attention in this general context to the protection otherwise available through employee participation on VW's supervisory board and to the risk that those authorities might use their position to 'defend general interests contrary to the economic interest of the company'.[81] 'General considerations that shareholders may put their personal interests before those of workers' were not sufficient to justify the restrictions as necessary to preserve jobs.[82]

[77] *Commission v Belgium* (n 16) at [48]–[52]; cf *Commission v France* (n 16) at [50]–[51]. The Court also ruled in *Commission v France* at [46] that particularly stringent justification was required where powers were to be exercised *a priori* (ie requiring prior approval for the transaction) as opposed to *ex post* (ie requiring the state to intervene to unpick the transaction once done). This distinction, criticized on the facts by AG Colomer in his opinion in the *BAA* (n 11) and *Commission v Spain* cases (n 16) at [38]–[40], seems unsustainable (*ex post* intervention powers will in practice normally necessitate applications for prior approval) but was not abandoned by Court in the *Spain* case—see ibid at [78] 'ex post facto opposition . . . is less restrictive than a prior approval'.

[78] *Volkswagen* case (n 7) at [70], [71]. The Commission criticized this as an 'economic policy' justification, as in *Commission v Portugal* (n 6), and the Court referred to but did not adopt this reasoning.

[79] Ibid at [74].

[80] Ibid at [79]. It will be recalled that such disproportionality was invoked in the *KPN* case (n 16) as a component of the restriction rather than to disallow justification, but here it is relevant to the claim of minority protection.

[81] *Volkswagen* (n 7) at [79].

[82] Ibid at [80].

This broad ruling on social policy justification of capital restrictions is likely to be of the greatest importance. It is clearly similar in orientation to the rejection of national structural policies in *Commission v Portugal* and *Commission v Italy.* On the other hand the Court did not invoke the argument in *Commission v Spain* that for justification to be available the industry in question must have a public service or essential economic interest function. The fact that VW was just a car manufacturer did not apparently rule out such justifications.

3. Horizontal effect

I have argued elsewhere[83] that the developing case law on horizontal effect of the services and establishment freedoms, notably in the *Laval* and *Viking Line* cases[84] is applicable also to golden share-type cases.

In *Laval* and *Viking* the Court held the defendant trades unions bound by the relevant freedoms and accordingly prohibited from forcing employers to enter into pay negotiations and a national collective agreement, with the effect of restricting their access to the relevant national market.[85] The Court held in *Laval* that (contrary to the view widely held before that decision) it was not only public and regulatory authorities that were bound by the freedoms. Compliance with Article 56 TFEU, on freedom of services 'is also required in the case of rules which are not public in nature but which are designed to regulate collectively provision of services' and applies to 'exercise of their legal autonomy by associations or organisations not governed by public law';[86] similarly in *Viking* the referring court asked the European Court if 'Article [49] has horizontal direct effect so as to confer rights on private undertakings which may be relied on against another private party and, in particular a trade union in respect of collective action'. The Court ruled that it was clear from the case law that 'abolition of obstacles to free movement of persons and services would be compromised if the abolition of state barriers could be neutralized by obstacles resulting from the exercise by associations or organizations not governed by public law of their legal autonomy [citing earlier case law mainly on private regulatory bodies or workers]'.[87] It added that 'it does not follow [from that case law] that that interpretation applies only to quasi public organisations or to associations exercising a regulatory task and having quasi legislative powers. There is no indication in that case law that could validly support the view that it applies only to [such

83 See the essay cited at n 1.

84 Case C-341/05 *Laval un Partneri Ltd v Svenska Byggnadsarbetareförbundet and others* [2007] ECR I-11767; and Case C-438/05 *International Transport Workers' Federation and others v Viking Line* [2007] ECR I-10779.

85 The terms sought by the union went beyond those the host state was entitled to impose on services operators under the relevant Directive.

86 *Laval* (n 84) at [98].

87 *Viking Line* (n 84) at [57].

organisations and associations]'; but the court then added 'furthermore it must be pointed out that in exercising their autonomous power pursuant to their trade union rights... trade unions participate in the drawing up of agreements seeking to regulate paid work collectively'.[88]

It is clear from these cases that a restriction of establishment or services need not be a state measure to fall foul of these freedoms.

There can be little doubt that this also applies to capital.

It is also clear that the powers in question need not be public powers. It follows that where states exercise private powers they are also subject to the freedoms. It seems strongly arguable that since the case law applies to private persons exercising private powers it follows *a fortiori* that it does to public persons exercising private powers. This is wholly in conformity with EU principles. As the Advocate General pointed out in the *KPN* case, Member States are bound by the treaties *qua* signatories and not *qua* state authorities.[89] Moreover, Member States are obliged by Article 4(3) TFEU (formerly Article 10 EC) to ensure fulfilment of the obligations arising out of the Treaty, to facilitate the achievement of the Union's tasks, and to abstain from any measure which could jeopardize the attainment of the objectives of the Treaty. Where a state can exercise a power in a way which has the object or effect of restricting a fundamental freedom it is bound to comply with the Treaties, whatever the legal basis of that power.[90] It appears to follow that if a state may exercise powers by virtue of a shareholding in a company then it must not do so in a manner which discriminates, nor in a manner which restricts the fundamental freedoms of others, however that share was acquired. Similarly if a share is acquired with the object of restricting such freedoms or its acquisition would tend to have that effect that is a breach of the Treaties by that state.

It may be argued that when states act as shareholders they do not exercise collective powers as did the trades unions in these cases; but such states are exercising public authority—their very status is to act for the collective benefit. And in any case this restriction is clearly intended to limit the nature of the private

[88] Cf ibid at [33]: 'Articles 39, 43 and 49 [freedoms of workers establishment and services] do not apply only to the actions of public authorities but extend also to rules of any nature aimed at regulating in a collective manner gainful employment, self-employment and the provision of services'.

[89] 'Treaty provisions on free movement of persons services and capital impose obligations on national authorities regardless of whether these authorities act as public powers or private law entities' A G Maduro in *Commission v Netherlands* (n 16) at [22] (author's translation) and again in *Federconsumatori* (n 6) at [22].

[90] See Case 249/81 *Commission v Ireland* [1982] ECR 4005—state conduct not involving national measures and having no binding effect (a buy Irish campaign) nevertheless if amounting to a national practice is contrary to Article 30 (now Article 34 TFEU) and again Case 45/87R *Commission v Ireland* [1987] ECR 783—public authority exercising contractual power bound by Article 30 EC Treaty (now Article 34 TFEU).

bodies that are to be subject to the case law; it is very doubtful that the Court would apply it to a public body.[91]

A third question provoked by these horizontal effects cases is—how far can *private persons* engaging in protectionist activity intended to inhibit free movement of capital be bound by the horizontal effect of the freedom? This is more speculative. It is doubtful whether where a private party engages for private purposes in conduct which falls short of discrimination (which is probably outlawed by *Angonese*[92]) the freedoms can be invoked. But there is room for development of a principle, and some authority, that where such a party engages in such conduct for public purposes, then on the analogy of a trade union which is entrusted by private law with the function of negotiating collective agreements with general effect, that party should be subject to the obligation not to obstruct the operation of the freedoms except in conditions permitted by EU law. Where a private party is entrusted with public functions under private law the treaty freedoms apply to that party because he acts as a surrogate for the state.[93]

One possible area for discussion of the application of this principle in the context of private persons exercising company powers impeding freedom of capital for protectionist purposes is the position of certain foundations in Nordic countries which hold voting shares, often with enhanced powers exercisable for the benefit of the company in the widest sense, including its continuity and independence and the interests of employees and the wider community in which it operates. Again, the company laws of some states confer public functions on boards in the sense that their fidelity obligation requires that they serve not only interests of shareholders but also a wider range of constituencies and the public interest. Such bodies and boards with wider public purposes are arguably acting as surrogates for the state. A particular example is the exercise of powers to frustrate takeover bids under the authority allowed under the Takeover Bids Directive,[94] in particular the 'reciprocity' power to block a bid from a company with a less open structure than their own.[95] It is clear from the legislative history that this was envisaged as having a public purpose—to level the regulatory playing field. Such powers are arguably worthy of being subjected to Treaty freedoms.

91 Perhaps company constitutions, given the breadth of their effect, do regulate a matter collectively.

92 Case C-281/98 *Angonese v Cassa di Risparmio di Bolzano* [2000] ECR I-4139.

93 Cases 266 and 267/87 *The Queen v Royal Pharmaceutical Society* [1989] ECR 1295; Case C-16/94 *Édouard Dubois et Fils SA and Général Cargo Services SA v Garonor Exploitation SA* [1995] ECR I-2421.

94 Directive 2004/25/EC (n 5), Article 12. For the legislative history and Swedish practice see R Skog, 'The Takeover Directive the Breakthrough Rule and the Swedish system of Dual Class Common Stock' (20004) 15 Eur Business L Rev 1439.

95 The legality of the Directive is beyond the scope of this paper—see J Rickford, 'The Emerging European Takeover Law from a British Perspective' (2004) 15 Eur Business L Rev 1379, 1402 ('contrary to well recognised Treaty principles'), developed in J Rickford, 'Takeovers in Europe: a UK Perspective' in T Baums and A Cahn (eds), *Die Umsetzung der Übernahmerichtlinie in Europa* (Berlin: de Gruyter, 2006) 88, 89; cf Wyatt and Dashwood (n 51) ch 20.

VI. State powers of corporate control—making sense of the golden shares cases

One can conclude from the case law at this juncture that for powers over company control and operations to be contrary to the capital freedom they must at least:

(1) be likely to deter investors (perhaps particularly investors from other Member States);

(2) be exercisable by states or state bodies (though the horizontal effects cases suggest that this is capable of some extension); and

(3) be operable in pursuance of a state measure[96] or state power[97] (of debatable, import given that all that is required appears to be some public interest purpose).[98]

Further factors regarded by the Court as relevant are whether the measure:

(4) creates a 'special' power for the state authority (relevant but apparently not necessary—*VW*);

(5) infringes mandatory state law (relevant—*VW*, but not necessary—*KPN*);

(6) departs from default state law (relevant—*VW*); or

(7) infringes proportionality (ie of capital stake to voting power) principles (which may be by reference to state law or to some abstract ideal of proportionality) (*VW* and *KPN*).

It has also been argued, in the light of the most recent cases on horizontal effect, that powers exercisable by private bodies may also be objectionable on similar grounds where such bodies are acting in the exercise of public functions or actually or purportedly for public purposes.

More sense needs urgently to be made of this catalogue. Items (1) to (3) seem to be necessary in all cases on the basis of the decisions. But the extent to which (4) to (7) are needed and in what combination is far from clear. For *KPN* and for the blocking minority and appointment power in *Volkswagen* a version of (7) was apparently necessary. Item (7) was also present in the other cases, at least in its 'ideal' form.

But these criteria give an uncertain and unsatisfactory guidance. How are the uncertainties attaching to golden share cases and horizontal effects cases to be resolved? It should be borne in mind that it is not the concern of the Court of Justice to impose some idealized version of company law on Member States' authorities, nor their own company law default rules, nor even their mandatory

[96] *KPN* (n 16) at [22]. [97] *Volkswagen* (n 7) at [27].

[98] See the discussion of *KPN* (n 16) above.

rules—it is to ensure that states do not adopt powers or actions which conflict with Treaty principles—ie, here, which have the object or effect of deterrence of inter-state investment.

The search for criteria for identifying objectionable interferences with freedom of capital should therefore focus on what investors may legitimately expect in a properly functioning internal market, rather than on any ideology concerned with the proper functioning of company law. The crucial step missing in the jurisprudence so far is the establishment of a logical connection between the criteria adduced for identifying objectionable restrictions and the mischief which the freedom is designed to meet.

We must address realities: it is notorious that Member States, in taking powers over companies, whether by public law or private law and whether by special provision or by acquisition of shares in the market place, often (perhaps always) intend to use those powers in pursuit of their industrial policies, frequently for protectionist or other purposes conflicting with Treaty principles. The issue is not, it is submitted, the legal means by which those powers are obtained, nor the nature of legal provisions under which they are exercisable, but the impact on investors of their actual or potential use. It follows from this reasoning, and, as we have seen, from the implications of the *Netherlands (KPN)* case and the authorities on the horizontal effects of the freedoms, that insistence that states are only subject to Treaty principles if they are acting under state measures is unsustainable. It is sufficient if they are pursuing political objectives. Or to put it another way, the 'state measure' requirement in *KPN* is met wherever states have or may have an industrial policy objective—privatization is merely an example. The proposed extension of the law into the field of actions by private bodies, which seems to be required by *Laval* and *Viking*, confirms this.

Similarly, insistence on qualifications by reference to actual or ideal company law provisions would only be justifiable if compliance with such provisions were an indicator of absence of the mischievous effect (or even conceivably an indicator that it would be less likely). As a matter of common experience, that is not so—whatever the character of a state's control power it has the potential for protectionist abuse; in some states such abuse is very likely, not disguised and even publicly paraded to deter unwelcome investors. Such potential is likely to deter investors—the mischief the Court has correctly identified. Moreover what applies to states also applies to bodies acting as surrogates of states, such as nationalized industries and state investment banks.

All this is, it is submitted, wholly consistent with general principles of the European economic constitution and far from original. More difficult is how to carry it through in terms of legal consequences in this sensitive context. Clearly where states *exercise* such powers in ways which are discriminatory or deter cross-border investment such exercises are open to challenge. But, as the Court has recognized, the very *existence* of the powers carries the risk of abuse—hence the test in terms of 'liability' to deter investors and the rule that discretionary powers must be transparent. In my view, this operates to reduce risks of deterrence of investors in legitimate cases. Such powers are objectionable as such, unless they are subject to a transparent and enforceable regime at domestic level, which ensures they are only used for legitimate purposes. If such a regime is in place then investment will not be unlawfully deterred because there is an assurance of the absence of abuse, or at least such deterrence will be reduced to the feasible minimum. The burden is on Member States to show that such regimes are effective as the Court itself ruled in the *France* and *Belgium* cases.

In the absence of such regimes the powers exercisable by states should be void as contrary to EU law; if they are attached to shares, the shares should remain valid, but be shorn of control rights.

There would surely be strong political opposition to this proposal and the Commission may well be unable to summon the necessary internal conviction to pursue it before the Court. But fortunately that is not necessary. Any shareholder in a company subject to such powers may pursue these arguments. A suitable test case might be brought by such a shareholder wishing to pursue or facilitate a takeover bid. A shareholders' association has already successfully challenged a 'golden share' in this way.[99] Damages will be available, as well as enforcement orders.[100] But it must be admitted that Court's litigation is scarcely the most efficient way of resolving disputes over company ownership.

Similar conclusions can, it is submitted, apply to company organs exercising private law powers for public purposes. It is often argued that private persons are subject to Treaty principles even when exercising purely private powers. This seems a step too far[101] and one the Court deliberately did not take in *Volkswagen*, *Laval*, and *Viking*. It is not necessary for purposes examined here. It is sufficient to leave the discipline of true market players to the market, autonomous regulation and competition law. But while the progression of the public law cases is in the right direction, the law should be more focused on the mischief to be addressed.

VII. A coda—back to the drawing board? The capital/establishment boundary

Since capital movements by definition cover 'direct investment', including (explicitly) the establishment and acquisition in whole or in part of companies and firms[102] and since Article 63 TFEU, unlike Article 49 TFEU, extends to

[99] *Federconsumatori* (n 6; disproportionate, but lawful in domestic law, control power reserved by local authority in articles under private law powers).

[100] As in the *Laval* and *Viking* cases (n 84). Cf Cases C-46 and 48/93, *Brasserie du Pecheur/Factortame III* [1996] ECR I-1029.

[101] See van Bekkum and others (n 64) 8. Many *contra,* eg Wyatt and others (n 51) 861–3; M Andenas, T Guett, and M Pannier, 'Free Movement of Capital and National Company Law' (2005) 16 Eur Business L Rev 757, 775.

[102] See the Capital Directive (n 9).

movements between the EU and third states, the capital freedom looks on its face to be a licence for third-country nationals and businesses[103] (and, but perhaps less worryingly for protectionist purposes, for EU nationals and businesses dealing with third states) to exploit EU law fundamental freedoms including in the field of control of corporate enterprise. Establishment and capital overlap and capital provides an escape hatch from the legal territorial limits on freedom of establishment by liberalizing establishment in fact.

A growing body of case law apparently responds to this threat by holding that in cases where both freedoms would otherwise apply freedom of establishment supplants (or in the gaming metaphor 'trumps') capital, thus excluding third-country beneficiaries. This case law is, however, difficult to reconcile with the Treaty and basic internal market principles. It is also, paradoxically, based on a surprisingly, even alarmingly, narrow view of the scope of establishment.

Acceptance of this case law at face value would lead to two major conclusions:

- first, much of the golden share jurisprudence is based on the wrong Treaty freedom
- second, the scope for third-country related exploitation of the capital freedom is far greater than, it is submitted, a more acceptable and viable view of the scope of establishment, and the implications of that scope for the scope of capital, under proper application of the Treaty, would suggest.

There is a wealth (or at least a profusion) of case law now on this matter, mainly very recent and much of it highly complex tax law. But the problem can be reasonably elucidated by reference to just three main cases, the beginning of the problems in *Baars*[104] and the most recent case *Commission v Italy*,[105] with its precursor *A and B*.[106]

1. *Baars*

The leading early case on the establishment/capital boundary is *Baars*.[107] This concerned the taxation of foreign shareholdings. The Netherlands law exempted Dutch taxpayers from wealth tax on 'substantial holdings' (defined as holdings of at least one-third and more than 7 per cent of the nominal value of the paid up capital[108]) in Dutch companies, but not foreign ones. Mr Baars challenged an assessment to tax on such a substantial holding (in fact 100 per cent) in an Irish company. The Dutch court asked whether this was contrary to (1) Article 52 (later

[103] Article 54 TFEU does not of course govern Article 63 TFEU; nor does the restriction in the General Programme requiring a 'real and continuous link' between a beneficiary of Article 49 and a Member State.

[104] Case C-251/98 *Baars* [2000] ECR I-2787.

[105] n 13.

[106] Case C-102/05 *Skatteverket v A and B* [2007] ECR I-3871.

[107] n 104.

[108] Ibid at [8]. The cumulative 1/3 and 7% tests seem obscure, but nothing turns on this.

Article 43 EC, now Article 49 TFEU) and/or (2) Article 73b (later Article 56 EC, now Article 63 TFEU).

In response AG Alber opined that 'the border' between 'simple investment' and 'actual establishment' 'should probably be set where a shareholder ceases to confine himself to provision of capital in support of a business... and *begins to become involved himself in the conducting of the business*... beyond simply exercising his voting rights, and to participate in a way which will enable him to exercise *real influence*' [emphasis added].[109] On the facts the case was clearly one of establishment because *Baars* held all the shares. The Dutch law was discriminatory and there was a clear infringement of establishment rights.

On the second question, on capital, AG Alber recognized that there was no need to answer given the conclusion on establishment. He nevertheless (in spite of his reference to a 'border', above) argued that establishment and capital freedoms could be applied 'in parallel':[110] 'the fact that freedom of establishment is in point does not preclude the simultaneous application of the rules on capital movements';[111] contrary to the position on establishment, for capital 'the size of the shareholding is immaterial,'... but... 'if the holding reaches a size which enables the investor to exercise *a decisive influence over the undertaking's decision making*, the right of establishment will *supplement* free movement of capital' and 'the investment would be protected by the EC Treaty under two separate heads' [emphasis added].[112] AG Alber thus took the view that, whatever the size of the investment, what is now Article 63 TFEU applied; but there was limited overlap, with current Article 49 TFEU applying as well, where 'decisive' (but earlier only 'real') influence over decision-making was possible. Because the Dutch law gave preferential treatment to investment in the Netherlands and was an obstacle to investment in another Member State it was discriminatory and also infringed the capital freedom.[113] Thus AG Alber took the view that where establishment and capital overlapped neither 'trumped' the other.

The Court decided the case solely on establishment. The Court noted that on the facts the taxpayer held all the shares. 'Article [49] includes the right to set up and manage undertakings'... 'So [a national] who has a holding... which gives.... *definite influence over the company's decisions and allows him to determine its activities* is exercising his right of establishment' [emphasis added—hereinafter referred to as the 'Narrow *Baars* Control test']. It was self-evidently always the case that such influence and power were conferred wherever there was a 100 per cent holding, as in the case of Mr Baars.[114]

This was a holding that freedom of establishment applied on the facts on the basis of a very high level of control. The exact meaning of the Narrow *Baars*

[109] Ibid at [33].

[110] Ibid at [21], citing C-302/97 *Klaus Konle v Republik Österreich* [1999] ECR I-3099 (Austrian law bars foreigners from acquiring land—held both establishment and capital freedoms applicable).

[111] Ibid at [48].

[112] Ibid at [50].

[113] Ibid at [54], [57], [61].

[114] Ibid at [26].

Control test is unclear: if a shareholder is able to 'determine a company's activities' what is added by a further requirement that he have a 'definite influence over its decisions'—presumably a weaker level of influence?—Surely a person able so to determine inevitably also has such influence? Unless perhaps the 'and' is disjunctive and *either* such influence *or* such determinative power would suffice. But this seems an unlikely interpretation.

It is far from clear that the Court decided that this Narrow *Baars* Control (whatever its precise meaning) was necessary, as opposed to merely sufficient, for establishment to apply. The Court noted that the Dutch law's 'substantial holding' level, 'does not necessarily imply control or management'... 'which are factors connected with the exercise of the right of establishment' and therefore did not necessarily affect freedom of establishment.[115] This was clearly *obiter*, but the test applied in this context is both weaker and vaguer than the Narrow *Baars* Control test ('control or management' are 'factors connected with' exercise of the right of establishment). The view that 'control or management' are 'factors connected with the exercise of the freedom' is clearly consistent with a much broader concept of establishment than its definition by reference to Narrow *Baars* Control.

It is very strongly arguable that the Court did not intend the Narrow *Baars* Control test to define establishment in the sense that it is always necessary for a person to have such decisive powers to be a beneficiary of the establishment chapter, for two reasons:

- first, the Court actually employed a more relaxed test when referring to the extent to which Dutch law affected establishment
- second, because, it is submitted, such a narrow test is not consistent with the Treaty.

A person exercises rights of establishment when he exercises powers to take up and/or pursue the relevant activities, including in particular, to set up and/or manage companies and firms. While it is indeed possible for a company to have a capital structure under which one, or sometimes, more, shareholders hold a sufficiently large block to be able to determine decisions (and this common continental pattern may have influenced the Court) it is of course entirely possible for the shareholders to hold their powers in so diffuse a form that such influence can only be exercised collectively. The same is true of founder-members at the pre-incorporation stage.[116] Such shareholders are entitled to the benefit of freedom of establishment.[117] Establishment clearly carries a flavour of influence, but the company law harmonization directives are surely lawful in requiring remedies to be conferred on shareholders as such (eg minority and outside shareholders under

[115] Ibid at [20].

[116] Consider for example the facts of *Centros* but with, say, seven partners acting as founders.

[117] To similar effect W Schoen, 'The Mobility of Companies in Europe and the Organisational Freedom of Company Founders' (2006) 3 Eur Company and Financial L Rev 122, 140–2.

the Takeover Bids Directive). Article 55 TFEU confers a right to national treatment on any shareholder (participant in capital).[118]

I would myself argue that wherever shareholders have powers of management and control collectively they are entitled collectively to the benefit of the establishment freedom and where they are so entitled collectively it follows that they are entitled individually. All shareholders—at least if they hold votes—participate in control. This may be controversial however. What surely is not is that it cannot be necessary that shareholders must individually exercise decisive influence to have the benefit of the freedom.

The Court definitely did not decide that the applicability of this Narrow *Baars* Control test, and consequently of the establishment freedom, excluded application of the capital freedom. It simply stated that, in view of the answer to the first question on establishment, it *was not necessary* to reply to the second, on capital.[119]

Nevertheless within seven months of the *Baars* decision, in *Überseering*[120] (the well-known case on migration of a company's main establishment to a real seat host state) the Court stated:

> as a general rule the acquisition by one or more natural persons residing in a Member State of shares in a company incorporated and established in another Member State is covered by the Treaty provisions on the free movement of capital, provided that the shareholding does not confer on those natural persons definite influence over the company's decisions and does not allow them to determine its activities. By contrast where the acquisition involves all the shares in a company having its registered office in another Member State and the shareholding confers a definite influence over the company's decisions and allows the shareholders to determine its activities, it is the Treaty provisions on freedom of establishment which apply (see, to that effect, Case C-251/98 *Baars* [2000] ECR I-2787, paragraphs 21 and 22).

While the Court did not actually state that in the latter case freedom of capital did not apply, and the point was *obiter*—the case was entirely based on establishment—that may well be regarded as implicit.

It is clear that none of the golden shares cases until *Commission v Italy* in 2009[121] adopt the view that where Narrow *Baars* Control applies capital does not. In all these cases there were caps on shareholding, which precluded Narrow *Baars* Control, and/or veto powers on company decision-making which clearly touched the power of the company's controllers 'to determine its activities'. In many cases board appointment powers were in issue. So these were clear establishment cases in *Baars* terms. In *Volkswagen*[122] it was explicit that one objective of the national measures was to frustrate undesirable (in German authorities' eyes) takeover

[118] Formerly Article 294 EC, the provision has now moved to the 'establishment' chapter, but the references in the capital chapter have thus been extended.

[119] Ibid at [42].

[120] Case C-208/00 *Überseering BV v Nordic Construction Company Baumanagement GmbH* [2002] ECR I-9919 at [77].

[121] n 13.

[122] n 7.

bids. Yet all these cases were decided exclusively on capital and the Court typically regarded establishment restrictions as 'consequential' on the restrictions on capital, so there was no need for separate examination of establishment.[123]

By contrast in a number of tax cases the Court found that the *Baars* test was satisfied in relation to the legislation in question on the ground that it was applicable to shareholdings which did carry such decisive influence and ruled that restrictions on capital were consequential and therefore did not require separate examination. Thus the UK law on 'controlled foreign companies', because it applied only to subsidiaries was to be considered as an establishment matter and capital did not justify examination.[124]

The unsatisfactory nature of the 'direct consequence' or 'merely a consequence' argument is illustrated by these two sets of cases. In the golden shares cases an establishment restriction is the direct consequence of a capital restriction: in the tax cases capital is a consequence of establishment. In both cases the invocation of causality, with presumably the implicit argument that the primary cause is the significant factor, is unconvincing. In all these cases the very transaction restricted is both a capital transaction and an establishment one. There is no causality, or sequence, but simultaneity and identity.

In yet other tax cases, or other issues in the same cases, the Court finds that both establishment and capital apply because the size of the shareholdings restricted may in some circumstances carry *Baars*-type control powers and in others not. The rational view of these cases is, it is submitted, that the Court is not holding that capital and establishment apply in parallel but that the legislation infringes both freedoms not simultaneously but distributively—establishment in cases for *Baars* control stakes and capital for others.[125]

The trend of these cases seems to be towards the position that establishment applies if, but only if, the *Baars* test is satisfied and capital applies only where it is not and the two are mutually exclusive with establishment trumping capital. The cases of *A and B*, decided in May 2007, and *Commission v Italy*, decided in March 2009, tend strongly to confirm this view. But it is hardly yet firmly established

[123] eg *Commission v Portugal* (n 6) at [55], [56]. In *Commission v Germany (VW)* (n 7) establishment was left unargued and the Court was content to decide entirely on capital although the restrictions clearly went to control and the objective was explicitly the frustration of takeover bids.

[124] C-196/04 *Cadbury Schweppes and Cadbury Schweppes Overseas v Commissioners of Inland Revenue* [2006] ECR I-7995 at [33] (but note the emphatic 'in any event' perhaps suggesting that examination of capital is not only unnecessary but positively inappropriate); C-201/05 *Test Claimants in the CFC and Dividend Group Litigation* [2008] ECR I-2875 follows *Cadbury* at [73], but see [89] apparently because consequential not even to be considered where material—cf *Commission v Italy,* discussed below.

[125] Arguably a genuinely parallel case is case C-207/07 *Commission v Spain* [2008] ECR I-111—government discretionary cap on shareholdings at 10% held in breach of both Articles 49 and 63—but perhaps capable of explanation on similar distributive grounds. The Court relied on case C-157/05 *Holböck* [2007] ECR I-4051 where the holding on capital was contingent (relied on by Henderson J (UK High Court) in *Test Claimants in the FII Group Litigation v Commissioners for HM Revenue and Customs* [2008] EWHC 2895 (Ch)) as a true parallel case however, and see *Commission v Germany (VW)* (n 7), where there was, however, no actual holding on establishment.

and is open to obvious criticism given the earlier jurisprudence, the Treaty texts, and the cases themselves.

2. *Skatteverket v A and B*[126]

The *A and B* case concerned the Swedish tax on close companies' dividends. This made an allowance against tax on dividends reflecting the employment costs of the company and its subsidiaries. But this was only made for employment in EU Member States, and not third countries.

The applicants were shareholders, each holding 1.7 per cent. They claimed an allowance against tax on their dividends for employees of a branch, established in Russia.

The Commission and the Netherlands argued[127] that the Swedish law 'affects the establishment of a branch and consequently falls solely within the field of freedom of establishment'. The Court went on to argue that 'since an examination from the angle of freedom of establishment would make it *superfluous* to conduct a separate examination...on...capital, it is necessary to consider first...establishment'.[128] Establishment entailed for companies within Article 54 TFEU the right to exercise their activity in the host Member State through a subsidiary, branch, or agency and that the Member State of origin was prohibited from hindering this.[129] The national measure 'has the principal effect of making the establishment of a branch by a Swedish company in a non-member country less attractive' and '[in] discouraging the creation of branches...fundamentally affects freedom of establishment and therefore comes *solely* within the scope of the Treaty provisions relating to that freedom'...'If that measure has restrictive effects on...capital, such effects must be seen as an unavoidable consequence of any restriction on...establishment and do not justify an examination of that measure in the light of Articles [63] to [65]...consequently there is *no need* to examine the measure...in the light of Treaty provisions...on...capital' [emphasis added].[130] The national measure 'fundamentally affects freedom of establishment within Article [49] et seq' and 'those Articles may not be relied upon in a situation involving establishment in a non-member country'.

So, since establishment was 'fundamentally' in point, the provision should be considered 'solely' from that perspective, even though establishment did not apply, and no consideration should be given to capital. It is not evident why establishment was 'fundamental' but capital not. Discouraging the creation of branches involves making the return realizable less attractive—both an establishment and an investment matter. If a subsidiary had been in issue the interest of that subsidiary in raising funds from its parent would have been a legitimate claim under the capital chapter.

126 n 106. 127 Ibid at [21]. 128 Ibid at [22]. 129 Ibid at [23] and [24].
130 Ibid at [25]–[28].

The *A and B* case was decided by reasoned order as a case where the same point had already been decided.[131] But the cases relied on (*Cadbury Schweppes*,[132] *Fidium Finanz*,[133] and the *Test Claimants in the Thin Cap Group Litigation*[134]) are not authority that, where establishment applies to the operation of a subsidiary company or branch, capital not only need not be considered where Article 49 applies but also shall not be considered even where it does not. The Advocate General's Opinion has not been published. There must therefore be some doubt about the authority of this case.

3. *Commission v Italy* (2009)

The latest *Commission v Italy* case is, however, more conclusive.[135] This is a 'golden share' case where (what is now) Articles 49 and 63 TFEU were applied according to the nature of the particular provisions of national law. This law enabled the state under the Articles of various privatized companies to: (a) block accumulation of shares bearing 5 per cent or more of voting rights; (b) block shareholder agreements to exercise 5 per cent[136] or more of such rights; (c) veto certain strategic transactions (eg merger, dissolution, and migration); and (d) appoint a non-voting director.[137]

The Commission challenged this under the current Article 63, but added that a challenge could equally be based on Article 49. Italy, citing *Cadbury Schweppes*, argued it should be considered exclusively on establishment.[138] AG Colomer reiterated his view[139] that 'the natural and most suitable context for evaluating... "golden shares" is freedom of establishment'. 'Such powers make the right to freedom of establishment less attractive either directly where they impinge on access to share capital, or indirectly where they reduce its allure by restricting the powers of the board relating to the ownership or management of the company'... 'the resulting restriction on free movement of capital is incidental rather than inevitable'... 'this is the case as regards measures which affect the composition of membership, but... is even more true as regards measures restricting company resolutions' of the (c) type.[140]

AG Colomer noted the

> high degree of practical relevance in view of that fact that free movement of capital applies [...] also between Member States and non-member countries. The implication

[131] Article 104(3) of the Rules of Procedure of the Court of Justice.

[132] n 124.

[133] Case C-452/04 *Fidium Finanz v Bundesanstalt für Finanzdienstleistungsaufsicht* [2006] ECR I-9521.

[134] Case C-524/04 *Test Claimants in the Thin Cap Group Litigation* [2007] ECR I-2107.

[135] n 13.

[136] There was also a ministerial power to reduce these 5% levels.

[137] A separate decree of 2004 prescribed criteria for operation of the powers, which the Court found inappropriate (ie insufficiently linked to the power) and disproportionate—not our concern here.

[138] *Commission v Italy* (n 13) at [11], [22].

[139] Cf the *BAA* and *Commission v Spain* cases (n 11 and 16).

[140] Opinion, at [44], [45].

is that, even if a measure such as a power of veto [...] were found to be incompatible with Article [49 TFEU], it would still be effective as against shareholders of non-member countries. By contrast, a finding that this extraordinary power contravened Article [63 TFEU], despite the secondary nature of the movement of money [...] which is precondition to the acquisition of a controlling shareholding, would leave the way open for non-EU shareholders to carry through [for example] the dissolution.[141]

So AG Colomer adopted the view that Article 49 was applicable because of the impact on shareholders of these powers in terms of their interference with powers of company management and the consequent impact on the attractiveness (or 'allure') of a holding in the company concerned and he appears to have taken this view regardless of the size or nature of the shareholding affected. But he was particularly concerned about the impact of a holding of breach of Article 63 on the ability of third-country shareholders to override the veto power. However, in the latter part of his opinion, considering justification of the Italian decree which laid down criteria for exercise of the powers, AG Colomer seems to accept that Article 63 alone applies to the (a) and (b) (5 per cent cap) restrictions and Article 49 to (c) (the veto power), arguing in the case of the latter that under the case law 'in order to ascertain whether a provision falls under one freedom or another it is necessary to look at the subject-matter of that provision', that national laws governing a holding of capital 'which gives *definite influence* over a company's decisions and *permits involvement in its activities* are covered by freedom of establishment'[142] [emphasis added—note the relative laxity of the influence/control criterion].

The Court did not follow AG Colomer either in his early argument that Article 49 alone applied or in his later approach applying Article 63 alone to the (a) and (b) (5 per cent+ holding) powers and Article 49 alone to the (c) veto power. It held that the (a)- and (b)-type blocking powers 'may' infringe both Article 49 and Article 63, but that the paragraph (c) veto power infringed only Article 49. First, on the question of the applicability of one freedom or another 'the purpose of the legislation concerned must be taken into consideration'.[143] Holdings allowing the holder to exercise narrow *Baars*-type control powers were within the ambit of freedom of establishment.[144] Direct investments, ie those 'which serve to establish or maintain lasting and direct links with the undertaking' enabling the investor 'to participate effectively in management or control', fell within Article 63.[145] National legislation not intended to apply only to shareholding enabling strict *Baars* control but which applies 'irrespective of size *may fall* within the ambit of both Article [49] and Article [63]' [emphasis

[141] Ibid at [47]. [142] Ibid at [62], [66], [78], [79].

[143] *Commission v Italy* (n 13) at [33], citing *Holböck* (n 125), which in turn cites *Fidium Finanz* (n 133), *Cadbury Schweppes* (n 124), and case C-446/04 *Test Claimants in the FII Group Litigation* [2006] ECR I-11753. [144] *Commission v Italy* (n 13) at [34].

[145] Ibid at [35]. This is not an assertion that other investments do not. It emerges later in the judgment that only such direct investments are a fact in point—see below.

added].[146] So a distinction needed to be drawn between the paragraph (a) and (b) 5 per cent powers and the paragraph (c) veto power. As to (a) and (b), it was clear on the facts that the 5 per cent holdings had to enable effective participation in management, which was covered by Article 63. But even at the 5 per cent level it was conceivable that in companies with large numbers of shareholders there might be narrow *Baars*-type control powers; furthermore the percentages were minima and greater holdings give an obvious power of control. So it was necessary to examine those powers in the light of both Article 49 and Article 63.[147]

As for the paragraph (c) veto power, since that 'clearly relates to decisions within the scope of management and therefore only concerns shareholders capable of exercising definite influence the power must be examined in the light of Article 49. Even if the effects of those criteria are restrictive of... capital those effects would be the unavoidable consequence of any restriction on freedom of establishment and would not warrant examination in the light of Article 63'... so the 'veto must be examined *solely* from the point of view of Article [49]'[148] [emphasis added].

So the powers were to be considered in the light of Article 63 and/or Article 49 according to the character of the shareholding in issue by reference to the size of the holding and the ownership structure––dispersion, etc. It is reasonably clear that the Court took the view that Article 49 applied, and Article 63 did not, where the *Baars* test was satisfied, and that Article 63 applied, and Article 49 did not, where the *Baars* test was not satisfied, even though on the facts the character of shareholding targeted by the Italian provisions was limited to 'direct' investment—ie conferring powers to participate effectively in management. In the case of the veto power because the decisions in question were ones for a high majority Article 49 alone applied and consequential effects on investment of the veto power were to be disregarded. But it should be noted that the test applied by the Court for application of Article 49 to the veto power was not the *Baars* test applied to the 5 per cent powers, but only a 'direct influence' requirement.[149]

VIII. Exclusive application of Article 49—extended Member State immunity in third-country cases

Finally on this case, it is worth comparing the territorial effect which would follow from AG Colomer's Opinion with the more stringent effect of the judgment. As he said in his 'Epilogue' the Italian concern was with third-country investors

[146] The Italian contention, based on *Cadbury Schweppes*, that only Article 49 TFEU applied was rejected.

[147] Ibid at [38].

[148] Ibid at [39].

[149] Compare para [38] of the judgment with para [39].

('extra-Community investor groups')[150] exercising strategic powers—eg to dissolve the business. As we have seen, his Opinion concludes that Article 63 TFEU alone applies to the powers in (a) and (b) (the 5 per cent powers) and Article 49 TFEU alone to (c) (the veto power over strategic decisions). Thus the EU law invalidity of the national provision would benefit third-country claimants in relation to (a) and (b), but not (c).

The judgment, by holding that Article 49 applies to the exclusion of Article 63 also to the (a) and (b) powers where the Narrow *Baars* Control test is satisfied, extends the immunity of national measures also into the (a) and (b) field to that extent. But of course, if the Court had adopted the AG's initial view that Article 49 alone applied to all three classes of power, there would have been no invalidity of national measures for such third-country cases at all. As will emerge below, I think this is the right answer, but for different reasons.

IX. Conclusion and proposal

1. Conclusion

Is this summary of the *Commission v Italy* case a safe, satisfactory, and stable basis for resolution of the issues in this field? It is submitted not, for the following reasons:

(1) The decision is far from clear—in particular as we have noted, on the (a) and (b) powers the strict *Baars* control test is applied to determine when Article 49 TFEU applies and Article 63 TFEU not with all the consequences that follow. On the (c) powers on the other hand only a 'definite influence' is required to have this effect. Assuming that this distinction is deliberate it seems impossible to find any justification for it, leaving a reasoned approach to defining this vital boundary in limbo.[151]

(2) Whichever test is applied the distinction between direct investment (which gives 'lasting economic links' and 'enables the investor to participate effectively in management or control'[152]) and establishment (whether based on the strict *Baars* control power test or some laxer version mentioned above) is very refined and hard to administer in practice, if discernible at all. Such refined reflections on the degree of control or influence operative in any case are, it is submitted, not a sound basis for important policy distinctions.

[150] Opinion para [91]—the notorious hedge funds may be in mind.

[151] AG Colomer adopts a different formula again—ie whether the holding 'gives definite influence over the company's decisions and permits involvement in its activities' (purporting to apply *Baars*, *X and Y*, and *Cadbury Schweppes*)—para [79] of the Opinion.

[152] See *Commission v Germany* (*Volkswagen*) (n 7).

(3) The narrow view which sets the bounds of Article 49 by reference to the Narrow *Baars* Control test are not reconcilable with the Treaty (including Article 55 TFEU), the subordinate legislation (such as the Takeover Bids Directive) nor with the general case law on establishment. If it is adopted on other areas it will, it is submitted, unduly curtail the scope of freedom of establishment, which is a fundamental guarantee for business activity by a wide range of business participants.

(4) The view that where establishment is in play it always trumps capital is not consistent with Articles 64 and 65 TFEU, which clearly envisage that, subject to defined exceptions, the capital freedom can operate in the establishment field. Article 49, second paragraph, has the converse implication.

(5) Adoption of a narrow *Baars* view for the bounds of establishment leads to a correspondingly narrow area for establishment to derogate from capital to the extent that it is concluded that establishment indeed trumps capital (as I argue below that it indeed does, but on different grounds). This produces a wide, and it is submitted undesirable range of rights for third-country related claims under Article 63 in areas of influence falling short of the very high levels of control required by *Baars*.

(6) The purpose doctrine enunciated in *Commission v Italy* is not consistent with Articles 63–65, which clearly envisage measures adopted for purposes other than restraining capital transactions falling within the chapter, and not consistent with principle. State measures restrict freedoms if that is their effect whatever their purpose.[153] The majority of the cases adduced to assert such a purpose test are in fact decided on the effects of the measures.[154] Whether a measure deters investors, or is likely to, is the correct test for applicability of the capital freedom, assuming it is (as it must surely be) a Treaty objective in its own right.

(7) There are major difficulties with arguments that the effects on one freedom are 'purely consequential' on the effects of the infringement of another. A realist may conclude that where establishment is in play the Court will now find effects on capital movements always thus consequential, to narrow third-country related remedies. As argued above, in many circumstances the two freedoms are concomitant, even identical, and it is not possible to discern causal links in either direction.[155] While

[153] It is trite law elsewhere that a purpose other than to regulate the freedom does not exempt the restriction, though it may found a justification.

[154] See eg *Cadbury Schweppes* (n 124) at [31]–[33]; *A and B* (n 106) at [25]–[27]; *FII Group Litigation* (n 143) at [36]; *Thin Cap Group Litigation,* (n 134) at [26]–[34]; *CFC and Dividend Group Litigation* (n 124) at [72], [73]; and *Fidium Finanz* (n 133) at [34], [44].

[155] AG Colomer in the *Italy* case (n 13) asserts (in a revealingly hyperbolic outburst at para [81]) that because the transfer of funds will have occurred earlier than the interference with their enjoyment this reduces the link with capital to 'the level of a schoolboy hypothesis'!

there may be cases where the impact of a national measure on one freedom may be so trivial it does not deserve consideration it is submitted that none of the cases considered here are examples where the impact on investors was *de minimis* in this sense.

2. Proposal

Hard cases make bad law. There is a danger the Court's understandable desire to reduce the scope of the capital freedom for territorial reasons will lead to a distortion of the freedoms. I suggest it is better to accept the natural meaning of the Treaty: that the freedoms operate in parallel when transactions are capable of being characterized as exercises of both freedoms.

But this does not mean that the capital freedom is a means of evading necessary and established restrictions on freedom of establishment. Article 65(2) makes it clear that 'the provisions of [the capital chapter] are without prejudice to the applicability of restrictions on the right of establishment which are compatible with the Treaties'. Establishment here must include establishment involving third countries and not be limited by the territorial scope of Article 49, for two reasons: first, it would be absurd if the provision applied as between Member States but did not as against third countries (giving less scope to Member States to regulate the latter); and second, it is clear from Article 64(1) and (2) that establishment in this chapter has that wider sense—ie applies to foreign establishment—see also *A and B*. It may be argued that this view of Article 65(2) is open to objection because it deprives Article 64 as it applies to establishment of all meaning (because that Article enables Member States in limited circumstances to adopt restrictions contrary to Article 63 involving establishment). It seems evident this view is mistaken: Article 64 removes the national measures entirely from the chapter; Article 65(2) does not. Article 65(3) disapplies the exception where it is shown that invocation of establishment in this way covers arbitrary discrimination or a disguised restriction on capital.

A proper application of Article 65(2) will thus allow Member States to restrict investment involving third countries, on legitimate establishment grounds—ie where this is not arbitrarily discriminatory nor really a disguised restriction on capital.[156] No such constraint applies to the laws 'grandfathered' under Article 64(1).

These difficult issues are best resolved by careful reference to the Treaty.

[156] What of *Fidium Finanz* (n 133) (where a Swiss provider of credit to borrowers in Germany was held to be engaging in a service rather than a capital transaction) and the capital/services overlap? This was an acute problem where the service in question was itself a capital transaction, ie the lending of money. The answer seems to be that the national legislative purpose was prudential regulation, also specifically excluded from capital under (what is now) Article 65(1)(b) TFEU.

Table 4.1 Analytical table of VW restrictions

Criteria / Possible Restriction	State Measure	Contrary to 'General Company Law'	Prohibited by Member State's Company Law?	'Specific right enabling more significant control'	Article 56 restriction
1. 20% voting cap	Yes [1]	Yes	Yes	No?[2] But 20% holdings already in place at time[3]	No, taken alone, but yes, combined with 2 [4]
2. 20% blocking minority	Yes [1]	Yes[5]	No, but NB contrary to default rule and not autonomous	No?[2] But ditto	No, alone, but yes, combined with 1
3. Supervisory Board appointment (2+2)	Yes[1]	Yes[6]	Yes	Yes[7]	Yes

Notes:
[1] Judgment at [26], [27]: 'fact that this agreement has become the subject of a national law suffices for it to be considered a national measure'.
[2] Germany said the effect was the same for all shareholders and conferred no special rights on the state [36]. At [47] the Court agrees: 'this power applies without distinction. In the same way as the cap on voting rights, it may operate to the benefit and detriment of any shareholder in the company'.
[3] [48] 'when the law was adopted the Federal State and the Land of Lower Saxony were the 2 main shareholders... and each held 20%'. See too Commission arguments at [34] and [35] of the judgment.
[4] Note that on 1 and 2 combined the Court rules, [52] 'By limiting the possibility for other shareholders to participate in the company with a view to establishing or maintaining lasting and direct economic links with it which would make possible effective participation in management or control, this is liable to deter direct investors from other Member States' and for 3 at [66] in substantially the same terms. No assertion that investors from other Member States are more deterred than those from Germany.
[5] See [46] 'derogating from general law, imposed by way of specific legislation'; [50]... 'a blocking minority... on a lower level of investment than would be required under general company law'.
[6] See [60]... 'constitutes a derogation from company law, which restricts rights of representation of certain shareholders... to 1/3 of the shareholders' representatives'... and [62]... 'thus enables them to participate in a more significant manner than their status as shareholders would normally allow'.
[7] 'specific right... derogates from general company law' [61]; 'gives possibility of exercising influence which exceeds levels of investment' [64].

5

When the State is the Owner—Some Further Comments on the Court of Justice 'Golden Shares' Strategy

Andrea Biondi

I. Introduction

The process of privatization and compatibility with the EU trade regulatory model of those mechanisms aimed at preserving some forms of state control on strategic economic sectors is one of the most 'emotionally' charged areas of internal market law. Often the true and genuine legal aspects become embroiled in what one may call an ideological debate. Apart from some (not unexpected) political overreactions, many commentators have moved to the high grounds of discussing conceptual issues such as the model of European corporate governance and the social implications that the judgments of the Court of Justice of the European Union might seem to predicate.[1] No doubt the dilemma of the golden shares litigation is how to ease the tension between the creation of rules of corporate organization that would facilitate intra-state regulatory competition on one side and the respect for Member State policy choices on the other.

It is also true that the Court's judgments made a certain language seem out of date and deprived it of any substantive meaning. As rightly noted, categories such as shareholder/stakeholder, private/public do not seem to be so useful in understanding the new realities of the European corporate regulatory model.[2] However, it seems to us that we have been here before, as every time European (legal) integration takes a leap forward, the same questions have been raised and

[1] See M Rhodes and B van Apeldoorn, 'Capitalism Unbound? The Transformation of European Corporate Governance' (1998) 5 J of Eur Public Policy 406; P Zumbansen and D Samm, 'The ECJ, Volkswagen and European Corporate Law: Reshaping the European Varieties of Capitalism' (2007) 8 German L J 1027. For an updated discussion see A Johnston, *EC Regulation of Corporate Governance* (Cambridge: Cambridge University Press, 2009).

[2] P Zumbansen and D Samm, 'The ECJ, Volkswagen and European Corporate Law: Reshaping the European Varieties of Capitalism' (2007) 8 German L J 1027, 1049.

the same dilemmas posed. It is such a long list of concerns, spanning from human rights protection and taxation to social security systems and labour law, that it would be impossible even to footnote. It is thus in our view preferable, as supported by Professor Rickford's contribution in this volume,[3] to focus upon and take stock of the many recent developments in this area and to insert them in their proper milieu, that is free movement law.

II. The golden shares *acquis* and the internal market

In such a habitat, the ECJ golden shares cases[4] seem comfortably settled as they comply with all the most fundamental (even constitutional?) principles of internal market law: the EU internal market is an 'objective' and not a 'subjective' concept as it focuses not on the aim of the national measure, nor on its protectionist intent, but on its effect, from which a cascade of implications flow: the EU internal market rules (and its ensuing prohibitions for Member States) extend over not only any national rules that 'physically' deny access to the market, but also over any measure which could produce an effect on trade.

As Professor Rickford in his contribution suggests, the golden shares case law is very much based on the idea that the Treaty will be triggered against either discriminatory national measures or when it is possible to ascertain some kind of excessive state influence which can in its turn have the effect of deterring investors. Consistently with other freedoms the Court has always been reluctant to introduce any kind of *ab limine* limitation; thus, the very strong rejection of a possible *Keck* analogy[5] in the area of capital in the *BAA* case.[6] Actually any kind of possible future use of an 'investments arrangements' criterion seems very unlikely in the light of the recent decisions in the area of free movement of goods where the Court rejected any extension of the *Keck* test to restrictions imposed on how to use a product.[7] Focusing on the effects implies further the irrelevance of the 'kind' of regulatory competence that is actually exercised by the Member State. In the golden shares *acquis* this is exemplified by the stubborn refusal to consider (despite the many efforts of the late Advocate General Ruiz Jarabo Colomer) the neutrality of the Treaty towards ownership rights enshrined in Article 295 EC (now Article 345 TFEU) as a shelter for Member States' 'power

[3] J Rickford, 'Protectionism, Capital Freedom and the Internal Market' in ch 4 of this volume.

[4] See inter alia Case C-483/99 *Commission v France* [2002] I-4781; C-503/99 *Commission v Belgium* [2002] I-4809; C-98/01 *Commission v United Kingdom* [2003] ECR I-4641; C-112/05 *Commission v Germany* [2007] ECR I-8995; C-326/07 *Commission v Italy*, [2009] ECR I-2291.

[5] Cases 267 and 268/91 *Keck* and *Mithouard* [1993] ECR I-6097

[6] C-98/01 *Commission v United Kingdom* [2003] ECR I-4641.

[7] Case C-110/05 *Commission v Italy* [2009] ECR I-519 and Case C-142/05 *Åklagaren v Percy Mickelsson and Joakim Roos* [2009] ECR I-4273. See on their implications for free movement law C Barnard, 'Trailing a New Approach to Free Movement of Goods' (2009) 68 Cambridge L J 288.

to influence economic life even through ownership of undertakings'.[8] Finally, far from being an ultra-deregulatory system, the European single market has always been structured on a series of checks and balances between the effective application of trade rules and the preservation of public values—preservations which are allocated both to supranational institutions and to Member State authorities. It has been suggested that the case law on golden shares is an example of intense scrutiny by the Court. The Court has been accused of failing to take into account that if golden shares' mechanisms are actually adopted by all Member States, this could indicate that there is a general interest here worth protecting. Further, a softer version of proportionality should have been preferable because of the delicate nature of the economic sectors involved. In reality, the Court has applied its standard two-test approach—breach and proportionality of the measure in question in the light of the aim of the measure—rather consistently. Thus, the acknowledgement of possible public aims such as public security[9] but at the same time the refusal to hear any purely economic ones. A little bit less celebrated, but still a significant judgment, is worth mentioning in this context. In a judgment of 2005[10] the Court was asked to rule on Italian legislation that provided for the automatic suspension of voting rights attaching to holdings exceeding 2 per cent of the capital of undertakings operating in the electricity and gas sectors, where such holdings were acquired by public undertakings that were not quoted on regulated financial markets and held a dominant position. The Court found in favour of the Commission, considering such a mechanism a restriction on capital movement between Member States, contrary to Article 56 EC (now Article 63 TFEU). The Court explained that 'effective' direct investment involves the possibility of participating effectively in the management and control of a company, and the suspension of voting rights means that the category of public undertakings concerned is precluded from participating effectively in the management and control of Italian undertakings operating in the electricity and gas markets.

It is interesting to discuss the possible justifications; the Italian Government essentially argued that such a measure was in conformity with the EU's aim of the liberalization of the energy sector. In particular, the objective pursued by the Italian legislation was to avoid anti-competitive attacks by public entities operating in the same sector in other Member States where public undertakings retained a position of advantage because of the lack of a real liberalization. In short, the Italian decree was necessary to remedy the 'asymmetry' existing in the competitive structure of the energy market. The Court dismissed such an argument as a purely economic one: an interest in generally strengthening the competitive structure of the market in question cannot constitute a valid justification for restrictions on the free movement of capital.

[8] AG Ruiz Jarabo Colomer Opinion in Case C-483/99 *Commission v France* [2002] I-4781; C-503/99 *Commission v Belgium*, [2002] I-4809 para 53.

[9] C-503/99 *Commission v Belgium* [2002] I-4809.

[10] C-174/04 *Commission v Italy* [2005] ECR I-4933.

Furthermore, despite being alerted to possible abuses, the Court—consistently with its case law on other economic freedoms—has not entirely turned a blind eye to other possible defences put forward by Member States. The Court has for instance gradually recognized some extra space for some kind of mandatory requirements.[11] In the *Volkswagen* case, for instance, although not applicable in the case at stake, the Court considered arguments based on workers' protection and on considerations of general interest and the preservation of a high level of employment.[12] Even faced with the application of openly distinctly applicable measures, the Court at least in theory accepted to look at certain extra Treaty grounds. For instance in *SEVIC*, a case on establishment, the Court was asked about the compatibility with EU law of a German measure that did not allow registration in the commercial registry of intra-community mergers.[13] The Court did not have any difficulties in concluding that the freedom of establishment for companies includes cross-border merger operations. Next, as regards the question of a possible breach, it was clear that German law had to be considered as a measure which had the effect of establishing a difference in treatment between companies. The Court although dealing with a distinctly applicable measure, accepted to look at possible justifications based on the necessity to protect creditors, minority shareholders, and employees, and to preserve the effectiveness of fiscal supervision and the fairness of commercial transactions.[14]

The second point that should be made on the intensity of the Court's review is that the application of the principle of proportionality in the golden shares context is not expressed in terms of balancing interests but by using some objective benchmarks such as transparency and legal certainty. It is indeed a well-established principle that any time the state intervenes in the market there is a specific obligation for the national political process to take into account its effects on the internal market.[15] This translates in practice in what you could term transparency requirements imposed on any state intervention into the economic sphere.

The Court of Justice seems to apply a global test that requires state machineries to restrict free movement only if the system devised is '*based on objective, non-discriminatory criteria which are known in advance, in such a way as to circumscribe the exercise of the national authorities' discretion, so that it is not used arbitrarily*'.[16] Any kind of restrictions should also be based on a procedural system which is easily accessible and capable of ensuring that a request for authorization will be dealt with objectively and impartially within a reasonable time and refusals to

[11] C-302/97 *Klaus Konle v Republik Österreich* [1999] ECR I-3099.

[12] C-112/05 *Commission v Germany* [2007] ECR I-8995 paras 74 and 80.

[13] C-411/03 *SEVIC Systems AG* [2005] ECR I-10805.

[14] See for a similar approach Cases C-208/00 *Überseering* [2002] ECR I-9919 and C-167/01 *Inspire Art* [2003] ECR I-10155.

[15] See in general the Opinion of AG Poiares Maduro in Joined Cases C-158/04 and C-159/04 *Alfa Vita Vassilopoulos v Elliniki Dimosio* [2006] ECR I-8135.

[16] Case C-157/99 *Smits and Peerbooms* [2001] ECR I-5473.

grant authorization must also be capable of being challenged in judicial or quasi-judicial proceedings.[17] In the context of free movement of capital—likewise—the Court explained that a system of prior authorization cannot be justifiable unless the investors are given specific indications as to the specific circumstances in which such restrictive measures are required. Thus any lack in transparency would be considered a violation of EU law as it:

> does not enable individuals to be apprised of the extent of their rights and obligations deriving from Article 73b [now Article 63 TFEU] of the Treaty. That being so, the system established is contrary to the principle of legal certainty.[18]

Hence the insistence in cases such as French and Belgian golden shares in indicating an *ex post* process of refusal instead of an *ex ante* authorization is the best regulatory approach to guarantee transparency and efficacy.[19]

III. The state as market participant—some lessons from state aid law

So far we are treading on familiar ground—any risk of tripping over? The application of a wide deterrence in the golden shares litigation is not totally unproblematic. No questions can be posed in those cases whereby the Member State acts squarely as a market regulator with the intention of preserving for itself certain prerogatives. Thus in the French, Belgium, or UK golden shares cases, the Court's judgments sanctioned the inability of the governments concerned, once a virtuous process of privatization had started, to take it to its logical conclusion— the dismantling of national barriers. The mortal sin of each in the first wave of golden shares litigation is identifiable in the failure, to borrow some US federalism language, to take into account out of state interests in exercising a perfectly lawful regulatory power. However, there are instances where it can be argued that the 'measure' in contention was adopted pursuant to the normal application of private company law. In short, to use Professor Rickford's expression, the question is whether free movement of use can be used as a challenge to ordinary company law.[20] Further is this the most efficient way of resolving disputes over company ownerships?[21] He rightly draws attention to cases such as *Viking* whereby the

[17] See for instance, Case C-205/99 *Analir and Others* [2001] ECR I-1271; Case C-372/04 *Watts* [2006] ECR I-4325; Case C-231/03 *Coname* [2005] ECR I-7287; C-458/03 *Parking Brixen* [2005] ECR I-8612; Case C-380/05 *Centro Europa 7* [2008] ECR I-349.

[18] Case C-54 /99 *Eglise de Scientologie* [2000] ECR I-1335 para 22.

[19] Case C-483/99 *Commission v France* [2002] ECR I-4781; C-503/99 *Commission v Belgium* [2002] ECR I-4809.

[20] See on this question also WG Ringe, 'Company Law and Free Movement of Capital' (2010) 69 Cambridge L J, forthcoming.

[21] Jonathan Rickford, 'Protectionism, Capital Freedom and the Internal Market' in ch 4 of this volume.

Court seems to suggest full directly horizontal effects.[22] It is thus safe to claim that after that decision, at least discriminatory actions taken by both the state and private actors that might have the effect of restricting the access of other market operators could fall within the scope of EU economic freedoms. This may well be the case for certain provisions of a corporate constitution aimed at limiting the possibility of acquiring the control of the corporation.

There are, however, other issues that are worthy of discussion. One might ask whether it is always a bad thing if the state decides to be involved? Does free movement law apply any time the state is participating in the market? These questions have been tackled head-on by Advocate General Poiares Maduro in his Opinion in the *Federconsumatori* case.[23] The question was whether Article 63 TFEU precludes national rules which enable a public body which retains a minority shareholding (33.4 per cent) in a privatized company to retain the power to appoint an absolute majority of the members of the board of directors. The Italian Government argued that this was just a 'neutral provision' as it was contained in the Italian Civil Code and that the decision was a voluntary one by the shareholders in the general meeting, 'in which the public body acted in its capacity as ordinary shareholder'. The Advocate General Opinion was a drastic one: first of all, for the purpose of determining whether the free movement of capital is restricted where the state enjoys special powers in an undertaking, it is immaterial how those powers are granted or what legal form they take. This is to prevent any possible circumvention of Treaty rules by astute Member States which could use civil laws instead of regulatory powers to escape their EU obligations.[24] He further argued that Member States are under a duty to respect the Treaty provisions on the free movement, both *ratione personae* in their capacity as signatories to the Treaty and *ratione materiae* when a national measure entails a discrimination which, in respect of the exercise of a transnational activity, imposes additional costs or hinders access to the national market for investors established in other Member States, either because it has the effect of protecting the position of certain economic operators already established in the market or because it makes intra-Community trade more difficult than internal trade. This principle—he argues—means that only if investors in other Member States can be sure that the public body concerned will, with a view to maximizing its return on investment, respect the normal rules of operation of the market, the conduct of the Member State will not trigger the application of EU law.

[22] Case C-438/05 *International Transport Workers' Federation and Finnish Seamen's Union, 'Viking Line'* [2007] ECR I-10779.

[23] Joined Cases C-463/04 and C-464/04 *Federconsumatori and others v Comune di Milano* [2007] ECR I-10419.

[24] See for instance C-171/08 *Commission v Portugal* pending before the Court of Justice, Opinion of AG Mengozzi delivered on 2 December 2009. In this case, the Portuguese Government argued that maintaining for 500 shares with special rights (class A shares) in Portugal Telecom was merely the direct and immediate result of the will of Portugal Telecom itself and, therefore, of the normal application of company law.

A possible criticism is that such a reconstruction leaves very little space for the Member States, because if any kind of actions attributable to the state have some form of regulatory effect it is difficult to imagine any situation when this regulatory effect would not fall short of the 'normal rules of operation of the market'. In other words, the Member States' objectives are never going to be maximizing profits alone, but their conduct will also be guided by other public policy objectives. It might be useful to address these points to draw a parallel with state aid law—the principal tool for regulating states intervention in the economy in EU law.[25] From an economic point of view, any form of positive intervention in the economy is routinely considered as being dangerous and 'virtually all state actions can affect international trade'.[26] In the EU regulatory framework, things are not so drastic and the whole regime of state aid is based on a balance between prohibitions and justifications. Furthermore, one of the benchmarks employed to check if the state measure unduly confers an advantage to the undertaking concerned is the so-called 'market investor principle'.

In order to determine whether a state measure constitutes aid it is necessary to establish whether the state has acted as a rational market investor, implying that state conduct would be immune from scrutiny if proven to be subject to the normal rules of operation of the market.[27] The application of the market investor principle has been variously criticized[28] but it does offer some useful lessons for the application of the free movement of capital. First and foremost, it is an application of the principle of equality, that is there is a specific obligation imposed on the state not to discriminate against private operators. If the state decides to enter the market it is subject to its rules. If it does not follow these rules, this would confer an undue advantage on the beneficiary.[29]

To go back to the free movement of capital, it is therefore the presence of an 'advantage' that the Court is actually sanctioning in these cases. For instance in the *Belgian Eurobond* judgment, the Court was confronted with such a question whereby the Government tried to demonstrate that issuing a Eurobond in the German market that gave subscribers the right to withhold certain taxes—a right which was not available to Belgian residents—was just a normal commercial operation and thus not falling within the scope of the Treaty.[30] The Court noted that the withholding of tax and the exclusion of Belgian residents were considered 'advantages' that only the state could have conferred and that created an obstacle to the free movement of capital.

[25] On this parallel, see Ringe (n 20).

[26] R Snape, 'International Regulation of Subsidies' (1991) 14 The World Economy 139, 140.

[27] See inter alia Case C-480/98 *Spain v Commission* [2000] ECR I-8717 and Case T-296/97 *Alitalia v Commission* [2000] ECR II-3871.

[28] See, for instance, M Parish, 'On the Private Investor Principle' (2003) 28 Eur L Rev 70.

[29] For an exhaustive discussion see L Rubini, *The Definition of Subsidy and State Aid* (Oxford, 2009) especially 246–60.

[30] Case C-478/98 *Commission v Belgium* ECR [2000] I-7587.

Likewise, the golden shares mechanisms are not just restrictions to entry but they are also a sort of state guarantee inducing investors to rely on the reassuring state presence. Golden shares are in fact sometimes perceived by the market itself as endowing the company at stake with preference in government procurement and investment, privileged access to decision-makers, concessionary terms of operation, and a favourable pricing structure. These conditions create a *de facto* advantage for the state that once again has to be challenged in terms of free movement. To continue with the analogy of the market investor principle, its application is not monolithic or susceptible to possible graduations. Both the Court and the Commission have acknowledged that a certain flexibility and margin of judgement should be reserved to the state in its capacity as investor as would be the case for any investor.[31] Further, it could also be argued that the maximization of profit is not always the only consideration to be taken into account.

In two famous cases dealing with large public holdings, the Court of Justice confirmed the necessity to look at considerations of a social nature or of a regional or sectorial policy. To borrow the language of Advocate General van Gerven in those cases, it is possible to imagine a reasonable investor, as opposed to a private investor:

> This does not mean that the requirement of profitability should be left out of account. The reasonable investor must in order to act responsibly secure a normal return on its investments even if in doing it may have regard to a wider social and economic context and over a longer time span.[32]

Once again, the golden shares cases are acknowledging that in certain strategic economic sectors state participation in the market should not be led by purely economic considerations, but should consider wider social and economic factors that think beyond short-term benefits subject to the requirements of transparency and proportionality.

Come to think of it, this seems to be a good guiding principle not just for national governments but for the whole EU business community.

[31] Case C-303/88 *Italy v Commission* [1991] ECR I-1433 and Case C-305/89 *Italy v Commission* [1991] ECR I-1603.

[32] Case C-303/88 *Italy v Commission* [1991] ECR I-1433 and Case C-305/89 *Italy v Commission* [1991] ECR I-1603 at paras 11 and 12 of the Opinion.

PART II

TAKEOVERS AND MERGERS

6

The Takeover Directive as a Protectionist Tool?

Paul Davies, Edmund-Philipp Schuster, and Emilie van de Walle de Ghelcke†

I. Introduction

The principal purpose behind the Takeover Directive[1] in the eyes of the European Commission was to promote the integration of the national economies constituting the 'single market' and to enhance the competitiveness of European industry as against non-European rivals by facilitating takeover bids, especially cross-border ones. As the Commission put it in its 2002 proposal,

> the Lisbon European Council placed this directive, which forms part of the Financial Services Action Plan, among the priorities as regards the integration of European financial markets by 2005. [...] Under the circumstances, the Commission considers it essential to provide a European framework for cross-border takeover bids as part of the Financial Services Action Plan. Such transactions can contribute to the development and reorganisation of European firms, a key condition for withstanding international competition and developing a single capital market.[2]

Although this rationale was buttressed with the familiar arguments about providing a level playing field and enhancing legal certainty, it is clear that the competitiveness and integration rationales were the dominant ones in the Commission's

† We wish to thank Domenico Benincasa, Jacques Buhart, Luca Enriques, Athanasios Kouloridas, Frédéric Pelèse, and Luigi Verga for valuable comments. We are also indebted to various European regulatory authorities for helpful clarifications and explanations of their respective legal frameworks. Finally, we want to thank all participants of the conference on 'Company Law and Economic Protectionism', held at Christ Church, Oxford.

[1] Directive 2004/25/EC of the European Parliament and of the Council of 21 April 2004 on Takeover Bids [2004] OJ L142/12 (the '*Takeover Directive*' or the '*Directive*').

[2] Commission of the European Communities, *Proposal for a Directive of the European Parliament and of the Council on Takeover Bids*, COM(2002) 534 final (Brussels, October 2002) (hereafter 'Commission's 2002 proposal') 3.

mind. Also, as Enriques has pointed out,[3] the level playing field rationale is, by itself, a rather uncertain guide to what, substantively, should be included in any particular EU legal instrument. Everyone would be playing by the same rules if, for example, the launching of a bid were made conditional upon the agreement of shareholders of the acquirer and of the employees of the target, but such rules would be inconsistent with the promotion of cross-border takeovers. The same point can be made about legal certainty. This is not to deny that common rules *of a particular character* and legal certainty *of a certain type* facilitate cross-border bids, but simply to point out that the substantive content of the Commission's 2002 proposal, or at least the elements of it that were to prove controversial, can be explained only on a rationale of facilitating bids and integrating the European capital market.[4]

This paper seeks to establish whether and, if so, to what extent the implementation of the Takeover Directive in the Member States has moved national laws (further) towards the position in which takeovers are available to a significant extent as a technique for 'the development and reorganization of European firms'. For this purpose, it focuses on one of the provisions in the Directive which was aimed at facilitating takeover bids, the board neutrality rule (BNR), contained in Article 9 of the Directive. In the very long debates over the Commission's proposals for a Takeover Directive, the BNR was at the centre of the political controversy about whether the European Union should attribute a significant role to takeovers. The Commission's 1996 proposal for a Takeover Directive contained a mandatory BNR[5] and it was primarily the European Parliament's objections to this provision, coupled with a late change of heart by the German Government of the day (departing from the common position agreed by all the Member State governments), which led to the failure of this first proposal at the very final stage of the European legislative process in 2001.[6] The Commission's 2002 proposal reiterated the suggestion for a mandatory BNR but, to address one set of objections which had been made to a ban on post-bid defences, the Commission coupled it with a proposal for the mandatory 'breakthrough' of certain pre-bid

[3] L Enriques, 'The Mandatory Bid Rule in the Proposed EC Takeover Directive: Harmonization As Rent-Seeking?' in G Ferrarini, K J Hopt, J Winter, and E Wymeersch (eds), *Reforming Company Law and Takeover Law in Europe* (Oxford/New York: Oxford University Press, 2004) 784.

[4] The integration rationale probably played an important role in regard of the mandatory bid rule, which is widely believed to have a 'chilling' effect on (domestic and cross-border) takeover activity, whilst providing minority shareholders with additional protection (and therefore arguably increasing market confidence). However, takeover bids are only the means to an end (ie a more competitive corporate landscape); consequently, the mandatory bid rule can also be seen as being in line with the 'competitiveness'-rationale in so far as it prevents inefficient takeovers.

[5] [1996] OJ C 162/5; COM(1995) 655, Article 8. There was an even earlier Commission proposal of 1989 (COM(1988) 823 final), which also contained a (somewhat weaker) form of mandatory BNR, negotiations on which were suspended in 1991. See V Edwards, 'The Directive on Takeover Bids—Not Worth the Paper It's Written On?' (2004) 1 Eur Company and Financial L Rev 416.

[6] Edwards ibid, 425–7. In fact, the very last vote on the Directive (in the European Parliament) was tied, so that, by convention, the proposal failed.

defences, ie that certain departures from the principle of one share/one vote and certain restrictions on the transfer of shares, existing prior to the offer, should not apply in the context of a takeover bid. So in the 2002 proposal a mandatory BNR was supplemented with a mandatory breakthrough rule (BTR).[7] Perhaps not surprisingly, this extension of the scope of the rules against takeover defences proved no more attractive to the other participants in the EU's legislative process. Eventually, agreement was reached between the Council (representing the Member States) and the Parliament on the final text of the Directive only on the basis that Member States could decide to opt out of the BNR (contained in Article 9) and/or of the BTR (contained in Article 11) when they came to transpose the Directive.[8] This compromise, which was proposed initially by the Portuguese Government and later elaborated upon by the Italian, was bitterly opposed by the Commissioner responsible for the Commission's proposal.[9] Whatever one thinks of the compromise, it clearly made the transposition decisions of the Member States more than usually significant.

This article proceeds as follows. Section II identifies the function of the BNR in facilitating takeover bids. Section III analyses the choices created by the Directive in relation to the BNR by the Directive. As we shall see, these choices exist both at the level of the Member State and at the level of the individual company. Sections IV and V report the evidence about the choices which have been made at both these levels. Section VI concludes.

II. The function of the Board Neutrality Rule

The BNR, as adopted in the Takeover Directive, prohibits the management of a target company from taking any action which may result in the frustration of a takeover bid for this company without obtaining post-bid shareholder approval for the specific defensive measure.[10] The only exceptions to this strict prohibition are the search for alternative bids (ie seeking a 'white knight') and the completion of measures within the company's normal course of business, if they were already started pre-bid. It might seem obvious that a rule prohibiting the board of a company from taking defensive measures against an unwelcome bid without the consent of the shareholders given after the bid has been launched would have a significant impact in facilitating bids, where the rule is present, and in constraining bids, where it is absent. However, there are two sets of arguments which can and have been made in support of the view that the BNR is less important than first impression suggests and even that it is trivial. These two sets of arguments

[7] See Article 11. [8] The optional provisions are contained in Article 12.

[9] Edwards (n 5) 430–1. The title of her article includes the phrase the responsible Commissioner used of the Directive as adopted (Not worth the paper it's written on). [10] See Article 9(2).

can be termed (1) the redundancy argument (which comes in three forms) and (2) the shareholder structure argument.

1. The redundancy argument

(i) The BNR adds nothing to national law

The first form of the redundancy argument is that a BNR adds nothing to restrictions already existing in a legal system constraining directors from acting contrary to the interests of the shareholders when deciding whether to take defensive measures in relation to a takeover bid. Those national restrictions either already require shareholder approval of defensive tactics or constrain the exercise of board discretion in the face of a bid so as to protect shareholders. This is an argument which is obviously highly contingent on the content of the corporate laws of any particular legal system to which it is being applied. Whether it is true or not in relation to any particular system requires an in-depth and sophisticated analysis of that system against the standard of the BNR.[11] It is obviously doctrinally possible for a set of corporate laws not to contain an explicit BNR but instead to contain a collection of more specific rules and standards which together produce the same overall effect. In fact, it is rather unlikely that a legal system without a BNR lacks any restraints at all on defensive measures. In most Member States the core duty of loyalty, for example, requiring directors to act in the best interests of the company would be engaged in a takeover situation, but, as we argue below, this constraint is probably not very effective.

However, this form of the redundancy argument is not convincing. First, it is unlikely that the argument that the BNR adds nothing to existing restrictions holds good in relation to many Member States of the EU.[12] The BNR, as articulated in Article 9, has three powerful features which the non-BNR provisions must match if this form of the redundancy argument is to be made out. First, the BNR is a general rule that covers any action the board may take which could potentially result in the frustration of the bid (subject to the two exceptions just mentioned and the positive requirement of the Directive that the board publishes its views on the offer).[13] Thus, the rule is not open to evasion by the creation of new defensive measures, such as, famously, the poison pill in the United

[11] For an application of this argument to the UK see D Kershaw, 'The Illusion of Importance: Reconsidering the UK's Takeover Defence Prohibition' (2007) 56 Intl & Comparative L Q 267.

[12] Of course, the Directive's BNR may be trivial if the national system already contains a domestic BNR, but the question we address here is whether a BNR, from whatever source, is a significant rule.

[13] See Article 9(5). The advice of the target's board to accept an offer, for instance, will often be a key factor for the bidder's success. A recent example is Kraft Foods' takeover offer for Cadbury, where the decision of Cadbury's board to agree to (and recommend) Kraft's offer ended a month-long fierce fight over the company, and financial journalists had little doubt that—with Cadbury's board 'approving' the takeover—it would be successful; see J Wiggins and L Saigol, 'Cadbury and Kraft agree £11.6bn deal' *Financial Times* (London, 18 January 2010).

States, which were not in mind when the more specific rules were formulated.[14] As important, a general rule will catch measures with defensive qualities which, while generally available, were not anticipated as being used for this purpose when the specific rules were drawn up.[15]

Second, the BNR is a rule, not a standard, and a rule which turns on the likely *effect* of the defensive measure in frustrating the offer, not on the good faith or proper purposes of the directors. Hence it is less susceptible to qualification or softening through *ex post* judicial decision-making. For example, a general duty of loyalty imposed on directors, requiring them to act in what they consider to be the best interests of the company, is not likely to be significantly constraining in relation to defensive tactics, because of the element of subjectivism in the formulation of the duty, coupled with the fact that in many Member States' laws the 'company' does not constitute a reference exclusively to the shareholders' interests or, at least, does not do so unambiguously. Even with more objectively formulated standards, such as the UK standard requiring directors to exercise the powers conferred upon them only for a 'proper purpose', courts are sometimes reluctant to apply the standard in such a way as to require directors to obtain shareholder authorization for defensive measures against what the court perceives to be an abusive offer.[16] In addition, takeovers are a time-critical operation from the bidder's perspective, and thus the prospect of having to litigate against the target's management will often render a transaction substantially less attractive for the acquirer—even where the chances of prevailing seem reasonably high. In short, the BNR is a bright-line *ex ante* rule, which avoids the uncertainty of meaning and interpretation associated with a more open-ended standard.[17]

Finally, the BNR requires shareholder authorization of defensive tactics in the face of the bid. Pre-bid shareholder authorization is not enough. How significant is the distinction between pre-bid and post-bid authorization? The issue is

[14] For the reasons given below, the poison pill is a US-specific example which cannot as easily be replicated in the European Union. So, in the EU the ingenuity of lawyers acting for target management would have to be exercised along different lines. The point is that scope is given for such ingenuity if the rule constraining defensive measures is not comprehensive.

[15] For example, the rulings of the British Takeover Panel bringing within the BNR decisions by targets to litigate against the bidder. See Panel Decision 1989/7, *Consolidated Gold Fields* (decision by wholly-owned subsidiary to seek to restrain in the US courts the bid for the British parent company as being a breach of US competition legislation required approval of parent's shareholders).

[16] This is true even in the UK where the dominant trend in the court decisions is to require shareholder approval under the proper purposes rule in all cases for defensive actions (see *Hogg v Cramphorn* [1967] Ch 254; *Howard Smith Ltd v Ampol Petroleum Ltd* [1974] AC 821). A minor strand in judicial thinking, nevertheless, is that a proper purpose is constituted by saving the company from an abusive takeover. See *Cayne v Global Natural Resource* (unreported, August 12, 1982, Chancery Division) (directors' purpose not to perpetuate their control over the company but to 'prevent it from being reduced to impotence and beggary' by a predatory bidder); and *Criterion Properties plc v Stratford UK Properties LLC* [2003] BCC 50. Since the adoption of a BNR in the UK City Code in 1968 there has been less need to litigate the issue under the proper purposes doctrine.

[17] For a general analysis of the distinction between rules and standards see L Kaplow, 'Rules vs Standards: An Economic Analysis' (1992) 42 Duke L Rev 557.

particularly important in the European Union because the issue of shares (or convertible debt or share warrants) requires shareholder authorization under the Second Directive, which also specifies pre-emption rights for the existing shareholders if the new shares are issued for cash.[18] However, that authorization can be given up to five years in advance of the particular exercise of the issue power by the directors.[19] Share issues constitute one of the core areas for defensive measures by target management and so the Second Directive is potentially important.[20] The poison pill, ie the shareholder rights plan, is thus not as easy to adopt in the EU as in the US, because the authority to put the plan in place does not lie exclusively with the directors, as it does in the US.[21] Nevertheless, the Second Directive does not require shareholder authorization post-bid where the decision to issue shares is taken by the board of directors in the framework of prior shareholder authorization. How much does the BNR add to the Second Directive?

The Takeover Directive applies the BNR from the moment the board of the target receives information about the bidder's decision to make a bid.[22] It would be straining credulity to suppose that significantly different shareholder responses would be obtained if the shareholders were asked to approve defensive measures just after that moment or just before it when rumours of a potential bid were widespread but the acquirer had not yet communicated its offer to the target board. In both situations, managers requesting authorization for the use of additional powers will be well understood by their shareholders as, in fact, asking for permission to 'defend' the company. Thus, the shareholders' decision will depend on the expected impact of the anticipated defensive measures on the share price—eg trading-off the risk of entrenchment-driven defences against the chances of obtaining a higher takeover premium due to the increased bargaining power of the board.

However, the powers most commonly used to 'defend' the target company can typically be used for multiple purposes, many of which clearly lie in the interest of shareholders. This is certainly true for the authority to issue new shares—probably the most important corporate power used for defending a target company.

[18] Directive 68/151/EEC [1968] OJ L65/8, Articles 25 and 29. Articles 25 and 29 refer to 'increases of capital'. However, it is clear that this means the issuance of shares, rather than an increase of the authorized capital (in those jurisdictions which have both concepts).

[19] Articles 25(2) and 29(5).

[20] It also is a defensive measure singled out for specific mention in Article 9(2).

[21] L A Bebchuk and A Hamdani, 'Optimal Defaults for Corporate Law Evolution' (2002) 96 Northwestern U L Rev 489, 513. It is unlikely that shareholder consent will be introduced via the US rules relating to increases in authorized capital, because US companies usually carry substantial levels of shareholder-approved authorized capital. A US-style shareholder rights plan, which excludes the acquirer from the rights, is also likely to infringe the European rule requiring equal treatment of shareholders (Second Directive, Article 42) but it is possible to craft an effective shareholder rights plan without infringing this principle. We discuss the recently introduced French example of this approach below in Section V.2. So, shareholder approval is the bigger obstacle.

[22] Takeover Directive, Articles 9(2) and 6(1). Member states may impose the BNR at an earlier stage 'for example, as soon as the board of the offeree company becomes aware that a bid is imminent'.

Before takeover rumours appear, shareholders will often be inclined to give the board the power to move quickly to raise finance for the company and to avoid the delays inherent in obtaining shareholder permission or offering pre-emption rights.[23] Thus, management seeking permission to issue shares (and on a non-pre-emptive basis) at a time when the company is not acutely perceived to be a potential takeover target will often succeed simply because the expected value of this decision is positive from the shareholders' point of view. Consequently, in the absence of a BNR shareholders may have to accept the cost of enhancing managerial discretion in relation to a bid in order to reap the benefits arising from management's increased discretion in a non-takeover scenario. Although it will be possible to make the pre-bid permission conditional in some jurisdictions (so that it does not apply once an offer has been announced), this step presupposes a sophisticated shareholder body and requires overcoming the typical collective action problems in shareholder decision-making. Therefore the BNR in effect imposes a requirement for shareholder permission post-bid, when the motives of the incumbent management are suspect, without the need for shareholders to amend the management's pre-bid proposals so as to impose that qualification. In other words, the BNR enables shareholders by simple vote to accept the benefits and avoid the costs of advance approval of share issues.

Whilst the Second Directive requires at least pre-bid shareholder authorization for share issues, there is no equivalent general EU law requirement in relation to the other main category of defensive measures, ie dealings with the assets of the company, for example, the conditional sale[24] of prized assets to a third party or the acquisition of assets which make the target less attractive to the bidder.[25] Although most Member States probably require shareholder approval, at least in listed companies, of sales of all or a substantial part of the company's assets, these rules still leave target management with considerable leeway in their dealings with the corporate assets—which the BNR restricts. Also, rules requiring specific shareholder approval for certain high-value transactions are typically triggered by thresholds tied to factors like asset values, profit generation, or the consideration of a transaction.[26] In terms of 'defence potential', however, other factors, like the synergy potential of sold assets or restrictions arising from competition law play a more important role, which will often allow management to make the

[23] See eg the vulnerability of British banks to short-selling during 2008 as they coped with the delays imposed by the need to obtain *ex post* shareholder approval. HM Treasury, *A Report to the Chancellor of the Exchequer by the Rights Issue Review Group* (November 2008) ch 1.

[24] The sale is conditional on the success of the takeover offer, so that, in the ideal situation, the target loses its attraction for the acquirer and the bid is withdrawn. A conditional sale of the 'crown jewels' also helps to meet the test that the sale must be in the best interests of the company. If it is in the interests of the company that the bid fail, a sale whose purpose is to achieve that end and which will be executed only if the bid succeeds more easily meets the core loyalty test than an outright sale.

[25] An acquisition is probably more difficult to put in place in a hurry post-bid than a sale.

[26] See eg the UK Listing Authority's Listing Rule 10 for the UK.

target company substantially less attractive for a particular bidder without even coming close to the relevant thresholds.

We thus conclude that, certainly in the case of EU law, and probably in respect of national rules, the BNR fills a regulatory gap.

(ii) Removal rights render the BNR unnecessary

The first form of the redundancy argument asserts that the BNR is unnecessary because other features of domestic law already constrain managerial discretion to an equivalent extent. Those constraints may be transaction-specific (such as the rules on share issues) or general standards for reviewing the exercise of discretion by directors (such as the core duty of loyalty). The second form of the argument proceeds on the basis that such constraints may not exist to an equivalent extent, but argues that such constraints are unnecessary provided that shareholders have effective removal rights over directors. To put the matter another way, governance rights can replace the BNR or its equivalents. Where there are strong removal rights, shareholders can ensure that the bid discretion possessed by management will be exercised in their favour by threatening to remove the directors later, if a wealth-maximizing bid fails through board opposition, or (more likely if shareholders suffer from collective action problems) an acquirer can solve the shareholders' co-ordination problems by mounting a takeover bid through the mechanism of a proxy fight to replace the existing directors with its own nominees. In the latter case, the absence of a BNR causes the acquirer to adopt a different acquisition technique but there is no impact on the chances of the acquisition occurring. This argument is well known in the United States in the form that it is the poison pill together with the staggered board[27] that chills acquisitions, not the poison pill on its own.[28]

However, it is far from clear that the delay involved in the requirement to make the acquisition through a proxy fight, even when the board is not staggered, is insubstantial. If, with even a non-staggered board, the opportunity to remove the incumbent management arises only once a year at the expiry of the directors' term of office, then the delay and inflexibility as to timing imposed on the potential acquirer, as well as the advance publicity as to its goals, would be inhibiting.[29] Put more generally, the removal strategy can operate effectively

[27] In the typical staggered board arrangement one-third of the board retires each year and thus can be replaced at the annual general meeting, but the others are irremovable before the end of their terms, except for cause (see Delaware General Corporation Law § 141(k)). A bidder will thus have to win a proxy fight in two successive years in order to be able to replace a majority of the board.

[28] L A Bebchuk, J C Coates, and G Subramanian, 'The Powerful Antitakeover Force of Staggered Boards: Theory, Evidence and Policy' (2002) 54 Stanford L Rev 887.

[29] Bebchuk and others, ibid, focus on the impact of the staggered board but note at p 912 that in company laws with 'effective annual terms' (EAT) for directors but without staggered boards 'because a significant delay might be required before a proxy contest can be launched, the ballot box route may not provide a sufficient safety valve against disloyal incumbents of EAT targets in some cases. Thus, incumbents of EAT targets sometimes have significant power to block offers that

as a substitute for the BNR only if an ordinary majority of the shareholders can at any time and without cause remove the directors from office and only if a small proportion of the shareholders are in a position quickly (and cheaply) to convene a meeting of the shareholders at which the removal power can be exercised. Even then it might be good policy to buttress the removal power with the equivalent of a BNR once the notice requisitioning the shareholders' meeting is communicated to the target board. Without that safeguard there would be opportunities for managerial opportunism in the intervening period, which is bound to be measured in weeks rather than days.[30] This is especially true for defensive actions which cannot easily be reversed after the bidder obtains control over the board, such as 'defensive acquisitions'. Additionally, the bidder will often be restricted in his ability to place his nominees on the target's board as a consequence of competition law.[31] However, the more important point is that by no means all Member States provide for director removal along these lines. In many EU jurisdictions removal is not available until the end of the term of office or a supermajority is required for removal or removal is not an act which can be carried out directly by the shareholders (because that power lies with a supervisory board) or the convening of meetings against the opposition of incumbent management is difficult.

(iii) Market responses to managerial entrenchment

The third form of the redundancy argument is that the BNR is unnecessary because the same effect can be produced through contractual arrangements between the company and the incumbent management. Again, this argument is founded on US experience. The argument is that the poison pill, at least to some extent, has been countered by the development, through contracting, of performance-related payment schemes for managers, at least where these generate significant pay-outs upon a change of control.[32] These arrangements,

shareholders would support'. See also J N Gordon, 'An American Perspective on Anti-Takeover Laws in the EU: The German Example' in Ferrarini and others (n 3) 549: 'The poison pill is, on its own, formidable.'

[30] Article 5(4) Directive 2007/36/EC of the European Parliament and of the Council on the exercise of certain rights of shareholders in listed companies [2007] OJ L184/7 imposes a minimum period of three weeks between the notice summoning the meeting and its happening, and the directors will have some further period to check the validity of the request from the shareholders and to respond to it. The provision also contains an exception for meetings convened in order to decide on takeover defences; even in this case, the minimum notice period is two weeks (see Article 9(4) Takeover Directive).

[31] Obtaining control over the target's board will often, in itself, already be subject to competition law approval.

[32] M Kahan and E B Rock, 'How I Learned to Stop Worrying and Love the Pill: Adaptive Responses to Takeover Law' (2002) 69 U of Chicago L Rev 871. The remuneration strategy may counteract the adverse effect of the poison pill on the number of takeovers, but the division of the bid premium as between shareholders and managers, by contrast, is significantly affected by the pill. Incentivized remuneration conditioned on a change of control can be viewed 'as a buyback

which have become very widespread in the United States, will powerfully affect management's response to an offer, if a successful offer triggers the vesting of share options (or some other financial bonus) under a performance-related remuneration scheme. Whilst this is a potentially effective market response to the poison pill, its effectiveness turns on the acceptability of high-powered remuneration schemes in the jurisdiction in question. Although performance-related pay for managers of listed companies has spread quite widely through the developed economies, the extent to which it has been embraced still varies from jurisdiction to jurisdiction. Where such schemes run against national corporate culture, this market response will be lacking or muted. In such jurisdictions, it may well not be the case that a manager will be significantly better off, at least on a lifetime basis, by taking a change-of-control payment rather than exercising discretionary powers so as to maintain him- or herself in office. Moreover, following the classical market for corporate control-rationale, such change-of-control payments will often be a consequence of a company's underperformance prior to the bid. The resulting 'reward for failure'-character of such arrangements will further reduce their acceptability.[33] The significance of this aspect was recently evidenced by the public outcry caused by the enormous payments to unsuccessful managers in the financial sector, even in jurisdictions like the US.[34]

(iv) The example of Germany

It might be useful to take a particular jurisdiction and see how the considerations mentioned above play out in a particular national setting. Germany, as seen above, led the last-minute opposition to the 1996 proposal for a takeover directive largely because it contained a mandatory BNR. Having secured that negative position in 2001, it then enacted at the end of that year a domestic Securities Acquisition and Takeover Act.[35] That Act starts from a board

by shareholders of the takeover-resistance endowment that managers were able to obtain from the legislatures and the courts during the 1980s' (Gordon [n 29] 555).

[33] Such considerations played an important role in Germany's 2009 regulation of executive remuneration (*Gesetz zur Angemessenheit der Vorstandsvergütung*, 'VorstAG'), which gives the supervisory board the power to alter the contractual remuneration arrangements in case of a deterioration of the company's situation. See the press release of the German Ministry of Justice (available at <http://www.bmj.de/managergehaelter>), which states that such a deterioration would, for example, exist where 'the company needs to lay-off employees and cannot pay dividends'. § 87 (2) AktG now allows an adjustment of the remuneration, where the continued payment of the contractually agreed remuneration would be 'inequitable' (*unbillig*) for the company.

[34] Even in the US, CEOs of (quasi-)failed financial institutions came under substantial criticism (and political pressure) over the enormous 'golden parachutes' they received; see eg J Anderson, 'Chiefs' Pay Under Fire at Capitol' *The New York Times* (New York, 8 March 2008), available at: <http://www.nytimes.com/2008/03/08/business/08pay.html>.

[35] *Wertpapierwerbs- und Übernahmegesetz*—'WpÜG'. For an brief overview of the WpÜG's history see eg A Zinser, 'Das neue Gesetz zur Regelung von öffentlichen Angeboten zum Erwerb von Wertpapieren und von Unternehmensübernahmen vom 1. Januar 2002' (2002) 56 Zeitschrift für Wirtschafts- und Bankrecht (WM) 15.

neutrality principle but then creates three exceptions to it. Most important, it provides that the management of German targets may take defensive measures if the supervisory board approves post-bid.[36] The Act also authorizes 'actions which a diligent and conscientious manager not subject to a takeover offer would have also taken'[37]—without imposing the requirement of supervisory board approval. Indeed, prior to the enactment of the 2001 Act, there existed an ongoing debate on whether or not German general company law contained an implicit BNR, which lost much of its force through the enactment of the WpÜG, which can be seen as the legislator's answer to the negative.[38] This certainly underlines the importance of a bright-line rule, as any degree of legal uncertainty allows management to use, or credibly threaten to use, corporate powers to defend the company at a much smaller cost.[39] When the second version of the Directive was adopted with an optional BNR, Germany chose to opt out of it, in order to preserve its domestic provisions.[40] Thus, on two occasions in recent history Germany has chosen to avoid a mandatory BNR in order to preserve its freedom to enact and maintain domestically what it sees as a less demanding takeover regime.

Why did Germany expend precious political capital in resisting EU legislative efforts to introduce a mandatory BNR? Can it be argued that the apparent freedom the WpÜG gives to management through the exceptions to the neutrality principle is illusory because other parts of German law, including those implementing the Second Directive, restore the shareholder primacy which the BNR espouses? The answer appears to be in the negative, ie the adoption of a

[36] §33(1) WpÜG. Under §33(2) WpÜG the management board may also obtain pre-bid shareholder approval for defensive measures (effective for 18 months at a time). This is the second exception to the domestic BNR. However, since shareholder-approved defensive measures also need supervisory board approval post-bid, little is gained (and something is potentially lost) by seeking shareholder authorization in advance, and so this particular provision seems to have been largely a dead letter. See T Stohlmeier, *German Public Takeover Law* (2nd edn, The Hague: Kluwer, 2007) 112 (its 'practical relevance [...] is, in any event, very minor').

[37] This does not give the managing board powers it would not otherwise have (eg to issue shares without shareholder authorization) but it does at least permit the managing board to perform the balancing act among stakeholder interests which the German duty of loyalty requires without taking account of the fact that shareholder interests might indicate that the bid should be facilitated. Thus, a company already pursuing an acquisition strategy could continue (and even accelerate?) it in the face of a bid, even if fully aware that the acquisition would render the company a less attractive target.

[38] See A Wolf, 'Der Mythos "Neutralitätspflicht" nach dem Übernahmerichtlinie-Umsetzungsgesetz' [2008] Zeitschrift für Wirtschaftsrecht (ZIP) 300 for an overview of the discussion.

[39] First, a credible threat to block the transaction will often result in hostile takeovers not being attempted. Second, even where they are, managers will not only take into consideration their chance of prevailing with their arguments in litigation, but they often will also enjoy a certain kind of liability privilege where they take decisions in an area of legal ambiguity (even where no statutory liability privilege applies, the ambiguity of the situation might have consequences in terms of insurance cover).

[40] § 33a WpÜG provides the company level opt-in to the EU's BNR. See Section IV below.

mandatory BNR in Germany would have been a significant departure from the existing law for the following reasons:

- prior shareholder approval for share issues (including share issues on a non pre-emptive basis) can be given up to five years in advance[41]
- acquisition of assets is subject only to the general core duty of loyalty, which views the company through a stakeholder rather than a shareholder lens[42]
- disposal of assets is subject only to the general duty of loyalty[43]
- removal rights for shareholders are constrained. During their term of office (typically around five years), members of the management board may be removed only by the supervisory board and only where good cause can be shown. Good cause may include a vote of no confidence by the shareholders, but such a vote only empowers (and does not require) the supervisory board to act.[44] Thus, the shareholders may be forced to proceed indirectly by removing the members of the supervisory board as a first step. Within the term of office (again usually around five years)[45] three-quarters of the votes cast are necessary for such a removal.[46] Of course, in co-determined companies this applies only to the shareholder representatives on the board. A shareholders' meeting may be convened by 5 per cent of the shareholders.[47]
- high-powered incentivized remuneration, especially where it involves payouts dependent on a change of control, is treated with caution in Germany. The Act has recently been further tightened so as to allow for downward revision of contractual pay arrangements in case of financial distress.[48] It also requires the supervisory board, which fixes the remuneration of the members of the management board, to ensure that such remuneration 'bears a reasonable relationship to the duties of such members and the condition

[41] §§ 202–204 *Aktiengesetz* ('AktG'). This is 'probably the most common defence': Stohlmeier (n 36) 114. The par value of the new shares may not exceed one half of the value of the share capital existing at the date of the authorization and the authorization of the supervisory board is needed for the issuance. There are no equivalents to the pre-emption or share issuance guidelines from institutional investors which cut down on the statutory freedom to give advance approval, as is the case in the UK. Contrast ABI, *Directors' Powers to Allot Share Capital and Disapply Shareholders' Pre-emption Rights*, December 2008 and Pre-emption Group, *Disapplying Pre-Emption Rights: A Statement of Principles*, 2006.

[42] W Underhill and A Austmann, 'Defensive Tactics' in J Payne (ed), *Takeovers in English and German Law* (Oxford: Hart Publishing, 2002) 96: 'In a takeover situation, management may take action frustrating the bid if this appears justified in balancing the different interests involved.'

[43] The *Holzmüller* doctrine may limit disposals (and possibly acquisitions) when they are very large, but on the latest authority it only applies in cases comparable to the original decision where the disposals reached 80% of the company's total assets: M Löbbe, 'Corporate Groups' (2004) 5 German L J 1057, 1078–9. The AktG requires shareholder approval only for the transfer of the entire assets of the company: §179a AktG.

[44] § 84 AktG.

[45] § 102 AktG.

[46] § 103 AktG, which contains a default rule to this end; the articles can provide for a removal by simple majority.

[47] § 122 AktG.

[48] See n 33 above.

of the company'.[49] The German Corporate Governance Code states more precisely: 'payments promised in the event of premature termination of a Management Board member's contract due to a change of control shall not exceed three years' remuneration'.[50]

2. The shareholder structure argument

The second main argument against the BNR is that it has no significance in concentrated shareholder jurisdictions and that these jurisdictions predominate in the European Union. The argument can be elaborated as follows. It is commonplace in the relevant literature to assign a *corporate governance* or *disciplining function*[51] as well as an *efficiency function*[52] to the market for corporate control, or, in other words, to identify two types of desirable control shifts. We need to consider the dispersed/concentrated distinction in relation to each function.

First, in companies with widely dispersed ownership structures ('Berle-Means companies'), even significant underperformance by the managers will often not lead to shareholder action, owing to rational apathy and collective action problems. Managers, therefore, have little to fear from their unorganized and apathetic investors. Being theoretically empowered, but practically unable, to 'fire' their managers, the market for corporate control here fulfils its disciplining function by providing an alternative mechanism to bring assets to more efficient use.[53] Shares trading below the fair value of the same assets under efficient management invites bidders to make a tender offer for the company's shares. The bidder, holding all or the majority of the shares after the offer, can now exercise the formerly unused powers to oust the current managers and run the company more efficiently. The effect is not limited to *actual* (observable) control transfers, however. In the face of a (realistic) takeover threat, managers have an *ex ante* incentive to do their best, as a hostile takeover will normally lead to them losing their job. From a policy perspective, employing this effect,

[49] § 87(1) AktG.

[50] 2009 edn, 4.2.3. See generally Gordon (n 29), arguing that cultural opposition to golden parachutes and the accelerated vesting of stock options on a change of control casts the discretion conferred on boards by takeover defences in an entirely different light, because the market reaction to the defences is not available or is significantly limited. The infamous recent criminal prosecution for corporate waste of former Mannesmann board members for the payment of post-takeover bonuses has no doubt also chilled pay-outs conditional on a change of control, though it should be noted that the payment in that case was gratuitous, not contractual. See BGH 21 December 2005, NJW 2006, 522 and C Milhaupt and K Pistor, *Law and Capitalism* (Chicago/London: University of Chicago Press, 2008) ch 4.

[51] On the market for corporate control, see the classical contribution by H Manne, 'Mergers and the Market for Corporate Control' (1965) 73 J of Political Economy 110; see also eg J C Coffee, 'Regulating the Market for Corporate Control: A Critical Assessment of the Tender Offer's Role in Corporate Governance' (1984) 84 Columbia L Rev 1145.

[52] See Coffee ibid, 1166, describing the synergy hypothesis.

[53] See eg R Gilson, 'A Structural Approach to Corporations: The Case against Defensive Tactics in Tender Offers' (1981) 33 Stanford L Rev 819, 841.

in principle, clearly makes sense, as more efficient corporate structures may be expected as a result, fitting in smoothly with the mentioned rationale of the Takeover Directive.

Second, and distinct from this corporate governance function, which primarily addresses problems of managerial agency costs, transferability of corporate control also serves a more general efficiency goal. In that sense, takeovers can be explained by what are normally referred to as 'synergies', where the target company's assets are of unique value for the acquirer.[54] Combining two firms' assets can create value—eg owing to economies of scale or scope—which even the most talented and diligent managers could not achieve for the target company's shareholders. Here, the issue turns away from corporate governance and agency costs; rather, takeovers are here explained as an operation of Coasian mechanisms, 'bringing together what belongs together'.[55]

Clearly, both motivations can give rise to takeovers, and both forms of control shifts are socially desirable and therefore compatible with the Directive's aims. However, it should be noted that the disciplining effect of takeovers is basically a remedy against shareholder apathy; it is the unsatisfied investors who choose to sell their shares, rather than to oust or more closely monitor the management, and—by leaving the share price languishing—trigger the functioning of the market for corporate control.[56]

In blockholder[57] companies, in contrast, the controller of the company *does* have sufficient incentives to monitor closely the managers' performance and,

[54] See Coffee (n 51) 1166. See also R Romano, 'A Guide to Takeovers: Theory, Evidence, and Regulation' (1992) 9 Yale J of Regulation 119, 125–9.

[55] There are, of course, other possible motives behind or explanations for corporate control transactions. Especially worth mentioning is the empire-building explanation, asserting that bidders actually overpay in takeovers, which can be founded in self-interest (eg higher managerial compensation) or simply in hubris. As Easterbrook and Fischel ('Corporate Control Transactions' (1982) 91 Yale L J 698, 707) point out, corporate law can ignore overpayment due to the self-deterring nature of wasting money (this is to say, it can ignore that when dealing with control transactions, not in general). This view was also implicitly embraced in the Directive, which does not try to address issues related to bidder overpayment (eg by means of obligatory approval by bidder shareholders). Moreover, as an expression of the agency costs of shareholders, empire building is itself constrained by the threat of a takeover of a company run by managers who destroy shareholder wealth through ill-advised acquisitions.

Another explanation of premiums paid by the bidder is the exploitation rationale, based on dispersed shareholders' inability to co-ordinate their actions when facing an inadequate bid (see eg L A Bebchuk, 'The Pressure to Tender: An Analysis and a Proposed Remedy' (1987) 12 Delaware J of Corporate L 911); this cannot be further analysed here, as the problems are mostly addressed by the mandatory bid and the sell-out rules; see P L Davies, 'The Notion of Equality in European Takeover Regulation' in Payne (n 42) 14–15. Exploitation of other stakeholder—another possible driver for takeover activity—is better dealt with by separate regulation; see also the *Report of the High Level Group on Issues Relating to Takeover Bids* (Brussels, January 2002) ch 4.2.

[56] See Manne (n 51) 113.

[57] The term 'blockholders' is used here to describe a shareholder of the company who, at least under normal circumstances, can exercise effective control over the company due to his shareholding.

where necessary, let better qualified people run the company.[58] Equally, managers in controlled companies are always confronted with a realistic threat of being ousted in case they underperform, as they face a vigilant 'principal' watching them permanently. This is to say that the market for corporate control (and contestability of control) is simply not needed in blockholder companies, as far as disciplining takeovers are concerned. To put it slightly differently: a blockholder will not normally sell his shares to a person whose only source of gains from the transaction is the replacement of the current inefficient management team; he would rather effect the change himself and keep all the value generated for himself (and free-riding fellow shareholders). Knowing that, we should not expect a potential bidder actually to propose such a transaction, as the research on its part is likely to constitute sunk costs. Therefore, there is neither demand nor supply on the market for corporate control in blockholder companies as far as disciplining takeovers are concerned; this seems to make questions about the contestability of control close to meaningless in this context and to leave no room for a BNR to operate.

Regarding the efficiency function of the market for corporate control, the situation is different. Obviously, even the most vigilant watchdog cannot easily cause the managers to create value that depends on a shift of corporate control.[59] However, the existence of blockholders by itself should not reduce the contestability (or, rather, transferability) of corporate control regarding such takeovers 'of the second kind'. Where the potential bidder has something to offer to the incumbent controller which the latter cannot achieve (a purchase price exceeding the value of the shares in the hands of the incumbent controller, even with the best available managers), the blockholder will have ample economic incentives to effectuate the transaction. Arguably, the acquirer will find it easier to convince the blockholder to sell than to secure agreement in a widely held company (where the acquirer has to deal with the managers or dispersed shareholders).[60]

However, the blockholder's response to restructuring offers is complicated by the potential for private benefits of control (PBCs). Although the blockholder, as

[58] See P L Davies and K J Hopt, 'Control Transactions' in R Kraakman and others, *The Anatomy of Corporate Law* (2nd edn, Oxford: Oxford University Press, 2009) 225, 233, explaining the shift of the agency conflict away from the management–shareholder relationship in controlled companies.

[59] Unless it is in a position to effect that shift by acting as acquirer, rather than as a target.

[60] This, of course, is oversimplifying the complex relationships between managerial ability and the potential for synergy gains. It can probably be expected that good managers (irrespective of whether the company has a dispersed shareholding or not) are likely to create more efficient company structures by employing all means available to them before being taken over (eg buying smaller competitors, entering complementary businesses where this creates value, and the like). This, however, only strengthens the point made: blockholder structures, it could be argued, are likely to render disciplining takeovers unnecessary *and* leave less scope for synergy-based takeovers (as managers make use of all options to create economies of scale/scope available without changing the current control structure). Simple measures, like the sheer level of public M&A activity, are therefore unsuitable for assessing the efficient functioning of the market for corporate control.

rational economic actor, can be expected to accept mutually beneficial offers,[61] this somewhat depends on an equal (or rather: unchangeable) distribution among the shareholders of the cash-flows generated by the company. PBCs, on the other hand, are benefits enjoyed by the blockholder (controller) of a company due to the controlling position, which are not shared with the outside (ie non-controlling) investors, and are typically associated with concentrated share ownership.[62]

The existence of PBCs naturally increases the per share value of the blockholder's shares as compared to the valuation of shares held by the outside investors. This, in turn, potentially diminishes the transferability of a controlling position. Where the incumbent controller derives much of the value of his shareholding from the enjoyment of PBCs,[63] socially desirable control shifts can be prevented by the fact that the potential acquirer, while creating a higher overall value, does so in a way which requires it to share the gains equally among all shareholders. In this case, it might not be able to meet the blockholder's (rational) price expectations.[64] This potential for decreasing the transferability of control in blockholder companies, which depends on differences in PBCs between the bidders,[65] can therefore impede the Directive's efficiency goal.

A good regulatory response to this problem of private benefits of control where there is blockholder control is hard to design.[66] Whatever the best solution, it is clear that the BNR is of only limited[67] relevance to it. The Directive attempts to tackle part of the free-rider problem by allowing the successful bidder to

[61] This is to say, he will accept the bargain where the potential acquirer is willing to pay a purchase price above the controller's current (or otherwise achievable) per share value.

[62] See eg C G Holderness, 'A Survey of Blockholders and Corporate Control' (2003) 9 Economic Policy Rev 51; A Dyck and L Zingales, 'Private Benefits of Control: An International Comparison' (2004) 59 J of Finance 537. The latter show that the size of PBCs varies from jurisdiction to jurisdiction. In some jurisdictions they are probably no greater than is appropriate for compensating blockholders for their monitoring efforts. In that situation PBCs do not constitute a barrier to control shifts since the incumbent controller will be relieved of the monitoring costs after a sale.

[63] Although often associated with 'tunnelling' or outright theft, PBCs can come in different forms, including synergies; eg Holderness ibid, 55.

[64] This is mainly due to free-rider problems on the part of the remaining shareholders, who will be reluctant to sell below the post-takeover share value; see L A Bebchuk 'Efficient and Inefficient Sales of Corporate Control' (1994) 109 Quarterly J of Economics 957, 966–7. See also Easterbrook and Fischel (n 55) 705–6.

[65] See Bebchuk ibid, 961.

[66] One suggestion made by Easterbrook and Fischel (n 55) is to allow an acquirer to squeeze-out the remaining shareholders at the pre-transaction value (ie the current share price), which allows shifts of corporate control to take place even where the acquirer produces most of his efficiency gains in the form of increasing future dividends (as opposed to retaining or increasing the PBC level of the incumbent controller). The Directive (Article 15), on the other hand, requires far stricter requirements to be met in order to squeeze-out minority shareholders, namely a 90% threshold and payment of the same price as in the block trade/bid.

[67] Arguably, the presence of a BNR allows *de facto* controlling shareholders with (substantially) less than 50% of the voting rights to prevent the success of a bid which offers a premium over the market price of the shares (thus being attractive to the outside investors), but leaves the incumbent worse off because he is not compensated for a loss of his current PBCs.

'squeeze-out' the remaining shareholders.[68] However, this right comes coupled with another core provision of the Directive that effectively exaggerates the PBC problem, the mandatory bid rule (MBR). This rule requires an offer at the same price to be made to the outside shareholders where there is a transfer of control shares from blockholder to bidder, thus preventing the bidder from compensating the blockholder for its additional (ie PBC) 'loss' arising out of the sale.[69]

Does this mean that the BNR is relevant only in jurisdictions where blockholding is unusual? Within the European Union, there are only two such jurisdictions, namely, the United Kingdom and Ireland.[70] However, since the UK has long imposed a BNR – indeed its BNR provided the model for the Directive—and Ireland similarly has enacted an equivalent rule long before the Directive's enactment, the debate over the Directive's BNR might be thought to be a storm in a teacup.

Whilst we accept that shareholder structure can render the BNR irrelevant, we argue that the view that the BNR has importance only in the UK is misplaced. We have three reasons for our view. First, the issue is not whether companies in a particular jurisdiction typically have dispersed shareholding or blockholder control but which category a particular target company falls into. In the UK there are some companies under blockholder control, even if that arrangement is far from typical. Equally, in jurisdictions where blockholder control is typical, companies with dispersed shareholding can be found. Whilst stressing the importance of controlling shareholders in continental Europe, Berglöf and Burkart have remarked that:

> most publicly traded firms in Europe are either widely held or family controlled. There is, however, a marked difference in the relative importance of these two categories across Europe. In Continental Europe, as in most other countries of the world, family controlled firms are in the majority.[71]

This is far from a claim that widely controlled companies are non-existent in continental Europe. The existence, but atypicality, of widely held companies in continental Europe may explain the willingness of many European Union states to adopt a BNR in advance of the Directive.[72] The BNR was relevant in these

[68] See Article 15, allowing the bidder to acquire the remaining shares where he obtains 90% or 95% of the target's shares. For the rather complicated calculation of the threshold and the respective Member State options see eg C van der Elst and L van den Steen, 'Balancing the Interests of Minority and Majority Shareholders: A Comparative Analysis of Squeeze-out and Sell-out Rights' (2009) 6 Eur Company and Financial L Rev 391.

[69] For this argument in more detail, see Davies and Hopt (n 58) 257–60. Adding the MBR also means that PBCs can prevent efficient takeovers even where the acquirer and the seller have the identical PBC-levels. See also EP Schuster, 'Efficiency in Private Control Sales—The Case for Mandatory Bids' (2010) LSE Law, Society and Economy Working Paper 8/2010, available at <http://ssrn.com/abstract=1610259>.

[70] M Faccio and L H Lang, 'The Ultimate Ownership of Western European Corporations' (2002) 65 J of Financial Economics 365, 379.

[71] M Burkart and E Berglöf, 'European Takeover Regulation' (2003) 18 Economic Policy 171, 181.

[72] Ibid, Table 1 (referring to the then 12 members of the EU).

jurisdictions but the atypicality of the widely held company reduced managerial opposition to the adoption of the rule.[73]

Second, the evidence suggests that the pressures of globalization and the expansion of the single market within the European Union have generated a discernible trend towards an increase in the proportion of companies not subject to blockholder control. In a study of Germany, France, Italy, and the UK, Franks and colleagues used a test of no shareholder with more than 25 per cent of the voting shares as the (relatively generous) test for that company being widely held.[74] On that basis there had been significant increases in the number of widely held companies in all three continental jurisdictions between 1996 and 2006, with the UK remaining steady at over 90 per cent. In France, the percentage of widely held companies increased from 21 per cent to 37 per cent, in Germany from 26 per cent to 48 per cent, and in Italy from 3 per cent to 22 per cent.[75]

Third, our analysis above assumed a binary division between dispersed shareholding and secure blockholder control (ie a blockholder holding at least 50 per cent of the votes in a company). An intermediate situation is one where a group of large shareholders have control of the company, so long as they act together, but the defection of one or more of them, together with the support of the majority of the non-controlling shareholders would be enough to transfer to an acquirer control over the company. One might term this situation 'insecure' blockholder control. The empirical evidence suggests that such control arrangements are quite common in Europe. Thus, Laeven and Levine report on a sample of 1,657 publicly traded firms across Europe in the late 1990s. Here, 34 per cent by number and 18 per cent by market capitalization had multiple large shareholders (a large shareholder being one holding 10 per cent or more of the voting rights), as opposed to having one controlling shareholder (50 per cent by number and 46 per cent by capitalization) or no controlling shareholder (16 per cent and 36 per cent).[76] In such a situation an acquirer is not without hope of effecting a control shift against the opposition of at least some of the leading shareholders.[77] In that context,

[73] See the similar argument by A Ferrell, 'Why Continental European Takeover Law Matters' in Ferrarini and others (n 3) 571–2.

[74] J Franks, C Mayer, P Volpin, and H Wagner, 'Evolution of Family Capitalism: A Comparative Study of France, Germany, Italy and the UK' EFA 2009 Bergen Meetings Paper, available at <http://ssrn.com/abstract=1102475>.

[75] Ibid, Table 2, panel B.

[76] L Laeven and R Levine, 'Complex Ownership Structures and Corporate Valuations' (2008) 21 Rev of Financial Studies 579, Table 2. In none of the countries studied did the proportion of listed firms with multiple large shareholders fall below 20% by number. These figures also suggest that the largest companies were more likely to have no controlling shareholder and that multiple (ie more than one) large shareholders were disproportionately to be found in smaller listed companies. Table 2 also supports our first point for it reports the existence of listed companies with no controlling shareholder in all jurisdictions, even if the proportion in some is very small (<5% in Italy, Austria, Portugal, and France).

[77] Precisely what level of support the acquirer needs to obtain to be successful will vary from case to case. In some instances acquisition of shares carrying a majority of the voting rights may be enough to give effective control; in other cases, where decisions important to the acquirer require

restrictions on the power of the management[78] to prevent or discourage the bid being put to the shareholders as a whole fulfil a function in facilitating bids even in companies one would not characterize as having a dispersed shareholding. Of course, leading shareholders can seek to counteract the risk of defection by contract, for example, shareholder agreements binding the signatories in some way to adopt a common policy towards acquirers. Thus, it may be that in the insecure blockholder situation the value of the BNR depends in part on other rules putting shareholder agreements in question where there is a bid. It is not the purpose of this paper to discuss the BTR but we note below (in Section V.2) in our discussion of France the increased significance of the BNR in a national jurisdiction which has adopted a 'mini' BTR directed at shareholder agreements.

Equivalently, a blockholder often does not have *de jure* control of the target (ie more than 50 per cent of the voting rights), but nevertheless is still able to exercise the majority of the voting rights in a typical general meeting. The practical relevance of this is evidenced by the 30 per cent threshold most European jurisdictions use as a trigger for the mandatory bid rule. This second type of insecure blockholders will typically be in control of the company's board at the time of the offer announcement. As we will argue below,[79] the BNR can significantly impede the ability of such blockholders to prevent unwanted offers from succeeding.

Taking these points together, it would be wrong to conclude that hostile takeovers (and more generally, the BNR) are a phenomenon confined to the UK. Whilst Martynova and Renneboog report that 80 of 130 hostile bids launched in Europe in the period 1993 to 2001 concerned UK or Irish targets, the remaining 50 by definition occurred elsewhere, with France (13) and Sweden (11) being particularly active markets.[80] Overall, the above analysis suggests that an EU-level prohibition on post-bid defensive measures by target management without shareholder approval could have a potentially significant impact. The argument can be made that a 'no frustration' or 'board neutrality' rule (BNR)[81] promotes the corporate governance benefits of takeovers in widely dispersed companies, whilst not impinging on the operation of companies controlled by secure blockholders.

supermajority approval of the shareholders, the acquirer may need to be certain that no hostile shareholder holds a blocking minority position.

[78] The management will have been appointed by the leading shareholders before defection and probably see their loyalty as lying with the non-defecting members of the group of leading shareholders.

[79] Section III.3

[80] M Martynova and L Renneboog, 'Mergers and Acquisitions in Europe' in L Renneboog (ed), *Advances in Corporate Finance and Asset Pricing* (Amsterdam: Elsevier, 2006). On the other hand, 17 of 29 countries studied had experienced no hostile bids in the period.

[81] These terms are generally used interchangeably, but 'no frustration' can be argued to be the better term, since Article 9 of the Directive does not require the board to take a neutral stance on the bid. Inaction (eg refusing the bidder access to the target's books), seeking a 'white knight', and recommending against the bid are all examples of non-neutrality that the Article allows. However, board neutrality seems to have become the accepted term and it has the advantage that its acronym (BNR) resonates with that for the breakthrough rule (BTR).

Where the blockholder or controlling coalition is insecure, a ban on post-bid defences encourages challenges by acquirers and thus promotes transfers of control to acquirers who can offer the benefits of economies of scale or scope.[82]

However, although the analysis suggests that a mandatory BNR encourages value increasing control shifts, it does not follow that the BNR is *necessarily desirable* in terms of creating value for shareholders *overall*. It is possible that the advantages of 'shareholder primacy' (ie increased chances of value increasing takeovers) are set off or outweighed by forgone benefits found in systems vesting discretion over control transactions in management. For instance, a shareholder-focused system can discourage employees from investing in firm-specific skills, as no credible promises of long-term employment are available.[83] A lack of a highly specialized workforce may well yield higher efficiency costs than prevented control shifts resulting from an entrenched management for certain firms or even sectors of the economy. We return to this point in our concluding policy proposal.

3. Evasion through pre-bid defences

The strongest criticism of the BNR is probably none of the above, but rather the argument that an effective BNR simply generates a strong incentive for incumbents to put in place defensive measures in advance of the bid.[84] A BNR simply does not bite on such measures. As we have noted,[85] the Commission's 2002 proposal sought to address this concern by adopting a BTR, whereby certain pre-bid steps with defensive qualities would cease to be effective post-bid, namely certain departures from the one share/one vote principle and certain restrictions on the transfer of shares. As with the BNR, the BTR ended up in the Directive as an optional rule.[86] We do not report systematically in this paper on the BTR. We simply note the following:

(1) A mandatory and comprehensive BTR was known in no Member State before the Directive was adopted, with the possible exception of Italy, even though the mandatory BNR had been adopted by a large proportion of the

[82] There remains room to argue, however, that transfers against the will of insecure blockholders or parts of a controlling coalition do not *per se* pass the efficiency test. Losses of PBCs on the part of the blockholder or coalition are not necessarily completely set off by equivalent efficiency gains caused by the control shift. In other words, transactions could impose negative external effects on blockholders. Contrary to what is sometimes asserted, PBCs are not necessarily illegal, and there are good reasons for legislators to take into account such efficiency losses; see Schuster (n 69).

[83] This is a central theme in the 'varieties of capitalism' literature; see P Hall and D Soskice, 'Introduction to Varieties of Capitalism' in P Hall and D Soskice (eds), *Varieties of Capitalism: The Institutional Foundations of Comparative Advantage* (Oxford/New York: Oxford University Press, 2001) 30.

[84] J Arlen and E Talley, 'Unregulable Defences and the Perils of Shareholder Choice' (2003) 152 U of Pennsylvania L Rev 577.

[85] Section I, above.

[86] Articles 11 and 12. The options created track those for the BNR.

Member States. However, a number of Member States had 'mini BTRs', ie rules restricting the adoption of certain pre-bid defences.

(2) Very few Member States adopted the BTR on transposition of the Directive.[87]

(3) Apparently, no company has chosen not to opt out of the BTR. We do, however, consider the relevance of the absence of a mandatory and comprehensive BTR for Member State and company choices in relation to the BNR.

III. The choices created by the Directive

1. Introduction

The aim of this paper is to investigate the choices made by the Member States in the course of the transposition of Article 9 of the Takeover Directive and by companies thereafter. The first step in such an exercise is to identify the choices created by the Directive. In any case where the EU's legal instrument takes the form of a directive some choices are created for Member States. Unlike a regulation, a directive does not automatically become part of the Member State's legal order upon enactment through the EU's legal process, but rather it needs transposition into national law by an act of each Member State's legislative process. Further, a directive 'shall be binding, as to the result to be achieved [...] but shall leave to the national authorities the choice of form and methods'.[88] In the case of the Takeover Directive, however, Member State level choices were given a particular significance because of the default status ultimately accorded at EU level to the BNR. Agreement was reached between the Council (representing the Member States) and the Parliament on the final text of the Directive only on the basis that Member States could decide to opt out of the BNR (contained in Article 9) when they came to transpose the Directive.[89]

2. Member State choices

(i) Opting out or not?

Article 12 of the Directive provides that Member States 'may reserve the right not to require companies [...] which have their registered offices within their territories' to observe the BNR. Although the Member States' choice is

[87] Bulgaria, Estonia, Latvia, and Lithuania have chosen not to opt out of the BTR.

[88] Article 288 TFEU (formerly Article 249 EC).

[89] Article 12. A similar provision was made in relation to the BTR, which we do not discuss in detail in this paper.

untrammelled, the language used to express the option (as an opt-out) signals the implementation favoured by the drafters (or, rather, shows its history).[90] More important, if a Member State chooses to opt out of the BNR, it must provide a counter-option for any particular company to opt 'back' into it, on a reversible basis.[91] The corporate-level decision to opt back in (or reverse this decision at a later date) is to be taken by the shareholders in accordance with the rules applicable in that jurisdiction for adopting changes to companies' articles of association.[92] Such corporate decisions are to be communicated to the national authorities of the state of incorporation and of any other state where its securities are admitted to trading on a regulated market.[93] Thus, decisions on the corporate level become important as well and are discussed below.

(ii) Reciprocity or not?

There is a further refinement to the default status of the BNR. Article 12 uses the concept of 'reciprocity' to introduce a further option—or rather another potential double option: one for the Member State and—depending on this Member State choice—one for the company. Reciprocity, a novel concept in takeover regulation, refers to the question of whether the acquirer is subject to the BNR. The Member State may give companies subject to the BNR, if they receive a bid from an acquirer not subject to the same restrictions, the power in relation to that bid to escape from the BNR which would otherwise be applicable to them. If the Member State chooses not to make this option available, that is an end of the matter. However, if the Member State chooses the opposite course, then the company through its shareholders can authorize the management to take defensive action, which would otherwise be caught by the BNR, if subject to a bid from a company 'which does not apply the same Articles'[94] as it does. The crucial point about this authorization is that it can be given in advance of the offer, provided the shareholders do so within the 18-month period before the launch of the bid in question. Article 12 does not specify any particular procedure for the giving of general meeting authorization to take up the reciprocity exception, nor does it require such decisions to be communicated to the authorities, though they must be disclosed.[95]

The reciprocity exception in its current form is probably one of the oddest results of the compromise that finally led to the adoption of the Directive. As

[90] J Winter, 'The Need for a Regulatory Framework—EU Company Law at the Cross-Roads' in Ferrarini and others (n 3) 18.

[91] Article 12(2). The set of companies to which the Directive applies are those whose securities are admitted to trading on a regulated market within the EU: Article 1(1).

[92] To use the UK term. In other jurisdictions the document is often referred to as the company's 'statutes' or sometimes as its 'charter'.

[93] Article 12(2).

[94] Article 12(3); 'Articles' here refers to Article 9 and/or Article 11.

[95] Article 12(3) to 12(5). However, a convenient way of complying with the disclosure requirement may be for the Member State to add reciprocity decisions to opt-in decisions as needing disclosure to the national authorities.

mentioned above, the 2001 proposal was turned down primarily because of disagreement over the BNR. One of the Member States' concerns[96] was that the BNR would lead to a general disadvantage of European companies as against their US rivals, because the latter typically can employ powerful defensive tactics, which would no longer be possible for their EU counterparts. The High Level Group, although clearly unconvinced by the argument, consequently suggested that the *mandatory* BNR be confined to bids by European listed companies for other European companies.[97] Instead, the reciprocity exception has finally been adopted in addition to an *optional* BNR. This substantially complicates the whole framework of the Directive and directly counteracts the aim of harmonizing national takeover rules.[98]

Perhaps because it was drafted at such a late and contentious stage in the Directive's adoption process, there are also many unsolved questions about the scope of the reciprocity exception. A central one concerns the point at which the option arises. There is no doubt that a Member State may choose to make the reciprocity exception available to companies when they are considering opting back into the BNR in situations where the Member State has decided to opt out of the rule. It is much less clear whether a Member State can decide to qualify its decision *not* to opt out of the BNR by making the mandatory BNR subject to the reciprocity exception.[99] However, a number of states on transposition took the view that they were free to apply the BNR on a mandatory basis, but subject to the reciprocity exception, and implemented such a regime in their national laws.[100] As we shall see below, the functions of the reciprocity exception are different when it operates as a qualification (a) to an otherwise mandatory BNR imposed by the Member State or (b) to a corporate decision to opt back into the BNR—as are the incentives for the Member State to make it available in the two cases.

A second important interpretative uncertainty about the reciprocity rule arises where a target, subject to the BNR but with the reciprocity exception, receives offers from two or more bidders, one or more of which is subject to the BNR and

[96] The point was primarily raised by Germany; see M Becht, 'Reciprocity in Takeovers' in Ferrarini (n 3) 648.

[97] See *Report of the High Level Group on Issues Related to Takeover Bids* (n 55) 42.

[98] Considering exclusively the Member State choices regarding BNR, BTR, and the reciprocity exception, there are 16 different possible regulatory outcomes. Note that at the time of the Directive's adoption, the EU had 15 Member States.

[99] The wording of Article 12(3) suggests rather strongly that the reciprocity exception is available only in the former case since it refers to 'companies, which apply' Articles 9 or 11. For arguments that the reciprocity exception is available in both cases see J Rickford, 'The Emerging European Takeover Law from a British Perspective' (2004) 15 Eur Business L Rev 1379, 1397–8 and for arguments against A Maréchal and A Pietrancosta, 'Transposition de la directive OPA: des incertitudes entourant le recours à la clause de réciprocité' (2005) 203 Bulletin Joly Bourse 797.

[100] The following made this choice in relation to the BNR: France, Greece, Portugal, Slovenia, and Spain. The opt-out version of the BNR ultimately adopted by Italy is also subject to reciprocity.

one or more which is not. Can the target apply the reciprocity exception against all the bidders or only against the ones not subject to the BNR? The French legislator has taken the view that defensive measures can be adopted by the target in relation to all the bidders in such a case.[101] Other national legislation is ambiguous on the point. If the French view is incorrect, then target management is presumably able to take defensive measures only if these are targeted at particular offerors, for example, the issuance of warrants[102] which become effective only if a particular offeror or offerors, not subject to the BNR, obtain control. It would be improper for the warrants to be triggered by an offeror subject to the BNR obtaining control. By extension, it could be argued that warrants issued when only one bidder, not subject to the BNR, is in the field would equally have to be designed in this way, lest a bidder subject to the BNR later enters the field or be discouraged from doing so. Irreversible or non-conditional defensive measures would not be permitted because they might deter a bidder subject to the BNR from making a bid.

(iii) The function of the reciprocity exception

Why would a Member State seek to make the reciprocity option available and why would the shareholders of the target seek to take it up? Where the Member State does not opt out of the BNR (and assuming the reciprocity option is indeed available in this situation), it is not obvious why the principle of shareholder decision-making should be departed from in the case where the bidder is not subject to the BNR.[103] The anti-entrenchment gains for the target do not depend on whether the bidder is subject to a BNR. However, on a longer-term perspective there may be something to be said for the Member State's adopting the reciprocity exception. Suppose the world consists of only two states, one (A) with and one (B) without a mandatory BNR. Other things being equal,[104] over time the proportion of businesses in the two states together not subject to the BNR will increase. This is because it will be easier for state B companies to acquire state A companies than vice versa, but state A companies, once acquired by state B companies, will no longer be subject to the BNR—or rather their holding companies will not. If state A takes the view that the BNR is an important element in securing efficient management of companies,[105] it may make sense for state A to give state B or its companies an incentive to become subject to the BNR by adopting some version

[101] Commercial Code, Article L233-33. [102] See below Section V.2.

[103] J McCahery, L Renneboog, P Ritter, and S Haller, 'The Economics of the Proposed European Takeover Directive' in Ferrarini (n 3) 645; Rickford (n 99) 1402, suggesting the reciprocity option is inconsistent with Treaty provisions.

[104] Which, of course, they will not be. Suppose, for example, state A generates new businesses rapidly whilst state B does so hardly at all. Furthermore, we put aside possible consequences from the product markets, which could give country A companies, who are successful, an edge over country B companies, which may survive in an inefficient state purely owing to entrenchment (as control is not contestable in such companies, where they are widely held).

[105] The corporate governance rationale for the BNR is discussed briefly above in Section II.2.

of the reciprocity rule.[106] On this analysis state A has to trade off the reduced impact now of the BNR (as a result of the adoption of the reciprocity exception) against the increased impact of the BNR in the future.

However, it is doubtful whether the reciprocity option contained in the Directive is apt to secure this longer-term goal. It requires reciprocity on the part of the bidder only at the time of the acquisition and not the subsequent maintenance of the BNR after the acquisition has been effectuated. Within the EU, therefore, it is doubtful whether the reciprocity qualification to the mandatory BNR fosters the overall adoption of that rule, because companies in jurisdictions where the BNR is not mandatory can make opportunistic use of the opting in facility—opting in as potential acquirers but not opting in or opting out, after having previously opted in, as potential targets.[107] With regard to acquirers from outside the EU, the impact of the reciprocity exception is even less clear. Article 12(3) allows reciprocity where a company is subject to an offer from a company 'which does not apply the same Articles as they do' (or is controlled by such a company). Since a non-EU company, even if it is subject to the equivalent of a BNR, will not be in that position as a result of applying Article 9, it can be said that reciprocity will always be available against a non-EU company.[108] If the non-EU company is in fact subject to a BNR, this seems an indefensible result. There will exist no incentive to non-EU companies or countries to adopt the BNR because the reciprocity option will still be open to EU targets faced with bids from such companies. Perhaps for this reason the French transposing legislation makes the reciprocity exception available if the bidder does not apply the BNR 'or equivalent measures'.[109] Similarly, the Italian implementation also employs the wider concept of 'equivalency'.[110] Even if a non-EU bidder can take advantage of being subject to the equivalent of the BNR, the bidder is still required to be in this state only at the date of the bid and not to maintain that rule thereafter, so that the incentive for non-EU jurisdictions, as well, is to provide only an opt-in to/opt-out from the BNR for companies within their jurisdiction.[111]

[106] State A will have an interest in state B companies being subject to the BNR so long as state B companies carry on operations in state A.

[107] Of course, this overstates the ease with which companies can play the system. Member states may impose constraints on the speed with which companies can reverse an opting in decision, and companies may misjudge whether they are potential acquirers or potential targets.

[108] At least to the extent this is not barred by international agreements; see *Report of the High Level Group on Issues Related to Takeover Bids* (n 55) and recital 21 of the Directive. Denmark, for instance, seems to embrace this view, by applying the reciprocity exception to all non-EEA bidders; see § 81c (5) of the Danish Public Companies Act.

[109] Commercial Code Article L233-33. On the other hand, the French provision appears to make the reciprocity option available whenever there is a bid from any 'entity' that does not apply the BNR or its equivalent, whereas the Directive suggests that reciprocity is available only in the case of non-BNR companies. Thus, it is doubtful whether the Directive allows reciprocity against a bid from an individual or a non-corporate entity, whether the bidder is within or without the EU.

[110] Article 104-ter comma 1 Legislative Decree 1998 no 58.

[111] There is an entirely contrary argument, based on recital 21 of the Directive, to the effect that targets can invoke the reciprocity exception only against bidders which have chosen not to opt

It seems more likely, therefore, that the drafting of the Directive in relation to reciprocity, and decisions by Member States whether to invoke it, are driven more by economic nationalism, ie a desire to ensure that in the process of global consolidation companies headquartered in their jurisdictions should more often be acquirers than targets. We return to this point below in Section IV.1.

Where the Member State chooses not to make the BNR mandatory, its decision whether to allow opting in by companies subject to reciprocity raises a different set of considerations. The Member State's aim, presumably, is to alter the incentives that operate upon the company when deciding whether to opt in or not. It is thought that opting in on the basis of reciprocity will be more attractive to shareholders in some cases than opting in without it.[112] Whether and in what circumstances this is a convincing analysis of the company-level incentives is discussed below.

Overall, in relation to the BNR the choices which the Directive gives the Member States can be set out as follows:

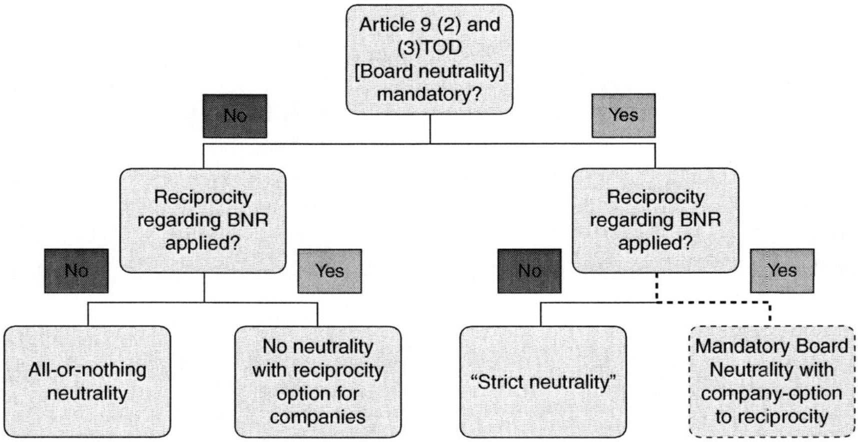

Figure 6.1[113] Member State choices regarding the BNR

into the BNR, in which case all non-EU companies would be outside the range of the reciprocity exception, even if they are not subject to the equivalent of the BNR—an equally odd result. The argument is somewhat weakened by the reference to international agreements to which the EU is a party in the same sentence, which rather strongly suggests that third countries are to be included.

[112] K J Hopt, 'Obstacles to Corporate Restructuring: Observations from a European and German Perspective' in M Tilson and others (eds), *Perspectives in Company Law and Financial Regulation* (Cambridge: Cambridge University Press, 2005) 380.

[113] As pointed out above (see text to n 98), it is unclear whether the reciprocity exception is in fact available in combination with a mandatory BNR under the Directive. This choice is marked by the dotted lines in Figures 6.1 and 6.2.

3. Company level choices

The company may have no choices to make at all. If the Member State chooses to impose a mandatory BNR and not to make reciprocity available as a qualification to the mandatory rule, then the company has nothing to decide. If, however, the Member State chooses to make reciprocity available as a qualification to the mandatory BNR, the company, by way of shareholder decision, has to decide whether to take it up.[114] Further, if the Member State chooses not to make the BNR mandatory, it must give the company the right to opt back into the BNR (by shareholder decision) and may choose to allow it to do so on the basis of reciprocity. In this case the company has two choices to make. The position can be put as in the following figure.

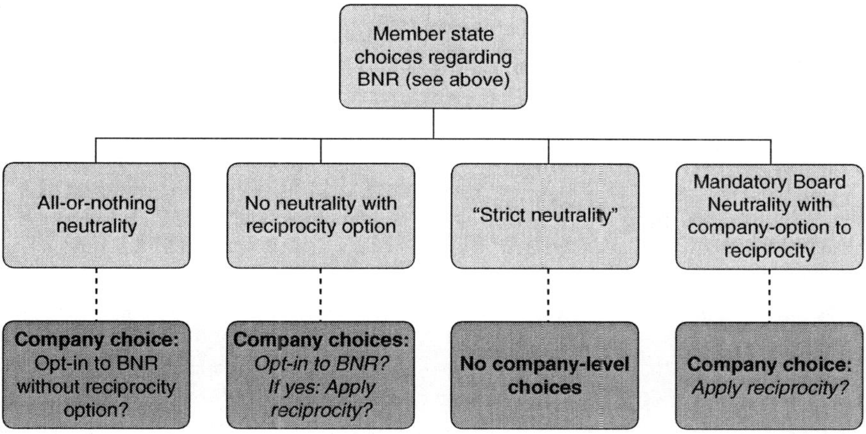

Figure 6.2 Company-level choices regarding the BNR

What is the incentive structure of the shareholders if faced with any of these options? Let us look first at the company's decision to opt back into the BNR, where reciprocity is not available (ie the far left-hand box on the bottom line of Figure 6.2). All these optional decisions are to be taken by the shareholders, in the case of this decision typically by supermajority vote because the Directive mandates that the shareholders should take the opting back in decision 'in accordance with the rules applicable to amendment of the articles of association'.[115] The shareholders' decision to opt into the BNR will presumably be motivated by a desire to maximize the market value of the shares, by capturing both the disciplinary and restructuring benefits of the takeover or the threat of it. However,

[114] But see the Portuguese and Danish implementation, Section IV below.
[115] Article 12(2).

the Directive does not significantly help the shareholders to put their preference into operation. In the absence of management initiative, the shareholders must take the initiative to secure the opt-in and the Directive does nothing to help them overcome their co-ordination problems, which are likely to be severe in a dispersed shareholding company. To the contrary, by insisting on a supermajority vote, the Directive accentuates the shareholders' difficulties. Where shareholding is concentrated and the controlling shareholders wish to preserve their PBCs, there is probably not much the Directive could have done to facilitate a shareholder opt-in decision, other than mandating the BNR as the default rule in national law, and thereby reversing the direction of the opt-in/opt-out mechanism.[116] By insisting on a supermajority vote, the Directive makes it even easier for large shareholders in insecure blockholder companies to stymie a resolution to opt back in.

Overall, the Directive's provisions on opting back in go against the modern theory that default rules should be constructed so as to counteract shareholders' co-ordination problems and thus give the management or controlling shareholders the burden of securing an opt-out from default.[117] It is perhaps not surprising that we found no case to date in which the shareholders of a company had opted back into the BNR where the Member State had chosen not to make it mandatory.

Moving on to the next box in the bottom row of Figure 6.2, we consider the case where the shareholders may opt back in either with or without reciprocity. If we have correctly identified the motives for shareholders to wish to opt back into the BNR, then the addition of a reciprocity qualification would not seem attractive to them.[118] If the reciprocity option is adopted, it will reduce the chances of an offer being made for the shares or of a competitive bidding situation arising if an offer is made. Moreover, the management of an acquirer not subject to a BNR is likely to be less strongly accountable to its shareholders than one that is subject to a BNR and so is more likely to contemplate overpaying for a target (for empire-building reasons, for example) than one that is so subject. Thus, by applying the reciprocity rule the shareholders of the target are potentially excluding offers from the most attractive acquirers. At the same time, such offerors are likely to be the favoured choices for the target's management, as a less accountable bidder will typically have more leeway offering them to keep their jobs or giving 'golden

[116] In this case, insecure blockholders would have reason to fear opposition in case they try to opt out of the BNR. This reverse opt-in mechanism was enacted by Italy in a recent change of its takeover law; see Section IV.2 below.

[117] See Bebchuk and Hamdani (n 21). Regarding the merits of and problems associated with the Directive's optional arrangements see also G Hertig and J McCahery, 'Company and Takeover Law Reforms in Europe: Misguided Harmonization Efforts or Regulatory Competition?' (2003) 4 Eur Business Organization L Rev 179.

[118] The reciprocity qualification to the opt-in needs renewal every 18 months if it is to continue to be effective, but the Directive does not stipulate a supermajority vote for this decision: Article 12(5).

handshakes'. Thus, the management may use their bargaining power to divert a higher proportion of the bid premium to themselves than would be the case in the absence of the reciprocity rule.[119] Consequently, if shareholder-initiated opt-ins to the BNR by companies were to be made, we would not expect them to be accompanied by decisions in favour of reciprocity.

Where the Member State has imposed a mandatory BNR but has allowed the companies to qualify the mandatory rule by opting for reciprocity by shareholder decision (ie the far right-hand box), the burden of initiating action is placed on the management/controllers of the company, because reciprocity here qualifies a BNR which applies to the company without shareholder decision. So, in this instance the modern theory about default rules is complied with: those who would benefit from the change must persuade the shareholders to qualify a default which is apparently in the shareholders' interests. In dispersed shareholding companies, the shareholders' co-ordination problems are partly addressed by this formula, because it is the management that needs to convene the meeting and put the reciprocity proposal to the shareholders. If shareholders' responses to requests for pre-bid authorization of defensive measures where the bidder is not subject to reciprocity are exactly the same as their response to a post-bid request for authorization of defensive measures in such a case, then management has no incentive to seek pre-bid authorization.[120] If, however, as argued above,[121] a significant number of shareholders may in fact treat voting on pre-bid authorization differently from deciding whether to accept an offer, once it is made, then there may be advantages for management in seeking to make use of the reciprocity qualification. In short, the management may find the burden of persuading the shareholders (even where they are highly sophisticated) less heavy pre- than post-bid, despite the fact that the only purpose of the reciprocity resolution is to increase the management's defensive powers if a bid materializes. One argument the management could (and most likely will) use to win support for the proposal is the positive effect a strong bargaining position could have on the premium paid by an acquirer.

Whilst the reciprocity qualification to the mandatory BNR is irrelevant where the company has a secure single controlling shareholder (absent unusual circumstances, the management will always do what the controlling shareholder wants), the reciprocity rule may have attractions for non-secure blockholders. Assume that multiple large shareholders (or a single insecure blockholder) have enough shares to control the company's general meeting (because of the apathy of the non-controlling shareholders) but fear that an offer put to the shareholders individually would prove attractive to a sufficient proportion of the non-controlling shareholders to permit the offer to succeed. Similarly, the controller might fear

[119] Cf the discussion in Section II.1.(iii) above.

[120] Unless the managers want to avoid the time constraint linked to post-bid decision-making.

[121] Section II.1.(i).

that dramatically more shareholders might show up in a post-bid general meeting deciding about defensive measures than in a 'normal' meeting. Such fears could be founded in the notion that, after announcement of a bid, the proportion of more activist shareholders (especially event-driven hedge funds) increases dramatically. Hedge funds acting as arbitrageurs will favour the bidder and seek to secure the success of the bid, by accepting it and voting against defensive measures, if asked to do so. The latter worry might be further amplified by the EU's more recent attempts to facilitate (cross-border) exercise of voting rights.[122] There might also be a particular post-bid risk where one of the large shareholders defected to the acquirer.

The controllers fear in other words that their control of shareholder meetings might be undermined in what is in effect a postal ballot of all the shareholders. In such a case the blockholders might wish to give the board of the target (ie themselves, in essence) the power to escape from the BNR; after all, they are able—under 'normal circumstances'—to control the board's decision whether or not to take defensive measures in the face of any particular bid, and can therefore screen out unwanted bidders. As mentioned above,[123] increasing the managerial discretion can be regarded as value-increasing from the non-controlling shareholders' point of view *ex ante*; thus, rational shareholders will sometimes vote in favour of such a proposal.[124] Even where the management would not be able to convince a rationally acting shareholder body of the advantages of increased defensive powers, a reciprocity proposal could still prove successful, where a sufficient amount of shares are in the hands of rather passive investors. Their apathy will (rationally) be higher in an *ex ante* ballot, where the expected costs are still discounted by the uncertainty of the reciprocity rule's relevance, than in a post-bid scenario, where the wealth effect of defence is predictable with near certainty. In addition, some of the involved institutions might be conflicted or financially unsophisticated, with weak incentives to force the company to implement a value-increasing strategy. Again, this effect is likely to be greater *ex ante* than *ex post*.

In short, the reciprocity exception operates here as a way of watering down the mandatory BNR and of preserving management or (insecure) blockholder control. Management or blockholders might prefer not to be subject to a BNR at all but that choice is not available to them. Instead, they can reduce the range of situations in which their control will be tested, especially if the reciprocity option is given a wide scope by being available, for example, against all non-EU bidders or in all situations where one of the bidders is not subject to the BNR.[125] As we shall see below, opt-outs by companies where the BNR has been made mandatory by the Member State, which has also made the reciprocity exception

122 See Directive 2007/36/EC (n 30).

123 Section II(1).(i).

124 See Section V.2 regarding some French companies making use of this possibility.

125 See Section II.1.(ii) and (iii) above.

available, is the one area where we have found significant company-level decision-making—though not in all jurisdictions where the exception has been made available.

IV. The choices made—Member States

1. Transposition choices

We have scored the choices made available to the Member States, as set out in Figures 6.1 and 6.2 above, in the following way. We assign three points to Member States that decided to make the BNR mandatory. In a second step, we assign one point for the decision *not* to make the reciprocity exception available. The highest score (4) is thus assigned to those states which have chosen not to opt out of the BNR and have not applied the reciprocity exception, and the lowest score (0) to those states which have made the BNR optional and have given companies opting back in the freedom to do so on the basis of reciprocity. A Member State that does not make the BNR mandatory but does not make the reciprocity exception available scores 1. So, the higher the score, the more friendly to bidders is the Member State, as far as the BNR is concerned.

As pointed out above, the decision to make reciprocity available on the company level is of rather minor importance in practice. Combined with a non-mandatory BNR it does not seem to influence the outcome of the rules ultimately applicable to the companies to any meaningful extent. As an add-on to a mandatory BNR the reciprocity exception can have some practical consequences (as will be seen in the French example), but certainly to a far lesser extent than the decision whether the BNR is mandatory in the first place. For example, a Member State combining a mandatory BNR with a reciprocity exception effectively opens its market for corporate control at least regarding all *domestic* takeovers; in addition, the UK, as a very important originator of cross-border bids, and any other state which has made the BNR mandatory will also benefit from this choice. It was our intention to account for these differences in practical impact by assigning a substantially higher 'score' to the opt-out or not decision than to the reciprocity choice.[126] Of course, such a score necessarily involves an element of judgement, as it can hardly be quantified to what extent one choice is more important than the other. Our method of scoring also leads to unambiguous results in the sense that the score directly translates into a specific combination of choices made by the Member State.

[126] The '0'/'1' division is somewhat debatable. If the alternative for the shareholders to opting in with reciprocity is not opting in at all, then it can be argued that '0' is the better choice from the bidder's point of view (ie for bidders subject to a BNR). However, if the comparison is with opting in without reciprocity, '1' is clearly more bidder friendly.

Table 6.1 sets out the results of our scoring.

Table 6.1 Member State implementation scores: BNR

Country	BNR Score
Austria	4
Belgium	0
Bulgaria	4
Cyprus	4
Czech Republic	4
Denmark	0
Estonia	4
Finland	4
France	3
Germany	0
Greece	3
Hungary	0
Ireland	4
Italy	2
Latvia	4
Lithuania	4
Luxembourg	0
Malta	4
Netherlands	0
Poland	0
Portugal	3
Romania	4
Slovakia	4
Slovenia	3
Spain	3
Sweden	4
United Kingdom	4

Fourteen Member States (out of twenty-seven) chose not to opt out of the BNR and not to make the reciprocity exception available. Five further states did not opt out but made the reciprocity exception available. All the remaining eight Member States opted out of the BNR on the basis that the reciprocity exception was to be made available as well, ie they maximized the choices available to their companies. However, since we found no companies to have opted back into the BNR, the Member State choice as between making reciprocity available or not has had no practical significance in relation to the opting back in decision. What does seem to be the case is that the incentive provided by the reciprocity option for companies to opt into the BNR is weak.

Italy, to which we assigned a score of '2', calls for a special explanation. Since enactment of the Directive, Italy has adapted its rules regarding the BNR (and the BTR) several times, starting from a strict BNR. In its latest version,[127] Italy still maintains its formal opt-out of the BNR, adopted in 2008,[128] together with a reciprocity option—a choice that would generally yield a score of zero according to the methodology described above. However, while the application of the BNR remains optional in Italy, the 'direction of choice' has been reversed, as the BNR was adopted as a default rule. As a consequence, Italian companies will be subject to the BNR *unless they opt out* of the rule by amending their articles of association.[129]

As we have argued above,[130] the mechanism employed for implementing the optional arrangements may have an important impact on the rules finally applicable to the companies. Apart from alleviating the co-ordination problems among shareholders, reversing the direction of the choice mechanism also alleviates the problems connected to the supermajority requirement for opt-in decisions[131] required by the Directive. In a 'typical' opt-out jurisdiction, a blockholder in a *de facto* controlling position with significantly less than 50 per cent of the voting rights[132] can effectively block any opt-in proposal by his fellow shareholders, even if they overcome the collective action problem. This also leads us to assigning a score of '2' to Italy. As the value of the rules *per se* is not objectively quantifiable, our aim must be to assign scores with 'ordinal accuracy'; for our purposes, this means that we try to assign higher scores to more pro-shareholder choices. In these terms, Italy's score can be explained as follows. The choice restricts management discretion to a greater extent than the rules in countries scored '0' (ie where the BNR is optional and reciprocity is available), because in the latter, a supermajority needs to support the BNR to put it in place, while in Italy 33 per cent[133] of the shareholders are sufficient to block an opt-out decision.

Similarly, Italy's new framework constrains management (and/or insecure blockholders) to a larger extent than countries with a score of '1' (ie where the BNR is optional, but no reciprocity exception exists), as an equivalent shareholder majority would always adopt *more, or at least equally, bidder-friendly* rules in Italy, as it would in a typical '1'-scored country. Where a supermajority of shareholders supports adopting a 'strong' BNR, it can do so in both cases. Where only a simple majority favours such rules, a BNR will apply in Italy (because the

[127] See Legislative Decree no 146, Article 1(3), 25 September 2009 (published in the GU no 246 of 22 October 2009), which amended Article 104 of the Legislative Decree no 58 as of 1 July 2010.

[128] See also below, text to n 148, for more details.

[129] Fiat recently announced that it will amend its articles of association to allow its board of directors to take defensive measures without prior shareholder approval. Other Italian companies can be expected to follow Fiat's example (see S. Bocconi, 'A Pizza Affari è l'ora delle 'pillole antiscalate'—Torino dà il via, i big studiano le difese'—Carriere della Sera (31 August 2010)).

[130] Section III.3.

[131] Article 12(2); see also above Section III.3

[132] Depending on the national corporate law and the expected attendance of the relevant general meeting, a blockholder with around 15%–25% will probably be able to block any supermajority-requiring decision.

[133] In the new Italian takeover regime opting out of the BNR presupposes an amendment to the articles of association of the company. This requires a supermajority of 2/3 of the voting rights.

company cannot opt out), while a company in a '1'-country would be unable to opt in. Where a majority, but not a supermajority, favours increasing management discretion, it is true that a reciprocity exception can be adopted in a jurisdiction like Italy,[134] but not in a country scored '1'. However, this situation in Italy would lead to the BNR still being applicable in favour of all bidders who are themselves subject to a BNR,[135] while the same shareholder body, on the other hand, would not apply any form of the BNR in a country scored '1'. Finally, where a supermajority of shareholders favours authorizing the managers to take defensive action as they think fit, the BNR will apply neither in Italy nor in any jurisdiction scored '1'.

As regards jurisdictions scored '3', Italy never yields a more pro-shareholder outcome when comparing equivalent shareholder bodies' choices, but in one case (where a supermajority exists which favours increasing management discretion), a company subject to Italian law will not apply the BNR (ie opt-out), while this option does not exist in countries with a score of '3'.[136] The score of '2', therefore, seems to properly reflect the relative 'bidder friendliness' of Italy's new rule.

Also worth mentioning are Denmark and Portugal, both of which seem to have adopted an 'automatic' reciprocity rule: in contrast to the Directive's requirements, they do not require regular shareholder approval for the reciprocity exception to kick in, but rather apply the rule in any case. While this seems irrelevant in the case of Denmark,[137] as it has opted out of the BNR, and no company seems to have opted back in again, this could be significant in Portugal (a '3'-country).[138]

2. Comparison of pre- and post-transposition position

We have discussed so far the choices which the Member States made in implementing the BNR. Given the options made available to the Member States, it is not surprising that the resulting pattern of regulation is not uniform across the EU. However, it would still be possible for the Commission to claim that the Directive had made progress towards a single market in which companies were more open to takeovers, if the BNR were more widespread post-Directive than it had previously been.

Table 6.2 sets out our assessment of the national positions on the BNR before and after the transposition of the Directive. In assessing the 'after' position we

[134] The reciprocity decision does not require a supermajority decision under the new law, unless the decision requires a change of the articles, for example, to give the board the right to issue shares free of pre-emption rights.

[135] Because a simple majority can only adopt the reciprocity exception, but will be unable to opt out entirely from the BNR.

[136] However, it might be questioned whether the difference between Italy's choice and a typical '3'-scored jurisdiction has much practical relevance, since this will mainly concern secure blockholder cases where the BNR is less relevant; see above Section II.2.

[137] For the rule, see § 81c (5) of the Danish Public Companies Act.

[138] See also below Section V.2.

Table 6.2[1] Member State BNR scores before and after the Takeover Directive

Country	BNR score before	BNR score after
Austria	4	4
Belgium	0	0
Bulgaria	4	4
Cyprus	0	4
Czech Republic	4	4
Denmark	0	0
Estonia	4	4
Finland	0	4
France	4	3
Germany	0	0
Greece	4	3
Hungary	4	0
Ireland	4	4
Italy	4	2[2]
Latvia	0	4
Lithuania	4	4
Luxembourg	0	0
Malta	0	4
Netherlands	0	0
Poland	0	0
Portugal	4	3
Romania	0	4
Slovakia	4	4
Slovenia	4	3
Spain	4	3
Sweden	4	4
United Kingdom	4	4

[1] Many states had a BNR before transposition but reciprocity was in effect unknown. We have used the scoring deployed above in Table 6.1 but have assigned 0 to the situation where there was no BNR and 4 to the situations where there was.
[2] The BNR is the default rule in Italy, but shareholders can vote to opt out of it; see Section IV.1.

have taken the most recent set of rules. In some jurisdictions, such as Hungary, Italy, and Poland, an initial set of policy choices with regard to the transposition of the Directive was subsequently altered.[139] As we noted in Section II, the absence of a BNR pre-Directive does not mean there were no controls over board discretion once a bid had been launched. Equally, it is possible that a Member State may have made progress towards a BNR post-Directive without actually getting to the position where it applied a ban on defensive action across the board. However, we are not aware of any state falling within this category.

It might be argued that all Member States have made some progress in a bidder-friendly direction because all Member States must now make the BNR

[139] We will return to the reasons for this below.

option available to companies in their jurisdictions (with or without reciprocity), if they do not impose it as a mandatory rule. Thus, the shareholders of German or Dutch companies may now opt into the BNR. Whereas previously they could not commit the board in advance to a 'no frustration' response to a bid, this option is now available. However, in the face of the difficulties of exercising that choice and the fact that we could find no examples of opting back in,[140] we do not find it convincing to argue that a move from no or a limited BNR to an optional BNR constitutes a step in a bidder-friendly direction, and we have not so treated it in Table 6.2. Finally, even if examples of this could be found, management-inspired opting into the BNR by potential acquirers as a shield against potential targets invoking the reciprocity exception is not a step in a bidder-friendly direction, when comparing pre- and post-Directive national laws. This is because, before transposition, reciprocity was not an element in Member States' takeover laws, so that opting in by potential acquirers operates only so as partially to counteract the bidder unfriendly and newly introduced reciprocity exception, thus at best restoring the *status quo ante*.

If these arguments are accepted, then only Cyprus, Finland, Latvia, Malta, and Romania show a significant shift in a bidder-friendly direction through their introduction of a mandatory BNR without reciprocity. Apart from Finland, however, the capital markets in these jurisdictions are particularly small.[141] As far as Malta is concerned, the pre-implementation general company law was already strongly influenced by UK law, and it included a UK-type 'proper purposes doctrine'. This might make the actual changes effected through the adoption of a 'bright-line' rule appear somewhat smaller than in other jurisdictions.[142] Regarding Finland, the adoption of the BNR took place through a non-binding 'recommendation' in the Helsinki Takeover Code; nevertheless, Finland seems to be satisfied that this, in combination with general corporate law, meets the standards required by Article 9 of the Directive.[143] Otherwise, no other Member State with a significant market capitalization adopted the mandatory BNR where it previously did not impose it.

In 15 Member States the law remained broadly as it was. Those Member States used their BNR choices to maintain the status quo. Five countries can be classified as moving moderately in a less bidder-friendly direction, through the introduction of reciprocity exception to a previously mandatory BNR. This group consists of France, Greece, Portugal, Slovenia, and Spain. Finally, two states moved in a

[140] See the discussion below in Section V.

[141] The market capitalizations of those jurisdictions are: Latvia: GBP 1.15 bn; Malta: GBP 2.50 bn; Cyprus: GBP 6.3 bn; Romania: GBP 7.4 bn. The aggregate of these four jurisdictions corresponds to about 2/3 of the Czech capital market or 1% of the UK market.

[142] s 136A (3) (e) of the Maltese Companies Act 1995, inserted in 2003. Regarding the relevance of the proper purposes doctrine, see also text to n 16 above.

[143] Which is indicated, inter alia, by the absence of an opt-in possibility for Finnish companies.

significantly less bidder-friendly direction, Italy and Hungary. In both cases a previously mandatory BNR was made optional, and the reciprocity exception applied.

The quite widespread take-up of the BNR on a mandatory basis in large part reflects the fact that the BNR was quite widely established in Member States' legal systems prior to the adoption of the Directive.[144] We return to this point in Section V below.

Despite the number of Member States scoring '4' after transposition of the Directive, the post-transposition state of the takeover laws in the Member States was overall less favourable to the BNR than it had been previously. It is perhaps not surprising that the Member States as a whole have not moved in a direction more favourable to the BNR. The effect of the options created by the Directive was to leave the decision on whether to adopt a BNR to the legislative processes of the Member States, subject to the minor qualification that companies must be free to opt into the BNR if the Member State chooses not to make it a mandatory rule. For the reasons mentioned briefly above and examined more fully below,[145] this option has been of no practical significance so far and seems unlikely to become more than a minor feature of takeover practice. Leaving it aside, one can say that since takeover legislation has been on the agendas of all Member States for the past couple of decades following the takeover boom of the 1990s,[146] it is not surprising that Member States which were in favour of the BNR had adopted it in advance of the Directive. In short, the Directive added nothing (or virtually nothing) to the Member State-level impetuses in favour of the BNR and, where these impetuses existed, they had already resulted in the adoption of the rule.

However, this does not explain the discernible shift away from the full mandatory BNR in the post-Directive period in a significant number of Member States. It may be that the Directive, by causing Member States legislatively to address once again the issue of the BNR (if only to provide the company-level opt-in to the Directive), caused the domestic political forces pro and con the BNR once again to deploy their strengths in favour of their preferred position. In the majority of states, the outcome of this renewed policy debate was the same as the pre-Directive position. This explains the large number of Member States whose score in Table 6.2 remained the same, pre- and post-transposition (whether the pre-Directive position was a 0 or a 4).[147]

[144] Nine of the fourteen '4' states were also '4' states before transposition; see also M Goergen, M Martynova, and L Renneboog, 'Corporate Governance Convergence: Evidence from Takeover Regulation' ECGI Law Working Paper 33/2005 at 28 (70% of all EU countries required shareholder approval of defensive measures by 2004. Unfortunately, this figure does not distinguish between pre- and post-bid approval.)

[145] See Section V.1.

[146] Martynova and Renneboog (n 80) 2.

[147] It is conceivable that some '0' states moved in the direction of the BNR in the transposition process but fell short of adopting it fully. We are not aware of this in any of the Member States.

In a minority but nevertheless significant number of states the policy debate triggered by the need to transpose the Directive led to a recalibration of the competing arguments and a different legislative outcome. In some cases the outcome was in favour of the BNR (Cyprus, Finland, Latvia, Malta, and Romania). In a larger number of cases (including some economically significant countries) the result was a move away from the mandatory BNR. This is most obvious in the two states which abandoned a pre-existing mandatory BNR, ie Italy and Hungary. The Italian debate was particularly lively,[148] involving as it did three successive legislative responses to the BNR. The first was to maintain the pre-existing BNR; the second was to make it an opt-in rule for companies as Article 12 of the Directive contemplates, and the third and distinctive approach was to make the BNR as a whole a default rule (ie to allow companies by shareholder vote to opt out of the BNR entirely and not just as against companies not subject to the BNR).[149] Hungary, too, initially implemented the Directive by maintaining its pre-existing mandatory BNR but then made the BNR optional.[150] What we cannot estimate is whether the existing mandatory BNR would have been maintained in these two countries had the Directive not required transposition. The fact that post-Directive both countries initially confirmed their existing BNRs but then substantially modified them might suggest that the transposition process itself was relatively unimportant. It was the events subsequent to the transposition which brought about the reversal of the positions adopted at transposition. In the case of Italy that event was the collapse of the stock markets in 2008 and the fear that Italian companies would easily be taken over by foreign (especially non-EU) bidders.[151] In the case of Hungary the triggering event for the reversal was a bid by a foreign acquirer for a large domestic company in a sensitive sector of the economy, ie the bid for MOL, the largest Hungarian oil company, by OMV, an Austrian company.[152]

In the case of the Member States which maintained the BNR which had previously existed, but made it subject to a shareholder option to take up the reciprocity exception to the rule, the case for the Directive itself contributing to this development is stronger. The notion of reciprocity seems to have been generated by the policy discussions over the Directive. None of the pre-existing Member

[148] It is set out in G Ferrarini and G Miller, 'A Simple Theory of Takeover Regulation in the United States and Europe' (2009) 42 Cornell Intl L J 301, who adopt an interest group analysis which we have found helpful.

[149] See also Section III.3 above. The new rule applies from 1 July 2010. See Legislative Decree no 146, Article 1(3), n 127 above. The change to the existing law was led by the industry and CONSOB (the competent Italian regulator) who both took the view that the crisis-driven opt-out of the BNR was no longer justified. For a description of the new takeover regime in Italy see F Mucciarelli, 'Le difese' in *Le nueve leggi civile commentate*, n 1, 2010, 92–100.

[150] Initial implementation by Act CLXXVI of 2005; amendment by Act CXVI of 2007.

[151] The relevant law was Legislative Decree no 185, 29 November 2008, Article 13. It might have been thought that the reciprocity exception would have been enough to meet this point.

[152] For this reason Act CXVI of 2007 is colloquially referred to as the '*Lex MOL*'.

State BNRs was subject to a reciprocity exception. Having first generated the idea of reciprocity and then having made it available in the Directive,[153] it is perhaps not surprising that a number of Member States took it up. In particular, 17 of the 27 EU Member States had a mandatory and unqualified BNR pre-transposition. Six introduced the reciprocity exception to that mandatory rule post-transposition. The significance of the reciprocity option depends, of course, on the willingness of companies to make use of it. If no use is made of it, it will have no greater significance than the option for companies in jurisdictions with non-mandatory BNRs to opt into rule, which none has done. We examine this below in Section V.

(i) Transposition choices and economic nationalism

A final question is whether there is an association between decisions by Member States to qualify a pre-existing mandatory BNR (either by opting out of it altogether or by making the reciprocity exception available) and the resurgence in the forces of economic nationalism in the European Union.[154] The question is particularly pertinent in relation to the introduction of the reciprocity exception to the mandatory BNR, since that exception permits the taking of defensive measures against out-of-state acquirers (unless they are subject to a BNR as well). The exception does not deter same-state acquirers. It is difficult—and politically impossible—for the European Commission to challenge decisions made by Member States by taking up options explicitly provided for in the Takeover Directive. However, any association between choices under the Directive and economic nationalism can be tested indirectly by looking at Commission challenges to non-takeover but related legislation by Member States on the grounds that it infringes either or both of the Treaty provisions on free movement of capital or freedom of establishment within the EU.[155] In these situations the Commission is explicitly acting to protect the interests of acquirers from other Member States. The non-takeover legislation in question typically does not apply across the board, but only to companies in 'sensitive' areas of the economy, which is sometimes equated with recently privatized companies.[156] The restrictions imposed have been many and various but at their core involve either state approval for the acquisition of non-trivial shareholdings in the companies covered and/or the retention by the state of powers to veto significant management decisions.

[153] Or, at least, arguably having done so. See text to n 99 above.

[154] Analysed by Hopt (n 112).

[155] A summary of surveillance and enforcement actions taken by the Commission in the area of capital movements is available at <http://ec.europa.eu/internal_market/capital/analysis/index_en.htm> (last accessed 1 August 2010).

[156] The companies may or may not be listed on a regulated market and thus within the scope of the Takeover Directive.

Table 6.3 Overview of BNR scores, Commission infringement procedures, and (adverse) ECJ rulings

Country	BNR Score Before	BNR Score After	Commission Challenge	Adverse Court of Justice Decision
Austria	4	4	NO	
Belgium	0	0	YES	C-503/99
Bulgaria	4	4	NO	
Cyprus	0	4	NO	
Czech Republic	4	4	NO	
Denmark	0	0	YES	
Estonia	4	4	NO	
Finland	0	4	NO	
France	4	3	YES (2)	C-483/99
Germany	0	0	YES	C-112/05
Greece	4	3	YES (2)	
Hungary	4	0	YES (2)	
Ireland	4	4	NO	
Italy	4	2	YES (4)	C-58/99; C-326/07; C-174/04; C-463, 464/2004
Latvia	0	4	NO	
Lithuania	4	4	NO	
Luxembourg	0	0	YES	
Malta	0	4	NO	
Netherlands	0	0	YES	C-282; 283/04
Poland	0	0	YES (2)	
Portugal	4	3	YES (4)	C-367/98
Romania	0	4	NO	
Slovakia	4	4	YES	
Slovenia	4	3	NO	
Spain	4	3	YES (2)	C-463/00; C-207/07
Sweden	4	4	NO	
United Kingdom	4	4	YES	C-98/01

Table 6.3 sets out in summary form the position roughly since 2000. Whilst not conclusive, it suggests a correlation between lower scores on the transposition of the Takeover Directive and the adoption of other legislation protective against takeovers by foreign acquirers which either the Commission thinks or the Court of Justice has found to be in breach of the Treaty provisions.[157] Of the states with a mandatory BNR before and after transposition only the UK and Slovakia have been the subject of a Commission challenge, and only the

[157] Information about particular infringement cases is available on: <http://ec.europa.eu/internal_market/capital/analysis/index_en.htm#infringments> (last accessed 1 August 2010). In some cases the Commission has not taken its case to the Court because the Member State implemented the requested changes. This was so in the cases of Hungary in relation to Act CXVI of 2007 and Italy in relation to the acquisition of stakes in domestic banks.

UK has been subject to an adverse Court ruling.[158] Except for Slovenia, all the states which either abandoned an existing mandatory BNR (Italy, Hungary) or qualified it with the introduction of the reciprocity exception (France, Greece, Portugal, and Spain) have been the subject of one or more Commission challenges to recently introduced protective legislation, which have led in some of the cases to decisions from the Court adverse to the Member State. There were also Commission challenges to protective legislation in all six countries (Belgium, Denmark, Germany,[159] Luxembourg, Netherlands, Poland) which adopted the mandatory BNR neither before nor after the implementation of the Directive.

V. The choices made—companies

1. Opting into the BNR

Companies have not chosen to opt into the BNR where these rules have not been made mandatory by Member States. We have already indicated above that the default is a difficult one for the shareholders to alter.[160] From a shareholder perspective, seeking to open up the company to offers, we may speculate that the opting-in provisions of the Directive do not substantially strengthen the hand of the shareholders as against incumbent management (plus controlling shareholders). In other words, although the BNR provides an effective legal device for making the company attractive to bidders, it does not make it easier for shareholders to secure the passing of resolutions opposed by the management (or management plus blockholders). A resolution to opt into the BNR—which requires a supermajority[161]—is not any easier to secure in the presence of controlling

In other cases the procedure is still ongoing, either because the complaint has been referred to the Court of Justice, whose decision is awaited, or the Member State's response to the Commission's request for amendments to the domestic law is not yet clear.

[158] This concerned a share cap in the airports operator, British Airports Authority, which effectively made it bid-proof. After the adverse judgment of the Court of Justice, the cap was removed and the company was later acquired by the Spanish company, Ferrovial (with associates). The acquisition was financed with large amounts of debt which the company has subsequently struggled to repay.

[159] The German challenge was to the special law for the Volkswagen company. Its more general protectionist legislation did not attract a Commission challenge, but for a sceptical account of these rules see Hopt (n 112).

[160] See Section III.3.

[161] Article 12(2). It sets a particularly stiff hurdle. In the case of Sweden all the shareholders present at the meeting must vote in favour of opting in and there is a quorum requirement of 90% of the shares. Opting in for a Swedish company is, in consequence, practically impossible, though the Swedish requirements are an outlier and other Member States use more attainable supermajority requirements. (Sweden has different levels of requirement for changes in the articles, according to the nature of the change. See Companies Act, ch 7, ss 42–45. The most demanding level has been chosen for opting in.)

shareholder opposition[162] than any other resolution of the shareholders which is so opposed. Further, had the shareholders' position as against management (and controlling shareholders) changed in favour of an increase of the non-controlling shareholders' influence before the transposition of the Directive, in many jurisdictions there are other steps they could (and would) have taken to render the company more attractive to potential bidders, even in the absence of the opting in arrangements. An example of alternative action might be replacing the incumbent board with directors more ready to contemplate selling the company.

However, opting in needs to be considered also from the point of view of management (plus controlling shareholders). From their point of view, the incentive to opt in is to *avoid* the use of the reciprocity exception by potential targets which the company might wish to acquire. Performance-based remuneration, perhaps combined with golden shares or high self-confidence, can also play a role in the management's incentive to opt in. This incentive is perhaps at its strongest where the company has nothing to fear from a BNR, for example, where there is a blockholder with *de jure* control of the company without resort to disproportionate voting rights, so that the BNR in no way threatens the blockholder's position. However, the strength of this incentive depends upon the reciprocity exception being available to potential targets and those targets having taken up the exception. In relation to potential targets in those countries scoring 4[163] in the above table, the incentive for potential acquirers to opt in for the purpose of avoiding reciprocity does not exist, because reciprocity is not an option for the targets. This is the case for potential acquirers both from within those jurisdictions and those incorporated in another Member State. Fourteen countries,[164] including the UK, fall within the category of jurisdictions that provide potential acquirers with no incentive to opt in.

Even in relation to the seven[165] countries scoring 0 (where reciprocity is available), the incentive to potential acquirers (whether from those or other jurisdictions) to opt in depends on whether potential targets in those jurisdictions have taken up the reciprocity exception. As we have stated, where the BNR is not mandatory, there have been no opting in decisions so far, whether on the basis of reciprocity or otherwise. So, this incentive to opt in as a potential acquirer is currently very weak.

Overall, we find no evidence of companies opting into the BNR where this is not mandatory and for the reasons given above, we do not find this situation surprising. The incentives for company controllers (whether management or blockholders) to opt in are weak or non-existent, whilst the incentive for non-controlling shareholders are strong, but the Directive does nothing to

162 As argued above (Section II.2), this is particularly important with regard to insecure (< 50%) blockholders.

163 Likewise, this argument would also apply to countries scoring 1, but no country has chosen this option.

164 These are Austria, Bulgaria, Cyprus, Czech Republic, Estonia, Finland, Ireland, Latvia, Lithuania, Malta, Romania, Slovakia, Sweden, and the UK.

165 ie Belgium, Denmark, Germany, Hungary, Luxembourg, the Netherlands, and Poland.

help them overcome opposition from the controllers to the opting in decision. However, we have still not considered the final company-level option which may be available, ie to take up the reciprocity exception to the mandatory BNR where a Member State has chosen to make it available (ie '3' states). Here we do find significant company-level activity in one such state, and so our task is to explain its presence in that state and its absence in the others.

2. Taking up the reciprocity exception to the mandatory BNR

Where the BNR is mandatory but the shareholders may introduce a reciprocity exception to the rule, the incentives to act or not would appear to be as follows. Non-controlling shareholders would probably not be in favour of introducing the exception, unless they had a very high degree of confidence that the management would use the discretion vested in them to advance the interests of the shareholders as a class (for example, by negotiating a higher price with the bidder or encouraging an auction). Unlike with an opting resolution where the BNR is not mandatory, the shareholders do not have to take any action to secure the application of the BNR; the burden lies with the controllers of the company if they wish to introduce the reciprocity exception to the mandatory BNR. They need to persuade the shareholders to pass a resolution adopting the reciprocity exception, though the Directive does not require supermajority support for the resolution. They will also need to seek periodic (in effect, annual) renewal of the authority given by the resolution.[166] In terms of the controllers' incentives to take that initiative, much turns on how highly they rate the chance of their company being subject to an offer from an acquirer which is not subject to the BNR. Acquirers from outside the EU are likely not to be subject to a BNR and this will also be true for acquirers from some important EU Member States, such as Germany. So, the incentive for controllers of potential targets in category 3 countries to seek to introduce the reciprocity exception is quite strong, unless there is some more easily adopted or more effective way open to them of achieving protection against acquirers.

France, Greece, Portugal, Slovenia, and Spain fall within the category of having made the BNR mandatory but subject to reciprocity (ie they scored 3). As far as we could establish, no company has taken up the reciprocity exception to the mandatory BNR in Greece, Slovenia, or Spain. Portugal is a somewhat exceptional case, as the implementing legislation seemingly does not call for pre-bid authorization by the shareholders for the reciprocity exception to apply.[167] Rather, it automatically applies as against bidders not subject to 'the same rules'. This clearly does not meet the requirements set out in Article 12(5) of the Directive.[168]

In relation to France, however, over a quarter of the CAC 40-companies have taken up the reciprocity exception. Although this uptake does not (yet) seem to have provided a sufficient incentive for companies in other jurisdictions to opt

[166] Article 12(3) and (5). [167] See Article 182(6) of the Portuguese Securities Code.

[168] The same seems to be true for Denmark, which did not, however, make the BNR mandatory. Absent company-level opt-ins, the rule is therefore virtually irrelevant at the moment.

into the BNR to avoid the reciprocity exception—possibly because the French companies are seen as unattractive takeover targets for other reasons—we do here have a not insignificant corporate level response to an option made available by the legislature and one which stands out in contrast to the absence of corporate level responses to legislative options in other countries.[169] It is therefore worth investigating, independently of its impact on the choices of other companies, why these large French companies have taken up the reciprocity exception to the mandatory BNR.

Part of the answer might be that the French legislature did not simply make the reciprocity exception to the mandatory BNR available, but also provided a mechanism through which the company could take defensive action. This was the issuance of defensive warrants[170] (*bons Bretons*—after Mr Thierry Breton, the Minister of Economy, Finance, and Industry at the time), based, though with some significant differences, upon the US 'poison pill'.[171] By 2008 seven companies[172] among the CAC 40 had secured resolutions from their shareholders taking up the warrants option. The advantage to companies of a legislative specification of a defensive mechanism which can be used to introduce the reciprocity exception is that doubts arising from general company law about the legality of this type of defensive measure are eliminated or at least significantly reduced.[173] Further, this particular legislatively endorsed defensive measure has no continuing impact on the company's future operations, if it is successful.[174] However, the company is not bound to introduce the reciprocity exception through defensive warrants. French companies which have sought prior shareholder authorization for the issuance of warrants in the face of a takeover from a company not subject to the BNR have also often sought authorization simply to issue fresh capital in those circumstances, whilst others have sought pre-bid authorization for post-bid share issues but not for the issuance of defensive warrants.[175]

Nevertheless, it seems unlikely that one can explain the take-up of the reciprocity exception in France simply on the grounds that the legislature has designed

[169] And to some extent in France itself where no company has chosen to opt into the BTR.

[170] Commercial Code Articles L233-32.II and L233-33.

[171] In particular, the requirement for shareholder approval for the creation and issuance of the warrants. Where the reciprocity exception does not apply, the issuance of the warrants requires shareholder approval post bid: Commercial Code Article L233-32.III. In the US the shareholder rights plan can be adopted on the authority of the board alone, without either pre- or post-bid shareholder approval, assuming, as will invariably be the case, that the company has sufficient authorized but unissued capital. The French scheme also allocates warrants to the acquirer in respect of the shares it already holds—but not, of course, those it has contracted to acquire in the bid—thus respecting the principle of equal treatment of shareholders.

[172] Air Liquide, Bouygues, Essilor, Pernod Ricard, Peugeot, Saint Gobain, Veolia Environnement. See Herbert Smith, *Overview of defences used by companies listed on the CAC 40 to prevent unsolicited takeover bids*, February 2008 (available on <http://www.herbertsmith.com/NR/rdonlyres/64ED9941-EF44-4B7D-B560-FC4087038A43/5567/DefencesOPA_Eng_Feb2008.pdf> [last accessed 1 August 2010]).

[173] See the discussion in Section II.1.(i).

[174] If the bid is withdrawn, as it is overwhelmingly likely to be in the face of the dilutive effect of the warrants, the warrants lapse: Commercial Code Article L233-32.II.

[175] For example, Dexia, EADS, LVMH, Sanofi-Aventis. See Herbert Smith (n 171).

an effective mechanism for making use of it—especially as some companies which have taken up the reciprocity option have not made use of defensive warrants. It is more likely that an explanation can be found in the structure of the shareholdings in French companies. France is known as a country in which state ownership of and intervention in the corporate sector has traditionally been extensive, but also as one in which that role has been substantially reduced in recent decades.[176] Although in the French privatizations the initial aim was to put in place long-term, stable shareholders (*les noyaux durs*), who would discourage takeovers, those holdings too have been eroded since the 1990s.[177] The result is a shareholding structure in large companies which, whilst certainly concentrated, is less so than in many other continental European countries. Becht and Mayer calculated the median size of the largest voting block in the CAC 40 at 20 per cent in the late 1990s, substantially bigger than the UK median figure of 10 per cent but also significantly smaller than that for the other European countries studied, where it was often in excess of 50 per cent and in no other continental European case did it fall below 34 per cent (the Spanish figure).[178] Later work put the percentage of listed companies in France where no single shareholder held more than 25 per cent of the votes at 37 per cent in 2006, as compared with 16 per cent in 1996.[179]

Thus, one can think of France as a country with control in many companies in the hands of multiple large shareholders. This control may be effective in the normal run but is insecure and subject to challenge from an acquirer which may be able to wrest control away from the blockholders by acquiring the shares of the non-controlling shareholders and, possibly, inducing one of the controlling coalition of shareholders to defect. In this situation the controlling shareholders may have an interest *ex ante* in strengthening management against an acquirer by authorizing pre-bid, defensive measures to be taken post-bid. The pre-bid authorization of defensive measures is a form of commitment by the multiple large shareholders to keep control of the company in their own hands and not to sell out to an acquirer. Furthermore, as pointed out above, the change in the shareholder structure typically associated with the announcement of a bid—from a more passive institutions/private investor-mix towards a more activist/hedge-fund-dominated structure—can make this strategy seem even more plausible. The relative lack of interest of the non-controlling shareholders in defensive measures may well not be replicated once a bid is made. However, the arguments in favour of the resolution may not always persuade the shareholders. In 2008 two resolutions (at Capgemini and Vallourec) authorizing defensive share warrants were

[176] V A Schmidt, *The Futures of European Capitalism* (Oxford: Oxford University Press, 2002) esp 117.

[177] B Clift, 'Second Time as Farce? The EU Takeover Directive, the Clash of Capitalisms and the Hamstrung Harmonization of European (and French) Corporate Governance' (2009) 47 J of Common Market Studies 55, 68–9.

[178] M Becht and C Mayer, 'Introduction' in F Barca and M Becht (eds), *The Control of Corporate Europe* (Oxford: Oxford University Press, 2001) 19. The European jurisdictions studied were Austria, Belgium, Germany, Spain, France, Italy, Netherlands, Sweden, and the UK.

[179] Franks and others (n 74) Table 2, panel B.

withdrawn from the AGM agenda at a late stage, apparently for fear they would not be accepted by the shareholders; and although the resolutions proposed at other companies were passed, and passed comfortably, they were among the resolutions receiving the lowest levels of shareholder support.[180]

There is a third element in the explanation of the willingness of French CAC companies to take up the reciprocity option. This relates to the range of alternative defensive mechanisms available. The reciprocity exception is far from a complete protection against an unwelcome bid. It may have the virtue (from the adopting shareholders' point of view) of being usable against US or German companies, which are rarely subject to the equivalent of the BNR, but it is not a protection against a bid from an acquirer located in any jurisdiction where the BNR is mandatory, such as the UK or Sweden. One might expect French controlling shareholders whose position is insecure to seek a protective device that operates across the whole range of acquirers, especially as France has opted out of the breakthrough rule. However, France has long had and still maintains a mini-BTR which catches two pre-bid defences which might otherwise be popular, namely, the voting cap and restrictions in the articles on the transfer of shares.[181] In this context pre-authorized defensive measures may be seen as a useful supplement to the traditional French defensive measure—double voting rights—which some half of the CAC 40 have in place but which again constitute a far from unbreakable defence.[182] Thus, for large French companies whether to seek shareholder authorization pre-bid for the taking of defensive measures post-bid (and notably the issuing of defensive warrants) is a far from straightforward question. There is some risk that the shareholders will not approve the resolution, in which case the company may simply have signalled to the market that it is a potential takeover target. Even if the resolution is approved, it will not be effective in the face of a bid from an acquirer subject to the BNR. On the other hand, pre-bid authorization of post-bid defensive measures may substantially reinforce the defensive measures otherwise available to the company. In the light of these considerations it is perhaps not surprising that the take-up of the reciprocity exception among the CAC 40 has been significant, but not the majority response.[183]

180 HQB Partners, *CAC 40 2008 AGM Season – Trends and Observations*, available on <http://www.hqbpartners.com/upload_files/French%202008%20AGM%20Season%20Review.pdf> (last accessed 1 August 2010) and ibid, *An Overview of the CAC 40 2009 Annual General Meeting Season*, Table 1, available on <http://www.hqbpartners.com/upload_files/CAC%2040%202009%20AGM%20Season%20Review.pdf> (last accessed 1 August 2010).

181 Articles L233-34 and L225-125 of the Commercial Code; Article L231-43 of the General Regulation of the AMF.

182 Herbert Smith (n 171). French companies also tend to have strong disclosure provisions in their articles, giving them advance warning of possible bids, which may be triggered at the 0.5% level and every 0.5% thereafter, requiring shareholders to disclose their intentions as against the company. Some 95% of CAC 40 companies have such provisions.

183 Some 27.5% of CAC 40 companies have in place pre-bid defensive authorization of post-bid defensive action (of one sort or another), as compared with over 50% having double voting rights but only 15% voting caps: ibid.

This analysis may also explain the failure of companies in Spain to take up the reciprocity option. Voting caps are a widely used mechanism in Spanish companies, more frequently used than in any other Member State.[184] This mechanism can provide a truly powerful protection for an incumbent controller, even far below *de jure* control. Thus, a voting cap might be a more attractive pre-bid defence, because it applies across the board, than pre-bid authorization of post-bid defences, which needs to be renewed, in effect annually.

Greece, our third country allowing the reciprocity exception to the mandatory BNR, allowed for pre-bid authorization of defensive measures before the implementation of the Directive. In addition, Greece adheres rather closely to the one share/one vote standard, disallowing, for instance, the issuance of multiple voting shares.[185] From this perspective, the lack of usage of the reciprocity option on the company level might be rather surprising. However, it might be an interesting observation that of the eleven *recently listed* companies examined by ISS,[186] seven used pyramid structures to enhance control and one made use of a shareholders' agreement. This constitutes a significantly higher proportion than in the larger sample drawn from all listed companies (where the one share/one vote principle seems to be more closely followed). One explanation might be found in the implementation of the Takeover Directive, which might have made controllers search for other mechanisms to entrench their control—preferably one that is applicable against all bidders.

Finally, we attempt to explain the non-take-up of the reciprocity exception in Slovenia. Although Slovenian company law does not seem to provide for the typical pre-bid protection devices for incumbents that are available in Spain, no Slovenian company has made use of the reciprocity option so far. In part, this could be explained by the ownership structure of Slovenian companies, with state funds controlling 44 per cent of all listed companies at the end of 2004.[187] Another 25 per cent of the companies are controlled by domestic non-financial companies and 6 per cent by foreign investors, which in average hold 48 per cent and 52 per cent of the shares, respectively.[188] Although the level of ownership concentration is somewhat lower than in other emerging markets (though still high, with the largest voting block averaging 35 per cent of the shares), this partly seems to be the result of relatively high employee stock ownership as a conse-

[184] ISS Europe, ECGI, and Shearman & Sterling, *Report on the Proportionality Principle in the European Union*, External Study Commissioned by the European Commission (2007) 20, available at: <http://ec.europa.eu/internal_market/company/docs/shareholders/study/final_report_en.pdf> (last accessed 1 August 2010).

[185] Ibid, 18.

[186] Ibid, 49.

[187] N Cankar, S Deakin, and M Simoneti, 'The Reflexive Properties of Corporate Governance Codes: The Reception of the "Comply or Explain" Approach in Slovenia' (2008) Centre for Business Research, University of Cambridge Working Paper no 371, available at <http://www.cbr.cam.ac.uk/pdf/WP371.pdf>.

[188] A Gregoric and C Vespro, 'Block Trades and the Benefits of Control in Slovenia' (2009) 17 Economics of Transition 175, 180.

quence of the privatization modalities.[189] Combined with German-type co-determination rules, a coalition between managers and employees might well be regarded as offering sufficient defensive potential against unwanted bidders.[190] In addition, the relative illiquidity of the Slovenian capital market[191] also makes sudden post-announcement shifts in shareholder structures (eg from passive investors towards event-driven hedge funds) far less likely.

VI. Conclusion

One of the Commission's main aims when it proposed a directive on takeovers as long ago as 1989[192] was to secure the introduction of a mandatory BNR in all Member States. Judged by that standard, the Directive as adopted was clearly a major setback for the Commission. The Directive left the decision whether the BNR should be mandatory to the legislative process of each Member State, which, of course, was where the decision lay before the Directive was adopted. To that extent, the Directive simply reproduced the *status quo ante*. However, the Directive did cause all Member States to revisit the policy underlying their existing provisions on the BNR, even if it left them free to determine the mandatory nature of the BNR as they wished, and so caused them consciously to re-affirm or amend their existing national positions.[193] The fact that more than half the Member States[194] imposed a mandatory BNR after transposition of the Directive reflects more than anything else the fact that the mandatory BNR was a feature of Member States' takeover laws before the Directive was adopted.[195] It was no doubt this type of consideration which led the Commissioner responsible for the Directive to remark at the time of its adoption that it was 'not worth the paper it was written on'.[196]

This view of the Directive's provisions on the BNR also suggests that investigation of the results of Member States' transposition of the Directive would not yield anything interesting: the status quo would simply be maintained. The results we report in this paper certainly do not indicate that the overall configuration of Member States' takeover laws in relation to the BNR has changed dramatically

[189] Ibid, 177. [190] Ibid. [191] Cankar and others (n 186).

[192] The initial proposal for a directive on takeover bids was presented by the Commission on 19 January 1989, see n 5. The first report published by the Commission regarding the harmonization of takeover rules, the so called 'Pennington report', dates back to 1974 (COM Doc XI/56/74).

[193] Those states wishing to maintain (as close as possible) their 'score 0' status quo (eg Germany) or who chose this regulatory option after the Directive came into force (eg Hungary) were required to legislate for the company-level opt back in. In fact, in all states the Directive generated a need to reflect upon the national takeover law, including therefore the national provisions on the BNR, as part of the process of transposition of the Directive as a whole, although, in some cases, a Directive-compliant BNR was achieved by encouraging and overseeing amendments to self-regulatory arrangements (eg in Finland).

[194] Fourteen out of the total twenty-seven Member States; see Table 6.1 above.

[195] However, in some countries the decision to adopt a BNR will have been influenced by the expectation of a binding European rule to that end. Such expectations probably existed throughout the 15 years prior to the Directive's adoption.

[196] See n 9 above.

post-transposition. Neither, however, do they show that the status quo has simply been maintained. Unfortunately for the Commission, the changes we have identified show that overall the Member States' takeover rules are now located somewhat further away from the Commission's ideal of a comprehensive, mandatory BNR than was the case before the adoption of the Directive. Only five out of the eleven states that did not have a mandatory BNR before decided to implement it as a consequence of the Directive. At the same time, almost half of the formerly mandatory BNR countries diluted their former choice after the Directive.[197]

However, this headline figure is the product of *three* types of Member State choice (ignoring the choice made by those Member States which simply maintained the status quo). Some chose to adopt a fully mandatory BNR, not having previously imposed such a rule; some moved from a fully mandatory BNR to an optional BNR; and some qualified the previously fully mandatory BNR with the reciprocity exception. We need to look separately at each set of choices.

The decisions by Member States to adopt a fully mandatory BNR, where no BNR was previously imposed, can be claimed by the Commission as an outcome of the Directive which was in line with its original policy objectives. Five Member States[198] took this decision, ie moved from a score of '0' to a score of '4' as a result of transposition. It is also realistic to think that that these national decisions would not have been taken, had the Directive not required the Member States to revisit their takeover rules and indicated to them that the Directive's preferred position was the adoption of a fully mandatory BNR. However, these were all countries with very low levels of hostile takeover activity where, with the possible exception of Finland, the adoption of a mandatory BNR was not a significant decision and where following the Directive's preferred option of a mandatory BNR may have seemed the path of least resistance. Regarding the latter argument, it should also be taken into account that four of these states (again with the exception of Finland) joined the EU after the Directive had been adopted. Given the amount of European legislation in company and securities law, one might expect that the substantial changes these countries had to undergo in order to adopt the *acquis* somewhat weakened possible political resistance.

The weakness from the Commission's point of view of the adoption of a policy of national choice in relation to the BNR is demonstrated by the decision of two states (Hungary and Italy) to abandon a previously fully mandatory BNR in favour of an optional BNR.[199] In terms of economic impact, the decision by these two states to adopt an optional BNR outweighed the decision by the five states just mentioned to adopt a fully mandatory BNR by a factor of three, with Finland representing 88 per cent of the market capitalization of the latter group

[197] This is true for seven of the sixteen relevant countries; see Table 6.2 above.

[198] Cyprus, Finland, Latvia, Malta, and Romania.

[199] Hungary moved from '4' to '0' in our scoring; Italy from '4' to '2'. For the explanation of the '2' score see Section IV.1 above.

of five.[200] This also seems to make it more likely that—with the exception of Finland—the countries that now apply a fully mandatory BNR, where they previously simply attached little significance to such a rule owing to their relatively small capital markets, did not regard the change as an important one. Although the transposition process was not the cause of the decisions taken in Hungary and Italy, the principle of national choice contained in the Directive permitted those states to respond as they did, whereas the Commission's proposed mandatory BNR would have closed off this option.

However, in terms of both numbers of states and economic impact, a bigger move away from the fully mandatory BNR occurred in the case of those five states[201] which moved from a fully mandatory BNR to a BNR qualified by the reciprocity exception, ie they moved from '4' to '3' on our scoring. In this category of case, however, it is arguable that the terms of the Directive as adopted contributed to the decisions taken by these Member States. Certainly, none of the Member States had adopted a reciprocity exception before the Directive and there might well have been considerable uncertainty about its legality. In fact, we suspect that a national rule with the same content as Article 12(3) would have been objected to by the Commission because of its impact on both third-country bidders and bidders from other Member States—especially if the Member State had precisely followed the reciprocity option later included in the Directive (ie it produced an outcome equivalent to a score of 3 by our definition).[202] The Directive itself seems to have conferred legitimacy on the reciprocity exception, by making it available as an option in Article 12(3) The adoption by some states of the reciprocity exception to the BNR is perhaps our most important result, especially given its late inclusion in the Directive and the doubts expressed subsequently by commentators as to whether it was intended to be available as a qualification to the mandatory BNR or only to the company-level voluntary opt-in to the BNR.[203]

[200] That is, in terms of companies (by market capitalization) being subject to the respective regulatory outcomes. See Table 6.4 and Figure 6.3 below.

[201] France, Greece, Slovenia, Spain, and Portugal.

[202] In this case (score 3), the outcome would not restrict any domestic, but only cross-border (including intra EU) acquisitions. To be sure, in theory the question whether or not the current framework is in line with primary EU legislation is still live, but it has far less practical relevance (see the discussion in Section IV.1). In addition, the fact that a score-3 result might have been incompatible with the Treaty before enactment of the Directive does not necessarily mean that it still is. As the BNR is now—to a certain extent—harmonized across the EU, the precondition for access to each Member State's market for corporate control is generally available on the company level (through the compulsory option to take up a mandatory BNR). This certainly removes some of the 'protectionist twist' from this regulatory option.

[203] The compatibility of a 'score 3'-outcome with primary EU law may also bear some relevance in deciding its scope under the Directive. While a country with a score of 0 creates equal conditions for both domestic and EU-companies, in terms of access to the takeover market, a score of 3 could theoretically be seen as creating a certain bias towards domestic restructurings. Although the general availability of the BNR to all companies (via the opt-in) can be regarded as eliminating this problem, this probably also depends on the factual difficulties of making use of it. As pointed out, no companies *actually* make use of the device, which calls into question whether the availability to companies of the option, in itself, is enough to insulate the concept against Treaty-incompatibility.

Our overall conclusion, based on an analysis of the formal rules adopted pre- and post-transposition, is that that there has been a significant shift away from bidder friendliness in the transposition process. Expressing the results of Table 6.1, not in terms of the number of states but in terms of the importance of their national capital markets, we find that countries retaining the status quo (ie the same level of bidder friendliness) constituted 61 per cent of EU market capitalization, those moving in a less bidder-friendly direction constituted 37 per cent of EU market capitalization, and those moving in a more bidder friendly direction constituted a mere 2 per cent of EU market capitalization (see Figure 6.3 and Table 6.4 below). As we suggested in Section IV, there is some evidence that the revision of takeover rules has been influenced by the growth of economic nationalism and a desire by Member States to preserve corporate headquarters and employing entities within their own territories. As shown below, this concerns a large proportion (by value and in numbers) of European listed companies.

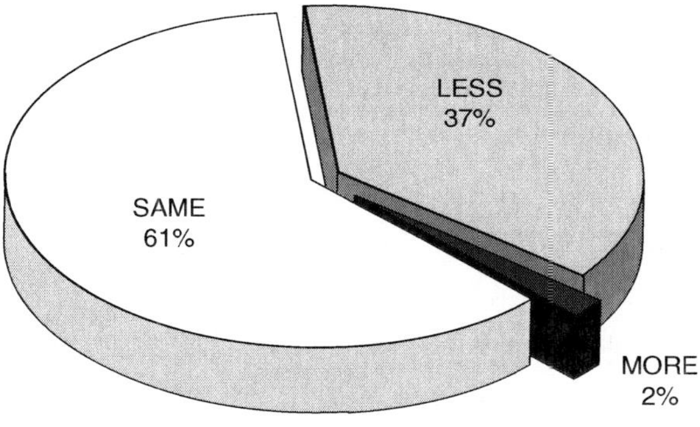

Figure 6.3[203] Changes in BNR status and size of capital market

See also the discussion at n 99 above. As Table 6.1 demonstrates, where Member States have not made the BNR mandatory, they have uniformly made the reciprocity qualification available to companies opting back in (ie there are no states which score '1' under our system; all the non-mandatory states score '0').

[204] Sources: own calculations based on data from the Federation of European Stock Exchanges (available at: <http://www.fese.be/en/?inc=art&id=3>), NYSE Euronext (available at <http://www.euronext.com/fic/000/054/615/546152.xls>), NASDAQ OMX Group (data for the Scandinavian countries available at <http://nordic.nasdaqomxtrader.com/digitalAssets/66/66299_statistics_december_2009_eur.pdf>; data for the Baltic states available at <www.nasdaqomxbaltic.com/market>); London Stock Exchange (available at: <http://www.londonstockexchange.com/statistics/markets/markets.htm>); Wiener Börse AG (available at: <www.wienerborse.at/prices_statistics/statistics/monthly/monatsstatistik.html>) (all last accessed 18 March 2010). All data based on end-of-year 2009; the attempt was made to exclude foreign issuers, secondary listings, and non-regulated markets (to which the Directive does not apply), although some inaccuracies may persist.

Table 6.4 Changes in BNR scores and size of domestic capital markets

COUNTRY	BNR Score Before	BNR Score After	Change in BNR	Market capitalization (MEUR)
Austria	4	4	SAME	79,511
Belgium	0	0	SAME	181,059
Bulgaria	4	4	SAME	6,031
Cyprus	0	4	MORE	7,157
Czech Republic	4	4	SAME	31,265
Denmark	0	0	SAME	131,000
Estonia	4	4	SAME	1,850
Finland	0	4	MORE	141,000
France	4	3	LESS	1,356,491
Germany	0	0	SAME	900,772
Greece	4	3	LESS	78,505
Hungary	4	0	LESS	20,888
Ireland	4	4	SAME	42,720
Italy	4	2	LESS	457,126
Latvia	0	4	MORE	1,317
Lithuania	4	4	SAME	3,220
Luxembourg	0	0	SAME	73,219
Malta	0	4	MORE	2,844
Netherlands	0	0	SAME	389,759
Poland	0	0	SAME	105,157
Portugal	4	3	LESS	68,478
Romania	0	4	MORE	8,402
Slovakia	4	4	SAME	3,614
Slovenia	4	3	LESS	8,462
Spain	4	3	LESS	584,569
Sweden	4	4	SAME	330,000
United Kingdom	4	4	SAME	1,949,352

Our analysis in the previous paragraphs has been based on the formal rules adopted by the Member States. However, our results also shed light on the issue of the design of company-level default rules and on the question of whether the burden of reversing the default should be placed on the management of the company or on the shareholders. The Directive uses company-level defaults in three important areas. First, all Member States which do not make the BNR mandatory must allow companies by shareholder decision to opt into it;[205] second, Member States may permit companies opting back in to the BNR to do so on the basis of reciprocity;[206] third, it seems Member States may make the mandatory BNR subject to a company-level decision, again taken by the shareholders, to apply the reciprocity exception.[207]

205 Article 12(2). 206 Article 12(3).

207 Ibid. Regarding the acceptability of this option see the discussion at n 99 above. As a matter of fact, five states made use of this option.

In the most important of these cases—the decision whether to apply the BNR or not—the Directive therefore requires shareholder action *to restrict* management's discretion. The default is permissive of management—the default is that the BNR does not apply[208]—and the burden of reversing it lies on the shareholders; indeed, they can reverse the default only by supermajority vote.[209] We could not identify a single Member State where the possibility to opt back in, in fact, played any practical role.

We suggest that this (negative) result gives support to the contention of Bebchuk and Hamdani[210] that where the legislature has two ways of expressing the default rule (as restrictive of management or as permissive in relation to management, but in each case reversible by shareholder decision), then the better policy is to choose the restrictive form of the default. This is because the collective action or co-ordination problems of the shareholders make it more likely that an inefficient pro-management default will persist than that an inefficient default constraining management will do so. In the latter case management will easily be able to put the question to the shareholders as to whether the default should be reversed; in the former case, shareholders may be ill-placed to raise the issue and the management (as well as insecure blockholders) will have no incentive to do so. After all, it is very unlikely that shareholders of all companies in '0'-scored countries simply consider the concept chosen by their legislator as the most efficient approach. This point is further emphasized by the abovementioned intention of Fiat, one of Italy's largest listed companies, to opt out of the BNR. The plan to deviate from the restrictive default rule in favour of management's discretion was announced only weeks after the respective changes to the Italian regulation. As mentioned, we could not identify a single shareholder decision running in the opposite direction (ie restricting managerial discretion) in any Member State throughout the preceding four years.)

By contrast, the default in relation to the reciprocity qualification to the mandatory BNR[211] is that reciprocity does not apply, so that the default is, in relation to management, the more constraining of the two forms of the BNR.[212] If management wishes to move to the less constraining form of the BNR, it must seek shareholder approval (which this time can be given by ordinary majority vote). We reported that in the case of France[213] there had been significant voting activity by shareholders of CAC 40 companies in relation to the reciprocity exception, where management had initiated resolutions at annual general meetings seeking pre-bid approval for defensive measures to be taken post-bid against acquirers

208 If the reciprocity exception were widely adopted, that might mean that the default was constraining of the management of acquisitive companies, who might seek to reverse it. However, as we saw in Section III(iii), that situation does not currently obtain.

209 Article 12(2).

210 n 21.

211 Since there has been no opting back into the BNR, the issue of whether to do so with or without reciprocity has not arisen. However, since the default is that there is no mandatory BNR, it would seem that here too the default is the form of the rule that constrains management less.

212 Article 12(3).

213 See above Section V.2.

not subject to the BNR. This similarly supports the Bebchuk/Hamdani analysis. However, we did not find evidence of shareholder voting on the reciprocity exception in the other three[214] countries that made it available in relation to the mandatory BNR. We sought to explain this on the basis of, partly, the availability in those jurisdictions of pre-bid defences which operated generally (ie not only in relation to acquirers not subject to the BNR) and which would therefore be more attractive to management and insecure blockholders, than the reciprocity exception and, partly, of the structure of shareholdings which rendered the controllers' need for bid defences less pressing (and the entrenchment desire of management unachievable).[215]

This leads us to our reform proposal. It is clear that the Commission's initial vision of a mandatory, cross-EU BNR is not attainable. The optional nature of the BNR will therefore in all likelihood have to be retained when the Commission comes to review the Directive in 2011.[216] However, the optional nature of the BNR could be retained whilst restructuring and simplifying it. Our results could be seen as providing some support for an optional approach to the BNR which makes the option solely a company-level choice and which reformulates the default so that the BNR applies unless the shareholders (by ordinary resolution) choose to disapply it. Such a recasting of the law would seem to have two main advantages. First, it would keep the Member States, whose policies are often influenced by economic nationalism, out of the decision-making process.[217] The applicability or not of the BNR could become a matter for company-level decision-making alone. This would be a gain for the Commission's goal of promoting the internal European market, as compared with the provisions of the Directive.

On the other hand, the reformulated option would imply that the Commission gave up on its original objective of imposing a mandatory BNR across the internal market. However, this is probably no bad thing. The 'varieties of capitalism' literature (distinguishing between 'co-ordinated' and 'liberal' market economies)[218] has taught us that there is more than one way of organizing efficient production in a capitalist system and, as important, different Member States have made

[214] This excludes the case of Portugal, as the reciprocity exception applies as an automatic qualification to the BNR; the Portuguese formulation of the reciprocity exception thus does not make it a default rule and so puts it outside the analysis of Bebchuk/Hamdani. See above Section V.2.

[215] One can also note that the low take-up of the reciprocity exception at company level has also reduced the incentives of the controllers of companies in jurisdictions where the BNR is not mandatory to opt into that rule. Irrespective of any non-controlling shareholder pressure to opt in, incumbents in such jurisdictions might have an incentive to opt in as potential acquirers, as a way of preventing potential targets from invoking the reciprocity exception against them. As things stand, that incentive exists only in the case of companies whose acquisition strategy is focused on France.

[216] Article 20.

[217] EU level decision-making does suffer—or at least traditionally has suffered—from the defects of inflexibility and an over-commitment to mandatory rules, but it does manage to dilute national particularism and the influence of purely national elites. See Ferrarini and Miller (n 147).

[218] See Hall and Soskice (n 83) 31.

different choices. From this perspective, imposing rules reflecting one model of firm organization across all Member States, as the Commission traditionally has been committed to doing, is likely to impose significant costs on those Member States which have adopted a different model, whilst conferring only modest gains on those which have already adopted the preferred model.[219]

Central elements in the difference between co-ordinated market economies and liberal market economies are the immediacy of the accountability of management to shareholders and the extent to which management is in a position to make credible long-term commitments to employees in return for human capital investment by the latter. The hostile takeover (or a real threat of it) can be seen as a powerful element in providing for immediate management accountability to shareholders and, in consequence, restricting the ability of management to make credible commitments to employees. Under our proposal a company would be free to choose the form of the BNR (mandatory or otherwise) which best fitted its business circumstances.[220] Where real value can be generated through a more 'entrenched' system, shareholders are likely to approve changes proposed by the management.

Since the company's business model and shareholder body may change over time, it would not be appropriate to make the choice for or against a BNR a once-and-for-all decision. However, the issue of how often the controllers of the company would need to seek shareholder review of the prevailing choice is likely to be a sensitive one. The present 18-month rule for the reciprocity exception in effect requires the shareholders to renew the authorization at successive annual general meetings. In the light of the 'varieties of capitalism' discussion, such a short renewal period might have the disadvantage of being both too short to reap the benefits usually associated with a lower degree of managerial accountability and too long to make use of the disciplinary function of the market. In particular, it would not permit management to make credible long-term commitments to the employees or other stakeholders, as this time horizon does not sufficiently exceed the time frame within which the company will be bound by contractual agreements already. It might therefore be appropriate to allow shareholders to commit the company to opt out of the BNR for periods of up to, for example, five years. However, some form of renewal should, in our view, be introduced. As ownership concentration typically decreases gradually following the initial listing, a once-and-for-all, or hard-to-change rule might otherwise (in the long run) lead

[219] See G Hertig and J McCahery, 'A Legal Options Approach to EC Company Law' in G Ferrarini and E Wymeersch (eds), *Investor Protection in Europe* (Oxford/New York: Oxford University Press, 2006). The Commission's policies can be argued to be doubly incoherent because they do not consistently follow the same model. Thus, its employment law proposals have traditionally followed the 'co-ordinated' model whilst its recent company and financial law proposals have reflected more strongly the 'liberal' model.

[220] This is of course very close to the position Italy has ended up in as a result of its most recent reforms, except that Italy does not require the periodic shareholder revalidation of the opt-out choice which we advocate below. See Section IV.1.

to similarly entrenched structures as in states currently scored zero. Blockholders would have a particularly strong incentive to opt out of the BNR before changing their position from *de jure* to (only) *de facto* controlling. As the pace and strategy of a blockholder's post-IPO divestiture can hardly be foreseen by investors, we do not believe that too much confidence should be put in market forces in this respect.[221]

Thus, opting out of the BNR would replace opting into it, as the Directive currently contemplates. However, the removal of the Member State from the decision-making process on the applicability of the BNR would have a major impact, not only in states which have chosen not to make the BNR mandatory, but also in those states, such as the UK, which have taken the opposite approach. Under our proposal, the UK would no longer be able to insist that the no frustration rule applied to the management of British companies provided the shareholders had voted to remove it. It seems to us that it might be rational for shareholders to decide in some cases to give management more autonomy than the mandatory BNR entails, for the reasons given above, and the disapplication mechanism would be a method, at least in non-securely controlled companies, for the shareholders to commit themselves to a regime of relative management autonomy.[222] This is not an area, it seems to us, where the legislature can clearly say that one approach is obviously more efficient than the other, as the advantages and disadvantages of different models will more likely depend on company- or sector-specific criteria, rather than on a company's state of incorporation. If the shareholders can genuinely decide (and periodically review their decision) whether the rule of post-bid shareholder approval of defensive measures or whether pre-bid approval of defensive measures serves their interests better, we should let them do so.

[221] This is relevant, because in the initial period, where the blockholder holds relatively large proportion of the company's votes (and capital), investors will not see the BNR as having an impact on their wealth (since the incumbent controls the decision in the presence as well as in the absence of a BNR). Only as the blockholder moves to significantly lower proportions of the share capital, or gives up his control completely (through dilution or further share dispositions), the wealth effects for shareholders kick in. It is therefore very hard for investors to assess the net-cost of a charter arrangement to this end.

[222] Or the shareholders might think that the board would be able to do a better job negotiating with a bidder on their behalf it if was not subject to a prohibition on post-bid defences. As we have noted above (text to n 122), the pre-bid decision to opt out of the BNR is likely to be taken by a differently constituted shareholder body than the one which might be asked to approve defensive measures post-bid, because of post-bid activities of arbitrageurs.

7

Varieties of Corporate Governance and Reflexive Takeover Regulation[1]

Andrew Johnston

I. Introduction

This comment is going to examine in greater detail the way in which the optionality provisions of the Takeover Directive[2] accommodate different national varieties of corporate governance and capitalism. It will then briefly address the question of protectionism under the Directive before looking at the use of reflexive regulation in European directives more generally in order to accommodate national varieties of capitalism.

EU law has always been concerned to strike a balance between market integration and the national interest in regulation. However, the Member States differ significantly in their approaches to company law and labour law. There is little or no consensus on the balance between these two areas, the functions they perform, the interests which should be protected, or the methods the law should employ. This posed particular difficulties for the initial vision of European integration, which anticipated that a single market would be created as divergent national regulations were replaced with positive supranational reregulation. As time wore on, and political agreement could not be reached on the terms of the proposed directives, it became clear that it would be impossible to draw up a single set of rules acceptable to all Member States. Imposing a uniform approach to regulation of these more controversial areas would entail significant transition costs for a significant proportion of the Member States, and it is far from clear that those costs would necessarily be outweighed by the benefits of fewer 'barriers' to cross-border dealings. Moreover, it is increasingly recognized—at a theoretical level at least—that changes to one aspect of the legal governance of economic relations

[1] I am grateful to Tonia Novitz and Phil Syrpis as well as participants at the conference on 'Company Law and Protectionism' for helpful comments on this chapter. All errors remain my own.

[2] Directive 2004/25/EC of the European Parliament and of the Council of 21 April 2004 on takeover bids [2004] OJ L142/12.

at national level is likely to have unpredictable spill-over effects into other areas. So, for example, as we will see, changes to takeover regulation may affect adjacent areas such as industrial relations and corporate finance. This goes some way to explaining the political opposition with which proposals for a Takeover Directive were met, and which forced the European Commission to compromise on its vision for market integration on the basis of uniform takeover regulation.

In proposing a European Takeover Directive based on the British City Code (with a strict prohibition on defensive measures by management and a mandatory bid rule), the European Commission appears to have assumed that it was a technocratic measure creating and regulating a market for corporate control without any significant effect on the Member States' freedom to determine how employment relationships should be governed. Of course the Member States did not share this view, and it took some 30 years to reach agreement on an appropriate compromise.[3] As adopted, the Takeover Directive uses reflexive regulatory techniques to increase market integration without imposing uniformity on the Member States or requiring them to subscribe to one particular model of corporate governance. These techniques had already been widely used in directives in which the protection of employee interests was prominent, such as the European Works Council Directive, the General Directive on Employee Information and Consultation, and the European Company Statute. All these instruments are the product of significant compromise, having emerged from earlier proposals which took a more prescriptive approach to employee participation. Similarly, the extension of the reflexive approach to the Takeover Directive was a response to the complexity of the regulatory context.

II. The problem of harmonizing takeover regulation

Any instrument which intends to impose top-down harmonization of national systems of takeover regulation faces formidable obstacles. There is no clear consensus—either in theory or in practice—on what the rules should be. The difficulty is perhaps clearest with regard to the question of whether defensive measures by management should be prohibited.[4]

From a theoretical perspective, neoclassical law and economics, best exemplified by the work of Easterbrook and Fischel, contends that allowing management latitude to take defensive measures can only be a source of unaccountability and therefore agency costs for shareholders.[5] More broadly, because some takeover

[3] On the long history of the Takeover Directive, see A Johnston, 'The European Takeover Directive: Ruined by Protectionism or Respecting Diversity?' (2004) 25 Company Lawyer 270.

[4] However, analogous arguments to those which follow can also be made in relation to pre-bid structures which depart from proportionality between shareholding and control.

[5] F H Easterbrook and D R Fischel, *The Economic Structure of Corporate Law* (Cambridge, MA: Harvard University Press, 1991).

bids will be frustrated, potential bidders will be discouraged from monitoring for underperforming management, will launch fewer bids, and corporate control will be reallocated to a higher valued use more rarely, resulting in fewer social gains. Easterbrook and Fischel therefore argue that 'managers should remain passive and let investors decide whether to tender'.[6] A legal framework which requires this will ensure that there is an adequate supply of potential bidders in the economy, which Manne viewed as a public good.[7]

In contrast to the orthodox approach taken by financial economics, a more institutional perspective on law and economics contends that shareholders are not the corporation's only residual claimants, and that their welfare is therefore not an adequate proxy for social wealth. This approach is perhaps best exemplified by the work of Margaret Blair, who contends that regulatory systems which give management greater security and autonomy make more credible the implicit commitments given by managers to employees and other stakeholders who have incomplete contracts with the company.[8] More specifically, employees will not make vulnerable investments in firm-specific human capital (which cannot readily be redeployed on the labour market) without some kind of assurance that they will share in the gains produced by their specialization to a particular company's assets. This cannot be embodied in a legally binding contract because the returns to specialization cannot be known in advance. Accordingly, managers use non-binding, 'implicit contracts' which are underpinned by trust and repeated interaction between the parties. These supports may be supplemented by procedural law, including the grant of legal rights to employees to information about, or even participation in, corporate governance. Procedures such as these ensure credible information exchange and enable the parties to adapt their implicit contracts and expectations to changing circumstances.[9] These implicit contracts and the quasi-rents generated by investments in firm-specific human capital are not easily observable or valued by outsiders, including the capital market, and cannot be protected by specific regulation because they differ from firm to firm and sector to sector. Indeed, it can be argued—following Coase—that these contracting and observability problems are the very reason for governance of such relationships within the firm rather than on the market.[10] In the absence of some kind of protection against removal from management, a hostile bidder can remove incumbent management, install their nominees, and expropriate the contractually unprotected expectations of employees.[11]

[6] Ibid, 171.

[7] H Manne, 'Mergers and the Market for Corporate Control' (1965) 73 J of Political Economy 110.

[8] M Blair, *Ownership and Control: Rethinking Corporate Governance for the Twenty-First Century* (Washington DC: Brookings, 1995).

[9] O Williamson, *The Economic Institutions of Capitalism* (New York: Free Press, 1985) 302–4.

[10] R Coase, 'The Nature of the Firm' (1937) 4 Economica 386

[11] For the classic discussion of the expropriation explanation of hostile takeovers, see A Shleifer and L Summers, 'Breach of Trust in Hostile Takeovers' in A Auerbach (ed), *Corporate Takeovers: Causes and Consequences* (Chicago: University of Chicago Press, 1988).

If the EU were starting from scratch, and creating a regulatory system before any firms had come into existence, this theoretical controversy would not give rise to great difficulty. The regulator could simply select a preferred model and impose appropriate rules. However, in practice the regulator is trying to impose regulation on national systems which already exist and differ significantly not only in terms of the doctrinal division of functions between labour and corporate law, but also in terms of the mechanisms and orientation of corporate governance more generally. These differences have been explored in some detail in the academic literature on 'varieties of capitalism', which draws a broad distinction between 'Liberal Market Economies' (LMEs), such as the UK and the US, and 'Coordinated Market Economies' (CMEs), such as Germany or the Netherlands.[12] In LMEs, a number of areas which impinge on corporate governance, including corporate finance and employment, are primarily co-ordinated by means of markets and hierarchies, with the latter being subject to considerable control by markets. In contrast, in CMEs non-market relationships play a greater role in co-ordinating these areas, with greater reliance on implicit contracting, consensual decision-making, and strategic interaction.[13] The existence of different 'varieties of corporate governance'[14] calls into question the idea that takeover regulation, which is a key aspect of any national corporate governance system, can and should be fully harmonized.

From a supranational perspective, takeover regimes which permit defensive measures and pre-bid structures that depart from proportionality are obstacles to free movement of capital because they distort patterns of cross-border investment from what they would be in the absence of those rules. They also hinder the cross-border consolidation of European enterprise. From the perspective of LMEs, which generally adopt a shareholder value approach to corporate governance, those takeover regimes are objectionable because they preclude the operation of a market for corporate control, and therefore undermine the principal mechanism by which managers are made accountable to dispersed shareholders. These two perspectives exercised a strong influence on the various proposals for a Takeover Directive, placing the creation of a pan-European market for corporate control at its heart.

However, from the perspective of CMEs, takeover regimes which permit defensive measures and departures from proportionality provide corporate management with a degree of autonomy from shareholders, and therefore provide a firmer foundation for implicit contracts which depend on continuity of

[12] See eg P Hall and D Soskice, 'Introduction to Varieties of Capitalism' in P Hall and D Soskice (eds), *Varieties of Capitalism* (Oxford: Oxford University Press, 2001) and B Amable, *The Diversity of Modern Capitalism* (Oxford: Oxford University Press, 2003). LMEs and CMEs should be seen more as ideal types rather than as a taxonomy which is capable of dealing exhaustively with all aspects of all national systems.

[13] Hall and Soskice (n 12) 8–9.

[14] See for example S Vitols, 'Varieties of Corporate Governance: Comparing Germany and the UK' in Hall and Soskice (eds) (n 12).

management. Such regimes are institutionally complementary to other aspects of national varieties of capitalism, such as pluralist corporate law, participatory industrial relations, and insider systems of corporate finance, with which they have co-evolved. Through their interactions, these different aspects of national systems of capitalism govern corporate resource allocation and ensure managerial accountability to a nationally specific set of corporate constituencies. From their perspective, a market for corporate control risks disrupting this balance of accountability by prioritizing managerial accountability to the shareholder constituency, and therefore risks creating spill-over effects into adjacent areas of law and the economy. The CME perspective was rejected by the Commission, which dismissed the European Parliament's various attempts to include greater protection for employees in the Directive on the basis that 'they have no place in these provisions... only the holders of securities can decide whether or not to sell them and they are therefore the only parties concerned by it'.[15] The Winter Group too rejected any relaxation of the proposed prohibition on defensive measures on the basis that the target board's 'claims to represent the interests of shareholders or other stakeholders are *likely* to be tainted by self-interest'.[16]

Since the Member States are scattered along a spectrum between LME and CME with regard to the way in which their corporate governance systems are co-ordinated, the proposed introduction of powerful norms of managerial passivity drawn from an LME generated a great deal of political opposition from those Member States located closer to the CME end of the spectrum. Prohibiting defensive measures and imposing a breakthrough rule was intended to reduce managerial autonomy and make managers more responsive to the demands of shareholders as mediated through the share price. However, these rules would also weaken the credibility of informal managerial undertakings, undermining the willingness of employees and others to invest in the specialization which gives certain national systems of production their competitive advantage.

III. The move to reflexive regulation

Faced with the difficulty of reconciling these contradictory demands, a reflexive approach to takeover regulation was adopted. The decision to make the most controversial provisions of the Directive optional was a pragmatic response on the part of the Italian presidency of the European Commission to the political deadlock facing the third draft of the Directive. However, similar reflexive solutions had already been adopted in relation to a number of supranational regulations dealing with the rights of employees. Under this approach, the regulatory

[15] COM(2001) 77 final at 5.

[16] *Report of the High Level Group of Company Law Experts on Issues Relating to Takeover Bids* (Brussels: 2002) 21, emphasis added.

measures which are most characteristic of either LMEs or CMEs—and therefore most politically controversial—are introduced by means of reflexive regulatory techniques such as optionality or bargaining against default rules.

Reflexive regulation harnesses existing self-regulatory capacity on the part of Member States or individual companies, and steers it in the regulator's desired direction but without imposing specific outcomes.[17] Using procedural regulation in this way often means that the differences between jurisdictions become smaller and less pronounced, but it also leaves room for experimentation at the level of Member States or individual firms. This is particularly beneficial where it is not clear what the optimal rules are, or indeed, whether a single set of rules is appropriate for all the Member States. Reflexive regulation offers itself as a middle ground between a return to legal formalism and instrumental regulation.[18] It enables law to have some influence over the complex social systems in its environment, whilst its procedural and reflexive orientation reduces the risk that it will irritate them by introducing inappropriate norms.[19]

So, for example, the European Company Statute requires bargaining between management and employee representatives over participation in the new entity—the *Societas Europaea* (SE)—against default rules which will apply in the absence of agreement.[20] The default rules and their application are determined—according to a complex formula—by the rules governing the existing companies which are forming the new entity. This enables individual companies to establish (or not) an employee participation system which fits well with their wider governance environment, while preventing them from using the regulation as a means to escape mandatory national-level employee participation. This complex regulatory compromise ought to ensure the continued viability of employee participation schemes in CMEs without forcing LMEs to introduce employee participation if this would damage existing complementarities between corporate finance and corporate governance, and without creating strong pressure for SEs comprised of companies formerly incorporated in LMEs to bargain for any level of employee participation. It can be seen from this that the question of employee participation—a key institution of many CMEs—is left to the national political

[17] See generally G Teubner, 'Substantive and Reflexive Elements in Modern Law' (1983) 17 L & Society Rev 239–85; G Teubner, *Law as an Autopoietic System* (Oxford: Blackwell, 1993); S Deakin, 'Reflexive Governance and European Company Law' (2009) 15 Eur L J 224. For detailed discussion of the use of reflexive regulation in this context, see A Johnston, *EC Regulation of Corporate Governance* (Cambridge: Cambridge University Press, 2009) ch 6.

[18] C Joerges, 'Integration through De-Legalisation? An Irritated Heckler' (2007) European Governance Papers (EUROGOV) No N-07-03 (available online at <http://www.connex-network.org/eurogov/pdf/egp-newgov-N-0703.pdf>) (last accessed 12 July 2010) 7.

[19] G Teubner, 'Legal Irritants: Good Faith in British Law or How Unifying Law Ends up in New Divergences' (1998) 61 MLR 11.

[20] The European Company Statute consists of Council Regulation (EC) 2157/2001 on the Statute for a European company (SE) [2001] OJ L294/1 and Council Directive 2001/86/EC supplementing the Statute for a European company with regard to the involvement of employees [2001] OJ L294/22.

process and—perhaps—bargaining on the part of the social partners in countries which do not impose mandatory participation.[21] The European Works Council Directive adopts a broadly similar approach of requiring bargaining against default rules.[22] However, in this case, the default rules are standard, giving a stronger steer to the bargaining process. The General Directive on Employee Information and Consultation[23] is the successor to the failed proposal for a Fifth Company Law Directive which, in its strongest form, had sought to impose employee participation on all public companies in the EEC. It abandoned its predecessor's prescriptive approach and uses reflexivity in two distinct ways. First, it is a minimum harmonization directive, which, in theory at least, allows the Member States to impose more far-reaching obligations on companies than those specified in the Directive where they consider them appropriate for the national context. Second, it is a framework directive, which allows the Member States considerable discretion both as regards the institutional form of the regulation and as to whether this area should be regulated prescriptively or left to agreement of the social partners.[24]

Accordingly, reflexive harmonization was already a familiar part of the European regulatory landscape, at least as regards instruments relating directly to the governance of the employment relationship.[25] The extension of the reflexive approach to the Takeover Directive broke new ground because, for the first time, optionality was applied to provisions which went beyond employee rights in the strict sense (although as we have seen the position of employees in the event of a takeover was central to the political controversy). There are clear parallels between the way the Takeover Directive deals with defensive measures and the way the European Company Statute deals with employee participation. Under the compromise solution, both the prohibition on defensive measures and the breakthrough rule were made optional, although Member States which opt out are required to allow companies to opt back in again.[26] From the perspective of varieties of corporate governance, the primary significance of this is that the Directive can accommodate the preferences of both LMEs and CMEs. LMEs can continue to use an active market for corporate control to ensure managerial accountability to shareholders. CMEs do not have to prohibit defensive measures altogether and can therefore rely on managerial autonomy as one means of

[21] For a discussion of the obstacles to voluntary establishment by firms of employee co-determination, see eg D Sadowski, J Junkes, and S Lindenthal, 'The German Model of Corporate and Labor Governance' (2000) 22 Comparative Labor L & Policy J 33, 42–8.

[22] Council Directive 94/45/EC on the establishment of a European Works Council or a procedure in Community-scale undertakings and Community-scale groups of undertakings for the purposes of informing and consulting employees [1994] OJ L254/64.

[23] Council Directive 2002/14/EC establishing a general framework for informing and consulting employees in the European Community [2002] OJ L80/29.

[24] Articles 4 and 5 of Directive 2002/14/EC.

[25] On the role of flexibility in European labour law interventions, see P Syrpis, *EU Intervention in Domestic Labour Law* (Oxford: Oxford University Press, 2007) ch 5.

[26] Article 12 of Directive 2004/25/EC.

underpinning specialization by employees and other stakeholders. At the same time, individual companies which do not value managerial autonomy and wish to subject themselves to greater capital market discipline but which are located in Member States that do not prohibit defensive measures are then able voluntarily to opt into the prohibition. This decision is a matter reserved for the general meeting by the Directive.[27] Since any decision voluntarily to opt into the prohibition will be disclosed to the capital markets,[28] we might expect the consequent greater contestability of control to be reflected in the company in question's share price. A voluntary opt-in by a company in a Member State which has opted out will also send a clear signal to employees and other stakeholders that managers are subject to removal by hostile takeover and that their informal undertakings may not be honoured by their successors. Such companies will therefore either incur much higher transaction costs in giving legal protection to stakeholder expectations or—more plausibly—will adopt production strategies which do not depend on firm-specific human capital.

Davies and others' interesting finding that no companies have chosen to opt in to a prohibition on defensive measures might reflect the existence of strong complementarities between national corporate governance regimes and the production strategies pursued by companies. Since this is a decision for the general meeting, it might be taken as indicating a lack of concern on the part of existing shareholders about existing levels of managerial entrenchment, or perhaps as demonstrating patience on their part. It might also reflect shareholder acceptance that continental managers continue to play the role of 'mediating hierarchs'[29] in more pluralist systems of company law, as opposed to the highly incentivized (economic) agents of the shareholders they have become in LMEs. Alternatively, it might, as neoclassical theorists would argue, reflect either the collective action problem facing shareholders, to which a market for corporate control is the solution, or the ability of majority shareholders to extract private benefits of control at the expense of the minority.

A fully reflexive directive would arguably also have allowed companies in Member States which have opted in to a prohibition on defensive measures to opt out of that prohibition, subject once more to full disclosure to the capital markets. Managers of companies in LMEs would have to persuade the general meeting that they intend to pursue production strategies involving employee specialization, and that in order to do so they require greater autonomy from the short-term demands of the capital markets.[30] Of course, it might be suggested

[27] Ibid. [28] Ibid.

[29] M Blair and L Stout, 'A Team Production Theory of Corporate Law' (1999) 85 Virginia L Rev 247.

[30] A similar argument could perhaps be made as regards mandatory employee participation, although of course it ought to be for the employees—as the beneficiaries of the rights—rather than the shareholders, to decide whether to opt out. This would, however, remove the possibility of using law as a 'beneficial constraint' to steer the operation of the economy as a whole: see W Streeck, 'Beneficial Constraints: On the Economic Limits of Rational Voluntarism' in J Rogers

that general meetings in LMEs would be very unlikely to opt out of the neutrality rule, given existing complementarities between patterns and methods of corporate finance and production strategies. However, Italy's reported decision to reinstate its—recently suspended—prohibition on defensive measures but to allow individual companies to opt out of it in their statutes appears to open up the possibility of companies opting out (albeit that Italy is generally considered difficult to classify as either an LME or CME[31]). It will be interesting to see both whether any Italian companies adopt such a constitutional provision, and also whether such a course of action is legally permissible under the Directive.[32]

This reflexive explanation of the Takeover Directive is important because, when viewed in the light of national varieties of corporate governance, the Directive should be viewed as an attempt to strike a workable balance between integration and national diversity, rather than as a failed attempt to impose a shareholder value model on all national systems of corporate governance. Leaving aside the controversial optional provisions, a number of other provisions of the Takeover Directive increase market integration, in the sense of being broadly encouraging of cross-border investment. As Davies and others note, a mandatory bid rule was introduced for the first time in the Netherlands and its threshold reduced in Greece, the Czech Republic, and Spain. This may enhance market integration by assuring small shareholders that they will share in takeover premia, and therefore encouraging them to invest across borders, counteracting the home country bias of many investors. The price for this, as is widely recognized, is a reduction in the disciplining effect of any market for corporate control as it deters partial bids which might otherwise be launched. As Davies and others note, the mandatory bid rule contained in the Directive may deter some transfers of corporate control. However, market integration rather than industrial consolidation should be the principal aim of the Directive. Sell out rights—which allow non-tendering shareholders to sell their shares following a successful bid—similarly protect investors from pressure to tender, but might also be viewed as raising the price paid for corporate control. Squeeze out rights—which allow a successful bidder to force out non-tendering shareholders—remove the risk of free riders, and therefore reassure bidders that, if successful, they will be able to internalize all the

Hollingsworth and R Boyer (eds), *Contemporary Capitalism: the Embeddedness of Institutions* (Cambridge: Cambridge University Press, 1997).

31 Hall and Soskice (n 12) 21.

32 Italy introduced a board neutrality rule and partial breakthrough rule in 1998. It was suspended by Article 13 of Legge 185/2008 (*decreto anti-crisi*) apparently in response to the financial crisis and the fall in share prices. However, the Council of Ministers decided to reinstate the rule from 1 July 2010. See Il Sole 24 Ore, 18 September 2009 (Riccardo Sabbatini, 'Cadono le barriere anti-Opa'). The *Agenzia Stampa Quotidiana Nazionale* similarly reported that from 1 July 2010 the assembly of shareholders would once again have to authorize defensive measures, although this rule could be derogated from with a provision in the company's statutes. No further details were available at the time of writing.

benefits accruing by virtue of their control of the company.[33] These rights were introduced for the first time in the Czech Republic, Greece, and Spain. The extension of this rule to more Member States ought to encourage more cross-border bids. The relevance of these provisions in practice will vary depending on the incidence of takeovers at national level, which will be strongly influenced, inter alia, by national takeover regulation, the choice of options, and the existing structure of shareholdings. The common rules introduced by the Directive ought to enhance market integration in the form of cross-border capital flows. However, the optional rules reserve freedom to the Member States to determine whether hostile takeovers are desirable at national level in the first place, given their effects in prioritizing the interests of shareholders over all other constituencies.

The double reflexivity of the optionality provisions should be emphasized: they allow both Member States and individual companies to tailor takeover regulation to their particular requirements. This allows an appropriate balance to be struck between the supranational interest in market integration and the national or firm interest in having appropriate and efficient corporate governance. The EU uses reflexive regulatory techniques to harness the self-regulatory capacity of Member States, the capital markets, and individual companies rather than require them to subscribe to a particular variety of corporate governance.

IV. The danger of protectionism

Achieving regulatory differentiation by granting flexibility to the Member States does create a risk that the Member States will act strategically in pursuit of protectionist goals. Whether the Member States have actually used the flexibility permitted by a particular directive for protectionist purposes is an empirical question. Davies and others' paper suggests that the risk of protectionism inherent in the Takeover Directive has not materialized to date to a significant extent. As regards the board neutrality rule, Latvia introduced it for the first time, whereas Hungary revoked its existing rule. In Hungary, in line with the requirements of the Directive, the general meeting can insert a provision in the articles forbidding management from taking defensive measures, although in practice the articles of public companies do not currently contain such provisions.[34] The changes to Hungarian law may have been specifically motivated by the threatened hostile takeover of MOL by an Austrian company OMV, in which

[33] On the economic rationale for squeeze out rights, see G Yarrow, 'Shareholder Protection, Compulsory Acquisition and the Efficiency of the Takeover Process' (1985) 34 J of Industrial Economics 3.

[34] Z Lengyel and B Sahin-Toth, 'Hungary' in *The International and Comparative Legal Guide to Mergers and Acquisitions 2009* (Global Legal Group, 2009) ch 20.

the Austrian government had a significant shareholding.[35] However, it should also be noted that Hungary requires companies with over 200 employees to have one-third employee representation on the supervisory board.[36] A permissive approach to defensive measures would certainly be institutionally complementary with employee co-determination at supervisory board level, and so it may be that Hungary is emerging from transition as a CME.[37] Italy's temporary suspension of its prohibition on defensive measures was discussed above. In contrast, as Davies and others show, the breakthrough rule has not resulted in any significant changes, with only Latvia adopting it in full, and the other Member States maintaining their pre-directive positions.

Even where Member States have taken the option not to prohibit defensive measures altogether, the impact of the Takeover Directive should not be overstated. Managers will not have carte blanche to take defensive measures when faced with a takeover bid because existing national restrictions will continue to apply. Furthermore, it must be emphasized that a more permissive approach to defensive measures reduces the overall likelihood of transfers of corporate control, regardless of the nationality of the corporation which is bidding for control. This makes takeover regulation a rather blunt instrument with which to achieve protectionist goals. Such a course of action was in any event open before the introduction of the Directive because the Court of Justice would have been unable to review national systems which merely permit managers to take defensive measures or allow shareholders to exercise their (disproportionate) voting rights.

Finally, where specific protectionist measures are introduced outside the framework of takeover regulation (eg in relation to particular industries) and therefore beyond the scope of the Directive, the Court's jurisprudence in general—and its robust approach to golden shares in particular—has long demonstrated itself able to distinguish between national measures which are

[35] Act CXVI of 2007 is widely nicknamed 'Lex MOL', although the company is not mentioned by name. Besides revoking the existing prohibition on defensive measures, it included a number of other measures aimed at protecting 'strategic' companies from takeover (see n 38 below).

[36] However, since 2006, it has been possible for public companies to adopt a one-tier board, in which case they must bargain with their employees over participation rights. See L Neumann, 'Employee board representation in Hungary's new company law' (2006, SEEurope, available online at <http://www.seeurope-network.org/homepages/seeurope/file_uploads/hungary_changesin-companylaw112006final.pdf>) accessed 20 January 2010.

[37] The categorization of the variety of capitalism found in Hungary, along with other countries of Central and Eastern Europe, remains a matter of some controversy: see A Nölke and A Vliegenthart, 'Enlarging the Varieties of Capitalism: The Emergence of Dependent Market Economies in East Central Europe' (2009) 61 World Politics 670, 671–2. Nölke and Vliegenthart classify them under the new category of 'dependent market economies' which have 'institutional complementarities between skilled, but cheap, labor; the transfer of technological innovations within transnational enterprises; and the provision of capital via foreign direct investment'. There certainly appears to be a role for employee investments in firm-specific human capital in this account.

protectionist and those which are justifiable responses to market failure in its various guises.[38]

Accordingly, although the Takeover Directive creates scope for Member States to pursue protectionist goals, to date this does not appear to have happened significantly, if at all. Moreover, the Directive does not materially increase the pre-existing risk that Member States will instrumentalize takeover regulation for protectionist purposes.

V. Does European law favour CMEs over LMEs?

The final issue which will be considered in this comment is Davies and others' suggestion that any attempt to defend the optionality provisions of the Takeover Directive on the basis that they accommodate different national varieties of capitalism poses a 'widespread and fundamental' challenge for the 'single market project' more generally. They suggest that, if CMEs have to be accommodated by the Takeover Directive, then similar respect should be shown for the regulatory preferences of LMEs, which would be adversely affected by 'the importation of institutions from co-ordinated economies which might undermine, for example, the flexibility of liberal labour markets, for example, restrictions on working hours or on the employment of atypical workers'.

A couple of comments will be made in response to this suggestion. First, it is far from clear that the rules being introduced in, for example, the Directive on Temporary Agency Work,[39] are characteristic of CMEs rather than LMEs. CMEs are widely regarded as gaining competitive advantage, inter alia, by means of labour specialization and incremental innovation in systems of diversified quality production.[40] In fact, the governance structures which underpin these processes of specialization by 'insider' employees quite often operate to the disadvantage of 'outsiders' who have short-term, casual labour relationships. LMEs, in contrast, gain legitimate competitive advantage through radical innovation.[41] Their institutions ensure, inter alia, that capital can be allocated swiftly and effectively into growth industries, and that it is cheap and easy to

[38] In the context of the discussion of Hungary above, it is worth noting that the European Commission sent a formal notice to Hungary challenging the compatibility with the Treaty of various provisions of the Act CXVI of 2007, including a right for the Hungarian Energy Office to appoint a member of energy companies' boards, and a requirement of bidder approval in relation to takeovers of companies of strategic importance. See IP/07/1681, 13 November 2007. The infringement procedure was closed when Hungary repealed the allegedly offending provisions.

[39] Directive 2008/104/EC of the European Parliament and of the Council of 19 November 2008 on temporary agency work [2008] OJ L327/9.

[40] See for example W Streeck, 'Productive Constraints: On the Institutional Conditions of Diversified Quality Production' in W Streeck (ed), *Social Institutions and Economic Performance* (London: Newbury Park, 1992).

[41] Hall and Soskice (n 12) 38–9.

incorporate and dissolve companies. While it may be true that some companies in the UK seek to gain competitive advantage through exerting their superior bargaining power over non-unionized, agency labour in order to lower wage costs, this is neither essential to the competitive advantage of the UK as an LME, nor legitimate. The essential point is that companies in both CMEs and LMEs use agency workers, and the Directive seeks to strike a balance between the corporate interest in having access to a flexible supply of labour and the labour interest in supplying labour on reasonable terms, rather than prevent the use of agency labour altogether.

Second, as was noted above, directives which govern the employment relationship have long made use of reflexive techniques in order to achieve political agreement. Indeed, the use of reflexive regulatory techniques was pioneered precisely in those areas in which the regulatory traditions of the Member States differed. The Directive on Temporary Agency Work is no exception.[42] It contains reflexive provisions allowing the Member States to decide whether to introduce specific regulation or to allow the social partners to implement the requirements of the Directive so as to ensure compatibility with national systems of industrial relations.[43] More importantly, there is further reflexivity allowing the social partners to derogate from the Directive's core provision that the basic working and employment conditions of agency workers should be 'at least those that would apply if they had been recruited directly by that undertaking to occupy the same job'.[44] Further, Member States are allowed to impose a 'qualifying period' before the obligation kicks in.[45] The key point being made here is that the Directive does not prevent LMEs from making widespread use of temporary agency labour in order to respond flexibly to changes in product market demand. It remains open to them to contract for their labour requirements in this way. What they cannot do is gain competitive advantage over companies in other Member States by paying lower wages to agency workers than they do to workers they have recruited themselves. The Directive therefore cannot be viewed simply as discouraging corporations in

[42] The history of the Agency Work Directive is almost as tortuous as that of the Takeover Directive, being traceable back to the 1974 Social Action Programme, the subject of failed negotiations between the social partners under Article 139 in 2001 and 'continually reprocessed and watered down' in response to opposition from 'certain Member States': see N Countouris and R Horton, 'The Temporary Agency Work Directive: Another Broken Promise?' (2009) 38 Industrial L J 329, 329.

[43] See Article 11 and para 16 of the Preamble to Directive 2008/104/EC.

[44] Article 5. 'Basic working and employment conditions' are defined in Article 3(1)(f) to include duration of working time, holidays, and pay. Article 5(4) allows a derogation where the social partners agree and an 'adequate level of protection is provided'.

[45] Countouris and Horton (n 42) 333. They emphasize that this will allow the UK to implement the Directive on the basis of a TUC-CBI agreement providing for a 12-week qualifying period (in contrast to the 6-week period envisaged by the Commission), effectively excluding 55% of British agency workers from the protection offered by the Directive.

LMEs from using agency labour.[46] Indeed, Article 4(1) even requires Member States which impose restrictions on agency work to justify their restrictions on the grounds of general interest.[47]

The Directive on Working Time[48] is similarly a reflexive regulatory measure. Based on Article 137(2), its ostensible goal is to ensure worker health and safety,[49] but it too contains a number of derogations which were 'political concessions granted to the UK and other Member States'.[50] Article 17(1) allows the Member States to derogate from the core limitations on working time where 'on account of the specific characteristics of the activity concerned, the duration of the working time is not measured and/or predetermined or can be determined by the workers themselves'. Article 22 also gives Member States the option of not limiting the working week to 48 hours, provided they require employers to obtain the workers' agreement to work more than 48 hours, prevent employers from subjecting workers who refuse to detriment, and require employers to maintain records of the hours worked by such employees and make them available to the regulatory authorities. These derogations appear adequate to accommodate Member States which do not wish to prevent companies from requiring employees to work long hours, although they are not exactly encouraging of this course of action. While long working hours may characterize entrepreneurial start-ups engaged in radical innovation, and therefore amount to one of the sources of competitive advantage of LMEs, it seems strongly arguable that the Directive makes adequate provision for the diversity of the Member States in this regard. Indeed, it appears specifically to recognize the role of the entrepreneurial employee by making specific reference to derogation in relation to 'managing executives or other persons with autonomous decision-taking powers'.[51]

[46] In fact the Directive does not seek to prevent the Member States from allowing corporations to use agency labour in order to evade the application of, for example, the European Works Council Directive: although Article 7(1) requires that Member States must count agency workers for the purposes of the thresholds in relation to the 'temporary work agency', Article 7(2) merely gives the Member States an option as to whether agency workers should be counted towards the threshold for a Works Council in the company in which they are temporarily employed.

[47] Countouris and Horton (n 42) 336. They emphasize that this will affect Member States such as France and Italy which have laws restricting the use of temporary agency work.

[48] Directive 2003/88/EC of the European Parliament and of the Council of 4 November 2003 concerning certain aspects of the organization of working time [2003] OJ L299/9.

[49] R Hobbs and W Njoya, 'Regulating the European Labour Market: Prospects and Limitations of a Reflexive Governance Approach' (2005) 43 British J of Industrial Relations 297, 310. They emphasize that there is 'only weak and equivocal evidence to support the imposition of a 48-hour weekly limit on the grounds of protecting the health and safety of workers'.

[50] Ibid, 299. Article 18(1) of the 2003 Directive's predecessor contained an opt-out which was widely used by UK companies: C Barnard, S Deakin, and R Hobbs, 'Opting out of the 48 Hour Week: Employer Necessity or Individual Choice? An Empirical Study of the Operation of Article 18(1)(B) of the Working Time Directive in the UK' (2003) 32 Industrial L J 223. Indeed the UK was initially the only Member State which implemented the individual opt-out: see Hobbs and Njoya (n 49) 304.

[51] Article 17(1) of Directive 2003/88/EC.

In fact, the true equivalent of imposing a prohibition on defensive measures on CMEs would be imposing mandatory employee co-determination on LMEs, something which was proposed in the first draft of the Fifth Directive, made optional in the second draft of the Directive, before being abandoned altogether and superseded by Directive 2002/14/EC. Likewise, earlier proposals for a European Company Statute which took a prescriptive approach to employee participation were abandoned in favour of the reflexive solution outlined above. Instead, it remains a matter for the Member States to decide whether to impose mandatory co-determination, although those that do so might have to justify that choice if their rules are challenged as a restriction on free movement of capital.[52]

[52] On the possibility of justifying mandatory co-determination, see Johnston (n 17) ch 5.

8

Cross-Border Restructuring—Company Law between Treaty Freedom and State Protectionism

Jesper Lau Hansen

Company law governs two important methods of restructuring, that of mergers and of takeovers, that may be applied within the European Union and are as such protected by the freedom afforded by the Treaty. Both entail a change of control that may conflict with the desire of a Member State to protect certain industries and maintain its influence by special regulation in the form of golden shares and the like. This chapter explores this conflict to establish the balance of interests reached by the Court of Justice of the European Union in recent case law.

I. Scope of chapter and observations on protectionism

Protectionism has a nasty ring to it, and well deserved according to the broad economic consensus. Few things gather more support among economists than the proposition that free trade is beneficial to society and that state protectionism prevents that.[1] And yet protectionism is widely embraced by elected politicians, has been for generations, and shows no decline, especially not now that we have just experienced a global crisis, which may even linger on for some years. It may be useful to speculate why protectionism displays such an attraction to politicians and the great masses that vote for them.

To serve and protect, is often how the state defines its role and this is what most of the electorate has come to expect of it. Viewed in this light, protectionism

[1] Free trade is used here as shorthand for all activities connected with economic intercourse across borders, including the movement of people, goods, services, and capital. The 1957 Treaty of Rome was in this way a treaty to provide 'free trade' within the signatory Member States and thus created a common, later renamed internal, market and the Treaty's Four Freedoms should be viewed as integrated elements in this wider concept.

describes the stance the state will take in order to do what it does best, that is, to regulate society and direct its subjects and resources according to its policy. Protectionism is more, though, than mere regulation; it has an exclusive element, that of warding off somebody, usually somebody foreign. This then, is what shall serve as a first stab at a pragmatic definition of protectionism in this chapter: actions by a state to ensure its capability to control by legislation, decree, or other means resources that might otherwise be controlled by foreigners. Although directed at foreigners, protectionism does not necessarily discriminate; it may subject foreign and own nationals to the same treatment, but as a policy it is normally only described as protectionism, if at all, when made with special attention to the anticipated activities of foreigners.

The continued popularity of protectionism is only partly explained by a persistent lack of knowledge about basic economic facts among the general public; it is also assisted by a close relationship to those very facts by some. The benefits of free trade fall, as is the case with those derived from creative destruction, to society at large, but they do not necessarily fall on all, and as a former prime minister of the United Kingdom once astutely observed, there is no such thing as society, there are only individuals. Thus, the benefits may befall some, and the more negative consequences such as job losses may fall on others. Even in a redistributing welfare society, that may create problems for politicians seeking re-election. To put it crudely: the benefits of free trade are buried in the annual statistics; its problems are all over the front page and the six o'clock news.

All this is not to deny the benefits of free trade and the urgent need to curb protectionism, it is simply to remind us that the state may have sensible and bona fide reasons to interfere in the economy, which must be observed when drawing the line between the acceptable and the unacceptable actions of the state. For that reason, in this chapter 'protectionism' will be used solely to denote the unacceptable actions, ie actions that violate the state's obligations in international law. This has the added benefit of preserving the sinister connotations of the phrase, which may prove useful in the public debate.

Furthermore, the scope of this chapter is limited to company law and the possibilities of restructuring that it provides. Within company law a distinction is usually made between restructuring by way of merger or by takeover. Although the distinction is merited by the different legislation available, the practical difference is negligible as evidenced by the fact that professionals routinely refer to this area as M&A (mergers and acquisitions). The common denominator is the change of control that is most often a necessary prerequisite to the restructuring.

The broader concept of protectionism is in this setting transformed to the narrower question of when a Member State of the EU violates its obligations under European law.[2] The 1957 EEC Treaty Article 221 (now Article 55 TFEU)

[2] 'European law' is in this chapter used to avoid a distinction between the present former regime, where primary Treaty law and secondary law derived from it could be described as 'Community

provided national, ie non-discriminating, treatment to citizens of other Member States in respect of investment in companies or firms covered by Article 58 (now Article 54 TFEU) after a transition period of three years. Freedom of establishment according to Article 49 TFEU provides the right for physical persons or legal persons according to Article 54 TFEU to establish themselves in another Member State. The scope provided by the free movement of capital was less evident, but the Court of Justice has found that Article 1 of Directive 88/361 that was adopted on the basis of Articles 69 and 70(1) EEC still has an indicative value for the purposes of defining the notion of capital movements, even though its basis in the Treaty has since been replaced by Article 73b et seq of the EC Treaty (now Articles 63 et seq TFEU), because Article 73b EEC substantially reproduces its contents.[3] The nomenclature in respect of movements of capital annexed to Directive 88/361 is not exhaustive, but Points I and III set out in Annex I and the explanatory notes appearing in that annex, indicate that direct investment in the form of participation in an undertaking by means of a shareholding or the acquisition of securities on the capital market constitute capital movements within the meaning of Article 63 TFEU. The explanatory notes state that direct investment is characterized, in particular, by the possibility of participating effectively in the management of a company or in its control. Consequently, interference by a Member State with those two freedoms in relation to company law would amount to protectionism.

II. Protectionism in company law

Protectionism in company law will usually take the form of interference with the mechanisms that allocate power and hence control within a company. These mechanisms are traditionally treated within company law under the title of corporate governance. The governance structure of a company may vary among jurisdictions as it is one area that has so far escaped harmonization within the EU; however, it is possible to discern some common mechanisms. As a creature of our legal imagination, the company does not exist and has to rely on physical persons to act on its behalf, ie to manage it.[4] Furthermore, the company is usually relied upon as a vehicle to attract investment from outside investors and they will require some sort of supervision of their investment and how it is used. Thus, a company will usually comprise at least two bodies vested with the management of the company and the supervision of management.

law', and the coming regime resulting from the Lisbon Treaty, whereby the said law can be described as Union law, as the transfer of regimes has had only a negligible effect.

[3] Case C-222/97 *Trummer & Mayer* [1999] ECR I-1661 para 21.

[4] This is readily accepted in all jurisdictions. In English law, reference could be made to Lord Coke's observations in *Sutton Hospital*, (1612) 10 Co Rep 23a, 77 ER 960.

The power to appoint managers, or directors as the most senior managers are often called in company law, is usually vested with parties who have a special interest in the company, although it can be done by self-appointment.[5] The most widespread way of appointing directors is by letting a general meeting of shareholders vote on who should be appointed. This probably owes its popularity to the fact that it provides the shareholders *qua* investors with the possibility of changing management if they are disappointed with the way the company is being run. In this way, being able to vote for management provides shareholders with a measure to counter the inherent risk in their investment, ie that the company will not turn the expected profit. It should be noted that shareholders are not the only investors who may appreciate such powers; other investors who may have made direct loans (banks) or bought debt instruments (bond holders) may require certain control rights to secure their investment, including the right to appoint directors.[6] But as these investors are normally not entitled to share the profits of the company, as are shareholders, they are less interested in maximizing the profitability of the company and often prefer economic security, in the form of pledges, mortgages, and liens, which provide better cover of their limited claims against the company.

Consequently, a company is usually governed by directors, who are ultimately in charge of managing the company, and the directors or a considerable part of them are appointed by a general meeting of shareholders, who vote to fill vacancies by using the votes applicable to their shares and in this way supervise management.[7]

In this setting, voting according to the rights attached to shares issued by the company is the mechanism for control of the company. Interference with this mechanism can be done in several ways. A share does not have to provide voting rights. It is distinct from a bond and is defined by the fact that it grants a right to the residual proceeds of the company. Whether it provides voting rights and to what extent is not a defining character of a share, but depends on the conditions approved by the company that issued it and the investor who subscribed for it and reflects the parties' opinion on the balance of risk and reward.[8] Thus, shares may be vote-less, provide a fraction of the votes provided by other shares of the company or a multiple thereof, or may only provide voting rights in certain

[5] Although it is rare in its most naked form, some jurisdictions, such as the Dutch regime of corporate governance, display this feature, but most often self-appointment is provided *de facto* and not *de jure* by relying on the passivity of those legally empowered to appoint, eg the appointment of directors by way of proxies to the board collected from disinterested shareholders.

[6] Other control rights may be more specific, eg the right to approve or veto certain actions or decisions.

[7] As the general meeting normally only congregates once a year, a specific body may be set up to supervise management. Where such a body is missing, supervision is done by the general meeting, notably by deciding on the annual accounts presented to them.

[8] See WG Ringe's discussion of the OSOV principle in ch 10 of this volume.

circumstances or in respect of certain decisions.[9] Whereas these voting rights are determined by the shares that provide them, the overall votes available may be limited by provisions in the articles of association of the company, notably by setting a ceiling over how many shares may be owned by one person, which ultimately limits the votes available to any shareholder (holding ceiling), or more directly by limiting the votes available to any one shareholder irrespective of how many votes the shareholder owns (voting ceiling). As these measures are easily circumvented by distributing shares among related parties, they are often supplemented by provisions that define the concept of 'related parties' and dictate that they should be treated as one shareholder. These measures are known as control enhancing mechanisms (CEMs) and are all intra-company measures insofar as they are determined by the articles of association of the company.[10] As such they are subject to disclosure by way of the First Company Law Directive that requires Member States to operate company registers where articles of association of limited liability companies are made publicly available.[11]

Most and sometimes all of the intra-company CEMs just described are available in the company law of the individual Member States, although it may vary within the different jurisdictions as to which measures are considered lawful. Even where a CEM is lawful within a Member State, it may be almost unknown as the use of the different CEMs appears to display a considerable path dependency.[12] For example, a share that increases its voting rights depending on the holding period of its owner (loyalty share) is lawful in Denmark and the other Nordic Member States but practically unheard of, whereas multiple voting rights attributed to a particular class of shares are ubiquitous. This difference is interesting as the holder of the said class of shares usually owns the shares for a considerable period of time and could use loyalty shares as a substitute for the class distribution of voting rights.

[9] Some preferential shares are vote-less as long as they pay a specified dividend, but acquire voting rights in years where the specified dividend is not paid. This is known, inter alia, in Germany and Finland. According to the new Danish Companies Act of 2009, a share with a right of representation carries no votes in ordinary decisions of the general meeting but can participate in more important decisions requiring a qualified majority. Other shares may provide additional votes if held by the same owner for a defined period, which is known in France. The benefit is to reward 'loyalty' to the company, ie its management; the drawback is a lock-in effect that hampers transfer of control. See ch 10.

[10] Other forms of CEM that are not intra-company measures comprise cross-holdings and pyramidal ownership that rely on agreements and co-operation among shareholders outside the remit of the individual company (inter-company measures).

[11] Cf on disclosure Article 2 of the First Council Directive 68/151/EEC of 9 March 1968 on co-ordination of safeguards which, for the protection of the interests of members and others, are required by Member States of companies within the meaning of the second paragraph of Article 58 of the Treaty, with a view to making such safeguards equivalent throughout the Community. Later amended by Directive 2003/58/EC.

[12] This path dependency is probably explained simply by the prevalence of tradition within advisors such as commercial lawyers and the preference for recognizable measures among their clients as there appear not to be any legal obstacles.

The question of protectionism becomes relevant in company law when a company's home Member State makes use of one or more of these measures to provide control.

III. Where to expect protectionism

The level of engagement by the Member States of the EU in commercial enterprises, utilities, and the like has changed considerably over the years. In the reconstruction period following the devastations of World War II, the level was quite high with many different industries being either vigorously regulated or nationalized outright. In fact, the embryonic beginning of the EU in the European Coal and Steel Community of 1951 could be viewed as a (supra-)nationalization of these industries, and the powers provided for a High Authority (now the European Commission) in the ECSC Treaty are testament to the belief in technocratic planning that was shared by most at the time. It was, after all, a period when it was widely believed that the Soviet Union was a powerhouse that would eventually provide better living conditions to its citizens by way of central planning. Following the sclerotic 1970s, a disenchantment with central planning set in and a wave of privatization swept across Europe that has persisted, albeit with occasional highs and lows, until the Financial Crisis of 2008 that may have signalled a change or at least a renewed interest in more direct involvement by Member States into areas as diverse as the production of cars and banking. This latest development is, however, too early to be fully understood and this chapter will instead focus on the era of privatization.

Contrary to popular belief, the wave of privatization of the 1980s and 1990s did not necessarily entail deregulation. Member States often continued to pursue their policy and retain their influence over company management, either through sector legislation or by interference with the control mechanisms of the newly privatized companies to maintain their influence even after privatization. While sector legislation as legislation in general may be contrary to the Treaty's freedoms or provisions on competition and amount to protectionism, the focus of this chapter is on the use by Member States of intra-company CEMs as measures to interfere with and possibly obstruct cross-border restructuring.

In this respect, the decisions of 4 June 2002 by the Court of Justice in case C-367/98, *Commission v Portugal*, case C-483/99, *Commission v France*, and case C-503/99, *Commission v Belgium*, are of particular interest.[13] Here the Member State used legislation to provide the necessary CEM. Portugal prohibited foreign

[13] Available online at the Court's homepage and reported as [2002] ECR I-4731, [2002] ECR I-4781, and [2002] ECR I-4809, respectively. On the decisions and the cases leading up to them, see E Flynn, 'Coming of Age: The Free Movement of Capital Case Law 1993–2002' (2002) 39 CML Rev 773–805.

acquisition of more than 25 per cent of newly privatized companies and required a prior consent by the relevant minister to the acquisition of 10 per cent or more irrespectively of nationality. France used legislative powers to provide special rights to a state-owned share (a.k.a. a golden share) in the oil company Elf-Aquitaine, whereby the prior consent of the relevant minister was required in respect of acquisitions of one-tenth, one-fifth, or one-third of its shares, two ministers were granted the right to appoint a director each, and the relevant minister was provided with a power to veto any agreement to divest the majority in four subsidiaries. Belgium also assigned by way of legislation special rights connected to a golden share in two energy companies (SNTC and Distrigaz) which enabled the relevant minister to veto transfers of the energy net or other decisions of strategic importance to the companies and conferred on the relevant minister the right to appoint two directors in each company with power to request the minister to annul management decisions deemed to be contrary to government energy policy. Although the Advocate General proposed a more cautious approach leaving considerable room for Member States to make such arrangements, the Court of Justice found them to be contrary to the principles of free movement of capital and the freedom of establishment and as such to constitute protectionism as defined here. These findings by the Court were re-affirmed by a so-called second generation golden share cases that differed slightly by virtue of the fact that the CEMs were incorporated into the articles of association of the companies.[14]

Although the golden share cases are well known and are now considered settled law, it is nevertheless useful to look more closely at AG Colomer's Joint Opinion of 3 July 2001 in the original three cases as it raised some questions that continue to merit attention. The Advocate General found the Portuguese public law provision on 25 per cent acquisitions to be discriminatory and contrary to what is now Articles 49 and 63 TFEU, but accepted the other non-discriminating CEMs, including those of the French and Belgian cases, as valid regulations of property rights by Member States within Article 345 TFEU. According to AG Colomer, Article 345 TFEU, with its long pedigree in European law originating in the Schumann Declaration, would allow Member States to pursue their economic policy through the possession of securities, administrative authorization, provisions in the articles of association, or any other means allowed in private or public law.[15] Considering the prevalence of nationalization of industries at the time of

[14] The first golden share cases cited in n 13 above all concerned CEMs provided by legislative measures, but the second generation golden share cases reached the same outcome even where the CEM was provided for in the articles of association. See the Court's decision of 13 May 2003, *Commission v United Kingdom* [2003] ECR I-4641, regarding the newly privatized airport operator BAA, which was already pending at the time of AG Colomer's Opinion. Other second generation cases concerned the decision of the same date in Case C-463/00, *Commission v Spain*, [2003] ECR I-4581, and the Court's decision of 28 September 2006 in Joined Cases C-282/04 and C-283/04 *Commission v Netherlands*, [2006] ECR I-9141 that concerned the sequential privatization of postal services (KPN and TPG).

[15] Cf para 65 of his Joint Opinion.

the founding treaties, this is a likely interpretation. More generally, he rejected that the Member States were faced with the choice of either outright nationalization or a full abstention towards privatized companies,[16] which would require a justification of any interference based on the *Gebhard*-like test of imperative requirements in the general interest.[17] If a Member State could nationalize a company, it could also settle for the less intrusive option of regulating ownership among the shareholders; if it could overtake the entire management, it could limit itself to decide on certain more important decisions, as long as the Member State did not use these powers to discriminate against citizens of other Member States.

One inherent weakness of this argument was the recognition that Article 345 TFEU did not set aside the other provisions of the Treaty and that the Member States may in fact violate their Treaty obligations even when pursuing their policy in respect of privatized companies.[18] On this, at least, the Court of Justice agreed. The Court stressed that the prohibition in Article 73b (now Article 63 TFEU) went beyond the mere elimination of unequal treatment on grounds of nationality,[19] and found that the CEMs amounted to impediments that were likely to render the free movement of capital illusory.[20] Having settled that the CEMs were restrictions, the Court turned to their justifications and found the Member States' arguments insufficient. In this test of general interest, the Court cannot be expected to substitute the opinion of elected politicians with that of its own and consequently, the test will not so much turn on whether the measure in question pursues a reasonable objective but on what is basically a proportionality test that may be subdivided into different aspects, notably whether the measure is suitable for the purported objective, whether it goes further than necessary, and to what extent it constitutes a violation of the Treaty. It was in respect of this test

[16] Ibid, para 60 and again in para 66. In para 41 reference is made to the Commission's Communication on certain legal aspects concerning intra-EU investment ([1997] OJ C220/15), where the Commission acknowledges that Member States are free to nationalize companies as this is within Article 222 (now Article 345 TFEU).

[17] The Commission had pointed to the Court's decision of 30 November 1995 in Case C-55/94 *Gebhard* [1995] ECR I-4165 regarding the freedom of establishment. On this test and the distinction between justification of measures that are either discriminative or just a non-discriminating hindrance for inter-state activity, see J Lau Hansen, 'Full Circle: Is there a Difference between the Freedom of Establishment and the Freedom to Provide Services?' in M Andenas and W H Roth (eds), *Services and Free Movement in EU Law* (Oxford: Oxford University Press, 2002) 197–209. For a later and fuller argument that the four freedoms are now treated by the Court in a similar manner, see P Oliver and W H Roth, 'The Internal Market and the Four Freedoms' (2004) 41 CML Rev 407.

[18] *Gebhard* (n 17) para 68. See also the unsuccessful attempt in para 81 of the opinion to distinguish the Court's decision of 1 June 1999 in Case C-302/97 *Konle* [1999] ECR I-3099.

[19] See inter alia para 40 of Case C-483/99 *Commission v France*. This line of reasoning was restated in the other decisions of that day.

[20] Ibid, para 41. The Court found the free movement of capital in the form of direct investment so closely connected to the freedom of establishment, that it made only a cursory reference to the violation of the latter freedom, cf para 56 of Case C-483/99 *Commission v France*. This line of reasoning was restated in the other decisions of that day.

of proportionality that the Court found the CEMs to be unjustified. As expected, the Court did not reject the argument of the Member States that certain industries could be of strategic importance which could merit special regulation to safeguard public policy, eg the oil supply as in the French case, but restricted the scope for the public measures that could serve as CEMs, notably that they should appear objective and enable the citizens to estimate their application and citizens should have a legal remedy, eg recourse to the courts, to ensure the objective application of the measures.[21]

The outcome of the golden share cases could at first glance appear to present a paradox as to the use of CEMs. It is perfectly legal according to the national company law of most Member States to have CEMs and a Member State may own shares in national companies and yet a Member State is forbidden to make use of the same measures that are available to other shareholders. Provisions that serve to determine the suitability of shareholders and that may grant public authorities the right to refuse ownership of shares in companies within certain important sectors such as banking are mandated by European law,[22] but are in violation of European law when applied by the Member States in connection to a golden share. Interference with managerial decisions by a Member State may constitute a CEM that amounts to protectionism if provided by a golden share because it may dent investors' desire to invest in the company, while it is considered appropriate by European law to interfere with other managerial decisions, eg on remuneration of directors[23] although it may discourage investors from investing no less if the company is prevented from rewarding its talent as it sees fit.

This treatment of CEMs in European law may be less of a paradox than it first appears. Although the CEMs applied in the first three cases were familiar features of company law, and in the second generation cases even placed in the articles of association where they would appear alongside other CEMs, their introduction

[21] The Court noted that such particular interest could be acceptable in industries 'involving the provision of services in the public interest or strategic services', cf para 43 Case C-483/99 *Commission v France*. This line of reasoning was restated in the other decisions of that day. In particular, the Court of Justice accepted the French Government's decision that the safeguarding of supplies of petroleum products in the event of a crisis was within the ambit of a legitimate public interest, cf para 47.

[22] See, inter alia, Article 12 of Directive 2006/48/EC of the European Parliament and of the Council of 14 June 2006 relating to the taking up and pursuit of the business of credit institutions that calls for Member State scrutiny of shareholders with qualifying holdings to ensure 'sound and prudent management'.

[23] Following the excessive risk taking by financial institutions that led to the present financial crisis and which appears to have been driven by a no less excessive remuneration of the risk takers, it has become popular European policy both at a European level and at the national level to regulate this area of a company's internal affairs, see, inter alia, Commission Recommendation complementing Recommendations 2004/913/EC and 2005/162/EC as regards the regime for the remuneration of directors of listed companies, 30 April 2009, C(2009) 3177; Commission Recommendation on remuneration policies in the financial services sector, 30 April 2009, C(2009) 3159; and Statement from the European Corporate Governance Forum of 23 March 2009 on director remuneration.

was not the outcome of an ordinary decision among the shareholders whereof the Member State happened to be one; they were introduced by the Member State and made possible by the special powers available to the Member State that are not available to ordinary shareholders. Thus, the Member State acted 'in its capacity as a Member State'.[24] As pointed out by AG Manduro in the Dutch golden share case, the Member States are bound not by their possession of public authority but as signatories to the Treaty.[25] That a Member State may be obliged by the Treaty in a way that its citizens are not is apparent also from the readiness of the Court of Justice to apply incorrectly implemented directives vertically, ie between the Member State and a citizen,[26] and its reluctance to do the same horizontally among citizens.[27] Although the Court has in recent cases been willing to enforce the Treaty's freedoms vis-à-vis organizations without public authority, it has only done so in respect of organizations that provide collective regulation of a public law nature.[28]

This view of the Member States as prevented from using CEMs that may be available to its citizens is further supported by yet another case on golden shares by the Court of Justice in respect of the German car manufacturer, Volkswagen.[29] Here, the Court points to the difference between CEMs that are available to shareholders and subject to their own decision and CEMs imposed by legislation without the possibility of avoiding them.[30] The point is made at the outset of the Court's reasoning and would appear to suggest that CEMs that are available to shareholders according to national company law are not restrictions at all. It could be argued that the presence of CEMs in respect of a company would discourage the free movement of capital irrespective of who instigated them, but

[24] The Court pointed this out in para 48 of the British *BAA* case (n 14), where the articles were subject to the approval of the relevant minister, and has consistently emphasized this in the later cases even where the Member State arguably has behaved as a shareholder, see para 22 of the Dutch golden share case (n 14).

[25] Para 22 of the Dutch golden share case (n 14).

[26] The conditions necessary for applying a directive vertically (direct effect) are summarized in the Court's decision of 19 January 1982 in case 8/81 *Becker* [1982] ECR 53 para 25.

[27] On the rejection of horizontal direct effect see, inter alia, the Court's decision in Case C-91/92 *Faccini Dori* [1994] ECR I-3325 para 20.

[28] See the Court's decision of 11 December 2007 in Case C-438/05 *Viking Line* [2007] ECR I-10779, and decision of 18 December 2007 in Case C-341/05 *Laval* [2007] ECR I-11767. Both cases concerned workers' unions in the Nordic countries, where there is a long tradition of close co-operation between unions and government, which has left the area mostly regulated by collective agreements and an absence of legislation. The advert of European legislation on social issues, notably directives that have to be implemented by Member States, presents a challenge to this traditional reliance on collective agreements among the industrial parties. See the report by the European Parliament, *Challenges to collective agreements in the EU*, 30 September 2008 (2008/2085(INI)).

[29] Decision of 23 October 2007 in Case C-112/05 *Commission v Germany* [2007] ECR I-8995. If the distinction between first and second generation cases mentioned in n 14 above is applied, the case would be a first generation case as the CEM were provided by special acts pertaining to the company. The legislation was not, however, due to privatization as opposed to a period of prior nationalization, but to the re-organization of the company after World War II.

[30] Ibid, para 40.

that is to ignore the fact that the obligation not to impede this freedom rests on the Member States and not on the citizens *qua* shareholders.

IV. Where not to expect protectionism

Based on this reading of the Court of Justice's case law, protectionism is within the realm of the Member States and not applicable as a label on the actions of private citizens. Restructuring by way of a takeover, whether it is done by acquisition or by merger, should not provide cases of protectionism as long as the involved parties are private and the Member States do not impede their decision. This is not to ignore that the Member States pay great attention to takeover activity that plays out on their territory, nor that there seems to be an almost universal belief among Member States that their home market is open and vulnerable compared to all the rest. But the takeover bid and how it is greeted by the target company and its shareholders is essentially a private affair. As mentioned in Section II above, the distribution of powers within a company is dependent on the negotiation of the involved parties. To use phrases like 'shareholder democracy' is inapt and likely to mislead as nobody is born a shareholder but acquires that position by a voluntary transaction involving a payment that reflects a balance of risk and reward. It is unnecessarily simplistic to assume that there exists such a thing as a typical distribution of powers. The more relevant questions are what mechanisms of control are available to the shareholders and how have they used them. Both questions require a certain amount of transparency; the former of company legislation, the latter of the company's articles of association. Where ample transparency is provided, paternalism is unwarranted.

In spite of this, the question of protectionism has been discernible as a false note ringing throughout the long and difficult negotiations of Directive 2004/25/EC on Takeover Bids. The proposal was originally intended as a Thirteenth Company Law Directive, although it was aimed only at the subset of companies that are publicly traded and concerned what was essentially a matter of securities regulation, ie the conditions for making a public takeover bid.[31] It did, however, also comprise elements that pertained to the internal affairs of the company and as such involved company law. Originally, the mandatory bid rule was the only such element. It was believed to solve the risk of abuse by the majority

[31] On the history leading up to the proposal for the present Directive, see R Skog, 'The Takeover Directive: An Endless Saga?' (2002) 13 European Business L Rev 301, who is critical of the concept of a breakthrough rule suggested by the Winter Group. Also on the proposal for the present Directive and critical of the mandatory bid rule, see J Lau Hansen, 'When Less Would Be More: The EU Takeover Directive in its Latest Apparition' (2003) 9 Columbia J of Eur L 275, who argues that the Directive should aim at governing the bid and its conditions and leave out provisions on corporate governance as these are not suited for harmonization.

of shareholders of the minority and whereas that is a questionable outcome,[32] it does serve as a deterrent to takeovers by making them more expensive, especially when combined with the very useful concept of 'parties acting in concert', which may explain the rule's popularity with both politicians and established business interests.[33] Later, other elements were added that would equally interfere with the distribution of powers that the individual shareholders had either introduced themselves or accepted when they made their investment. Thus, the anti-frustration rule in Article 9 of the Directive goes against the basic tenet of company law in Germany and many other Member States: that it is not for the shareholders to decide the future of the company, but for the management taking all stakeholders' interest into account. One may disagree with this view and argue that it ignores the conflict of interest between the management of the target company and a bidder, which bid has to be considerably above the market price to entice enough shareholders to take up the offer and can only be justified by the expectation of an improvement in profitability that apparently has escaped present management. But it is difficult to argue that a Member State should not be allowed to afford such powers on management in privately owned companies or that shareholders, who have volunteered to invest under such a regime, should be protected against it. Another element is the breakthrough rule in Article 11 of the Directive, which strives to annul multiple voting rights that some shareholders have paid for and to remove restrictions on voting that were inserted into the articles of association by the shareholders.[34] Fortunately, two out of these three company law elements have been subjected to an opt-out provision in Article 12, which permits Member States to make the two controversial provisions in Article 9 on the anti-frustration rule and Article 11 on the breakthrough rule optional, leaving the companies to decide.[35] The Member States' near universal use of this

[32] Lau Hansen ibid, 289–94.

[33] Article 2(1)(d) of Directive 2004/25/EC. The Directive thus provides the world with a brand new anti-takeover measure that may serve to insulate management against unwelcomed transfers of control and may even prevent existing shareholders from organizing a mutual front vis-à-vis management, because any acquisition of shares in the contest of power may trigger the mandatory bid rule.

[34] The rule is very strange indeed. There is no reason why vote differentiation should prevent takeovers, it simply allocates who has the necessary power to accept the offer and there is no empirical evidence backing the claim that takeovers are hampered by such arrangements. However, where vote differentiation could serve as a hindrance to takeovers, ie where multiple voting rights accrue over time and as such are unavailable for the bidder, the Directive has specifically cut these shares out of the Directive by the definition in Article 2(1)(g) that applies only to the kind of voting differentiation governed by different classes of shares that does not hinder takeovers. Another strange thing is the exception from the breakthrough rule's attempt to equalize vote differentiation, which would appear to apply the one share/one vote principle (see ch 10), but not in respect of shares that are issued with no votes at all, cf Article 11(6). Apparently, equality is too good to share with all. In this respect, the requirement that the share has compensated voting rights for specific pecuniary advantages would appear to be unnecessary. Whenever a share is issued with less or no voting rights compared to other shares, they will be compensated by a lower price either at subscription or at the acquisition in the secondary market.

[35] A Member State may opt out, whereby it does not implement one of the two Articles 9 and 11, but it then has to allow a company to opt in and voluntarily introduce these provisions in its articles

possibility as documented by a recent Commission report[36] has ensured that the important question of corporate governance has not been harmonized by a Directive, which is basically only about how to make an offer to many recipients in one go.

Rather than being relieved that harmonization of an area has not occurred where most would agree that it should not because there is no one size that would fit all and little room for paternalism where sufficient transparency is provided,[37] the Commission in its report seems to worry about protectionism and concludes that '[t]he number of Member States implementing the Directive in a seemingly protectionist way is unexpectedly large'. What is here identified by the Commission as protectionism is the Member States' reluctance to interfere with the control arrangements agreed and applied by private parties. This is arguably a very wide application of the concept of protectionism that would appear to rest on the proposition that existing control arrangements favour nationals of the Member State and so to preserve them will prevent nationals of other Member States from enjoying the freedom of establishment and the free movement of capital provided by the Treaty. But this argument is to make private parties the pawns of their Member State. The obligation to refrain from interference with the Treaty's freedoms rests on the Member States, not on their nationals who are free to interact and make private arrangements on investment and on the distribution of control that these investments may imply, and that condition should be extended by the Treaty's freedoms and not restricted by them. It is a dangerous road to travel if one begins to argue that any naturally existing differences among Member States should be construed as an impediment to the free movement safeguarded by the Treaty, not only because it could lead to the conclusion that Member States are not allowed to support their national culture, language, or history, but also because it would open up all private contracts to a scrutiny that should only be applied to Member States.

The Directive on Takeover Bids went much further than was necessary to regulate what is essentially a simple question of securities trading and was used to introduce a harmonization in various areas of corporate governance that ended up alienating most of the Member States and for that reason permitted a possibility

of association. If the Member State does not avail itself of Article 12, it has to implement Articles 9 and 11 and make the provisions mandatory for the companies, effectively harmonizing these aspects of corporate governance.

[36] *Report on the implementation of the Directive on Takeover Bids*, Commission Staff Working Document, 21 February 2007, SEC(2007) 268. The anti-frustration rule is implemented by 18 Member States, however, only one of these (Malta) did not already have it in its national law. Apparently, the Member States who did not have it, used Article 12 to avoid harmonization. The breakthrough rule has been implemented only by the Baltic States and Italy, whereas all others have availed themselves of Article 12 to avoid harmonization.

[37] The view that corporate governance should not be harmonized has been consistent with the recent reports, including the overview of national corporate governance codes made in 2002 by Weil, Gotshal & Manges LLP and by the Winter Group in their report, *A Modern Regulatory Framework for Company Law in Europe*, 4 November 2002, which recommends that legislative initiatives should be directed at providing transparency.

to opt out of the controversial parts that is difficult to reconcile with the principle of subsidiarity in Article 5 TEU. Since then, Commissioner McCreevy has made a commitment only to regulate at a European level where there is clear empirical evidence calling for Community action.[38] When the Directive is up for revision, this commitment should be invoked to ensure that regulation is made only insofar as harmonization is really necessary, which is most likely not the case in respect of private arrangements of control in commercial affairs such as companies, whether they rely on CEMs or not. This would be in line with the Commission's drive to make legislation slimmer and more efficient. The Directive should govern how to make a takeover bid, the issues that should be addressed by the bid, how long the bid should be open, how it should be accepted, how to ensure an equal treatment, and solve the question of competing jurisdiction among supervisory authorities. A directive on takeover bids should not include provisions that are of a corporate governance nature, that is, it should not proscribe a mandatory bid rule, which is essentially a question of minority protection which has the unfortunate capacity to serve as an impediment to takeovers, nor should it require management to be passive when faced with a takeover bid, if national law requires them to safeguard the interests of the company and its stakeholders as is the case in Germany and some other jurisdictions, or provide a breakthrough rule which aims at invalidating property rights that have been paid for and which should be safeguarded by Article 345 TFEU. This is not to say that these questions of corporate governance should not be harmonized. They could be, but it should be done in legislation intended for that purpose and subject to the proper consideration afforded to such drastic measures and not as an appendix to a directive on takeover bids. These important questions should not be distracted by the fact that Member States may dislike takeovers among private companies and the disruption that they bring and prefer the status quo, because that does not in itself amount to protectionism.

V. Conclusion

Protectionism that may prevent cross-border restructuring by way of merger or acquisition may be expected where a Member State applies its public authority to introduce control enhancing mechanisms (CEMs) in a particular company. It is irrelevant that the CEM in question may be available in national company law.

[38] The Commissioner instigated a pan-European investigation of whether CEMs would reduce the performance of companies. The report was inconclusive, see ISS, *Report on the Proportionality Principle in the European Union*, 18 May 2007. With a resolve that regrettably is unusual among politicians when faced with a lack of empirical backing for their policy, the Commissioner abandoned further initiatives, see speech 3 October 2007 to the EP Legal Affairs Committee. It may be argued that the lack of empirical evidence invalidated only the actions intended against CEMs, but not regulation intended to make them more transparent as suggested by the Winter Group (see n 37).

Whether it is a shareholder or not, the Member State is obliged to observe the Treaty's freedoms, in this respect notably the freedom of establishment and the free movement of capital, in a way that provides it with less leeway than private shareholders. It should not be ignored that the Member State has a right, and often a popular mandate to go along with it, to serve and protect its citizens as it sees fit. By signing up to the Treaty, a Member State accepts the restrictions on its powers that translate into the freedoms afforded to the EU's citizens by the Treaty. It is important that these limitations are not construed too narrowly, as that may provoke a backlash not just by the governments of the Member States but also by the electorate.

In respect of the interference by a Member State with companies that is deemed vital to public policy, the point made by AG Colomer in the original golden share cases should be remembered; the Member State always has the option of nationalization in lieu of regulation. The option to nationalize has not been a favourable one for some years now, but recent events such as bank and other bail outs may have made it more appealing again. The Court of Justice of the European Union appears to have reached a sound balance by accepting on the one hand the interest of Member States to safeguard their control over certain strategic industries while at the same time maintaining the responsibility of each Member State to honour the obligations that it has assumed under the Treaty and requiring that such control measures conform to the requirements usually associated with public law, ie clarity, objectivity, and access to judicial review.

Where the Member State neglects to regulate the distribution of powers within privately owned companies within its territory, it should be respected as a valid choice even if it may be governed by a keen self-interest to preserve companies in the hands of its nationals. The reluctance of Member States to implement the provisions of the Directive on Takeover Bids that would interfere with the distribution of powers between private parties in national companies should not be viewed as protectionism, but as the natural consequence of respecting another very important freedom so basic that it is not in the Treaty: the freedom of contract. Not all differences among the Member States that may impede cross-border activity are necessarily a restriction, and the Member States' acceptance of such differences should not be viewed as protectionism. Protectionism is a sinister concept and rightly so; it is important to employ this term only where strictly appropriate.

9

Mechanisms of Ownership Control and the Issue of Disproportionate Distribution of Power

Ulf Bernitz

I. The public policy element in European company law

In the legal system, company law forms part of private law. However, this does not mean legislation in the field of company law would be value neutral. To the contrary, the many differences in the shape of the company law of the EU Member States often reflect differences in underlying economic conditions and in public policy considerations, past and present. The very fact that company law legislation is normally of a prescriptive character is in itself an expression of the public element involved.[1]

The public policy element is particularly visible in the EU company law directives. Indeed, in the absence of such elements, aiming at facilitating European economic integration, there would be no legal basis for EU legislation. Normally, the company law directives are based on the Treaty articles on freedom of establishment. An important example is the EU Directive of 2004 on Takeover Bids,[2] known as the Thirteenth Company Law Directive or the Takeover Directive, establishing a legal regime at EU level in relation to public offers to take over companies. It is primarily this Directive which forms the legal background of this article.

The Takeover Directive is based on what is now Article 50(2)(g) of the TFEU.[3] This Treaty provision offers a legal basis for measures aiming at co-ordination 'to the necessary extent' but no general legal basis for approximation (harmonization) of laws. It forms part of the Treaty articles on freedom of establishment.

[1] I am inclined to stress the public policy element in company law more firmly than it is stressed in the article by Jesper Lau Hansen in ch 8 of this volume.

[2] 2004/25 EC of 21 April 2004, OJ L 142/12.

[3] See Recital 1 of the Directive. Before the Lisbon Treaty the Article number was 44(2) EC Treaty.

The scope of Article 50 is expressed in Article 50(1) TFEU where it is stated that the aim of the provisions of this Article is 'to attain freedom of establishment'. Article 50(2) TFEU lists in eight subsections measures of different kinds aiming at enhancing freedom of establishment. Subsection (g), the one relevant here, states, as read in conjunction with the first sentence in Article 50(2), that the European Parliament, the Council, and the Commission shall carry out the duties devolving upon them under the preceding provisions (ie on freedom of establishment):

> by coordinating to the necessary extent the safeguards which, for the protection of the interests of members and others, are required by Member States of companies and firms . . . with a view to making such safeguards equivalent throughout the Union.

Expressed in briefer language, the object of Article 50(2)(g) TFEU is to co-ordinate safeguards within Member States company law to the extent necessary in order to attain freedom of establishment within the Union.

A more resolute expression of the EU public policy interest is to be found in the preamble to the Takeover Directive. Recital 3 of the Preamble of the Directive states:

> It is necessary to create Community-wide clarity and transparency in respect to legal issues to be settled in the event of takeover bids and to prevent patterns of corporate restructuring within the Community from being distorted by arbitrary differences in governance and management cultures.

The Takeover Directive is based on the view that takeovers should be encouraged as an instrument for EU company restructuring plans. Takeovers have even been considered to be a 'condition for the survival' of European undertakings within the context of international competition and a condition for the establishment of a European financial market.[4] An important aim has been stated to be to ensure an equal 'playing field' and hence an equal chance for the success of takeover bids in the various Member States via an action implemented at EU level.[5]

These are far-reaching ambitions, not necessarily fully within the legal basis offered by Article 50 TFEU.[6] To quote the Recital, should EU law aim at purifying 'arbitrary differences in government and management cultures' embedded in the company law of Member States? Certain aspects of this important issue will be discussed in this article. It seems timely to do so. The Directive provides in Article 20 that the EU Commission shall examine the Directive after five years of application, ie in 2011, in the light of the experience in applying it

[4] Council Legal Service Note 2003, 8134/03, JUR 169, DRS 37, CODEC 412, see paras 24 and 39.

[5] Para 39.

[6] When reading the Preamble of the Takeover Directive one observes that the words 'necessary' or 'necessary measure' have been inserted in a great number of the paragraphs. However, a legislative measure does not become necessary according to the Treaty only because its necessity is claimed in preamble statements. Little is to be found in the text of the Directive or in the background reports about the substance of the necessity prerequisite.

and, if necessary, propose its revision. That examination shall include a survey of the control structures and barriers to takeover bids that are not covered by the Directive. There is certainly no lack of such control-enhancing mechanisms.

This article contains four subsequent parts. Section II gives a description of the Directive and its aims and limits with particular reference to the so-called breakthrough rule. Section III presents different European mechanisms of ownership control, based on the 2007 *Report on the Proportionality Principle.* In Section IV, the system of multiple voting rights as applied in the Nordic countries will be discussed, using Sweden as example. In Section V conclusions are drawn.

II. The Takeover Directive and the structure of company ownership

The Takeover Directive aims at harmonization on the EU level of the law and practice of the Member States in relation to public offers to take over companies.[7] The primary purpose of the Directive is to introduce a common European framework for the handling of takeover transactions. It includes rules on, inter alia, transparency and duty of information, honest practices, and protection of minority shareholders and creditors. The Directive contains special provisions on, inter alia, the squeeze-out right of the offeror and the sell-out right of the offeree company. However, the Directive leaves many important legal issues within the field to be handled in the future in accordance with the national company law of the Member States.

Special attention is paid in the Directive to different restrictions on the transferability of securities, provided for in the articles of association or agreed with the company as obstacles to takeover bids. During the legislative process the multiple voting rights, in the Directive called multiple-vote securities,[8] was regarded as a principal target, functioning as an obstacle to takeover activity. Primarily, this view was based on the fact that the multiple voting rights system deviates from the 'one share/one vote' principle and thus does not give each shareholder a voting power proportional to his share in the capital.[9] As a result, Article 11 of the Directive, the so-called breakthrough rule, provides that multiple-vote securities shall carry only one vote at the general meeting which decides on any defensive measures.[10]

[7] On the background, see, inter alia, G Ferrarini and others (eds), *Reforming Company and Takeover Law in Europe* (Oxford: Oxford University Press, 2004), R Skog, 'The Takeover Directive—an endless Saga?' [2002] EBLR 301 ff.

[8] The Directive defines multiple-vote securities as 'securities included in a distinct and separate class and carrying more than one vote each', Article 1(g).

[9] Paras 26–27 of the Council Legal Service Note.

[10] Article 11(3)(3) of the Directive. The Council Legal Service took the view the breakthrough rule could legitimately be adopted on the basis of what is not Article 50(2)(g) TFEU, paras 34–35

This measure was a primary concern for the Nordic Member States, where the system of multiple voting rights forms a core part of the ownership structure of the larger companies and their system of corporate governance. A compromise solution was found in the end. The Directive gives the Member States the option to keep the multiple voting rights system although, according to the drafting of the Directive, the opt-out from the breakthrough rule constitutes the exception.[11] However, Member States making use of this option are required to offer companies the alternative to opt in for the breakthrough rule by a decision taken by their general meeting.[12] When implementing the Directive, the Nordic Member States have made use of the opt-out option, ie the breakthrough rule in Article 11 has not been introduced in their national company law. However, as required by the Directive, companies are given the option to opt in for the breakthrough rule, but this option is hardly used and normally considered unattractive.[13]

The breakthrough rule, functioning as a prohibition on the right to exercise multiple voting rights in takeover situations, is not exactly the same thing as an outright prohibition of the multiple voting rights system as such. The breakthrough rule does not hinder the exercise of multiple voting rights in conjunction with other decisions taken at the general meetings of shareholders, such as the election of the board of the company. However, from the viewpoint of economic realities, the difference would be slight. In a multiple voting rights system, it is the core function of the shares with high voting rights to make it possible to control the target company in takeover situations. If the high vote shares are deprived of that function, they would lose most of their economic justification. This explains the strong reaction of the Nordic countries against the introduction of the breakthrough rule and the pressure for an opt-out clause.

In fact, the breakthrough rule was tailored to fit the Nordic multiple vote system while leaving other types of such systems untouched. Multiple-vote securities is defined in Article 2(1)(g) of the Directive as securities included in 'a distinct and separate class'. This definition covers the Nordic system but excludes other similar voting differentiation systems, eg the French system offering long-time owners of shares double voting rights after one year of ownership and the more varied Dutch systems. Also, securities not carrying voting rights at ordinary

and the Conclusions of the Council Legal Service Note. See also the contributions in this volume by Lau Hansen (ch 8) and Ringe (ch 10).

[11] Article 12(1) of the Directive. On the limits and framing of this option, see eg P Krüger Andersen, 'The Takeover Directive and Corporate Governance: The Danish Experience' [2002] EBLR 1461 ff.

[12] Article 12(2) of the Directive.

[13] In the Swedish Bill to Parliament on the Takeover Act of 2006, it was predicted companies would make little use of the opt-in possibility, Government Bill 2005/06:140, p 69. A decision to opt in requires a resolution at the company's general meeting requiring a nine-tenths majority. For further information, S Johansson, 'Chapter on Sweden' in P van Hooghten (ed), *The European Takeover Directive and its Implementation* (Oxford: Oxford University Press, 2009) 707 ff. Johansson confirms the opt-in option is not in practical use.

general meetings are not covered by the Directive unless Member States decide otherwise.[14]

In 2007, the Commission published a comprehensive report on the implementation of the Directive (the *Implementation Report*).[15] As stated in the conclusions of the *Implementation Report*, a large number of Member States have shown strong reluctance to lift takeover barriers. Most Member States seem to have made use of options offered in the Takeover Directive. The breakthrough rule has hardly been a success as it has been implemented fully in the three Baltic states only. The Commission has also initiated an expert study on the proportionality between ownership and control in EU-listed companies, the 2007 *Report on the Proportionality Principle in the EU* (the *Proportionality Report*),[16] partially based on a background paper by R Adams and D Ferreira.[17] As the *Proportionality Report* clearly demonstrates, there are many other systems of ownership control practised in Europe which should deserve close scrutiny from the viewpoint of obstacles to takeovers versus European integration just as much as multiple voting rights systems.[18]

In my opinion, the problems of obstacles to takeover activity were hardly handled in a satisfactory way during the legislative process leading to the enactment of the Directive. Whether, and if so, to what extent, the multiple voting rights system functions as an obstacle to takeover activity should not be assessed solely, or even primarily, on the basis of a theoretical, one share/one vote, analysis. Instead, taking the basic aims of the Takeover Directive into regard, it is important to access in what way the multiple voting rights system is actually functioning. It is also important to access other systems for company ownership control practised within the EU.

In this context, it is worth noting that in the United States company law has the status of state law and is far from uniform, albeit Delaware law holds the leading position.[19] Multiple voting rights systems are frequently practised in the US. The many existing differences in company law between the different American states and the existence of multiple voting rights does not seem to hamper the existence in the United States of a market far more integrated than is the case within the EU and a high level of takeover activity. These facts might cast some doubts on the presumptions behind the Takeover Directive.

[14] Recital 11 of the Preamble.

[15] Commission Staff Working Document, *Report on the Implementation of the Directive on Takeover Bids* (Brussels, 21 February 2007), SEC (2007) 268. The period for transposition of the Directive into national law ended on 20 May 2006, see Article 21(1) of the Directive, but a number of Member States did not meet that deadline.

[16] External study commissioned by the European Commission, undertaken by Institutional Shareholder Services in collaboration with Sherman & Sterling LLP and the European Corporate Governance Institute (ECGI).

[17] R Adams and D Ferreira, 'One Share, One Vote: The Empirical Evidence' (2008) 12 Rev of Finance 51.

[18] On the cause of development, see Ringe's contribution in ch 10 of this volume p 209.

[19] See for a useful comparison of the legal development C Forstinger, *Takeover Law in the EU and the USA* (The Hague: Kluwer, 2002). See also Ringe (n 18).

III. Different European mechanisms of ownership control

As mentioned above, there exist a number of systems of corporate governance and ownership control within the EU Member States, including different systems of control of shares or other securities holding special controlling rights. This spectrum of systems was studied in depth in the *Proportionality Report*.[20]

It is important to note the term *proportionality principle* as used in the *Proportionality Report* and this chapter has a particular meaning, referring to the relation between ultimate economic risk and control. The *Report* uses the following definition:

> Proportionality between ultimate economic risk and control means that share capital which has an unlimited right to participate in the profits of the company or in the residue on liquidation, and only such share capital, should normally carry control rights, in proportion to the risk carried.

The *Adams—Ferreira Paper*[21] uses the term disproportional ownership in a similar sense, ie mechanisms that separate voting rights from cash flow in corporations.

In 2002, the *Report of the High Level Group of Company Law Experts* (the so-called *Winter Group Report*)[22] made the assessment that the holders of the rights to the residual profits and assets of a company are best equipped to decide on the affairs of the company as the ultimate effects of their decisions will be borne by them. This view made the *Winter Group Report* favours the one share/ one vote principle and suggests that multiple voting rights be abolished in relation to take-overs. The primary aim of the *Proportionality Report* has been to identify existing diversions from the proportionality principle in the Member States, to analyse the relevant regulatory framework, to evaluate their economic significance, and to find out whether the diversions have an impact on EU investors.

The *Report* uses the term control enhancing mechanisms (CEMs). It identifies 13 different types of CEM, divided into three different subtypes: CEMs leveraging voting power, CEMs used to lock-in control, and other mechanisms.

In summary, CEMs leveraging voting power include:

(1) *Multiple voting rights shares*

This type comprises the Nordic system of multiple voting rights. It also includes the Dutch systems of multiple voting rights, widespread in the Netherlands and more varied in their application, and the French system of double voting rights as a kind of loyalty premium for shareholders who have had shares in their hands for a longer period (more than a year).

[20] For earlier discussion, see, eg M Barca and M Becht, *The Control of Corporate Europe* (Oxford: Oxford University Press, 2001), A Nilsen, 'Finance, Hostile Takeovers, and Worker Participation—A Cross-National Survey of Business Preferences' in U Bernitz (ed), *Modern Company Law for a European Economy—Ways and Means* (Stockholm: Norstedts Juridik, 2006) 97 ff. *The Proportionality Report* includes a comprehensive bibliography.

[21] See n 17 above.

[22] *Report of the High Level Group of Company Law Experts on Issues Related to Takeover Bids* (Brussels, 10 January 2002). Professor Jaap Winter presided over that group.

The system of multiple voting rights is used to some limited extent in the United Kingdom.[23] As mentioned, it also functions in the United States.

(2) *Non-voting shares, ie shares with no voting rights and which carry no special cash-flow rights such as a preferential dividend*

This system is not so much used according to the *Proportionality Report*.

(3) *Non-voting preference shares, normally with a preferential (higher or guaranteed dividend)*

This system is commonly used in some countries, primarily the United Kingdom, Ireland, and Italy.

(4) *Pyramidal structures*

This system occurs when an entity controls a corporation that in turn holds a controlling stake in another corporation; a process that can be repeated (box in box).

The system is widely available and widely used within the EU Member States.

CEMs used to lock in control include:

(5) *Priority shares, ie shares granting their holders specific powers of decision or veto rights in a company*

This system seems to be used primarily in the Netherlands.

(6) *Depository certificates*

This system is characterized by a differentiation between the underlying share and the certificate which does not hold voting rights but only the financial rights. Also this system is primarily used in the Netherlands.

(7) *Voting rights ceilings, ie a restriction prohibiting shareholders from voting above a certain threshold irrespective of the number of voting shares they hold*

This system is available in many EU countries and is used in particular in Spain.

(8) *Ownership ceilings, eg systems not permitting investors to take a participation in a company above a certain threshold*

This system is available in many EU states and used primarily in Italy and Greece.

(9) *Supermajority provisions*

ie systems which require certain important decisions to be supported by a majority of more than 50 per cent of the votes plus one. In most cases, the idea is to protect minority shareholders. This system seems to be normally available.

[23] In principle, Germany eliminated by legislation the use of multiple voting rights in 1998. However, such rights had never played an important rule in Germany; German barriers to takeovers are of different types. See, eg, T Baums, 'The Regulation of Takeovers under German Law' [2004] EBLR 1453 ff and Section IV below.

(10) *Golden shares*

ie priority shares issued for the benefit of government authorities, are normally used to give governments or government-controlled vehicles special rights in partially privatized companies, eg to block takeovers or veto certain important decisions.

The system has to a certain extent been used in a number of Member States. Golden shares, defined as Member States holding securities in the offeree company which confer special rights on the Member States, are explicitly excluded from the breakthrough rule, provided these special rights are compatible with the Treaty.[24] However, the Court of Justice has struck down golden shares systems in a number of cases as incompatible with the right to free movement of capital according to what is now Article 63 TFEU.[25]

Other CEMs include:

(11) *Partnerships limited by shares*

Particular legal structures in certain member states, eg differentiation between partners with unlimited liability and sleeping partners with limited liability.

(12) *Cross-shareholding*

Situations where company X holds a stake in company Y which, in turn, holds a stake in company X. A variety is circular shareholdings: company A holds a stake in company B, company B in company C, and company C in company A. This system is generally available in the Member States. According to the *Proportionality Report*, Sweden is the country where cross-shareholdings are used the most. It is also fairly common in France and the Netherlands.

(13) *Shareholders agreements*

These are generally considered to be legally available as part of freedom of contract. According to the *Proportionality Report*, they are particularly common in Italy with France as number two.

This overview of the types of control enhancing mechanism available in the EU countries shows that there exist many ways in which ownership control of companies can be exercised and undesired corporate restructuring stopped. Other systems also exist which fall outside the definition of control enhancing mechanisms

[24] Article 11(7) of the Directive.

[25] Formerly Article 56 EC Treaty. See, eg Case C-367/98 *Commission v Portugal* [2002] ECR I-4731; Case C-483/99 *Commission v France* [2002] ECR I-4781; Case C-463/00 *Commission v Spain* [2003] ECR I-4581; Case C-98/01 *Commission v United Kingdom* [2003] ECR I-4641; Case C-112/05 *Commission v Germany (Volkswagen)* [2007] ECR I-8995. A limited golden share arrangement in order to secure vital natural gas supplies to Belgium was accepted in Case C-503/99 *Commission v Belgium* [2002] ECR I-4809, referring to the exemption for justifications on grounds of public policy or public security in what is now Article 65(1)(b) TFEU. See also the articles by Biondi, Lau Hansen, and Ringe in this volume.

used in the Report, ie 'poison pills' in contractual arrangements between the target (offeree) company and third parties (eg change of control clauses in convertible bonds). In certain Member States banks and other financing companies have wide possibilities to acquire shares in other companies. Thus, concentration of ownership control in the hands of banks is a well-known reality in Germany.

As follows from the *Proportionality Report*, very different systems or combinations of control enhancing mechanism are used in the Member States. It is easy to recognize the vast divergences existing in this respect between, eg the Netherlands, France, Germany, and Italy. Many divergences seem to have their background in national economic history and development and related disparities in national company law. Often, methods widely used in one country are not available or not much used in practice in another. They may not even be compatible with the national company law of other EU countries. The *Proportionality Report* has found pyramid structures, shareholders agreements, and multiple voting rights shares to be the most common control enhancing mechanisms. Obviously, quite different legal mechanisms can be used to achieve similar objectives.

The *Proportionality Report* has also studied theoretical and empirical literature on the causes and consequences of disproportional ownership. The *Report* has found that there is no robust answer to the question whether disproportional ownership creates social costs by destroying firm value. The *Report* reached the overall conclusion that the evidence on the control enhancing mechanism discount is tenuous.[26] The *Adams—Ferreira Paper* has made a special study of the effects of multiple voting rights on the value of outside equity. It has found a lack of evidence of negative effects of ownership disproportionality on outside equity value.[27]

In conclusion, the *Report on the Proportionality Principle* has clarified the system of multiple voting rights as just one of many different mechanisms used within the EU countries for ownership control. There seems to be no evidence indicating the multiple voting rights system would be more far-reaching or have greater effects than many other control mechanisms studied. As mentioned, the overall conclusion of the *Proportionality Report* is that the effects of all the different control mechanisms studied are tenuous.

IV. The system of multiple voting rights in Nordic, particularly Swedish, company law

Against the background of the *Proportionality Report* and its findings, we should take a closer look at the multiple voting rights system as applied in the Nordic Member States of the EU[28] and in Norway.

[26] *The Proportionality Report*, 9.

[27] Part 8 of the Paper 1 (n 17), in particular 85.

[28] See for an overview N Jul Clausen and K Engsig Sørensen, 'The 2003 Proposal for a Directive on Takeover Bids—Impact on the Regulation in Scandinavia', (2003) 45 Scandinavian Studies in L 89 ff.

There is a long tradition of inter-Nordic co-operation in the drafting of legislation, in particular within the field of private law, which has resulted in a fairly high degree of legal uniformity between the Nordic countries. The Companies Acts of the Nordic countries are to a considerable degree the result of legal co-operation and are largely based on the same guiding principles, even if the recently enacted new statutes include more differences than before, not least in drafting technique. Thus, it is possible in this article to concentrate on the Swedish legislation[29] and at the same time largely describe the principles of the law of the other Nordic EU countries, inter alia Denmark and Finland, and of Norway and Iceland,[30] two EEA countries.

Nordic company law has a distinct market orientation. The primary object of the legislation is to set up a general legal framework and to secure transparency and the protection of creditors and minority shareholders. The Nordic Companies Acts (including adjacent legislation) are kept relatively short and leave many issues to be solved by soft law developed within the business community or by the parties involved on the basis of freedom of contract, primarily within the articles of association. Thus, the new Swedish statute on Public Takeover Bids has left many issues to be handled by self-regulation.[31] Compliance with these regulations is mandatory for all companies whose shares are listed on the Stockholm Stock Exchange (part of the NASDAQ/OMX Group) since the Recommendation forms part of the listing requirements. Non-compliance would lead to the delisting of the company. The Recommendation contains detailed rules on the bidder's behaviour and duties of information and on the conduct of the target company.

In line with basic principles of Nordic company law, the Swedish Companies Act of 2005 provides that all shares shall carry equal rights in the company (Ch 4 Sec. 1) and may be freely transferred and acquired (Ch 4 Sec. 7). However, the Act makes it possible for a company to have, albeit within limits, other provisions in its articles of association. For example, the articles of association may include a clause pursuant to which a shareholder or other person shall be entitled to purchase a share which has been transferred to a new owner (Ch 4 ss 27–36).[32] Thus, there is a high degree of freedom of contract. The articles of association may prescribe that there shall be shares of different classes or the right to issue such shares (Ch 4 s 3). The classes of shares may differ concerning the right to participate in the profits or assets of the company, or the voting rights. Varying voting rights are allowed.

[29] See in English, The Swedish Companies Act 2005 in Translation (part of the larger publication *Swedish Commercial Legislation* (Stockholm: Norstedts Juridik, 2006)). For a general presentation of Swedish company law eg K Moberg, 'Company Law' in M Bogdan (ed), *Swedish Legal System* (Stockholm, 2010) 81 ff.

[30] In Icelandic company law, generally similar in particular to Danish law, differentiated voting rights and non-voting shares are permitted by law but the one share/one vote principle strongly prevails in practice, A Björgvinsdóttir, 'Icelandic Company Law' (2003) 45 Scandinavian Studies in L 60 f.

[31] Government Bill 2005/06:140 p 44 ff.

[32] The Swedish legal term is *hembudsförbehåll*.

In Sweden, there is a cap on differentiated voting rights since the coming into force of the Companies Act of 1944. A share cannot carry more than ten times the vote of another share.[33] This provision, when introduced, was not given retroactive effect. Companies which had a higher degree of voting differentiation according to their articles of association at the time that the 1944 Act took legal force were permitted to continue their previous practice. The legislator found it impermissible to give a new restriction on differentiated voting rights retroactive effect and thus permitted companies to keep their existing system. The Swedish legislator took the same position when the Companies Act of 1975 and the present Companies Act of 2005 were enacted.[34] However, today this grandfather clause has lost most of its practical importance.[35] It should be noted the ten votes cap has recently been removed in the Finnish and Danish Companies Acts, as it was considered to be an unnecessary restriction.[36]

Swedish company law permits preference shares having a secured right to dividend in relation to ordinary shares. It is also permitted to include in the articles of association caps on the maximum amount of votes per owner. Swedish company law does not permit shares, whether ordinary or preference, carrying no voting rights. In addition, there is a fundamental rule of Swedish company law that shareholders are to be treated equally, the equality principle.[37] Swedish company law does not know of golden shares or non-voting shares carrying specific pecuniary advantages.

In Sweden, the articles of association are kept by the Company Office,[38] a government authority, and are fully public. Companies must keep a public register of all shares and shareholders in accordance with the provisions of Ch 5 of the Companies Act, the share register. The information is easily accessible to the public at large on the Internet and in other publications.[39] Thus, the voting rights system applied by the companies is transparent.

[33] The Swedish Companies Act of 2005 states in Ch 4 s 5: 'No share may carry voting rights which are more than ten times greater than the voting rights of any other share.'

[34] It is clearly stated in s 8 of the transitional provisions of the Companies Act of 2005 that companies, in which there exist shares carrying voting rights which are more than 10 times greater than the voting rights of any other share, may issue new shares carrying the same voting rights as the already issued shares are carrying.

[35] The Ericsson Company, the large telecom company, kept its old system of multiple voting rights shares having a thousand times the voting rights of the other shares until 2004. This system has now been changed by agreement between the shareholders to shares having ten times the voting rights of the other shares.

[36] On the new Danish legislation, see Lau Hansen's article in this volume, Section II.

[37] Ch 4 s 1 of the 2005 Swedish Company Act: All shares shall carry equal rights in the company, unless otherwise provided.

[38] In Swedish Bolagsverket. See <http://www.bolagsverket.se>.

[39] D Fristedt and S I Sundqvist, *Ägarna och makten i Sveriges Börsföretag* (Owners and Power in Sweden's Listed Companies) (Stockholm, 2007), gives detailed information about the owners of all Swedish companies listed on the stock exchange and how they are interrelated (with explanatory text in English).

In practice, multiple voting shares are very widely used by Swedish companies, while preferential shares and caps on the maximum amount of votes are far less common. Multiple voting shares normally take the shape of dual classes of shares, using the ratio 10:1 between the high vote shares (so-called *A shares*) and the low vote shares (so-called *B shares*). The A and B shares will have the same par value. The purchase of A-shares is in no way restricted by legislation, but the articles of association may include post-sale purchase right clauses. In large companies, often both the A-shares and the B-shares are listed on the stock market. Someone who is aiming at preparing a takeover bid would normally prefer to buy A-shares. In such instances, the market price of the A-shares might be substantially higher than the B-shares.

The system of A and B shares is so widespread in Sweden that it has become a very common system of company ownership. Almost half of all companies listed on the Stockholm Stock Exchange have classes of shares with different voting rights, practically without exception with the voting ratio 10:1.[40] Only a few companies apply post-sale purchase right clauses to non-listed A-shares. Interestingly, only one listed company of importance includes in its articles of association a cap on the maximum amount of votes per owner.

An important part of the explanation of the widespread use of differentiated voting rights is the fact that issuing new B-shares is a standard method used by Swedish companies for acquiring new capital for expansion. The vast majority of the stock exchange listed companies practising differentiated voting are companies which were formerly owned by a small group of owners, often the founder(s) of the company, who then listed their company in order to attract capital from the public via the stock market. In such companies, normally only the low vote B-shares are listed on the stock market while the former group of owners retains high vote A-shares.

Swedish banks and other financing companies are permitted to a strictly limited extent only to acquire shares in companies unrelated to their business in order to make profits or to keep the shares as financial holdings. However, as an exception to this legal rule, Swedish banks and financing companies may acquire shares in such other companies in order to secure a claim, provided there is reason to assume that the bank or financing company would suffer significant loss otherwise. Such shares shall be disposed of as soon as it deemed appropriate and, at the latest, when this can be done without giving rise to a loss.[41]

[40] R Skog, 'The Takeover Directive, the "Breakthrough" Rule and the Swedish System of Dual Class Common Stock' [2004] EBLR 1446 f; for further information see Fristedt and Sundquist (n 39).

[41] Ch 7 s 2–11 of the Swedish Bank and Financing Business Act of 2004. The regulation, which was stricter before 2004, is more detailed than has been summarized here. The rules have a partially historical explanation; they have their origin in the failure of the Kreuger Group based on match monopolies in the beginning of the 1930s, a huge economic scandal which forced the Swedish state to intervene financially in order to save important banks from bankruptcy.

In companies differentiating between high vote shares and low vote shares it is normally in the hands of the owners of the former to take decisions on accepting takeover bids. However, this does not seem to cause a barrier to takeovers or function as a protectionist measure. Statistics show that in relation to the size of the markets takeover activity is at least as high in Sweden as in the United Kingdom, where multiple voting is permitted but rarely applied.[42] Generally, the United Kingdom is regarded as having the highest takeover activity within the European Union. Hostile takeovers are not so frequent in Sweden but do occur. The share of foreign ownership of Swedish listed companies has increased rapidly in recent years, from approximately 10 per cent at the beginning of the 1990s to a figure of between 35 and 40 per cent today.[43]

The factual situation and experience in the Nordic Member States does not support the presumption that the multiple voting rights system, as practised in these countries, would function as a particular obstacle to takeover activity.[44] To the contrary: the particularly high Swedish takeover activity would indicate that the major obstacles to increased European merger activity are to be found elsewhere.

V. Conclusions

The Takeover Directive will be re-examined by the Commission in 2011, including the Member States' option to retain the multiple voting rights system. It seems still to be an open question how detailed this re-examination will be and to what extent systems of control enhancing mechanisms other than multiple voting rights, which are able to function as obstacles to cross-border takeovers, will be subject to scrutiny. At present, the Commission seems to have reduced its ambitions.

In light of the developments and the conclusions drawn in the 2007 *Proportionality Report* it seems evident that the 2004 Takeover Directive was overly ambitious in its aim to encourage cross-border European takeovers and to a large extent has failed. The intended degree of harmonization has not been achieved as the Member States have made wide use of the options embedded in the Directive. The breakthrough rule has been implemented fully only in the three Baltic states. It was not warranted, as was done, to single out the Nordic type of multiple voting rights system as the primary target of action in order to

[42] Shares with differentiated voting rights: Some facts about listed Swedish companies. Memorandum published by the Swedish Ministry of Justice, 13 June 2007, R Boman, *Some facts about takeover activity in the Swedish stock market* (Report, 2002).

[43] Fristedt and Sundqvist (n 39) 19.

[44] See for a factual overview of takeover activity in Sweden R Skog, 'The European Union's Proposed Takeover Directive, the "Breakthrough" Rule and the Swedish System of Dual Class Common Stock' (2003) 45 Scandinavian Studies in L 293 ff, in particular 302 ff.

foster trans-border mergers and acquisitions. As concluded in this article, the facts do not support the presumption that the Nordic multiple voting rights system would function as a particular obstacle to takeover activity—to the contrary the Nordic States seem to belong to the group of EU countries that are most open to takeovers. The *Proportionality Report* demonstrates clearly that there exist within the EU Member States many other methods of ownership control of equal importance. The overall conclusion of the *Proportionality Report* is that the effects of all the different control enhancing mechanisms studied are tenuous. This result suggests it would be possible to reconcile the existence of different European models of corporate governance and ownership control with an integrated, well-functioning European market, ie it should be possible to preserve multiplicity. On this point, one should keep in mind that company law is state law in the United States and far from uniform; still there is a well-integrated internal market.

As already stated, the basic aim of the Takeover Directive, when enacted, was to facilitate corporate restructuring with the Union, primarily cross-border, by introducing an EU-wide, coherent, and transparent legal regime governing takeovers. In other words, economic progress should be facilitated by making it easier to break up established ownership structures, which were regarded as protectionist in nature. In the light of the economic crisis starting in 2007 one might question these aims of the Directive somewhat. The effects of control enhancing mechanisms are not necessarily negative. They would normally create an ownership structure characterized by the prevalence of only one or a limited number of controlling owners of the company, being the strategic and active, long-term owners, while the remaining shares often would be widely spread and held by many as a financial investment. It is to be expected that this type of corporate governance would foster a group of strong owners interested in a lasting relation with their company covering several business cycles and taking active part in the future development of the company. Many would consider this type of company ownership as predominantly positive. It seems the deliberations leading to the enactment of the Takeover Directive applied an over simplified view to the relationship between ownership control and cross-border takeovers. The picture has many facets and the EU as legislator and supervisor should be cautious in intervening as long as control enhancing mechanisms are not applied as a disguise for national protectionism. It should also be kept in mind that the EU legal basis for intervention in this area, Article 50(2)(g) TFEU, includes a necessity requirement.[45]

Would it be legally possible to repeal the possibility for the Member States to opt out of the breakthrough rule? Actually, the Takeover Directive is problematic from the viewpoint of objectivity in its present form. As has been clarified in the *Proportionality Report*, there exist in the Member States a number of

[45] See Section I above.

control-enhancing mechanisms having largely the same types of effect. Thus, within the type of measures leveraging voting power, the *Proportionality Report* has identified not only the Nordic multiple voting rights system but also several Dutch varieties of multiple voting rights systems, the French system of double voting rights after one year of shareholding, and systems differentiating between shares with voting rights and those without voting rights. Given this situation, a repeal of the possibility to opt out from the breakthrough rule, designed to hit only the Nordic model of multiple voting rights system but leaving measures with similar effects in other Member States intact, would be arbitrary and discriminatory as it would not be based on objective differences arising from underlying economic conditions in the Member States. It would be possible in this situation to invoke the fundamental EU law principle of non-discrimination.[46]

It would also be possible to attack such a possible legislative repeal on the basis of the general Union law principle of proportionality, not to be confused with the proportionality principle as used in the *Proportionality Report*, where it stands for proportionality between economic risk and ownership control in companies. The Council Legal Service gave the following description of the scope and content of the general proportionality principle in Union law in its note on the Takeover Directive:

> That principle is respected when the burden imposed on the parties concerned is appropriate and necessary in order to achieve the objectives legitimately pursued and is proportionate to the aims sought; when there is a choice between several appropriate measures, recourse must be had to the least onerous, and the disadvantages caused must not be disproportionate to the aims pursued.[47]

When applying the general proportionality principle, it is important to access how onerous and disadvantageous a prohibition would be for those who are caught by it. When applying the proportionality test as a general principle of Community law, the disadvantages caused must not be disproportionate to the aims pursued. As explained in Section IV, above, the multiple voting rights systems as practised in the Nordic countries form a core part of the whole ownership structure of the stock exchange listed companies doing business in these countries and their system of corporate governance. Nearly 50 per cent of the companies listed on the Stockholm Stock Exchange apply the system. A prohibition

[46] Article 18(1) TFEU. See also the prohibition in Article 65(3) TFEU on measures and procedures which constitute a means of arbitrary discrimination or disguised restriction on the free movement of capital. T Tridimas, *The General Principles of EU Law* (2nd edn, Oxford: Oxford University Press, 2006) 88 f. See, eg the cases dealing with aspects of agricultural regulations differentiating production in different Member States, Case 230/78, *Eridania v Minister for Agriculture and Forestry* [1979] ECR 2749 para 19, Joined Cases C-181, C-182, and C-218/88, *Deschamps and others v Ofival* [1989] ECR 4381, Case C-309/89 *Codorniu v Council* [1994] ECR I-1853.

[47] Para 43. The Court has formulated the proportionality principle in a similar way in, eg Case C-180/96 *United Kingdom v Commission* [1998] ECR I-2265 para 96. Article 5(3) TEU prescribes: 'Under the principle of proportionality, the content and form of Union action shall not exceed what is necessary to achieve the objectives of the Treaties.'

on the exercise of multiple voting rights in takeover situations would have far-reaching effects on the corporate ownership structure. At the same time these Member States have a high takeover activity, not hampered by the opt-out from the breakthrough rule. Under such circumstances, a specific action repealing the opt-out from the breakthrough rule would go beyond what is appropriate and necessary and thus be disproportionate and not in conformity with the general proportionality principle.[48]

Finally, in the light of the *Proportionality Report* the whole issue of obstacles to takeover activity was handled in a biased and unacceptable manner during the legislative process leading up to the enactment of the Takeover Directive. The Nordic model of the multiple voting rights system was singled out unfairly as an anti-integration device during the preparations of the Takeover Directive. The experience of the Nordic countries demonstrates that a transparent, non-discriminatory multiple voting rights system can very well be combined with successful companies, open markets, and a high level of takeover activity. It would have been far better and in line with proper legislative practice, had the *Proportionality Report* been conducted first. The conclusions reached in that report do not indicate that mechanisms of ownership control should be the priority for European company law reform projects. The issues involved are probably solved better by market-driven forces. In a longer perspective, it seems likely increased financial integration and other demand-driven factors will stimulate a factual development towards more convergence in the shape of corporate ownership control within Europe.

[48] The Council Legal Service gave very brief reasons for its original position that a prohibition without an opt-out clause on the exercise of multiple voting rights in takeover situations would be in compliance with the proportionality principle in EU law. It stated rather cryptically that the measures aimed to facilitate takeover bids seemed proportionate since they were temporary and did not limit the rights themselves, but rather the use of those rights, para 44 of the Council Legal Service Note.

PART III

COMPANY LAW AND FORECLOSURE OF MARKETS

10

Deviations from Ownership-Control Proportionality—Economic Protectionism Revisited

Wolf-Georg Ringe

I. Introduction

The global financial crisis that has beset these recent years has prompted a somewhat panicked rediscovery of the concept of national protectionism. This rediscovery has in turn reinvigorated the debate around the proportionality of ownership and control. Though the previous 20 years bore witness to a steady decline of multiple voting rights, preference shares, voting caps, and the like, and thus a strong tendency towards convergence and proportionality, in the wake of the economic crisis of 2008/09 there floats a new debate about the desirability of control-enhancing mechanisms. This debate can be seen in the discourse of policy makers that advocate the introduction of multiple voting rights to reward long-term shareholders in an attempt to curb the short-termism that is perceived by many to have provided the prevalent business incentive prior to the financial crisis.[1] Alongside such discourse there buds a renaissance in the use of golden shares, in the hope, inter alia, of protecting European industries against Sovereign Wealth Funds from the Middle and Far East.[2]

The purpose of this paper is to revisit some of the aspects of the one share/one vote (OSOV) debate in the shadow of the protectionist fears that have lurked in the corners of discussions since the beginning of the financial crisis. The EU abandoned its plan to make OSOV mandatory law in 2007, and the US does not have an overall OSOV rule either. Accordingly, EU Member States and US federal states and stock exchanges have free discretion to regulate this matter, and we will see that the question of ownership and voting relationship is answered very differently by states and companies, depending on regulatory convictions, market pressures, takeover fears, and other external influences. Nevertheless, up

[1] See below Section V.2. [2] See below Section V.1.

until recently, the prevailing view in most Western jurisdictions was to follow the OSOV principle to a large extent. The recent financial crisis has, however, given shape to new protectionist movements and could correspondingly revitalize those calling for deviations from a strict OSOV rule.

This paper is structured as follows: we shall begin with an overview of the current OSOV debate, including the EU's policy agenda as well as the approach taken by the Court of Justice of the European Union and the academic debate (II). Following that, the presence of deviations from OSOV in the business world will be explored, both from a current and a historic perspective (III). This will then allow us to evaluate the landscape seen by some to be developing as a consequence of the recent financial crisis (V). Finally, implications from this new perspective are drawn (VI).

II. The one share/one vote debate and European solutions

'OSOV' expresses in practicable terms the principle that one should ensure a proportionate allocation of share ownership and control in a company. 'Ownership' in this context can be equated with 'cash-flow rights'. The principle implies that any shareholder should own the same fraction of cash-flow rights and voting rights, thus attributing an amount of control to a shareholder that is proportionate to his shareholding. Inherent in the principle is the proscription of deviations from a proportionate allocation of ownership and control via so-called 'control-enhancing mechanisms' (CEMs).[3]

Many in the academic debate perceive proportionality as being rationally compelling on the observation that shareholders as the company's residual claimants have the strongest interest in maximizing firm value, and in the further belief that voting power should match economic incentives alone. Additionally, recent public debates about proportionality have assumed an emotional dimension: the idea that each share entitles the owners to equal influence has intuitive appeal. It has lead to slogans such as 'shareholder democracy' based on assumed parallels between societal and corporate governance.[4]

The ultimate objective of establishing an OSOV principle in the EU has been pursued on two levels, and with diverging methods and aims. Based on recommendations of an academic expert group, the Commission has pondered whether to introduce mandatory legislation, whereas the Court of Justice of the European Union has indirectly been working on a case law-based approach over the past years.

[3] Possible CEMs are, for instance, multiple voting rights, voting ceilings, non-voting (preference) shares, etc.

[4] The term 'shareholder democracy' is imprecise, as modern democracy would imply proportionality between influence and the number, rather than investments, of shareholders.

1. The High Level Group and Commission activity

Upon reaching an apparent deadlock in European company law around the year 2000, the European Commission asked an academic expert group to reconceptualize the EU's legislation in this field. In the resulting report of 2002, the European High Level Group of Company Law Experts stated that, 'proportionality between ultimate economic risk and control means that share capital which has an unlimited right to participate in the profits of the company or in the residue on liquidation, and only such share capital, should normally carry control rights, in proportion to the risk carried'.[5] However, the group did not advocate a full mandatory OSOV principle, but rather confined itself to suggesting a limited principle that would be effective in takeover situations.[6]

The Commission, in its subsequent 2003 *Action Plan on Company Law and Corporate Governance*, was more cautious about a clear statement with regard to the OSOV principle. Whereas it considered that there was a strong medium- to long-term case for establishing a 'shareholder democracy' in the EU, the Commission nevertheless observed that any initiative in this direction required prior research.[7] Stakeholders confirmed the need for such a study in their response to the spring 2006 consultation conducted on the future priorities of the Action Plan.[8]

Therefore, the Commission entrusted a consortium of Institutional Shareholder Services (ISS), associated to a European network of leading academics, the European Corporate Governance Institute (ECGI) and the law firm Shearman & Sterling with a study to report about the effects of such measures. The final report of this group was presented in 2007.[9] It provides a factual background to the issue of proportionality between capital and control. The report is accompanied by detailed surveys of the academic literature[10] and of the empirical evidence[11] on the 'one share/one vote' issue as well as by a detailed comparative

[5] *Report of the High Level Group of Company Law Experts on Issues Related to Takeover Bids* (January 2002) 21.

[6] For the reasons, see J Rickford, 'Invisible Hand or Dead Hand?—Reflections on the EU "One Share One Vote"' in European Policy Forum (ed), *One Share one Vote? Tomorrow's Companies: One Universal Model or Tailored Equity Structures?* (London: EPF, 2006) 67, 70 f.

[7] Communication from the Commission to the Council and the European Parliament, *Modernising Company Law and Enhancing Corporate Governance in the European Union—A Plan to Move Forward*, COM(2003) 284 final, 14.

[8] Directorate General for Internal Market and Services, *Consultation and Hearing on Future Priorities for the Action Plan on Modernising Company Law and Enhancing Corporate Governance in the European Union—Summary Report* (2006), <http://ec.europa.eu/internal_market/company/docs/consultation/final_report_en.pdf> (last accessed 8 July 2010).

[9] ISS, Shearman & Sterling LLP, and ECGI, *Report on the Proportionality Principle in the European Union*, available at <http://ec.europa.eu/internal_market/company/docs/shareholders/study/final_report_en.pdf> (last accessed 8 July 2010).

[10] M Burkart and S Lee, 'One Share-One Vote: the Theory' (2008) 12 Rev of Finance 1, 4.

[11] R Adams and D Ferreira, 'One Share-One Vote: The Empirical Evidence' (2008) 12 Rev of Finance 51.

legal study covering 16 Member States of the EU as well as Australia, Japan, and the US.[12] The study found that there was no economic evidence of a causal link between deviations from the proportionality principle and the economic performance of companies.[13]

On the EU level, 2007 saw increased activity in this field. In September, the European Corporate Governance Forum published a statement on the question of proportionality between capital and control.[14] In December of the same year, the European Commission published an impact assessment on the question of proportionality between capital and control in listed companies.[15] The document presents the pros and cons of possible policy actions, also including an evaluation of the consequences of not undertaking any regulatory action in this field. The impact assessment has been validated by the Commission's impact assessment board.[16] Having weighed the arguments advanced, then Commissioner McCreevy finally decided that there was no need for action at EU level on this issue.[17] The European Commission therefore stopped work in this area. Since this moment, the OSOV project on the European level has no longer been pursued.

Instead, the Commission focused on transparency requirements contained in existing EU legislation.[18] The Takeover Bids Directive,[19] the 2006 amendments of the Accounting Directives,[20] the Transparency Directive,[21] and the recently

[12] Shearman & Sterling LLP, *Proportionality between Ownership and Control in EU Listed Companies: Comparative Legal Study* (May 2007).

[13] See Adams and Ferreira (n 11).

[14] European Corporate Governance Forum, *Statement on the question of proportionality between capital and control*, available at <http://ec.europa.eu/internal_market/company/docs/ecgforum/statement_proportionality_en.pdf> (last accessed 8 July 2010); see also the paper by the European Corporate Governance Forum Working Group on Proportionality from June 2007, <http://ec.europa.eu/internal_market/company/docs/ecgforum/workinggroup_proportionality_en.pdf> (last accessed 8 July 2010).

[15] <http://ec.europa.eu/internal_market/company/docs/shareholders/impact_assessment_122007.pdf> (last accessed 8 July 2010).

[16] <http://ec.europa.eu/governance/impact/ia_carried_out/docs/ia_2007/d_2007_9803_iab_opinion_proportionality.pdf> (last accessed 8 July 2010).

[17] C McCreevy, Speech at the European Parliament's Legal Affairs Committee, 3 October 2007, Speech/07/592.

[18] A Johnston, *EC Regulation of Corporate Governance* (Cambridge: Cambridge University Press, 2010) 302 ff.

[19] Directive 2004/25/EC of the European Parliament and of the Council of 21 April 2004 on takeover bids, [2004] OJ L142/12.

[20] Directive 2006/43/EC of the European Parliament and of the Council of 17 May 2006 on statutory audits of annual accounts and consolidated accounts, amending Council Directives 78/660/EEC and 83/349/EEC and repealing Council Directive 84/253/EEC, [2006] OJ L157/87; Directive 2006/46/EC of the European Parliament and of the Council of 14 June 2006 amending Council Directives 78/660/EEC on the annual accounts of certain types of companies, 83/349/EEC on consolidated accounts, 86/635/EEC on the annual accounts and consolidated accounts of banks and other financial institutions and 91/674/EEC on the annual accounts and consolidated accounts of insurance undertakings, [2006] OJ L224/1.

[21] Directive 2004/109/EC of the European Parliament and of the Council of 15 December 2004 on the harmonisation of transparency requirements in relation to information about issuers whose securities are admitted to trading on a regulated market and amending Directive 2001/34/EC, [2004] OJ L390/38.

adopted Shareholders' Rights Directive[22] contain ample provisions on transparency. Then Commissioner McCreevy therefore saw additional transparency requirements as unnecessary.[23] The current regulatory stance thus seems to be threefold:

(1) a mandatory one share/one vote directive will not be introduced since its case has not been made;

(2) instead, the EU will continue to focus on more specific situations in which aspects close to OSOV become relevant. Some of the existing legislation in the field of securities markets already directly or indirectly addresses CEMs with a view to countering information asymmetry: This relates inter alia to rules on the exercise of control rights, on the prevention of conflicts of interest and on market transparency, including financial disclosure; and

(3) finally, the Commission conducted a 'third' consultation on shareholders' rights,[24] possibly further covering issues addressed by the already adopted Shareholders' Rights Directive.[25] This consultation, however, was conducted in 2007 and has not been followed up since then.

2. Court of Justice

At the same time, the Court of Justice of the European Union (CJEU) is pursuing a similar yet slower strategy towards deviations from OSOV. In the absence of any definite secondary law dealing with the issue,[26] the Court is currently assessing how far a reliance on *primary law* could provide similar results. More concretely, a number of judgments currently examine the scope and ambit of the free movement of capital provisions (Articles 63 ff TFEU) and how these can tackle the problem of CEMs. The capital freedom is one of the four fundamental freedoms contained in the Treaty. It was not until the Treaty of Maastricht that the full effectiveness of the freedom was developed, and consequently the EC Treaty has only mandated the complete abolition of all obstacles to capital movement since 1994.[27] In subsequent years, the Commission accepted this new task

[22] Directive 2007/36/EC of the European Parliament and of the Council of 11 July 2007 on the exercise of certain rights of shareholders in listed companies [2007] OJ L184/17. [23] Ibid.

[24] European Commission, *Fostering an Appropriate Regime for Shareholders' Rights—Third consultation document* (April 2007), <http://ec.europa.eu/internal_market/company/docs/shareholders/consultation3_en.pdf> (last accessed 8 July 2010); European Commission, *Synthesis of the Comments on the Third Consultation Document 'Fostering an Appropriate Regime for Shareholders' Rights'* (September 2007), <http://ec.europa.eu/internal_market/company/docs/shareholders/consultation3_report_en.pdf> (last accessed 8 July 2010). [25] n 22.

[26] Attempts to introduce a directive dealing with OSOV have failed. Moreover, the Takeover Directive—which addresses parts of the problem in a takeover context—is an only optional tool in this respect (see Article 12).

[27] J A Usher, *The Law of Money and Financial Services in the EC* (2nd edn, Oxford: Oxford University Press, 2000) 22 ff; D Chalmers and others, *European Union Law* (Cambridge: Cambridge University Press, 2006) 509; L Flynn, 'Coming of Age: The Free Movement of Capital

and published a communication on 'Certain Legal Aspects Concerning Intra-EU Investment' in 1997.[28] In this communication, the Commission explained the conditions for applying the free movement of capital and clarified necessary definitions. In the document, the Commission identified three major obstacles to the free movement of capital:

(1) prohibitions 'on investors from another EU country acquiring more than a limited amount of voting shares in domestic companies';
(2) 'measures applied without distinction to all investors, [...] in particular general authorisation procedures whereby, for example, any investor (EU and national alike) wanting to acquire a stake in a domestic company above a certain threshold [...] [must be authorised]'; and
(3) 'the rights given to national authorities, in derogation of company law, to veto certain major decisions to be taken by the company, as well as the imposition of a requirement for the nomination of some directors as a means of exercising the right of veto, etc.'

Measures of the first category are clearly discriminatory and are thus liable to violate fundamental freedoms. The second category applies to all investors without distinction, but concerns access to the market and hence violates the freedoms of establishment and capital in the absence of a justification.[29] The third category, special rights for public authorities, was at the time a less obvious violation of the free movement of capital. Its theoretical basis is that these special rights constitute 'national measures' under the *Gebhard* formula '[which are] liable to hinder or make less attractive the exercise of fundamental freedoms'.[30]

In the years following the communication, the Commission slowly proceeded to bring these special rights before the CJEU. In these proceedings since the end of the 1990s, the Court has abolished several national special rights in previously privatized undertakings, so-called 'golden shares'.[31] This is a term for one of the strongest deviations from OSOV and relates to a special share, usually held by the government, which entails specific rights that are unavailable to other

Case Law 1993-2002' (2002) 39 CML Rev 773. This fundamental freedom is considered as directly effective, see Joined Cases C-163/94, C-165/94, and C-250/94 *Criminal proceedings against Lucas Emilio Sanz de Lera and others* [1995] ECR I-4821 [41]–[47].

[28] [1997] OJ 220/15.

[29] Case C-302/97 *Klaus Konle v Republic of Austria* [1999] ECR I-3099.

[30] Case C-55/94 *Reinhard Gebhard v Consiglio dell'Ordine degli Avvocati e Procuratori di Milano* [1995] ECR I-4165 para 37.

[31] See on this E Szyszczak, 'Golden Shares and Market Governance' (2002) 29 Legal Issues of Economic Integration 255; H Fleischer, 'Case Note on the Golden Shares Cases' (2003) 20 CML Rev 493; C O Putek, 'Limited but not Lost—A Comment on the ECJ's Golden Share Decisions' (2004) 72 Fordham L Rev 2219; A Looijestijn-Clearie, 'All That Glitters is not Gold: European Court of Justice Strikes Down Golden Shares in Two Dutch Companies' (2007) 8 Eur Business Organization L Rev 429; S Grundmann and F Möslein, 'Die Goldene Aktie—Staatskontrollrechte in Europarecht und wirtschaftspolitischer Bewertung' [2003] Zeitschrift für Unternehmens- und Gesellschaftsrecht (ZGR) 317.

shareholders. Although the business of the company is privatized, a golden share retains the government's right to intervene in the share structure and management of the company. This includes special provisions designed to enable the executive to prevent takeovers or other changes of control.

The special rights attached to the golden type of 'share' can vary from case to case. Some golden shares confer the right to outvote all other shareholders at general meetings or to veto certain changes within the company, for example the sale of core assets. Others include provisions intended to ensure that no shareholder is beneficially entitled to an interest in more than a fixed proportion of voting shares. A third variant enables the government to nominate some of the directors. In some jurisdictions, golden shares can be created even under company law, while elsewhere, special legislation is needed to introduce state privileges in privatized companies. Golden shares are generally regarded as a separate class of shares. Consequently, any attempt to alter the state privileges requires the consent of the special preference class. The CJEU found in all but one of the cases before it, that these special rights violated the fundamental freedoms: the cases concerned France,[32] Portugal,[33] the United Kingdom,[34] Spain,[35] the Netherlands,[36] and Italy,[37] with the sole exception of Belgium.[38]

A full recounting of these proceedings is not necessary here;[39] the general gist of this case law is that the Court of Justice does not allow decisive state influence in companies if such influence unjustifiably favours the state over regular shareholders. In other words: the European Court has always found a violation of fundamental freedoms when—sometimes under the guise of market participation—the state has acted as a regulator.[40] Therefore, the Court does not distinguish between statutory law and provisions that are contained in the articles of association of the company.[41] Moreover, according to the Court's case law, infringement of Article 63 TFEU is no longer limited to discriminatory national provisions, but covers all norms that might hinder the free movement of capital, even if their effect is not discriminatory.[42] The decisive factor—in accordance

[32] Case C-483/99 *Commission v France* [2002] ECR I-4781.

[33] Case C-367/98 *Commission v Portugal* [2002] ECR I-4731.

[34] Case C-98/01 *Commission v United Kingdom* [2003] ECR I-4641.

[35] Case C-463/00 *Commission v Spain* [2003] ECR I-4581. More recently, see Cases C-274/06 *Commission v Spain* [2008] ECR I-26 (summary publication) and C-207/07 *Commission v Spain* [2008] ECR I-111 (summary publication).

[36] Joined Cases C-282/04 and C-283/04 *Commission v Netherlands* [2006] ECR I-9141.

[37] Case C-174/04 *Commission v Italy* [2005] ECR I-4933; Joined Cases C-463/04 and C-464/04 *Federconsumatori and others v Comune di Milano* [2007] ECR I-10419.

[38] Case C-503/99 *Commission v Belgium* [2002] ECR I-4809.

[39] For more details, see the literature cited in n 31 above.

[40] A Arnull and others, *Wyatt & Dashwood's European Union Law* (5th edn, London: Sweet & Maxwell, 2006) para 20-021.

[41] See especially *Commission v United Kingdom* (n 34).

[42] *Commission v Portugal* (n 33) paras 44 f; *Commission v United Kingdom* (n 34) para 43; see P Craig and G de Búrca, *EU Law—Text, Cases, and Materials* (4th edn, Oxford: Oxford University Press, 2007) 725.

with the above-mentioned Commission communication—has always been that the special right at stake conferred a benefit on the state as market co-ordinator.

More recently, the Court has gone beyond traditional golden shares and has tested general rules of company law as to their compatibility with the free movement of capital.[43] In the *Volkswagen* case, the Court had to assess the validity of the Volkswagen law, a statute that imposed specific measures on Volkswagen AG ('VW'), such as a voting cap and a special majority requirement for important company decisions.[44] Even though these measures did not necessarily favour the state as in the traditional golden shares cases before, the Court found them to be incompatible with the Treaty. The Court did not clarify, however, whether this finding was due to the fact that they indirectly favoured the state (which held 20 per cent of VW's shares) or whether a similar analysis would have been made if the sole benefit would go to private parties, ie regular shareholders.[45] The latter development cannot be excluded from being pursued by the Court in the next years.[46] This would mean that clearly simple rules of company law such as a voting cap (which was at stake in the *Volkswagen* case) could be tested directly against the free movement of capital. Its validity would then depend on whether it deters potential investors from other EU Member States. The development is, however, not certain, and for now it cannot be accepted as good law.

3. The academic debate

The academic debate, led on both sides of the Atlantic, has been turning around the question whether legislation that would make OSOV mandatory in any given country, but especially across the EU, would be socially desirable or not. There are diverging views in the literature as to whether OSOV implies such social value.

Proponents of the rule essentially argue that it efficiently aligns the interests within a company and that it facilitates takeovers while reducing the possibility of management entrenchment.

The quintessential OSOV supporting paper is that by Easterbrook and Fischel from 1983. The article emphasizes that deviations from an equal voting right in the company will create agency costs of management.[47] This essential assertion is based on two instances: first, and fundamentally, the two scholars argue that shareholders in possession of disproportionate voting rights will not make

[43] On the following, see J Rickford, 'Protectionism, Capital Freedom, and the Internal Market' ch 4 above, p 54; J Rickford, 'Free Movement of Capital and Protectionism after *Volkswagen* and *Viking Line*' in M Tison and others (eds), *Perspectives in Company Law and Financial Regulation* (Cambridge: Cambridge University Press, 2009) 61; WG Ringe, 'Company Law and Free Movement of Capital' (2010) 69 Cambridge L J 378.

[44] Case C-112/05 *Commission v Germany* [2007] ECR I-8995.

[45] Cf in more detail WG Ringe. 'Case C-112/05, *Commission* v. *Germany* ("VW law"), Judgment of the Grand Chamber of 23 October 2007' (2008) 45 CML Rev 537.

[46] Ringe (n 43).

[47] F H Easterbrook and D R Fischel, 'Voting in Corporate Law' (1983) 26 J of L and Economics 395, 409.

optimal decisions for the company.[48] Where a shareholder bears a higher economic risk than is reflected in his voting right (or vice versa, his voting rights are greater than his economic risk), his incentives to vote may be distorted. This is because he might be more willing to accept a risk when his financial interest is lower than his influence in the company actually is; conversely, if his financial exposure is greater than his equity share, he might not be in a position to make his voice heard in the same way as corresponds to his interests.

Secondly, the paper claims that disproportionate ownership structures have the further attribute of impeding corporate takeovers or changes of control and thus support the position of managers against shareholders.[49] Disproportionate voting rights can thus lead to an insulated management position, especially where the management is supported by or connected with the shareholder enjoying special voting rights.[50] This is relevant on three levels: First, differentiated voting rights facilitate control by an economic minority stake and thus make a takeover extremely difficult without a breakthrough rule which sets them aside during the period of a takeover bid. Secondly, circumventions of OSOV such as voting agreements may increase managerial discretion and discourage potential value-increasing takeovers.[51] Third, voting restrictions such as voting caps can represent important anti-takeover devices that discourage potential bidders from making an offer.[52] Moreover, it is recognized that deviations from OSOV permit an over-representation of minority interests in the company's governance, leading to the possibility that there will be diverging preferences among the members of the board. In this way, such schemes expose the firm to an uncompensated risk of making inconsistent or illogical decisions.[53]

These arguments can be complemented by a historical perspective. Behind the abolition of cumulative voting rights in various countries over the last decades can be found stories of plain abuse. The classic example is that of Germany in the 1920s, where many companies had shareholders with extremely high voting power, some comprising hundreds of votes (sometimes even thousands) per share.[54] At that time the excessive use of multiple voting rights—generally

[48] Ibid. Cf D R Fischel, 'Organized Exchanges and the Regulation of Dual Class Common Stock' (1987) 54 U of Chicago L Rev 119, 135; A Alchian and H Demsetz, 'Production, Information Costs, and Economic Organization' [1972] The American Economic Rev 777, 783.

[49] Ibid. This point is emphasized by a dissenting opinion in the Jenkins Report, *Report of the Company Law Committee* (London: HMSO, London 1962) 207–10.

[50] M Goergen and others, 'Corporate Governance Convergence: Evidence From Takeover Regulation Reforms in Europe' (2005) 21 Oxford Rev of Economic Policy 243, 253.

[51] R Crespi and L Renneboog, 'Coalition formation and shareholder monitoring in the UK' Discussion paper CentER, Tilburg University, 2002.

[52] Goergen and others (n 50).

[53] Easterbrook and Fischel (n 47).

[54] G Spindler, 'Kriegsfolgen, Konzernbildung und Machtfrage als zentrale Aspekte der aktienrechtlichen Diskussion in der Weimarer Republik' in W Bayer and M Habersack (eds), *Aktienrecht im Wandel—Band I, Entwicklung des Aktienrechts* (Tübingen: Mohr Siebeck, 2007) 440, 454; W Schubert and P Hommelhoff (eds), *Die Aktienrechtsreform am Ende der Weimarer Republik*, (New York/Berlin: de Gruyter, 1987) 89 f, 320 ff, 657 ff; cf K W Nörr 'Zur Entwicklung des

accepted by the courts—led to a situation where they were abused to erode shareholder rights for the sole benefit and entrenchment of the management. This in turn induced the German legislators in 1937 to make the availability of multiple voting rights dependent upon an authorization by the competent ministry.[55]

Finally, in the context of the topic under consideration here, the clear protectionist aspect of deviations from OSOV has to be mentioned.[56] In the same way as concentrated ownership is more likely to go hand in hand with government influence and is prone to support domestic elites,[57] CEMs often coincide with government policy objectives. The prime example is family-controlled firms where the family has disproportionate political influence, which they use to lock in a status quo advantageous to them.[58] This has a particular relevance within the European Union, where lawmakers have been trying over years to eliminate obstacles to cross-border investment.[59] Starting with the obvious example of golden shares,[60] and moving on to other CEMs like voting ceilings and quorum requirements,[61] these instruments can have the effect of locking up the different markets that the EU is aiming to open up.[62] The control position of established national elites—like the industrial networks in Germany or in France—may thus be reinforced.[63] Potential investors, whether or not they wish to acquire control in a foreign target company, are faced with established controllers, who can even reinforce their strong position with the help of CEMs. Moreover, an investor who desires to invest in other EU markets is faced with a multitude of different and opaquely disproportionate voting structures in other Member States, which significantly impede the possibility of investment or control acquisition in companies registered in other Member States. Conceptualized in economic terms, this means that these CEMs impose externalities by increasing the cost of capital in the EU.[64] Accepting that particular ownership structures might be functional in light of national complementarities, they might nevertheless be

Aktien- und Konzernrechts während der Weimarer Republik' (1986) 150 Zeitschrift für das gesamte Handelsrecht und Wirtschaftsrecht 155, 163.

55 Ibid, 456. Cf W Bayer and T Hoffmann, 'Mehrstimmrechtsaktien in Deutschland' [2008] Die Aktiengesellschaft R464, R466 ff.

56 See on this especially Rickford (n 6) 68, 69, 73, 83, 84; J Gordon, 'The International Relations Wedge in the Corporate Convergence Debate' in J Gordon and M Roe (eds), *Convergence and Persistence in Corporate Governance* (Cambridge: Cambridge University Press, 2004) 161, 165, 197; UK Law Society, Company Law Sub-Committee, *Minutes of 229th meeting (31 July 2007)*, available at <http://www.citysolicitors.org.uk/FileServer.aspx?oID=260&lID=0>.

57 Gordon (n 56) 163 f.

58 See on this R Morck, 'The Riddle of the Great Pyramids' NBER Working Paper 14858 (2009), 13. Economic evidence is consistent with this hypothesis: R Morck, D Wolfenzon, and B Yeung, 'Corporate Governance, Economic Entrenchment, and Growth' (2005) 43 J of Economic Literature 655.

59 A Arnull and others, *Wyatt & Dashwood's European Union Law* (5th edn, London: Sweet & Maxwell, 2006) paras 20–21 ff.

60 See above Section II.2.

61 These instruments were tested in Case C-112/05 *Commission v Germany* [2007] ECR I-8995.

62 Rickford (n 6).

63 Gordon (n 56) 197–8.

64 Rickford (n 6) 73 f.

inefficient from a transnational (European) perspective.[65] Consequently, there is an argument that—even if we are agnostic as to the potentially beneficial effect of OSOV for individual firms—EU law nevertheless requires its introduction because of its imperative to integrate the different markets and to overcome national boundaries. As explained above, deviations from OSOV may thus harm the development of a market for corporate control. The first proposal of the Takeover Directive—which would have taken a much stricter stance towards takeover-impeding obstacles—was rejected on the initiative of a few Member States (among them Germany) for this specific reason, ie that it would have facilitated takeover bids for domestic firms that these countries sought to protect.[66]

The key argument that has been raised *against* a mandatory OSOV rule is that deviations from a strict proportionality can be beneficial in certain situations. Entrepreneurs will be more willing to start a business or to expand it later by raising outside equity capital if they can make sure that they remain the strongest group in the company's decision-making process. Consequently, if such mechanisms (eg multiple voting rights) were not allowed, a lot of economic activity requiring outside equity capital (whether raised through IPOs or later capital increases) would not take place for the controllers' fear of losing their influence. From this perspective, deviations from OSOV facilitate the access to the public equity capital market for some companies (in particular small, family-owned companies).[67]

The second most relevant argument that has been made by opponents to a strict OSOV rule is that such a rule would interfere with the shareholders' sovereignty and independence. In many company law systems (like the UK and the US), the shareholders are principally free to arrange their internal affairs without much legislative intervention. In the spirit of contractual freedom, this would imply that shareholders generally can decide on their individual rights and voting allocation.[68] This is the essence of an argument made by many Scandinavian scholars and policy makers who refer to their largely available multiple voting rights and still very active takeover markets.[69]

[65] *Report of the High Level Group of Company Law Experts on Issues Related to Takeover Bids* (January 2002) 22-3.

[66] R Skog, 'The Takeover Directive—An Endless Saga?' (2002) 13 EBLR 301, 309 f; K J Hopt, 'Offene Märkte oder Abschottung?' in M D Kley and others (eds), *Aktie und Kapitalmarkt—Anlegerschutz, Unternehmensfinanzierung und Finanzplatz (FS v. Rosen)* (Stuttgart: Schäffer-Poeschel, 2008) 537, 544.

[67] M Goergen and others, Corporate Governance Convergence: Evidence From Takeover Regulation Reforms in Europe' (2005) 21 Oxford Rev of Economic Policy 243, 253.

[68] W Zöllner and U Noack, 'One share—one vote? Stimmrecht und Kapitalbeteiligung bei der Aktiengesellschaft' [1991] Die Aktiengesellschaft (AG) 117, 119, 127; U Noack, 'Das Aktienrecht der Krise—das Aktienrecht in der Krise?' [2009] AG 227, 234 f.

[69] U Bernitz, The Attack on the Nordic Multiple Voting Rights Model: The Legal Limits under EU law' (2004) 15 EBLR 1423; R Skog, 'The European Union's Proposed Takeover Directive, the "Breakthrough" Rule and the Swedish System of Dual Class Common Stock' (2004) 45

The third point made by the proponents of deviations from OSOV concerns its function within a concentrated ownership environment. Whereas they recognize the beneficial role OSOV could play in a dispersed-ownership environment, where it can help to discipline the board, mitigate agency costs, and overcome the rational apathy of shareholders, the effect would be quite different in a continental European system. In an environment characterized by large blockholders, the abolition of CEMs would not return control to the public equity markets, but would simply further strengthen the power of existing large shareholders, potentially enhancing their ability to extract private benefits of control to the detriment of minority shareholders.[70]

This leads to another line of argument, challenging the traditional view as propounded by Easterbrook and Fischel. According to some commentators, their argument is flawed in that it is based on the unrealistic presumption of homogenous or even 'identical' shareholders. This, however, is not the case: shareholders differ not only in the size of their respective stakes and influence within the corporation, but also in their strategic interests, financial or strategic investment perspectives, and the specificity of their investment.[71]

Furthermore, it should be noted that an implementation of an OSOV rule in legislation would probably be extremely difficult to achieve.[72] While it may be easy enough to insert such a provision into the relevant company law statute, it would most certainly be easily circumvented by other CEMs. On the one hand, pyramids and voting cascades can arguably be used to produce similar results as disproportionate voting rights. This is a technique that might be extremely difficult to tackle from a regulatory perspective.[73] Secondly, even if these avoidance strategies were not available, modern financial engineering, in particular financial instruments and derivatives, may be used to effectuate similar effects. Hence, the problem poses a difficult if not insoluble problem for every lawmaker.

Not all of these arguments are convincing, and some of them may even contradict each other. Much of the disagreement between the two positions can

Scandinavian Studies in L 293. They admit, however, that 'hostile takeovers are rare' (Bernitz ibid, 1429), which is the main problem of OSOV-deviations.

70 R J Gilson and J N Gordon, 'Controlling Controlling Shareholders' (2003) 152 U of Pennsylvania L Rev 785; A Khachaturyan, 'Trapped in Delusions: The One-Share-One-Vote Rule in the EU' (2007) 8 EBOR 335, 346 f.

71 Khachaturyan (n 70) 345. Cf A Khachaturyan and J McCahery, 'European Union Takeover Regulation and the One-Share One-Vote Controversy' in GN Gregoriou and L Renneboog (eds), *Corporate Governance and Regulatory Impact on Mergers and Acquisitions* (Amsterdam: Elsevier, 2007) 163, 175.

72 L Enriques, H Hansmann, and R Kraakman, 'The Basic Governance Structure: The Interests of Shareholders as a Class' in R Kraakman and others, *The Anatomy of Corporate Law* (2nd edn, Oxford: Oxford University Press, 2009) ch 3, 55, 60; M Burkart and S Lee, 'One Share-One Vote: the Theory' (2008) 12 Rev of Finance 1, 4.

73 The only possibility probably being tax law, see R W Morck, 'How to Eliminate Pyramidal Business Groups: the Double Taxation of Intracorporate Dividends and Other Incisive uses of Tax Policy' in JM Poterba (ed), *Tax Policy and the Economy, vol 19* (Cambridge, MA: NBER, 2005).

actually be explained and dissolved by putting more emphasis on the business environment in which the OSOV legislation is to operate and the basic conflicts which company law aims to solve. In a blockholder-dominated corporate culture like that of continental Europe, the basic agency conflict is between minority and majority shareholders.[74] Here, rules that allow for deviations from OSOV can aggravate this conflict. In such a system CEMs can, as the name suggests, enhance the already established control of a controlling shareholder and put him or her in a position that is virtually unassailable. Minority shareholders will never be able to introduce CEMs for themselves without the consent of the majority. This allows controllers to create corporate structures that can hardly ever be challenged by means of a hostile takeover. The consequence is well known: management entrenchment and private benefits of control.

In a dispersed shareholder environment like the UK or the US, however, allowing CEMs could actually make more sense. The main agency conflict in company law lies here between managers and shareholders—the latter often being unable to control the former effectively.[75] In such a situation, CEMs can overcome the agency conflict to a certain extent by assigning enhanced influence to some (minority) shareholders, who—owing to these disproportionate structures—will be in a position to supervise and control the management. In the end, this is probably one of the reasons why finding a clear solution to the problem is so difficult.[76] Neither is the economic contribution always cogent, nor do the legal arguments necessarily point in one direction or another. It is, however, important to note that the opposite case has not been made either: there is no convincing argument why deviations from OSOV should be always desirable. A more sophisticated solution must take into consideration the shareholder environment in which the OSOV operates or should operate, and the motivations and objectives for deviations from OSOV. The current international consensus lies somewhere between two positions: whereas most commentators accept that OSOV is the general starting point because it offers the best alignment of incentives, there is also agreement that under certain circumstances deviations can be justifiable. This is not to be misunderstood as a general carte blanche for every deviation in every situation. Deviations need to remain the exception and need to be justified. This justification may, for instance, be easier in a dispersed shareholder environment, or if the non-availability of CEMs would impede a value-creating IPO.

What we can take as a general consensus is consequently the following tenet: shareholders who control a proportion of total voting rights larger than

[74] L Enriques and P Volpin, 'Corporate Governance Reforms in Continental Europe' (2007) 21 J of Economic Perspectives 117, 122 ff.

[75] M Jensen and W Meckling, 'Theory of the Firm: Managerial Behaviour, Agency Costs and Ownership Structure' (1976) 3 J of Financial Economics 305.

[76] As explained, the results being inconclusive overall, the European Commission stopped working on the proposal for a mandatory OSOV rule in the EU. See above Section II.1.

their ownership rights have an incentive to extract value from the company at the expense of non-controlling shareholders.[77] Hence, especially in continental Europe, problems associated with blockholder ownership will be aggravated purely by the availability of CEMs. On the other hand, as discussed, the case for a *mandatory* OSOV rule has not been made. It seems to emerge that the preferred model would be a system where OSOV is the *default* rule, but deviations can be accepted in exceptional circumstances.

Based on this perspective, we will analyse the presence of OSOV in the business world and the possible impact of the recent financial crisis.

III. Presence of CEMs in companies

In the absence of any overall mandatory regulation across the EU or in the US, the decision about introducing a proportionate share structure is currently left to the individual states, and often even to the companies themselves. Accordingly, proportionality and deviations therefrom are applied to a varying extent by companies across jurisdictions, depending on market pressures, takeover fears, and other external influences. This section analyses the actual presence of CEMs in various countries and studies the extent to which the attitude of these countries has changed over time.

1. CEMs today

How common are deviations from the OSOV rule in reality? As a general rule, the Anglo-American world seems to be more OSOV-friendly than continental Europe. In the US, OSOV is today not a mandatory rule, but provided by Delaware law as a default rule so that companies deliberately have to opt out from it.[78] However, the listing standards of the New York Stock Exchange, Nasdaq, and other exchanges' requirements come close to an OSOV rule, banning at least the midstream introduction of deviations therefrom.[79] Overall, it is fair to

[77] Impact Assessment Board (n 16).

[78] Delaware General Corporate Law § 212(a): 'Unless otherwise provided in the certificate of incorporation [...], each stockholder shall be entitled to 1 vote for each share of capital stock held by such stockholder'.

[79] See eg NYSE Listed Company Manual §313.00(A): 'Voting rights of existing shareholders of publicly traded common stock registered under Section 12 of the Exchange Act cannot be disparately reduced or restricted through any corporate action or issuance. Examples of such corporate action or issuance include, but are not limited to, the adoption of time phased voting plans, the adoption of capped voting rights plans, the issuance of super voting stock, or the issuance of stock with voting rights less than the per share voting rights of the existing common stock through an exchange offer.'

say that OSOV remains the standard for American corporations;[80] even though some prominent companies retain dual-class shares.[81]

The situation in Europe is different. The final report on proportionality between ownership and control commissioned by the European Commission in 2007[82] identified a vast number of deviations from OSOV across the EU. Of all the 464 companies considered in the study, 44 per cent had one or more CEMs. The countries with the highest proportion of companies featuring at least one of these mechanisms were found to be France, Sweden, Spain, Hungary, and Belgium, which all had a majority of companies with CEMs or alternative mechanisms. The occurrence of those mechanisms varied from one country to another, but also between large companies and recently listed companies. Overall, the mechanisms mostly used were found to be pyramid structures, multiple voting rights, and shareholder agreements. However, this is not to say that tendencies towards OSOV are nowhere to be found.

The UK, for example, has seen a strong support for OSOV by institutional investors for years.[83] OSOV is the voting default provision in s 284 Companies Act 2006, but subject to an opt-out by the company.[84] Equally, the London Stock Exchange encourages listed companies to restrict themselves to one class of shares, although no official regulation has been made.[85] This may explain why—despite their availability[86]—studies on the UK show that multiple voting rights, voting right ceilings, or non-voting shares are used by a small fraction of companies only.[87] However, non-voting preference shares are commonly used in the UK.[88]

[80] P A Gompers, J Ishii, and A Metrick, 'Extreme Governance: An Analysis of Dual-Class Firms in the United States' (2010) 23 Rev of Financial Studies 1051. Cf S Martin and F Partnoy, 'Encumbered Shares' [2005] U of Illinois L Rev 775, 786; R B Thompson and P H Edelman, 'Corporate Voting' (2009) 62 Vanderbilt L Rev 129, 159 f.

[81] Examples are Google, Ford, or Echostar.

[82] See above n 9.

[83] Rickford (n 6) 78; P L Davies, *Gower and Davies' Principles of Modern Company Law* (8th edn, London: Sweet & Maxwell, 2008) 15–16; J Franks, C Mayer, and S Rossi, 'Spending Less Time with the Family—The Decline of Family Ownership in the United Kingdom' in R K Morck (ed), *A History of Corporate Governance around the World* (Chicago and London: The University of Chicago Press, 2005) 581, 604.

[84] Companies Act 2006, s 284(4).

[85] B Cheffins, *Corporate Ownership and Control—British Business Transformed* (Oxford: Oxford University Press, 2008) 317; B Cheffins, *Company Law—Theory, Structure and Operation* (Oxford: Oxford University Press, 1997) 472, 475; B Hannigan, *Company Law* (2nd edn, Oxford: Oxford University Press, 2009) 14–16.

[86] See M Siems, *Convergence in Shareholder Law* (Cambridge: Cambridge University Press, 2008) 114; J Lowry and A Reisberg, *Pettet's Company Law* (3rd edn, Harlow: Pearson, 2009) 296. For instance, multiple voting rights were enforced by the House of Lords in *Bushell v Faith* [1970] 1 All ER 53. However, it is generally accepted that all classes of shares must attach the same voting/dividend rights to all shares within that class. Listing Rule 9.3.1 states that a listed company must ensure equality of treatment for all holders of listed equity securities or listed preference shares who are in the same position, ie all shares of the same class must have the same voting rights.

[87] Deminor Rating, *Application of the one share—one vote principle in Europe* (2005) 11 ff. Amongst the UK companies examined by the Shearman & Sterling Study (n 12), only 5% had multiple voting rights in place. There were no non-voting shares at all amongst the UK companies examined in the study. See Shearman & Sterling Study (n 12) 12.

[88] Ibid, 13.

Another example is Germany, where multiple voting rights were abolished and voting ceilings largely restricted by law in 1998.[89] The German Corporate Governance Code recommends that companies adopt a one share/one vote structure.[90] However, for instance non-voting preference shares remain permissible. Consequently, there is no overall mandatory OSOV rule.[91] The proportionality study revealed that—while there were obviously no multiple or non-voting shares in Germany—few companies made use of non-voting preference shares or voting right ceilings.[92] In essence, therefore, Germany's companies come close to an overall OSOV standard.

2. Change

Even more than an overview of the current presence of CEMs in company law might it be promising to look at the change in their prevalence over time. This may turn out to be particularly helpful for the question that is to be scrutinized here: Why do attitudes to OSOV change, and how?

(i) United States

The US has had a long history of ups and downs with OSOV.[93] By the end of the nineteenth century,[94] common and preferred shares of US corporations usually had equal voting rights, thus reflecting a *de facto* OSOV situation.[95]

[89] The relevant provisions in the *Aktiengesetz* (§§ 12, 134) were amended by Articles 1(3) and 1(20) *Gesetz zur Kontrolle und Transparenz im Unternehmensbereich* ('KonTraG') of 27 April 1998, [1998] Bundesgesetzblatt I, 786.

[90] German Corporate Governance Code (2009), s 2.1.2: 'In principle, each share carries one vote. There are no shares with multiple voting rights, preferential voting rights (golden shares) or maximum voting rights'.

[91] The German Corporate Governance Code is based on the 'comply or explain' approach, see *Aktiengesetz* § 161.

[92] ISS Report (n 9) 18 ff. However, recently non-voting preference shares seem to be popular again: D Mohr, 'Totgesagte Vorzugsaktien erleben neue Blüte' *Frankfurter Allgemeine Zeitung* (Frankfurt, 12 December 2009) 21.

[93] The following deals primarily with the history of multiple voting shares, but a similar development can be seen for voting caps for instance, see L Enriques, H Hansmann, and R Kraakman, 'The Basic Governance Structure: Minority Shareholders and Non-Shareholder Constituencies' in R Kraakman and others, *The Anatomy of Corporate Law* (2nd edn, Oxford: Oxford University Press, 2009) 89, 91.

[94] For an analysis of the US landscape in the nineteenth century, see C A Dunlavy, 'Corporate Governance in Late 19th-Century Europe and the U.S.—The Case of Shareholder Voting Rights' in K J Hopt and others (eds), *Comparative Corporate Governance—The State of the Art and Emerging Research* (Oxford: Oxford University Press, 1998) 5.

[95] Dunlavy (n 94) 26 ff; H Henn and J Alexander, *Laws of Corporations and other Business Associations* (3rd edn, St Paul: West Publishing, 1983) 493, n 3; D Ratner, 'The Government of Business Corporations: Critical Reflections on the Rule of "One Share, One Vote"' (1970) 56 Cornell L Rev 1, 8; J Seligman, 'Equal Protection in Shareholder Voting Rights: The One Common Share, One Vote Controversy' (1986) 54 George Washington L Rev 687, 693 f; see also C Rohrlich, 'Corporate Voting: Majority Control' (1933) 7 St John's L Rev 218; G Ferrarini, 'One Share—One Vote: A European Rule?' (2006) 3 Eur Company and Financial L Rev 147, 162 f.

However, in the first two decades of the following century corporations showed an increasing tendency to restrict the voting rights of certain classes of shareholders.[96] In 1925, several leading corporations (including Dodge Brothers and Industrial Rayon Corporation) issued non-voting common shares.[97] Berle and Means pointed out that a number of legal devices had developed to form controlling minorities, such as pyramids, non-voting (preferred or common) shares, and the voting trust.[98]

After heavy criticism of these practices by Harvard Professor Ripley in 1926,[99] the American stock exchanges began to take a critical stance towards non-voting shares and began refusing to list companies that issued non-voting shares. Over the next decades, therefore, American firms showed a firm alignment between voting and financial interest.[100]

In the 1980s, the wave of hostile takeovers pushed companies into increased competition and repeatedly provoked the use of dual-class shares and other CEMs as a defence mechanism.[101] This was mainly done through the effectuation of dual-class recapitalizations, ie the issue of new shares with different voting rights.[102] Through the use of CEMs, corporate insiders were able—even with a relatively small share—to control the company and to successfully oppose a hostile takeover bid.[103] Thus, CEMs became popular again, owing to the increased competitiveness in the market for corporate control. The stock exchanges endorsed this move and liberalized their approach to CEMs in 1986.[104] Several reasons were given by the New York Stock Exchange, including the possible loss of listed securities to AMEX or NASD (both of which allowed the listing of securities with unequal voting power) and requests by NYSE-listed companies to be allowed to use dual-class recapitalization plans as defensive tactics against hostile takeovers.[105]

[96] L Loss and J Seligman, *Securities Regulation* (3rd edn, New York: Aspen, 2000) 1832 f.

[97] Ibid.

[98] A A Berle and G C Means, *The Modern Corporation and Private Property* (New York: Macmillan, 1933) 69 ff.

[99] See the discussion at Seligman (n 95) 694 ff.

[100] Thompson and Edelman (n 80) 159.

[101] Seligman (n 95) 700 f; Thompson and Edelman (n 80) 159 f; R Karmel, 'The Future of Corporate Governance Listing Requirements' (2001) 54 SMU L Rev 325, 343 ff; K Cunningham, 'Examination of Judicial Policy on Corporate Vote Buying in the Context of Modern Financial Instruments' (2008) 64 NYU Annual Survey of American Law 293, 307 f.

[102] Usually, a company issues a new class of common shares with voting rights superior to those of the original shares. The original shares typically receive compensation in the form of a higher dividend. One theory supporting management's decision to issue a new class of shares with superior voting rights is that if the new shares are friendly to management, they will vote to oppose a hostile takeover.

[103] Seligman (n 95) 700 f; Thompson and Edelman (n 80) 159 f; see also S Martin and F Partnoy, 'Encumbered Shares' [2005] U of Illinois L Rev 775, 785.

[104] Martin and Partnoy (n 103) 785.

[105] G A Jarrell and A B Poulsen, 'Dual-Class Recapitalizations as Antitakeover Mechanisms—The Recent Evidence' (1988) 20 J of Financial Economics 129, 131.

Consecutively, the Securities and Exchange Commission failed[106] to introduce a mandatory OSOV rule for all American stock exchanges and only gradually was able to persuade them to discourage at least a midstream adoption of dual-class shares.[107]

(ii) United Kingdom

Another episode is the change that can be observed in UK company law. Until the mid-1960s, dual-class shares were fairly prevalent in the UK.[108] It was only then—probably owing to market pressure and initiatives from institutional investors—that these CEMs began to disappear.[109] Today, listed companies in the UK rarely employ deviations from the one share/one vote rule.[110]

(iii) Germany

Germany, on the other hand, has seen a gradual reduction of various CEMs over the past century; until well into the 1920s, there had been no regulation on this matter, which led to the reported abuses and misuses. We know about many companies in which shareholders obtained more than 1,000 or even 10,000 votes per share.[111] The major company law reform in 1937 banned the introduction of new multiple voting shares, albeit subject to an exceptional permission for public interest, to be granted by the German ministry of business.[112] This exception was controversially discussed during the second major company law reform in 1965, but eventually left largely unchanged. Only in 1998 was legislation adopted to abolish this exception; existing multiple voting rights expired in 2003 and shareholders with such existing rights were granted compensation.[113] The 1998 reform also abolished voting ceilings, albeit only for listed companies.[114] However, other deviations from OSOV remained permissible. This applies for instance to non-voting preference shares, which have even gained importance since the 1980s.[115]

106 It was held that such a rule would be beyond the SEC's power: *Business Roundtable v SEC*, 905 F.2d 406 (DC Cir 1990).

107 See text accompanying n 79.

108 K Rydqvist, 'Dual-Class Shares: A Review' (1992) 8(3) Oxford Rev of Economic Policy 45, 47; B Cheffins, *Corporate Ownership and Control—British Business Transformed* (Oxford: Oxford University Press, 2008) 32 f.

109 Davies (n 83) 23–9; Franks, Mayer, and Rossi (n 83) 604.

110 Deminor Rating, *Application of the one share—one vote principle in Europe* (2005) 11 ff. Amongst the companies examined by the Shearman & Sterling Study (n 12), only 5 % had multiple voting rights in place. There were no non-voting shares at all. See Shearman & Sterling Study (n 12) 12.

111 W Schubert and P Hommelhoff (eds), *Die Aktienrechtsreform am Ende der Weimarer Republik*, (New York/Berlin: de Gruyter, 1987) 89 f, 320 ff, 657 ff; cf K W Nörr 'Zur Entwicklung des Aktien- und Konzernrechts während der Weimarer Republik' (1986) 150 Zeitschrift für das gesamte Handelsrecht und Wirtschaftsrecht 155, 163.

112 § 12(2) Aktiengesetz 1937.

113 *Gesetz zur Kontrolle und Transparenz im Unternehmensbereich* ('KonTraG') of 27 April 1998, [1998] Bundesgesetzblatt I, 786.

114 § 134(1) Aktiengesetz.

115 T Bezzenberger, *Vorzugsaktien ohne Stimmrecht* (Cologne: Heymanns, 1991) 36 ff. For the reasons, see U Hüffer, *Aktiengesetz* (8th edn, Munich: CH Beck, 2008) § 139 para 3. For very recent evidence, see Mohr (n 92).

The 1998 shift was further endorsed by the adoption of the 2002 German Code of Corporate Governance.[116] Section 2.1.2. provided: 'In principle, each share carries one vote. There are no shares with multiple voting rights, preferential voting rights (golden shares) or maximum voting rights'.[117] This voluntary instrument is backed up by a (mandatory) comply-or-explain provision in s 161 *Aktiengesetz*.

These developments may explain today's low presence of OSOV deviations in Germany, as found in the Shearman & Sterling study.[118]

(iv) Cross-country empirical work

There are few empirical studies that report any changes in the actual application of CEMs. One recent survey analyses the number of dual-class listed firms in a number of European countries[119] from 1995–2001. The authors find that the percentage of dual-class listed companies in the surveyed countries declined from 41 per cent in 1995 to 22 per cent in 2001.[120] None of the individual countries in the sample deviates from the general trend. This is attributed to a large extent to share-class unifications within already listed companies, and also to a drop in the listing of new companies with dual-class shares. As some countries no longer, or only under special circumstances, allow dual-class shares, a decline on average would have been expected. However, in 1999 and 2000 the proportion of companies with dual-class shares had dropped on average to around 10 per cent from 22 per cent in 1996. The decline is found across countries, including the ones where dual-class shares are traditionally widely used.

(v) Assessment

Drawing these different pieces of evidence together, we can see that the OSOV rule has never been set in stone. There have been important changes over time, sometimes triggered by market forces (as in the UK from the 1960s), sometimes by listing rules (as in the US from 1926), and sometimes by legislative intervention (as in Germany at various times). Nevertheless, upon a more in-depth examination it is possible to discover common motivations for the taking of certain regulatory positions on OSOV. Much apparently depends on the identity of the decision-maker. Upon the identification of the decisive forces behind the introduction or adoption of a more (or less) OSOV conforming approach below, we shall examine the possible motivations for the identified parties adopting their particular positions.

116 Available under <http://www.corporate-governance-code.de/index-e.html> (last accessed 8 July 2010).

117 This text remains unchanged until today.

118 Shearman & Sterling Study (n 12) 11 ff.

119 Denmark, Finland, Germany, Italy, Norway, Sweden, and Switzerland.

120 B Maury and A Pajuste, 'Private benefits of control and dual-class share unifications' Working Paper 2007, Table 3 (available at <www.hanken.fi/staff/maury/blog/files/Unification_4.7.07.pdf> [last accessed 8 July 2010]).

IV. Who decides about change?

Whose preferences or concerns the configuration of voting rights expresses depends largely on who had or has the power to specify or to alter voting rights. These rules can be written into company law or corporate governance rules[121] for example, in which case they may be taken to express the preferences of those who had the power to shape legislation. Otherwise they are specified in the individual articles of association when companies are incorporated or by later amendment; in this case, they may be taken to express the preferences of the (founding) shareholders or the management, depending on who has the power to set up or to alter the articles of the company.

In the examples given above, who wrote the rules about voting attribution, and what was their motivation?

The push by institutional investors in the UK[122] to encourage a general proportionality principle seems to be driven by a general preference for 'good governance' standards in the European sense, ie shareholder-friendly rules. UK institutional investors have constantly been driving for pro-shareholder laws or business standards and have been fairly successful over recent decades. As empirical evidence underlines, the proportion of shares in UK companies owned by institutional investors rose dramatically over the 1960s and 1970s, simultaneously with the advent of dispersed share ownership.[123] These institutions, holding a significant proportion of the shares in the UK market, consequently have had a strong incentive to support good governance of their portfolio companies.[124] Their influence tends to focus on issues that may be generalized across all companies, so as to economize on their decision-making costs through standard-

[121] Corporate Governance rules are here understood as 'soft law', ie a not mandatory best practices set of policies, usually together with a (mandatory) 'comply-or-explain' provision.

[122] See above Section III.2.ii.

[123] B R Cheffins, 'Law, Economics and the UK's System of Corporate Governance: Lessons from History' (2001) 1 J of Corporate L Studies 71, 82; A Johnston, 'Takeover Regulation: Historical and Theoretical Perspectives on the City Code' (2007) 66 Cambridge L J 422, 426; J Moyle, *The Pattern of Ordinary Share Ownership: 1957–1970* (Cambridge: Cambridge University Press, 1971). Their emergence seems to have been an unintended consequence of fiscal measures: See B R Cheffins and S A Bank, 'Corporate Ownership and Control in the UK: The Tax Dimension' (2007) 70 MLR 778.

[124] P L Davies, 'Institutional Investors in the United Kingdom' in T Baums and others (eds), *Institutional Investors and Corporate Governance* (Berlin: de Gruyter, Berlin 1994) 257; B A Black and J C Coffee, 'Hail Britannia? Institutional Investor Behavior Under Limited Regulation' (1994) 92 Michigan L Rev 1997, 2034 ff.

ized rules.[125] One of their particular aims[126] was to reduce the number of non-voting shares or other deviations from OSOV.[127]

Taking the contrasting example of Germany, we have seen there is a well-documented decline from OSOV methods spread over the entire twentieth century. Of particular importance, however, is the decision in 1998 to abolish in fact multiple voting rights and seriously restrict the use of voting ceilings.[128] This move was, unlike in the UK, not driven by (institutional) shareholders, but came through intervention by the lawmaker itself. The explanatory notes on the draft German legislation[129] state several reasons for the shift. First, increasing international competition for issuers requires German law to facilitate the financing of companies, to reduce the cost of capital, and to adapt to international standards.[130] Secondly, international capital markets presume an alignment of share ownership and voting rights (apart from different classes of shares like non-voting preference shares); a restriction of voting differentiations that result from the company's articles of association (like multiple voting rights) therefore strengthen both the standardization and tradability of shares and the German capital market.[131] Thirdly, instruments like voting caps impede (hostile) takeovers and are thus undesirable.[132] At the same time, the explanatory notes stressed that a certain minimum protection for minority shareholders in takeover situations was now provided by securities regulation,[133] insider trading law,[134] and a new takeover code.[135] The German motivation thus seems to be twofold: on the one hand, similarly to the UK, the change stems from the belief in the benefits of takeovers as a powerful corporate governance tool and the desire to reduce corresponding obstacles; on the other hand, the change was driven by the international competition of the financial markets.

[125] Black and Coffee (n 124); J Armour and D Skeel, 'Who Writes the Rules for Hostile Takeovers, and Why?—The Peculiar Divergence of U.S. and U.K. Takeover Regulation' (2007) 95 Georgetown L J 1727, 1771.

[126] For a general description of their programme, see J Armour, 'Enforcement Strategies in UK Corporate Governance' in J Armour and J Payne (eds), *Rationality in Company Law—Essays in Honour of DD Prentice* (Oxford: Hart Publishing, 2009) 71, 110 ff.

[127] B Cheffins, *Corporate Ownership and Control—British Business Transformed* (Oxford: Oxford University Press, 2008) 31; G Stapledon, *Institutional Shareholders and Corporate Governance* (Oxford: Clarendon Press, 1996) 58 f; Armour and Skeel (n 125) 1736 f.

[128] See above Section III.2.iii.

[129] *Entwurf eines Gesetzes zur Kontrolle und Transparenz im Unternehmensbereich* ('KonTraG') of 28 January 1998, Bundestags-Drucksache 13/9712.

[130] Ibid, 11.

[131] Ibid, 12.

[132] Ibid, 20.

[133] The new *Wertpapierhandelsgesetz* (Securities Trading Act, 'WpHG') had been adopted on 26 July 1994, [1994] Bundesgesetzblatt I, 1749.

[134] The German insider law (*WpHG* §§ 12 ff) had been amended twice in 1997 and 1998 by *Gesetz zur Umsetzung von EG-Richtlinien zur Harmonisierung bank- und wertpapieraufsichtsrechtlicher Vorschriften* of 22 October 1997, [1997] Bundesgesetzblatt I, 2518 and *Gesetz zur weiteren Fortentwicklung des Finanzplatzes Deutschland* of 27 March 1998 (*Drittes Finanzmarktförderungsgesetz*), [1998] Bundesgesetzblatt I, 529.

[135] At the time, Germany had a takeover code (*Übernahmekodex*), which was later replaced by the Takeover Act (*WpÜG*).

Yet it was other groups that were responsible for the changes that we observed in the US.[136] In the early twentieth century, strong minority shareholders formed controlling stakes in corporations by establishing CEMs like non-voting (preferred or common) shares and the voting trust.[137] After the 'OSOV period' between 1926 and through the 1980s, it was as a response to pressure exercised by managers that US companies began introducing deviations from OSOV.[138] An increasing amount of takeover activity led to fears amongst managers to cement their position via the use of CEMs. In comparison with European legal systems, US corporate law[139] is said to be more manager-friendly. Managers tend to control the agenda of annual meetings, are comparably difficult to remove, and have an enhanced discretion and managerial freedom.[140] This may explain why the US saw an increased use of CEMs following the takeover boom in the 1980s. So-called recapitalizations that resulted in dual-class share structures with disparate voting rights generally allowed the management to increase its voting control without increasing its equity stake.[141] Although these recapitalizations were adopted with shareholder approval, many commentators expressed concerns that the recapitalizations might allow the management to consolidate its control and protect itself from the discipline of the market for corporate control without adequate compensation to other shareholders.[142] This tendency in turn provoked the NYSE to amend its listing rules in the way described.[143]

Where is the golden thread? The picture that emerges from this historical perspective seems to be that lawmakers[144]—whether legislature, stock exchanges, or self-regulation—seem to be rather OSOV-friendly, whereas leaving companies—and especially their managers—the freedom to decide might incentivize them to deviate from a OSOV standard. As regulators and scholars have mostly argued that OSOV would properly align control and ownership, direct regulatory initiatives—such as in Germany or in the US—or self-regulation through standards set by powerful institutional investors—as in the UK—have led to pro-OSOV rules and practices. In contrast, especially managers and also shareholders have pushed in the opposite direction, away from OSOV, in an attempt to reallocate

[136] See above Section III.2.i.

[137] A A Berle and G C Means, *The Modern Corporation and Private Property* (New York: Macmillan, 1933) 69 ff.

[138] Jarrell and Poulsen (n 105); H de Angelo and L de Angelo, 'Managerial Ownership of Voting Rights—A Study of Public Corporations with Dual Classes of Common Stock' (1985) 14 J of Financial Economics 33.

[139] In particular Delaware corporate law.

[140] L A Bebchuk, 'The Case for Increasing Shareholder Power' (2005) 118 Harvard L Rev 833; L Enriques, H Hansmann, and R Kraakman, 'The Basic Governance Structure: The Interests of Shareholders as a Class' in R Kraakman and others, *The Anatomy of Corporate Law* (2nd edn, Oxford: Oxford University Press, 2009) ch 3, 55, 83.

[141] Jarrell and Poulsen (n 105) 130.

[142] Ibid.

[143] See above Section III.2.i.

[144] 'Lawmaker' is here to be understood widely, including self- and indirect regulation via soft law mechanisms like a voluntary best practices code.

Table 1. Policy changes towards OSOV

Country	*Change period*	*Observations*	*Main Driving Force*
US	1910–20	Increasingly dual-class shares	(Minority) shareholders
	1930s and 40s	Move towards OSOV	Stock exchanges
	1980s	Recapitalizations—increasingly dual-class shares and other CEMs	Managers; competition between stock exchanges
	1990s and 2000s	Gradual move back towards OSOV; midstream-adoption of dual-class shares discourages in listing rules	SEC, Stock exchanges
UK	1960s	Various CEMs gradually disappear	Institutional investors
Germany	1937–today	Gradual abolishment of CEMs in several steps	Legislation
	1998–2002	Abolishment of multiple voting rights, restriction of voting ceilings	Legislation; corporate governance rules

control away from ownership and to secure influence in their companies.[145] The German example from the 1920s shows that shareholders may even have been tempted to abuse CEMs so as to make the whole system of equity holding meaningless. Managers in the 1980s takeover battles in the US successfully invoked deviations from OSOV to fend off hostile takeover bids. Sometimes, these forces develop such a dynamic that stock exchanges—as in the same period—bow to them and lessen their standards.

V. The 2008/09 crisis and current developments

The general picture so far seems to be that the presence of CEMs comes in waves—very popular over a certain period, yet rigidly rejected in the next. Much depends, as we have seen, on the players—ie the crucial factor seems to be who the decision-makers in this process are and what their motivation is.

What influence does the 2008/09 crisis have in this respect, or what influence will it have? Arguably, there exists a possibility that due to revitalized economic patriotism, the next years will see an increase in the amount of deviations from the OSOV rule. It has been demonstrated that CEMs are a very powerful tool to increase the power of a small shareholder or even to reinforce the influence of an existing blockholder within a company. The renaissance of dual-class shares in the heat of the 1980s takeover wave in the US demonstrates especially well that companies intentionally employ the application of CEMs in order to protect their stake in times of crisis. Similarly, it is submitted that an increased use of CEMs could be a response to the current economic downturn.

[145] See Martin and Partnoy (n 103) 786.

Obviously, it is still too early to analyse these issues empirically or to obtain reliable financial data from the real-world companies. Nevertheless, there are a number of indicators that suggest that this development could reasonably become reality.

1. Protection from SWFs

First, the past months have seen an increased political discussion about the benefits of CEMs. The discussion has centred on the possible introduction of golden shares, which were seen as a tool to protect European markets from Sovereign Wealth Funds (SWFs) from the Middle East and from East Asia.[146] SWFs have increased their influence on global financial markets in recent years. Assets under management of SWFs more than doubled between 2001 and 2007 underpinned by growth in foreign exchange reserves due to the rising trade surpluses of some countries. Some governments have expressed reservations about SWFs because of the limited disclosure and transparency of some SWFs. Concerns have also been expressed about their multiplicity of objectives, making it difficult to assess the SWFs' activities and their impact on global capital markets. Another concern expressed by some governments is that SWFs may invest to secure control of strategically important businesses or sectors for political rather than commercial reasons, and could use these investments to advance their own national interests.

To this end, several countries have enacted protection measures. In 2007, the German Government announced that shareholders of the European aerospace company EADS were considering the possible introduction of golden shares in order to allow Germany and France to veto strategic decisions at this company.[147] Shortly after, the UK entered into the debate with Lord Mandelson, at the time EU Trade Commissioner and later British Secretary of State for Business, Innovation, and Skills, suggesting that golden shares could be used to protect strategically important European companies against foreign takeovers, especially from SWFs.[148] In a similar vein, a majority of Dutch MPs demanded the re-introduction of golden shares in Dutch companies.[149] In the end, Germany

[146] Another solution proposed by academics is vote suspension of equity owned by SWF, see R J Gilson and C J Milhaupt, 'Sovereign Wealth Funds and Corporate Governance: A Minimalist Response to the New Mercantilism' (2008) 60 Stanford L Rev 1345. For an overall discussion, see H Schweitzer, 'Sovereign Wealth Funds—market investors or "imperialist capitalists"? The European response to direct investments by non-EU state-controlled entities', ch 12, p 250.

[147] 'German Government Wants to Buy "Golden Share" in EADS' *Spiegel Online* (6 August 2007), <http://www.spiegel.de/international/business/0,1518,498327,00.html> (last accessed 8 July 2010).

[148] A Bounds and G Wiesmann, 'EU signals shift on using golden shares' *Financial Times* (London, 23 July 2007), <http://www.ft.com/cms/s/0/cfd2ca2c-38b4-11dc-bca9-0000779fd2ac.html> (last accessed 8 July 2010).

[149] *DutchNews*, 25 July 2007, <http://www.dutchnews.nl/news/archives/print/003388.php> (last accessed 8 July 2010).

amended its Foreign Trade Act[150] in 2008, establishing a review process for investments from outside the EEA if a company takes a stake in a German company of more than 25 per cent.[151] The government can approve a transaction with conditions. These conditions may, for example, take the form of a prohibition or limitation of the exercise of voting rights in the acquired company.[152] Similarly, the US' review process for foreign investments—undertaken by the Committee on Foreign Investments in the United States (CFIUS)—was amended in 2007/08 to accommodate concerns that the process in its previous form had been ineffective and too lenient.[153] Importantly, the new statute codifies the CFIUS review process itself as well as a number of related practices, sharpening CFIUS as a policy instrument. The formalization and extension of the review mechanism have raised the complexity of CFIUS, making it one of the most demanding foreign investment processes among the industrialized economies—not least for sovereign investors. One last example might be South Korea which is currently considering to allow domestic companies the use of 'poison pills' to help them fend off hostile takeovers as the influence of foreign investors grows in the country.[154] Despite criticism by investors groups, the Government has approved a revision of the country's commercial law that introduces a system aimed at protecting domestic companies from foreign funds by allowing them to issue new shares to existing shareholders at a pre-set low price, diluting the ownership value of a hostile bidder.[155]

2. CEMs to further sustainability

A second issue is that, as a response to the global financial crisis, dual-class share structures and multiple voting rights have reappeared on the political and academic agenda. Arguably, the financial crisis was at least partially caused or aggravated by incentives for short-term speculative success. Now, under the heading of sustainability of investment, commentators view differentiated voting rights

[150] *Außenwirtschaftsgesetz* ('AWG').

[151] *Dreizehntes Gesetz zur Änderung des Außenwirtschaftsgesetzes und der Außenwirtschaftsverordnung* [2009] Bundesgesetzblatt I, 770

[152] See on the new law eg O v. Rosenberg and others, 'Protektion statt offener Märkte? Die Änderungen des Außenwirtschaftsrechts in der Transaktionspraxis' [2009] Der Betrieb 831; H Krause, 'Die Novellierung des Außenwirtschaftsgesetzes und ihre Auswirkungen auf M&A-Transaktionen mit ausländischen Investoren' [2009] Betriebs-Berater 1082; H Müller and R Hempel, 'Änderungen des Außenwirtschaftsrechts zur Kontrolle ausländischer Investoren' [2009] Neue Juristische Wochenschrift 1638.

[153] The amending Foreign Investment and National Security Act (FINSA) was adopted on 26 July 2007 (PL 110-49), and the implementing Executive Order (EO 13456) was issued on 23 January 2008.

[154] S Jung-a, 'South Korea considers use of "poison pills"' FT.com, 9 November 2009.

[155] 'S. Korea to adopt "poison pill" system against hostile takeovers' *Yonhap English News* (2 March 2010) <http://english.yonhapnews.co.kr/> (last accessed 8 July 2010). Interestingly, the Government, however, refrained from considering other measures like 'golden shares' and multiple voting rights for fear of the rules being abused, see Jung-a (n 154).

as an incentive to convince shareholders of a long-term investment and hope that this attitude will create a more stable economic environment.[156] One example is the—newly rediscovered—French system of dual-class shares depending on the time-period that the shares were held.[157] The articles of association of a French company can attach a double voting right to shares that have been held for more than two years by the same shareholder.[158] Thus, French company law rewards shareholders with a longer-time investment. The intention behind this system is that the law aims to stimulate sustainable investment and a good relationship between shareholder and company, and tries to disincentivize a short-term or even intra-day holding of shares.[159]

This issue has been picked up in the UK by Lord Myners, Financial Services Secretary to the Treasury. On a number of occasions, he came up with suggestions on how to rearrange the relationship between share ownership and voting. In a TV interview, he suggested that consideration should be given to introducing differentiated voting rights in order to provide an incentive for institutional investors to take ownership more seriously.[160] He stated that greater voting rights given to long-standing investors would create more sustainable 'ownership' as compared to short-term financial investment, coining the phrase 'ownerless corporations'.[161] This suggestion has attracted much attention and debate, some

[156] U Noack, 'Das Aktienrecht der Krise—das Aktienrecht in der Krise?' [2009] AG 227, 234 f; R von Heusinger, 'Rettet den Kapitalismus' *Die Zeit* (Hamburg, 28 October 2004), who states that multiple voting rights will make the management more receptive for long-term decisions. Surprisingly, even the former chairman of Deutsche Bank, Rolf Breuer, favoured such a move, cf L Kamp and A Krieger, *Die Aktivitäten von Finanzinvestoren in Deutschland* (HBS 2005) 72.

[157] See on this A Constantin, *Droit des sociétés* (3rd edn, Paris: Dalloz, 2007) 188; R Mortier, 'La modernisation du droit des sociétés' [2008] La Semaine Juridique Entreprise et Affaires 2233; V de Beaufort, 'One Share—One Vote, Le Nouveau Saint Graal', Essec Centre de Recherche DR 06019, December 2006; A Outin-Adam and S Bienvenu, *'une action = une voix': Faut-il imposer une égalité entre participation au capital et détention du pouvoir?—Présentation du rapport Norguet adopté le 24 mai 2007 par la CCIP* [2007] La Semaine Juridique Entreprise et Affaires, act. 432; M Storck and U H Schneider, 'Doppeltes Stimmrecht für langfristig investierte Aktionäre im französischen Recht—Ein Beitrag zur "Nachhaltigkeitsprämie"' [2008] Die Aktiengesellschaft 700; L Enriques, H Hansmann, and R Kraakman, 'The Basic Governance Structure: Minority Shareholders and Non-Shareholder Constituencies' in R Kraakman and others, *The Anatomy of Corporate Law* (2nd edn, Oxford: Oxford University Press, 2009) 89, 92.

[158] *Code de Commerce*, Article L225-123: 'A voting right equivalent to twice that attributed to other shares may be attributed to fully paid shares which can be proved to have been registered in the name of the same shareholder for at least two years, depending on the proportion of the share capital they represent, by the memorandum and articles of association or a special shareholders' meeting.' Cf also Article L225-124 (as amended from 1 January 2009).

[159] D Norguet, *'une action = une voix' Faut-il imposer une égalité entre participation au capital et détention du pouvoir?* (CCIP report, 24 May 2007) 18 f.

[160] Lord Myners in the TV programme 'Leading Questions', interviewed by the BBC's Business Editor Robert Peston on Saturday 1 August 2009.

[161] J Croft and K Burgess, 'Opposition grows to "two-tier" share plan' *Financial Times* (London, 3 August 2009).

of it supporting,[162] although most commentators were sceptical, especially the institutional investors.[163] Lord Myners later went on to an even more radical proposal and suggested giving shareholders the ability to buy and sell their voting rights independently from their shareholding, ie a complete separation of ownership and voting rights.[164] According to this plan, shareholders who never vote could sell their voting rights to others who do want to vote. Again, reactions to this suggestion were mostly negative.[165] Finally, Myners proposed the introduction of the possibility to issue new non-voting shares to existing shareholders, allowing them subsequently to concentrate their engagement with the company on either a voting or non-voting position and thus fostering their identification with the company.[166] His remarks come in the context of growing concern that—owing to its liberal takeover laws—British firms might be at an increased risk of falling into foreign hands. This was highlighted by Lord Myners during the takeover of Cadbury plc by American competitor Kraft Foods Inc.[167] Despite his insistence that this fear is not merely xenophobic,[168] his remarks clearly seem to be based on national interests.

So far, the concerns and suggestions of Lord Myners have not been followed up by legislation in the UK. However, former Business Secretary Lord Mandelson urged the Takeover Panel to reconsider parts of the regulatory framework known as the City Code in order to make takeovers more difficult.[169] Some pressure groups even called for the adoption of a specific 'Cadbury's Law', to 'prevent hostile takeovers of British companies which are not in the public interest'.[170] Surprisingly, the Labour party included a call for such new regulation in its election manifesto for the 2010 general election.[171] Proposed rules to extend

[162] W A Allen, 'Disproportionate voting rights may be the way to better governance' *Financial Times* (London, 4 August 2009) 8.

[163] Cf ibid; J Russell, 'ABI leads attack on Myners over reform' *Daily Telegraph* (London, 1 August 2009); K Burgess, 'Investors wary of Myners' idea on voting rights' *Financial Times* (London, 4 August 2009) 16.

[164] W Hutchings, 'Myners proposes sale of voting rights' *Financial News* online (10 August 2009), <http://www.efinancialnews.com/story/2009-08-10/myners-proposes-sale-of-voting-rights> (last accessed 8 July 2010).

[165] S Jones, 'Big investors cool on Myners' idea of trade in voting rights rights' *Financial Times* (London, 11 August 2009) 1.

[166] T Tassell, 'Myners eyes new non-voting shares' *Financial Times* (London, 14 August 2009) 16.

[167] J Treanor, 'Too many UK firms fall into foreign hands, warns crusading Myners' *The Guardian* (London, 24 September 2009) 31.

[168] Ibid.

[169] J Eaglesham and L Saigol, 'Mandelson calls for radical reform of takeover rules for hostile bids' *Financial Times* (London, 2 March 2010) 19.

[170] A Hill, 'Protectionist "Cadbury's Law" is last thing UK needs' *Financial Times* (London, 16 March 2010) 18.

[171] H Ebrahimi and L Armitstead, 'Will Labour's "Cadbury's Law" lead to protectionism and harm Britain's businesses?' *Daily Telegraph* (London, 12 April 2010). The manifesto includes the call for a restoration of a public interest test in corporate takeovers (at least for utility or infrastructure companies), an amendment to the City Code so that two-thirds of shareholders must approve

the current public interest test from the media and public security sector to include utilities and infrastructure companies could take the form of new golden shares.[172]

3. Freedom of contract

Thirdly, many signs point towards the direction that some legislators across the EU might be poised to re-introduce 'flexibility' into company law. In a move to foster contractual freedom in the area, they propose to grant shareholders more scope to allocate their rights and powers internally and would thereby implicitly accept CEMs as not only legally possible, but also desirable. Take the example of Denmark, where the newly reformed company law leaves the permissibility of CEMs to be decided freely by the existing and future shareholders.[173] The present restriction on voting differentiation, whereby differences in voting rights of shares representing the same capital may not exceed the ratio of 1 to 10, is to be abolished, leaving it to the company and the investors to decide. It is also proposed that non-voting shares may be issued in all companies (with or without preferential rights to dividends), which until now had only been possible in private companies.[174]

A second example is Germany. The Association of German Jurists,[175] an influential academic but policy-oriented institution of German lawyers, at its 2008 annual meeting discussed the possible re-introduction of multiple voting rights, which had been abolished by German law in 1998.[176] Although in the end, after lengthy and controversial discussions, the Association did not take an actual decision or recommendation, the matter is still being discussed in Germany, and those voices championing multiple voting rights seem to be as emphatic as ever.[177]

the transaction, as opposed to the simple majority required at the moment. See Labour Party, *The Labour Party Manifesto 2010—A future fair to all* (12 April 2010) 1:7, 1:9 (available at <http://www.labour.org.uk/manifesto>). Moreover, the manifesto also contains a plan to limit the influence of short-term investors such as hedge funds, by excluding them from buying shares during bids and from voting on the transaction. However, the manifesto does not goes as far as unions had hoped, see A Hill, 'Labour's nutty Cadbury law would be bad for the UK' *Financial Times* (London, 13 April 2010) 20; N Pratley, 'Viewpoint: Save only two cheers for Labour's Cadbury Law' *The Guardian* (London, 13 April 2010) 25.

172 S Jagger, 'The hand of Mandelson' *The Times* (London, 13 April 2010) 34.

173 This goes back to the recommendations of a Committee on the modernization of Danish company law, which presented a Green Paper in November 2008. See J Lau Hansen, 'The Danish Green Paper on Company Law Reform—Modernising Company Law in the 21st Century' (2009) 10 EBOR 73. On the new law, see J Lau Hansen, 'The New Danish Companies Act of 2009' (2010) 11 EBOR 87, 89.

174 Lau Hansen (2009, n 173) 93.

175 *Deutscher Juristentag* (*DJT*).

176 W Bayer, *Gutachten E zum 67. Deutschen Juristentag* (2008), E109.

177 W Bayer and T Hoffmann, 'Mehrstimmrechtsaktien in Deutschland' [2008] Die Aktiengesellschaft R464, R466 ff. Cf U Noack, 'Das Aktienrecht der Krise—das Aktienrecht in der Krise?' [2009] AG 227, 235.

4. Assessment

It has to be emphasized that these are just a few motley instances to demonstrate that a general tendency towards a rehabilitation of CEMs can be found on multiple levels. This is to say that the three examples discussed above are not necessarily born from protectionist activities, nor do they necessarily impede cross-border trade. This paper's claim is more modest. It acknowledges that, for instance, the plan to enhance a long-term investment commitment by creating multiple voting rights is a well-meant policy measure. Equally, freedom of contract for shareholders is surely a laudable goal in itself.[178] Nevertheless, however good the intentions, we cannot deny that all of these measures can have protectionist *effects*. It has been long recognized that CEMs and other disproportionate structures have the effect of hindering cross-border investment. As explained, they tend to lock up national markets—on the one hand because investors are faced with established controllers, who can reinforce their strong position with the help of CEMs; on the other hand, politics may use such an instrument to support domestic elites.[179] Moreover, an investor who intends to invest into other EU markets is faced with a myriad of opaquely different and disproportionate structures in other Member States, which significantly hamper the possibility to invest and to acquire control in companies registered in other Member States. Expressed in a wider externality objective, this means that these CEMs increase the cost of capital in the EU.[180]

To be sure, there are also developments suggesting a movement in the opposite direction. For instance, the Swedish Stock Exchange has recently revised its takeover rules, requiring equal treatment of all shareholders irrespective of multiple voting rights and thus preventing bidders paying more for shares that have preferential voting rights in target companies.[181] However, in an overall assessment, CEMs, especially multiple voting rights, seem to have been reconsidered, and their advantages seem to be valued more than a few years ago. Particularly after the financial crisis, long-term investment is seen as a cure for the volatility of markets and promulgated as a solution for a more sustainable corporate culture. At the other end of the spectrum, golden shares and protection of markets towards non-EU markets, especially against SWFs from Asia, become popular again. In

[178] The opposite is true, however, for tendencies to shield European markets from Sovereign Wealth Funds, where the protectionist aim can hardly be ignored.

[179] See above n 56 and accompanying text. In particular, see J Rickford, 'Invisible Hand or Dead Hand?—Reflections on the EU "One Share One Vote"' in European Policy Forum (ed), *One Share one Vote? Tomorrow's Companies: One Universal Model or Tailored Equity Structures?* (London: EPF, 2006) 67, passim; J Gordon, 'The International Relations Wedge in the Corporate Convergence Debate' in J Gordon and M Roe (eds), *Convergence and Persistence in Corporate Governance* (Cambridge: Cambridge University Press, 2004) 161, 165, 197.

[180] Rickford (n 6) 73 f.

[181] 'Revised takeover rules and listing requirements on NASDAQ OMX Stockholm' *Euroinvestor* (28 August 2009) <http://www.euroinvestor.co.uk>.

the guise of 'freedom of contract', finally, the shareholders' freedom to deviate from OSOV is increasingly made possible.

VI. Implications

What can we learn from this? We have seen that over time the attitude of decision-makers—both on the law-making and on the business sides—has repeatedly developed and changed. At one point, OSOV was seen as the Holy Grail,[182] providing optimal alignment of incentives, facilitating takeovers, and leading to optimal governance structures. At another point in time, managers involved themselves in deviations from a strict proportionality, hoping to fend off strong competitive situations and trying to insulate themselves from takeover attempts. Various OSOV rules and practices have evolved primarily in response to either self-regulation, fear of regulation, or direct regulatory initiative, as regulators (and scholars) argued that OSOV would properly align control and ownership. In contrast, managers and shareholders have sometimes pushed in the opposite direction (away from OSOV), attempting to reallocate control away from ownership and seeking increased private benefits. States and stock exchanges have sometimes permitted these companies to redistribute voting control. In other words, OSOV is still the majority rule today, *notwithstanding* manager power, market pressures, and competition to the contrary. The (self-)lawmaker in the UK and in Germany are two examples that have produced a quasi-OSOV situation.

The threat now is that this equilibrium might be disturbed if companies and regulators start to introduce or even only facilitate deviations from OSOV, and not only for protectionist motives. Deviations are found high and low in the current debate and could become fashionable again. This appears problematic for the following reasons:

(1) Our analysis of historical developments has shown that whenever the market has been allowed to move away from OSOV, at some point the lawmaker—be it legislature, stock exchange, or self-regulation—would step in and correct the tendency. As long as current and future developments continue along these lines, there would be no problem. Contractual freedom would not necessarily pose a threat to this equilibrium. However, should the lawmaker decide to make a certain deviation from OSOV mandatory—as Lord Myners seems to suggest—unprecedented consequences could result. Historically, the lawmaker has always had the role of correcting drifts towards too much deviation from OSOV. At most, the lawmakers have granted contractual freedom. Making certain CEMs mandatory,

[182] Borrowing from V de Beaufort, 'One Share—One Vote, Le Nouveau Saint Graal', Essec Centre de Recherche DR 06019, December 2006.

however, is an unprecedented undertaking and probably an excessive legislative intervention.

(2) The general consensus, drawn from the academic debate, seems to be in favour of OSOV, although it is recognized that some deviation may be beneficial under exceptional circumstances. Hence the approach in most jurisdictions is to make OSOV not mandatory, but to leave it to the companies' discretion—albeit with strong encouragement (usually a comply-or-explain rule) to adhere to OSOV and—if necessary—regulatory intervention. What we can see from the enumerated instances above, however, is a growing popularity of measures that would introduce deviations from OSOV. These measures could potentially reverse the established relationship between rule and exception. In so far as these measures are based on a voluntary basis, they are innocent and largely correspond to what is already in place for example in the UK. When it comes to mandatory rules, however, caution is required. Particularly in the continental European context, mandatory deviations from OSOV could further add to protectionist sentiments and hinder the efficient development of a market for corporate control. But even in the UK, such new rules would probably do more to increase confusion than they would to bring eventual gains. In this sense, Lord Myners' proposals for instance, as far as they can be understood to be cast in mandatory terms, would arguably represent an alien object to British company law.

(3) Additional problems emerge in the continental European environment. Here, in a concentrated shareholder structure, CEMs and other deviations from OSOV reinforce the already existing strong position of blockholders.[183] In such a jurisdiction, already the availability of a certain CEM as a legal option may lead to its frequent adoption, since it favours and strengthens the position of a tentative controller, allowing them to extract private benefits of control. This might be an explanation for the popularity of the French 'double vote' under Code de commerce, Article L225-123.[184] Seen from this perspective, Germany's step to abolish many CEMs by mandatory legislation was a wise decision. If now continental jurisdictions like Denmark facilitate 'freedom of contract' for CEMs or Germany considers the re-introduction of multiple voting shares, these tendencies run contrary to the established experiences we have from the past.

To be sure, it is not this paper's intention to make a case for either introducing or abolishing OSOV at all costs. The empirical and economic evidence is—as discussed—inconclusive, and one should recognize that OSOV can (under certain

[183] R J Gilson and J N Gordon, 'Controlling Controlling Shareholders' (2003) 152 U of Pennsylvania L Rev 785.

[184] In France, 69% of the companies deviate from OSOV, see Deminor report (n 110) 19; de Beaufort (n 182).

circumstances) be beneficial, but also that it is not always so. This recognition of evidential inconclusivity must, however, extend to deviation from OSOV as well as adherence: There is no case for mandatory deviations from OSOV—ie the economic evidence does not suggest that multiple voting rights as in France (and discussed in the UK) are necessarily beneficial either. However, as we can learn from history, legislative or self-regulatory intervention has turned out to be necessary *in favour* of OSOV, if at all. Current developments make us believe that regulation could be planned to support moving *away* from OSOV. This cannot be deliberate—not in the UK, and certainly not in a shareholder structure as in continental Europe.

VII. Conclusion

The expediency of a OSOV approach remains a contentious issue. Since deviations from OSOV have tended to favour management entrenchment, excessive shareholder control, or inefficient structures in the past, lawmakers in various forms (the legislature, stock exchanges, self-regulators) have generally favoured the proportionality principle, although deviations can and should be permissible in certain circumstances.

This traditional picture has been contrasted with new developments. Following the recent financial crisis, academics and regulators seem to become increasingly supportive of possible deviations from a strict OSOV approach. Amongst the proposed measures are protections against Sovereign Wealth Funds, multiple voting rights to support long-term and sustainable investment, and a general freedom of choice for companies.

Most of these proposals appear to be ill-advised. In the continental European context, they would reinforce the existing blockholder-dominated share structures to the detriment of minority shareholders. But even in the UK, where the possible introduction of deviations from OSOV has been advanced, these suggestions have to be greeted with reservations. Historical analysis has taught us that the UK has fared very well with its optionality approach paired with pro-OSOV self-regulation.

If we share the general belief in the benefits of OSOV and simultaneously acknowledge that deviations can be appropriate under certain circumstances, we must come to the conclusion that it is the (self-)regulator's task to correct market forces that depart from this common ground. The current discussion, however, seems to leave well-established ground actively to support protectionist market forces.

11

Deviations from Ownership–Control Proportionality—Private Benefits and the Bigger Picture

Arad Reisberg

I. Introduction

The purpose of Wolf-Georg Ringe's excellent paper is to revisit some of the aspects of the one share/one vote (OSOV) debate 'in the light of the new protectionist fears that have surfaced since the beginning of the financial crisis'.[1] As he rightly notes, the recent financial crisis has given shape to new protectionist movements and could correspondingly revitalize deviations from a strict OSOV rule.[2] Ringe observes that OSOV is applied to a varying extent by companies, depending on market pressures, takeover fears, and other external influences. He is raising the question why do attitudes to OSOV change, and how?

In terms of methodology, Ringe emphasizes at the outset that it is not his intention to make a case for either introducing or abolishing OSOV. Indeed, this seems the right stance to take. The empirical and economic evidence is inconclusive as OSOV can, under certain circumstances, be beneficial.[3] But at the same

[1] Wolf-Georg Ringe, 'Deviations from Ownership-Control Proportionality—Economic Protectionism Revisited' ch 10 above.

[2] Connolly, for example, see this crisis in much wider terms and not as 'a justification but an excuse for the overbearing regulation that the enemies—in all countries, including Britain—of "Anglo-Saxon" capitalism had always longed for... the regulatory assault reflects an ambition of restoring a corporatist model of the state, seen by the EU as having been usurped by a perceived "Anglo-Saxon" victory in the Second World War. Further, the identification of risk-taking with anti-social or even criminal activity which has marked the attitudes of EU regulators and jurists, among others, implicitly rests on a theory of law, accepted by the European Court of Justice, that privileges the General Will over individual freedoms'. See, B Connolly, 'Regulation: reform or revenge? The crisis, the EU and British financial markets' (September 2009) L and Financial Markets Rev 414.

[3] For example, in light of renewed interest in the relation between shareholder protection and control arrangements, Vinaimont and Sercu thoroughly review the optimality of OSOV. They find that from the founder's perspective, OSOV is never optimal with imperfect foresight, and its optimality is surprisingly rare even with perfect foresight. See, T Vinaimont and P Sercu, 'Deviations

time, there is no case for mandatory deviations from OSOV.[4] The EU recognized this and as the European Commissioner for the Internal Market and Services, Charlie McCreevy, told the European Parliament's Legal Affairs Committee on 3 October 2007: 'there is no economic evidence of a causal link between deviations from the so-called proportionality principle and the economic performance of companies... there is no reason for action on the European level'.[5]

In light of the above, Ringe chooses to take what he describes as 'a current and historic perspective on the presence of deviations from OSOV in the business world'.[6] He revises the approach taken by the Court of Justice and the academic debate. He evaluates the new tendencies that are being discussed as a consequence of the recent financial crisis. Finally, he draws the implications from this fresh perspective. The paper's main findings are that there have been important changes over time (although as I will argue below, perhaps it is more accurate to classify these as 'trends'). In Ringe's words: 'the presence of [control-enhancing mechanisms] comes in waves—very popular over a certain period, yet rigidly rejected in the next'.[7] And that these changes are triggered by market forces (UK from the 1960s), listing rules (the US from 1926), or by legislative intervention (in Germany at various times).

So what does this teach us? And what influence does the current crisis have in this respect, or what influence will it have? Ringe suggests that an increased use of Control Enhancing Mechanisms (CEMs) could be a response to the current economic downturn. He points out a number of indicators that suggest that this development could reasonably become reality:

(1) protection from Sovereign Wealth Funds (SWFs);
(2) CEMs to further sustainability; and
(3) freedom of contract.

from "One Share, One Vote" Can Be Optimal: An Entrepreneur's Point of View' (1 January 2008) AFA 2004 San Diego Meetings; KULeuven DTEW Working Paper. Available at SSRN: <http://ssrn.com/abstract=302916> or doi:10.2139/ssrn.302916 (last accessed 21 November 2009).

[4] An important contribution in this respect is made by Adams and Daniel Ferreira. They review the empirical literature on the consequences of separating votes from cash-flow rights due to the adoption of explicitly disproportional ownership structures, and also the literature on control concentration when ownership is formally proportional. They conclude that there is no reliable indication that disproportional ownership destroys value for non-controlling shareholders by an amount that is larger than the value it creates for controlling shareholders. See R Adams and D Ferreira, 'One Share, One Vote: The Empirical Evidence' (December 2007) ECGI Finance Working Paper No 177/2007. Available at SSRN: <http://ssrn.com/abstract=987488> (last accessed 21 November 2009).

[5] Speech 07/592 by Commissioner McCreevy at the European Parliament's Legal Affairs Committee available at: <http://europa.eu/rapid/pressReleasesAction.do?reference=SPEECH/07/592&format=DOC&aged=1&language=EN&guiLanguage=en> (last accessed on 6 November 2009).

[6] Wolf-Georg Ringe, 'Deviations from Ownership-Control Proportionality—Economic Protectionism Revisited' at 210 (hereafter 'Ringe').

[7] Ibid, 231.

Interestingly, Ringe stresses that: 'It has to be emphasized that these are just a few motley instances to demonstrate that a general tendency towards a rehabilitation of CEMs can be found on different levels.'[8] In fact, he even provides evidence to the contrary:

> To be sure, there are also developments pointing towards the opposite direction. For instance, the Swedish stock exchange has recently revised its takeover rules, requiring equal treatment of all shareholders irrespective of multiple voting rights and thus preventing bidders paying more for shares that have preferential voting rights in target companies.[9]

II. My approach

This is a topical and important topic to write about and it is a pleasure to serve as a discussant of such a thoughtful paper dealing with the presence of deviations from OSOV. It is impossible to do this paper justice in the brief space I have available. The analysis by which Ringe comes to the above conclusion is a very exhaustive one. It has a strong legal component with plenty of references to previous cases and literature. My contribution will therefore be limited to additional clarifications. First, what I want to add is about two, which I am going to term deliberately and provocatively 'hidden truths' that I think this paper reveals, one about theory and one about practice in this area. I want to close also with a third potential 'hidden truth'. Before I go on, I should add one caveat: we all know the old chestnut about the difference between theory and practice. That is, of course, that in theory, there is no difference between theory and practice; but, in practice, it is a completely different story. So, please take my distinction with the necessary grain of salt.

The first 'hidden truth' relates to private benefits of control. The second highlights the changing landscape of the business world and the implications this has on the issues discussed. The third interesting issue, it seems to me, is the question of what difference it would make if one opts for describing the current situation as 'important changes over time', or as I will argue below as 'trends'.

III. Private benefits of control?

Let me begin with the hidden truth of theory. What I think is particularly interesting in the erudite paper that Ringe has provided is that it reveals one

[8] Ibid, 237.

[9] Ibid, 237. 'Revised takeover rules and listing requirements on NASDAQ OMX Stockholm' *Euroinvestor* (28 August 2009) <http://www.euroinvestor.co.uk>.

implicit issue, namely, the private benefits of control which may explain more fully the use of CEM and OSOV. Ringe states:

> In a blockholder-dominated corporate culture like in continental Europe, the basic agency conflict is between minority and majority shareholders. Here, rules that allow for deviations from OSOV can aggravate this conflict: In such a system, CEMs can, as the name suggests, even enhance the already established control of a controlling shareholder and put him or her in a position that is virtually unassailable. Minority shareholders will never be able to introduce CEMs for themselves without the consent of the majority. This allows controllers to create corporate structures that can hardly ever be challenged by means of a hostile takeover. The consequence is well known: management entrenchment and *private benefits of control*[10] [my emphasis].
>
> ...Hence, *especially in continental Europe*, problems associated with blockholder ownership will be even aggravated by means of the availability of CEMs[11] [my emphasis].

So the hidden truth, I would suggest, that confronts us is this: Private benefits may be the real issue at play here. As Wymeersch suggested, the 'new shareholder acts on the market for corporate control but does not control'.[12] But, of course, if private benefits is the real issue then there are a number of possible (well-known) ways/mechanisms the law can deal with this. First, mandatory bids (for example by way of majority at a 30 per cent threshold). Secondly, rules can ensure all shareholders benefit from a control premium. So are additional preventive measures needed? Well, Kalay and Pant's model develops a new empirical estimate of the private benefits of control which is the difference in prices of the stock and the synthetic stock.[13] Interestingly, when the control contest is only a possibility, shareholders optimally choose an OSOV structure. They conclude that this ability to deviate from OSOV when needed increases the value of the firm.

And so, if one believes that the traditional concentrated ownership pattern in Europe is put more and more under pressure,[14] then perhaps the answer is in the affirmative. More and more companies, it is suggested, have new dispersed ownership. In consequence, many companies have voluntarily abandoned their anti-takeover protection (especially in the Netherlands), they are now fully dispersed models and are now confronted with activist shareholders.[15] The new 'players' include professional investors, non-European (eg Indian, Russian, Chinese), European players (such as hedge funds, specialized governance funds, critical individuals), and institutional activists. In such an environment,

[10] Ibid, 221. [11] Ibid, 222.

[12] E Wymeersch, 'Good Governance—What Control?' in *Challenges for the Control of Corporate Europe* (Lisbon, 17 October 2007) 16.

[13] A Kalay and S Pant, 'One Share-One Vote is Unenforceable and Sub-Optimal' (1 November 2009). Available at SSRN: <http://papers.ssrn.com/sol3/papers.cfm?abstract_id=1558449> (last accessed 7 July 2010).

[14] E Wymeersch, 'Good Governance—What Control?' in *Challenges for the Control of Corporate Europe* (Lisbon, 17 October 2007) 16. [15] Ibid, 18.

private benefits could be dealt with in a number of ways. First, more focus should be given to systems to avoid private benefits (ie target conflicts of interest). Secondly, laws could be introduced against private benefits; for example, along the lines of the German *Konzernrecht*: prohibition in Group (similar laws in other EU countries: eg Italy, France)[16] or one could introduce conflicts of interest rules for shareholders as well (see, for example, the Israeli Companies Act 1999) or adopt more traditional measures, such as disclosures that need to be mandated or perhaps approved by the AGM (*contrats réglementés*). Ringe further asserts that:

> The threat is now that this equation might be disturbed if companies and regulators themselves will start to introduce or even only facilitate deviations from OSOV, and not only for protectionist motives. Deviations are found high and low in the current debate and could become fashionable again.[17]

If this is indeed the case then a number of alternative actions could also be fashioned:[18] First, one could require more disclosure about ownership (ie 'empty voting'[19] through disclosure). Secondly, states could be asked to report on CEMs (but, of course, this, in turn, raises questions such as how and at what price and who will vet this?). Thirdly, more attention should be given to the state as a shareholder. As Ringe notes, in the *Volkswagen* case, the Court of Justice had to assess the validity of the Volkswagen law, a statute that imposed specific measures on Volkswagen AG ('VW'), such as a voting cap and a special majority requirement for important company decisions.[20] And, finally, 'know your shareholder' (role of custodians) could be encouraged. Another interesting observation Ringe makes in relation to private benefits is that:

> ... Hence, *especially in continental Europe*, problems associated with blockholder ownership will be even aggravated by means of the availability of CEMs[21] [my emphasis].

I would like to suggest that these problems are, in fact, not unique to 'continental Europe'. As the following figure indicates, blockholder ownership can be traced outside Europe, for example, in a number of emerging economies as well. Whilst blockholding affects around 60 per cent of the total market capitalization in France, Germany, and Italy, similar patterns can also be seen in Brazil, Mexico, and Indonesia.[22] So, in fact, this observation may have wider implications.

16 Ibid, 26.

17 Ringe, 238.

18 E Wymeersch, 'Good Governance—What Control?' in *Challenges for the Control of Corporate Europe* (Lisbon, 17 October 2007) 28.

19 Where activist hedge funds borrow shares for short periods of time in order to vote at company meetings.

20 Case C-112/05 *Commission v Germany* [2007] ECR I-8995.

21 Ringe, 222.

22 It would have been interesting to see whether deviations from OSOV are also found outside Europe, but this is, naturally, outside the scope of Ringe's paper.

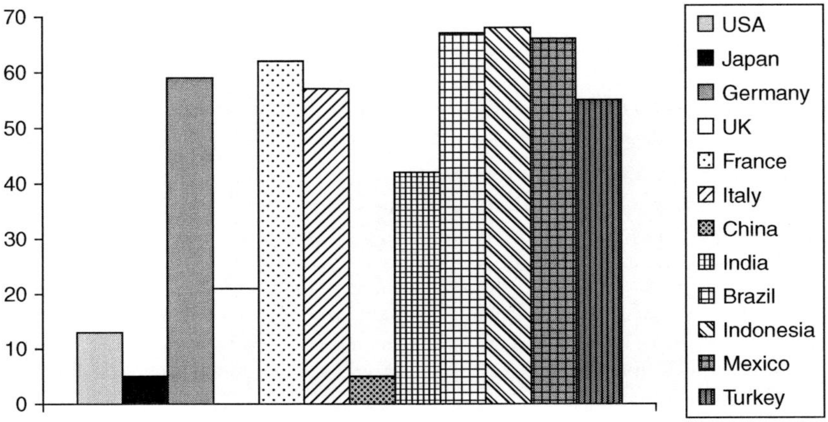

Figure 11.1 The extent of blockholding
Source: *Tomorrow' Company (2007 Report)* 33

IV. Changing business world?

We now turn to the 'practical' section of my commentary. Ringe's careful tour of recent practice on OSOV points out that the traditional understandings of the corporate law landscape may be misplaced or at least that traditional conception is being displaced. I think that, along the way, as he tells his story, his paper reveals another hidden truth, what I am going to call the 'hidden truth of practice'. That hidden truth is that, in practice, companies operate in an ever-changing business world, a more rapidly changing business practice with more pressures and complexity and with more diverse 'players' and conflicting interests at play. Although this is hardly a revelation, it may still underline or better explain or, in fact, provide a fuller account for some of Ringe's observations. To cut to the chase, the landscape is changing and the analysis should take account of this change. In particular, the change is in two dimensions, namely, a change in the landscape and a change in business practices (naturally, both feed each other).

With respect to the landscape, globalization now includes India, China, Russia, but even within Europe, Central European states, such as Poland, demonstrate strong nationalism against Western dominance. But the change is also manifested in more diverse and sophisticated players with various interests and stakes. Interestingly, *Tomorrow's Company 2007 Report* has plotted the relationship between types of shareholders and their tendency to exhibit the quality of stewardship along something they have termed 'the stewardship spectrum' (see Figure 11.2 below). At one end of the spectrum, founders tend to display their stewardship attributes very strongly, while at the opposite end, speculators exercise no stewardship responsibilities whatsoever. This raises a number of questions of what the differing approaches to ownership portend for the financial system, for companies, and for policy makers and regulators worldwide.

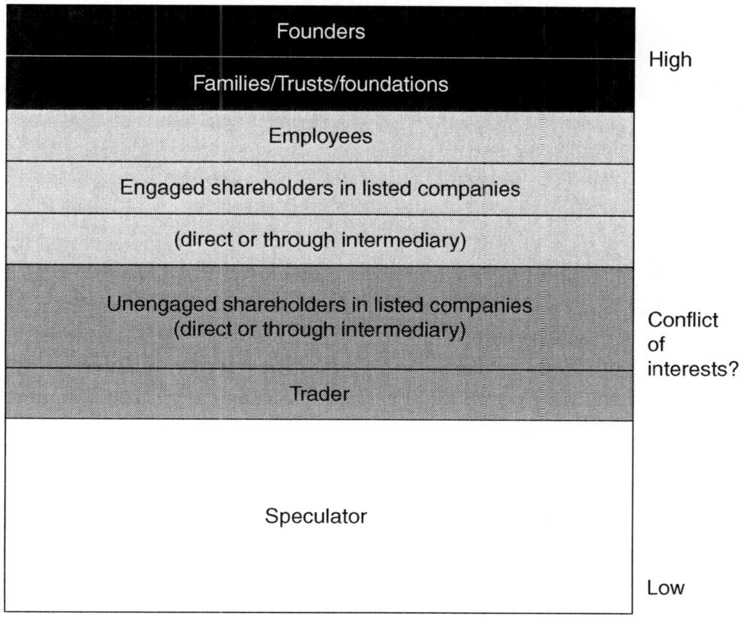

Figure 11.2 Stewardship spectrum
Source: *Tomorrow's Company (2007 Report)* 61

Turning to the second dimension, namely, change in business practices, the recent report, *Tomorrow's Global Company: Challenges and Choices* conducted by Tomorrow's Company[23] points out that the survival and success of a global company is bound up with the health of a complex global system made up of three interdependent subsystems: the natural environment, the social and political system, and the global economy. Global companies play a role in all three and they need all three to flourish. Facing the global challenges, arising from the analysis, the Inquiry team draw the conclusion that companies must expand the space in which they operate and to do this in practice requires a focus on three interlocking and mutually reinforcing priorities:[24]

- redefining success—defining and measuring success in a way that aligns and integrates the social, environmental, human, and financial aspects of companies' work

[23] 18 June 2009, available at <http://www.tomorrowscompany.com/publications.aspx> (last accessed 20 November 2009).
[24] Ibid.

- embedding values—defining, living by, and being judged by values that are publicly espoused and applied rigorously in challenging situations
- creating frameworks—supporting sound national regulatory frameworks and international agreements, working with governments, NGOs, and others to create them.

Moreover, in *Tomorrow's Global Talent*[25] it is argued that tomorrow's company will be operating in an era and a new business environment in which value creation depends on environmental and social issues as much as on economic ones—what they call the 'triple context'. More than ever, companies will need to think in terms of their own sustainability and that of the ecosystems and communities in which they operate. They believe this means that companies should think afresh about what they mean by 'talent'. At present most companies reserve the word 'talent' for high fliers who are destined to become top executives or high-level specialists. However, it is argued that this is too narrow a view for a world with multiple challenges, needing people with a wide range of capabilities.[26] The business world is in the midst of extraordinary change. Business leaders will need to take stock, scan their environments for possibility, and use this information to bypass cultural paralysis and fear.[27]

The hard and hidden truth here is that corporate law may also need to evolve in response to these changing social realities. Still it would be wrong, I think, to suggest that this is entirely novel territory for corporate law. In reality, corporate law has long faced multi-challenges and changing business realties, especially in the last few decades with the growth of diverse and complex investment mechanisms. Perhaps then it is not the practical challenges facing corporate law that are being pushed by the changing landscape, as *Tomorrow's Global Talent* suggests, but merely the application in practice of the principles that underpin it.

V. Finally: 'Trends' rather than 'changes'

In closing, I want to go back to where we started. You may recall that Ringe claims that there have been important changes over time: 'the presence of CEMs comes in waves—very popular over a certain period, yet rigidly rejected in the next'.[28] And that these changes are triggered by market forces (UK from the 1960s), listing rules (the US from 1926), or by legislative intervention (in Germany at various times). Ringe argues:[29]

What can we learn from this? We have seen that over time the attitude of decision-makers—both on the law-making and on the business sides—has repeatedly evolved

[25] Available at <http://www.tomorrowscompany.com/publications.aspx> (last accessed 20 November 2009).
[26] Ibid.
[27] Ibid.
[28] Ringe, 231.
[29] Ibid, 238.

> and *changed* [my emphasis]. At one point, OSOV was seen as the Holy Grail,[30] providing optimal alignment of incentives, facilitating takeovers and leading to optimal governance structures. At another point in time, managers betook themselves in deviations from a strict proportionality, hoping to fend off strong competitive situations and trying to insulate themselves from takeover attempts. Various OSOV rules and practices have evolved primarily in response to either self-regulation, fear of regulation or direct regulatory initiative, as regulators (and scholars) argued that OSOV would properly align control and ownership. In contrast, managers and shareholders have sometimes pushed in the opposite direction (away from OSOV), attempting to reallocate control away from ownership and seeking increased private benefits. States and stock exchanges have sometimes permitted these companies to redistribute voting control.

I would like to suggest that what Ringe describes as 'changes' should perhaps more accurately be classified or described as 'trends' rather than 'changes'. This, I believe, is not just a meaningless exercise in terminology, but rather could or should determine if and what action should be taken in this area. If, as Ringe indicates himself 'the presence of CEMs comes in waves—very popular over a certain period, yet rigidly rejected in the next'[31] then one should not contemplate that current developments necessitate regulation to support OSOV. If these are merely trends, then post crisis, the pressure to move away from OSOV will not be as strong. And so, one should not hurry up to plan and implement any countermeasures in this area. In this respect, the European Commissioner for the Internal Market and Services, Charlie McCreevy's speech from October 2007, I believe, still holds truth and provides an appropriate point for departure.[32]

> I have no doubt that enhanced transparency and better dialogue between companies and their shareholders would be useful for the market. Shareholders should use their existing voting rights to push for this. But a further layer of EU action is not the right way to go. Existing EU legislation—the Takeover Bids directive, the 2006 amendments of the Accounting directives, the Transparency directive and the recently adopted Shareholders' Rights directive already contain ample provisions on transparency. Therefore, I do not intend to propose any action on one-share, one vote.

[30] Borrowing from V de Beaufort, 'One Share—One Vote, Le Nouveau Saint Graal' (December 2006) Essec Centre de Recherche DR 06019.

[31] Ringe, 231.

[32] Speech 07/592 by Commissioner McCreevy at the European Parliament's Legal Affairs Committee available at: <http://europa.eu/rapid/pressReleasesAction.do?reference=SPEECH/07/592&format=DOC&aged=1&language=EN&guiLanguage=en> (last accessed on 6 November 2009).

12

Sovereign Wealth Funds—Market Investors or 'Imperialist Capitalists'? The European Response to Direct Investments by Non-EU State-Controlled Entities

Heike Schweitzer

I. Introduction

During the last three years or so, the international investment activities of Sovereign Wealth Funds (SWFs) have captured the attention of national and international policy makers and have raised serious concerns. There is a widespread fear that SWFs' investment decisions may be guided by political and geostrategic rationales rather than by the traditional market-oriented mind frame that can be presumed to govern private sector investments worldwide,[1] and that such a motivation may seriously harm the political and economic interests of the host states: SWF investments may pose risks to national security, they may lead to an appropriation of technological advantages by foreign states and thus compromise the national economy's international competitiveness, or they may simply distort competition by introducing non-market rationales and repeat the unfavourable continental European experiences with state intervention over the last century.

As Edwin M. Truman has observed, 'the growth of SWFs reflects a dramatic redistribution of international wealth from traditional industrial countries like the United States to countries that historically have not been major players in international finance and have had little or no role in shaping the practices, norms, and conventions governing the international financial system'.[2] The fact that a substantial part of this new wealth is not in private but in public hands has invited the suspicion that SWFs are (potential) instruments of competition between states for political and economic power—and thus as a new version of

[1] E M Truman, 'A Blueprint for Sovereign Wealth Fund Best Practices', Peterson Institute Policy Brief No. PB08-3, April 2008, 3.

[2] Ibid.

'mercantilism'.[3] Max Weber has used the term 'imperialist capitalism' to conceptualize the post-mercantilist interaction of modern states in a capitalist environment.[4] In his view, capitalist interests and the political system have become closely intertwined in the modern industrial state, as imperialist capitalism offers the greatest opportunities for profit—far greater than capitalism of a pacifist kind. Increasing opportunities for profit abroad emerge as territories open up politically and economically. These opportunities are captured by the imperialist state that politically assists economic expansion of its own public and private enterprises with the aim to acquire control of key economic sectors abroad as at home. The search for profit opportunities is paralleled by politically backed economic expansion as a specific form of competition among states. The imperialist impetus increasingly displaces the 'pacifist' expansion based upon open markets and 'freedom of trade'. Viewed in this light, SWFs may be seen as the instruments of commodity-rich states who use their growing economic power to exploit the capitalist system to their political and economic benefit. Societies committed to market capitalism must respond to defend their political interests and the benefits of the economic system they are committed to. They must not allow for a substitution of foreign state control for home state control of key industries as a follow-up to the broad privatization efforts of the last three decades.

Others have argued in favour of a more cautious approach. They have emphasized that the goals that SWFs pursue may be perfectly in line with the logics of markets with undistorted competition: SWFs may simply be an instrument for their owners to achieve higher rates of investment return and to diversify in order to reduce risk. If so, SWF investments may have the same beneficial effects as foreign investment generally: they bring liquidity to the markets and thus lower the costs of capital; moreover, they tend to flow to those projects that promise the greatest returns and thus enhance efficiency. The specific long-term investment horizon of SWFs may be particularly welcome as it can work as a stabilizing force.[5] The SWFs' investment activities during the financial crisis have tended to confirm this positive view: SWF investments have been most welcome, and

[3] See eg R J Gilson and C J Milhaupt, 'Sovereign Wealth Funds and Corporate Governance: A Minimalist Response to the New Mercantilism' (2008) 60 Stanford L Rev 1345; C Cox, 'The Role of Government in Markets', Keynote Address and Robert R Glauber Lecture at the John F. Kennedy School of Government, 24 October 2007, at <www.sec.gov/news/speech/2007/spch102407cc.htm> (last accessed 23July 2010). M Foucault, *Die Geburt der Biopolitik* (Frankfurt: Suhrkamp, 2004) 18. Foucault describes mercantilism as a specific organization of production and of trade according to the principle that, first, the state is to be enriched through the accumulation of money, that, second, the state is to foster the growth of its population, and that, third, the state is in an eternal state of competition with other states.

[4] M Weber, *Wirtschaft und Gesellschaft*, (5th edn, Tübingen: Mohr Siebeck, 1980) 524. For an English translation see Max Weber, *Economy and Society*, (University of California Press, 1978) vol 2, 918 ff (ch IX: The Economic Foundations of 'Imperialism'). See also E J Mestmäcker, 'Economic and Legal Foundations of Constitutional Liberty' [unpublished paper; on file with the author] for a precise summary and contextualization.

[5] See eg European Commission, 'A common European approach to Sovereign Wealth Funds' COM(2008) 115 final, 3 at 2.2.

several financial institutions have managed to recapitalize with the help of SWFs. In Western industrialized countries, no attempts of political instrumentalization have been reported so far.

The EU Commission has been one of the most outspoken advocates of a favourable approach towards SWF investments, in line with the proposals issued by the IMF[6] and the OECD:[7] it has emphasized the EU's commitment to free movement of capital, and has called for an approach which maintains 'the shared benefits of an open investment environment'.[8] In return, it expects SWFs to commit voluntarily to certain minimum standards of transparency[9] and good governance[10] which shall 'assuage public concerns'.[11] Any more aggressive reaction would run the risk to tip into protectionism—one of the most acute threats to a flourishing of the economy worldwide and to a rapid recovery of the international economy from the financial crisis.

The debate surrounding SWFs thus takes up the familiar question of how to deal with the states' direct engagement in markets, albeit this time with a view to non-EU states. With a view to the Member States' market activities, this theme has occupied EU law for a long time. Its starting point is the neutrality of EU law vis-à-vis questions of ownership. According to Article 295 EC (Article 345 TFEU), the European Treaties 'shall in no way prejudice the rules in Member States governing the system of property ownership'. EU law has thus taken a hands-off approach to the state ownership of firms and has refrained from subjecting the Member States to a duty to privatize. Instead, it has subjected public and private market actors to the same rules, including competition rules. When state entities engage in market activities, they must compete on equal footing and must not rely on privileges vis-à-vis private firms. In addition, the Member States are subject to specific rules: the free movement rules commit the Member States to the creation of an internal market characterized by the abolition of obstacles to the free movement of goods, persons, services, and capital; Article 86(1) EC (Article 106(1) TFEU) prohibits the Member States from enacting or maintaining in force any measure contrary to the competition rules in their relation to public undertakings and undertakings to which they have granted special or exclusive rights; a regime of European state aid control is to ensure that Member States will not distort market competition through the granting of subsidies and will not engage in subsidies wars among themselves; and public procurement rules shall constrain the broad discretion Member States enjoy in their

6 See the proposals for a voluntary Code of Conduct for SWFs: International Working Group of Sovereign Wealth Funds (IWG), Generally Accepted Principles and Practices (GAPP)—Santiago Principles, October 2008.

7 The OECD has identified 'Best Practices' for SWF investments in recipient countries—see OECD Declaration on Sovereign Wealth Funds and Recipient Country Policies, 4–5 June 2008; and the OECD Investment Committee report on recipient country policies and SWFs, approved by governments on 4 April 2008.

8 Commission (n 5) 3.

9 Commission (n 5) 10–11.

10 Commission (n 5) 10.

11 Commission (n 5) 8.

procurement decisions as they are not subject to the same competitive pressures as private actors would be.

The increased market presence of SWFs has raised the question of how to deal with the presence of *non-EU states* in European markets. Does it raise similar risks as the market presence of Member States, or are the concerns fundamentally different? Does Europe need a special legal regime—an extension of the rules addressed to the Member States to third-country states that want to engage in economic activities within the EU, for example, an intensified regime of entry control similar to the CFIUS review in the US, or a regime of European golden shares? Or can we rely on the existing general legal framework to address the relevant risks, in particular on the general rules of corporate law and capital market law at the level of the Member States, and on the competition rules at the level of the Member States and the EU?

This paper strives to address these questions in the following order: following a brief survey of the specific characteristics and relevance of SWFs (II) and the response that the increased economic importance of state-controlled foreign direct investment has received in the US (III), the general approach of EU law to the direct involvement of EU Member States in European markets shall be outlined (IV). The paper shall then ask how the presence of non-EU states in European markets can and should be addressed under EU law (V). Section VI will conclude.

II. Sovereign Wealth Funds—the phenomenon and questions it raises

1. Defining SWFs

The term 'Sovereign Wealth Funds' has become widely used to denominate state-owned investment vehicles which manage a diversified portfolio of domestic and international financial assets.[12] The first SWFs of this kind were established in the 1950s[13] by oil-rich countries with the aim to transform present-day revenue streams into a sustainable income that would reduce the country's reliance on

[12] For this definition see: Commission (n 5) 3. For another attempt to define SWFs see OECD, 'Foreign Government-Controlled Investors and Recipient Country Investment Policies: A Scoping Paper' (January 2009) 6: SWFs are 'special purpose investment funds or arrangements, owned by the general Government. Created by the general government for macroeconomic purposes. SWFs hold, manage, or administer assets to achieve financial objectives, and employ a set of investment strategies which include investing in foreign financial assets. The SWFs are commonly established out of balance of payments surpluses, official foreign currency operations, the proceeds of privatizations, fiscal surpluses, and/or receipts resulting from commodity exports'.

[13] The Kuwait Investment Board is generally named as the first SWF. It was set up by the Kuwait Government in 1953. In 1965, it was replaced by the Kuwait Investment Office (KIO), a subsidiary of the Kuwait Investment Authority (KIA) in charge of the management of substantial parts of the Future Generation Fund today, to which the state of Kuwait allocates 10% of the country's oil

its finite oil resources in the long term and to ensure inter-generational equity.[14] Since then, the number and size of SWFs has grown. The last decade in particular has seen a substantial increase in the total assets managed by SWFs,[15] which, according to general estimates, today amount to US $1.5–2.5 trillion. Despite the current financial difficulties of some SWFs, in particular Dubai World, the general prediction is that SWFs will continue to grow at a rapid pace.

A few features are common to all SWFs: they are funded and owned by a state, but managed separately from official reserves and have no or very limited explicit liabilities contrary, for example, to pension funds.[16] Apart from that, they are highly heterogeneous[17] and differ not only with regard to the origin of the funds managed, but also with regard to the goals pursued and their governance structure. The financial resources managed by SWFs may flow from official foreign exchange reserves, in particular where large balance-of-payments surpluses have accumulated (so-called 'non-commodity SWFs'[18]), or—even more typically—from fiscal surpluses resulting from the export of natural resources, eg oil and/or gas (so-called 'commodity SWFs'[19]).[20] The goals pursued by SWFs may include the intertemporal stabilization of income in highly volatile international markets for commodities,[21] the functions of a contingent pension reserve fund or a transformation of present-day revenue streams from the sale of the resources or other exports into sustainable long-term income in order to ensure inter-generational equity.[22] Potentially, SWFs may also pursue geostrategic and/or industrial policy goals. The relationship with the state-owner may also differ widely—some SWFs are thought to be under the direct influence and control of their government,[23]

revenues annually—see DB Research (Steffen Kern), 'Sovereign wealth funds—state investments on the rise' 10 September 2007, 4.

[14] Ibid. [15] For more precise numbers see below.

[16] See eg Commission (n 5) II.2.1; R Beck and M Fidora, 'The Impact of Sovereign Wealth Funds on Global Financial Markets' ECB Occasional Paper Series No 91 (2008) 6; R M Kimmitt, 'Public Footprints in Private Markets. Sovereign Wealth Funds and the World Economy' (2008) 87 Foreign Affairs 119, 120.

[17] See C Hammer, P Kunzel, and I Petrova, 'Sovereign Wealth Funds: Current Institutional and Operational Practices' IMF Working Paper November 2008, WP/08/254.

[18] See Kimmitt (n 16) 120–1: 'Non-commodity SWFs often arise from an exchange-rate intervention involving a domestic liquidity increase that has to be absorbed by issuing domestic debt to avoid unwanted inflation. Their net return depends on the difference between the yield earned on investments and the yield paid on domestic debt. The assets of this type of SWF therefore may be thought of more as borrowed money than traditional wealth. Non-commodity funds are frequently viewed critically: there is a concern that such SWFs are used as mechanisms to accumulate more foreign assets in an effort to keep the currency from appreciating' (ibid 122).

[19] Kimmitt (n 16) 120.

[20] See DB Research (Steffen Kern), 'SWFs and foreign investment policies—an update' 22 October 2008, 5. Other possible sources of funding include the proceeds of privatizations.

[21] See Kern (n 13) 4: 'SWFs may be a way to diversify the sources of income: they provide a liquidity pool which is replenished at times of favourable commodity prices or reserve inflows, and can be drawn upon at times when asset prices are low.' [22] Ibid.

[23] For example the CIC—see L C Backer, 'Sovereign Investing in Times of Crisis: Global Regulation of Sovereign Wealth Funds, State Owned Enterprises and the Chinese Experience' (2008) 19 Transnational L and Contemporary Problems 102, 250.

whereas others enjoy a large degree of independence in the management of the funds, aiming at a systematic, professional portfolio management. A wide variety of models exist also with a view to corporate governance structures within SWFs.[24] Finally, SWFs differ with regard to investment policies, risk management strategies, and disclosure policies.[25] While Norway's Government Pension Fund is typically cited as a role model for an independently managed, transparent SWF following well-established principles of good corporate governance[26] and acting essentially like a private investor,[27] the China Investment Corporation (CIC) remains under the overall direction of the Chinese Communist Party and state policy,[28] and its investment policy is to an important extent a reflection of the perceived political interests of China in the world. Along those lines, a recent focus of the CIC's investment activity has been the acquisition of control of natural resources abroad.[29] The overall level of transparency of most SWFs with regard to the value of asserts under management, investment objectives and strategies, target portfolio allocations, risk management systems and internal controls has so far remained low.[30]

2. Experiences with SWFs so far

With a view to the total assets under SWF management, SWFs are considered a source of investment of 'systemic importance' today.[31] Although the amount of US $1.5–2.5 trillion may appear small compared to a global equity market capitalization of US $50 trillion, the assets managed by all SWFs roughly equal the combined assets of all hedge funds and private equity firms. According to a widespread view, a politicized management of a significant portion of SWFs could inflict serious harm not only upon the targeted companies, but upon the world economy as a whole. At the same time, ownership of the wealth under SWF management is relatively concentrated. The top 10 SWFs manage significantly more than $100 billion each, and together represent 85 per cent of all sovereign assets.[32] Almost half of all sovereign assets are held by SWFs from the Middle East.[33] SWFs from the Asian region follow (29 per cent). SWFs from Russia and Norway manage around 16 per cent of all sovereign assets.[34] The Abu Dhabi Investment Authority (ADIA) with an estimated $875 billion under management, the Norges Bank Investment Management (NBIM) with an investment volume of around $400 billion, the Government of Singapore Investment

[24] For an empirical survey see J Aizenman and R Glick, 'Sovereign Wealth Funds: Stylized Facts about their Determinants and Governance', NBER Working Paper Series, Paper 14562, December 2008, 12 ff.

[25] See Hammer and others (n 17) 12–13.

[26] See <http://www.norges-bank.no/templates/article____69632.aspx>.

[27] See, for example, Beck and Fidora (n 16) 10.

[28] Backer (n 23) 250 ff.

[29] Backer (n 23) 262 ff.

[30] See Beck and Fidora (n 16) 5 ff.

[31] Commission (n 5) 3.

[32] Kern (n 20) 4.

[33] Kern (n 20) 4.

[34] Kern (n 20) 4.

Corporation (GIC) managing an estimated $330 billion, the Kuwait Investment Authority (KIA) with an estimated investment volume of $213 billion, and the China Investment Corporation (CIC), which—although established only in 2007[35]—already manages an estimated $200 billion[36] are among the largest single SWFs.[37]

Although these figures seem impressive, it is generally acknowledged that there have been no indications of an abuse or politicized management of SWFs in Western industrialized countries so far. Generally, the investments of SWFs appear to be relatively diversified across industry sectors.[38] In 2007/2008, SWFs have heavily invested into the US and EU financial sector,[39] apparently attracted by low share prices and the perception of a strategic opportunity.[40] They have been perceived as highly welcome investors during this period of turmoil, and although the transactions have included large-scale investments in single firms, their engagement has contributed to their perception as responsible market participants. In Germany, SWF investments into the car industry[41] have received high publicity recently. Investments into defence-related companies or firms active in the field of security-relevant technologies, on the other hand, have been extremely rare.[42]

Frequently, SWFs have been rather passive investors in the past, and have acquired small to medium stakes in the relevant target firms, refraining from claiming board seats or attempts to influence the business strategies or day-to-day business of the companies. The Norwegian NBIM, for example, has committed to a policy of not acquiring stakes exceeding 10 per cent. The majority of shareholdings are below 2 per cent. Such a policy is, however, not pursued by all SWFs. Some SWFs have opted for an active involvement and have acquired controlling stakes up to 100 per cent of the votes.[43] Recent SWF investments in the financial industry have generally followed an intermediate pattern: the stakes

[35] The CIC, equipped with an initial endowment of $200 billion, replaced China Central Huijn Investment Corporation which had been established in 2003.

[36] For a more thorough discussion of the CIC see Backer (n 23) 243 ff.

[37] For a brief overview of some important SWFs see, for example, Beck and Fidora (n 16) 9.

[38] They go into the real estate and construction sector, the commodities and energy sector, the technology industries, and into infrastructure and transportation—see Kern (n 20) 8.

[39] Kern (n 20) 7 ff. See also Beck and Fidora (n 16) 11–12; T Sun and H Hesse, 'Sovereign Wealth Funds and Financial Stability—An Event Study Analysis' October 2009, IMF Working Paper WP/09/239, 3–4: SWFs have contributed more than $50 bn of capital to financial institutions since November 2007.

[40] Kern (n 20) 10.

[41] See in particular Qatar's investment into VW/Porsche—'Einstieg von Katar in VW ist perfekt', Spiegel Online, 14 August 2009.

[42] An exception is the investment of Dubai International Capital's into the EU-based EADS in 2007. Dubai International Capital acquired a share of 3.12%.

[43] According to DB Research (Steffen Kern) 'Staatsfonds—Staatliche Investitionen in der Finanzkrise' July 2009, 23, 62% of all acquisitions publicly known have led to stakes of 20% or more in the target firm. 25% of all investments have led to the acquisition of 100%.

acquired have been minority stakes, but of a significant size[44]—frequently just below 10 per cent.[45]

3. Concerns regarding the investment activities of SWFs and other foreign state-controlled entities

The recent investments by which SWFs have acquired significant shareholdings such as to grant them considerable influence on, or even control of, the target companies have fuelled concerns that the occurrence of abuses will only be a matter of time. The notable absence of negative experiences does, however, indicate a certain imbalance of the debate: while SWFs have generally been good corporate citizens so far, acquisition sprees by state-owned enterprises (SOEs) have indeed raised the spectre of 'imperialist capitalism' at times. In fact, all incidences of state-controlled foreign direct investment which have raised public concerns have involved SOEs. This is, for example, true for the bid by China National Offshore Oil Corporation (CNOOC)—70 per cent owned by the Chinese Government—for the US-based Unocal Oil Company in July 2005 (a bid which was eventually withdrawn),[46] or the plan by Dubai Ports World (DP World)—a company owned by the government of Dubai—to acquire the London-based Peninsular and Oriental Steam Navigation Company (P&O), the fourth largest ports operator in the world, running, inter alia, major port facilities in New York, New Jersey, Philadelphia, Baltimore, New Orleans, and Miami; a plan which ultimately failed owing to political resistance in the US.[47] Similarly, attempts by Gazprom to integrate vertically into the energy sector of neighbouring states have raised concerns. In Germany, some discussion has ensued on an allegedly

[44] For example, China, through the CIC, has acquired a 9.9% stake in the Blackstone Group, and a 9.9% stake in Morgan Stanley. Singapore, through GIC and Temasek, has, inter alia, acquired a 9.9% stake in Merrill Lynch, an 18% stake in the UK-based Standard Chartered Bank Ltd and a 9% stake in UBS. Dubai, through DFG, DIFC, DIFX, and other funds has, inter alia, acquired a 28% stake in the London Stock Exchange, a 20% stake in Nasdaq, and a 28.4% stake in OMX. Qatar, through QIA, has acquired, inter alia, an 8.9% stake in the Barclays Bank, a 24% stake in the London Stock Exchange, and a 10% stake in OMX. With such stakes, the SWFs have in some cases become the largest single shareholders in the targeted financial institutions and will—individually and/or together—have an important position in these high-profile companies in the time to come.

[45] In many jurisdictions, the 10% threshold triggers special regulatory oversight. In the US, for example, the acquisition of a stake of 10% or more will allow the foreign investment control regime to kick in. Moreover, the acquisition of shares in banks from 10% upwards need separate approval by the SEC, and investor will obtain the status of a Bank Holding Company and become subject to specific supervision.

[46] For a discussion of this case see: J W Casselman, 'China's Latest "Threat" to the United States: The Failed CNOOC-Unocal Merger and Its Implications for Exon-Florio and CFIUS' (2007) 17 Ind Intl & Comp L Rev 155.

[47] See for a discussion of this case: D M Mostaghel, 'Dubai Ports World Under Exon-Florio: A Threat to National Security or a Tempest in a Seaport?' (2007) 70 Albany L Rev 583.

politically driven investment by the Russian investor Yusufov into the failing shipyard industry in Mecklenburg-Vorpommern.[48]

National legislation on foreign investment control has generally recognized that risks to public policy or national security are not specific to investments by SWFs. Foreign investment control regimes typically extend to all foreign acquisitions of substantial shareholdings indiscriminately of the identity of the acquirer. This paper shall focus on the specific risks that may result from cross-border investments by foreign government-controlled investment vehicles, in particular SWFs and SOEs.

III. The US reaction to foreign states' involvement in economic activities within the US[49]

In the US, a national security review of foreign acquisitions of US companies has been in place for some time now. The Committee on Foreign Investment (CFIUS), established in 1975 by President Gerald Ford as an inter-agency committee within the executive branch and chaired by the Department of Treasury, was originally designed as a mere monitoring body: it was to monitor the impact of inbound foreign investment and co-ordinate US investment policy. It was transformed into a system of formal review of foreign acquisitions of control of US firms through the 1988 Exon-Florio amendment[50] to the Defence Production Act of 1950, passed in reaction to growing political concerns about the increase of foreign direct investments in the US, in particular originating in Japan and the UK. The Exon-Florio amendment for the first time formally empowered the President to suspend or prohibit acquisitions that could result in foreign control of US companies if the transaction threatened to impair national security.[51] The President delegated the review of individual transactions to the CFIUS which was later statutorily established by the Foreign Investment and National Security Act of 2007. With the so-called 'Byrd-Amendment' of 1992,[52] CFIUS review

[48] See eg H Graupner, 'German shipyard creditors clear the decks for new Russian buyer' (18 August 2009) DW-World.

[49] For a description and discussion of the US regime of foreign investment control see eg G S Georgiev, 'The Reformed CFIUS Regulatory Framework: Mediating Between Continued Openness to Foreign Investment and National Security', (2008) 25 Yale J on Regulation 125 ff; R Prabhakar, 'Deal-Breakers: FDI, CFIUS, and Congressional Response to State Ownership of Foreign Firms' 2009, available on <http://www.ssrn.com> (last accessed 23 July 2010).

[50] Omnibus Trade and Competitiveness Act of 1988 § 5021, Pub. L. No. 100-418, 102 Stat. 1107 (1988) (codified at 50 U.S.C. App. § 2170).

[51] Prior to the Exon-Florio Amendment, foreign acquisitions could be blocked only if the President declared a national emergency or regulators found a violation of federal antitrust, environmental, or securities laws.

[52] National Defence Authorization Act for Fiscal Year 1993, Pub. L. No. 102-484 § 837, 106 Stat. 2315, 2463-65 (1992) (codified at 50 U.S.C. app. § 2170(b)(2000)).

became mandatory for all transactions where the acquirer is 'controlled by or acting on behalf of a foreign government'.

Despite the rather comprehensive regime of control already in place, the 2005 bid by CNOOC for Unocal and the plans by DP World to acquire P&O led to debates about the need to improve a previously lenient and allegedly ineffective investment control regime. In 2007, the Foreign Investment and National Security Act (FINSA)[53] was passed to amend the Exon-Florio Act, and has further been specified by an Implementing Executive Order of 23 January 2008.[54] The FINSA has once more extended the range of transactions falling under the CFIUS review. According to s 751(d) Defence Production Act in its current version, any merger, acquisition, or takeover is subject to review if:

... (1) there is a credible evidence that foreign entity exercising control might take action that threatens national security, and (2) the provisions of law other than the International Emergency Economics Powers Act do not provide adequate and appropriate authority to protect the national security.

The term 'national security' has deliberately been left undefined, in order not to curtail 'the President's broad authority to protect the national security'.[55] Some guidance is offered as to the factors that are considered in the security analysis. They include control of security-relevant technologies, relevance for national defence, and, since the entry into force of FINSA, also transactions involving critical infrastructure and energy assets. These factors are not conclusive, however. Generally, the term 'national security' is to be interpreted broadly and without limitation to particular industries.[56] According to one observer, the scenarios which CFIUS considers most worrisome in practice are the threat of a shut-down of critical facilities; of the removal of sensitive data offshore; of a denial of access to critical technology to the US Government; of the transferral of US-developed technology overseas; of a participation in espionage in government activities; and of aiding enemies of the US.[57] The fact that the acquirer was owned or controlled by a foreign state has repeatedly influenced the outcome of a CFIUS review in the light of these concerns.[58]

The CFIUS review procedure is a two-step procedure: In a first step, the committee decides in the course of a 30-day review whether a control proceeding is to be initiated. In practice, this is relatively rare. If a control procedure is initiated, the parties to the transaction will frequently withdraw the planned acquisition voluntarily.[59] Where the investors hold onto their plan, the control procedure itself will take place. It has to be completed within a maximum of 45 days. A specificity

[53] Pub.L. No. 110-49 (2007). [54] E.O. 13456.

[55] See the Regulations Pertaining to the Mergers, Acquisitions, and Takeovers by Foreign Persons.

[56] Regulations Pertaining to the Mergers, Acquisitions, and Takeovers by Foreign Persons.

[57] Prabhakar (n 49) 15. [58] For this hypothesis see Prabhakar (n 49).

[59] According to a study conducted by Georgiev (n 49), the US has initiated 25 control proceedings between 1988 and 2005. In 13 of these proceedings, the investor has retreated from an acquisition in response, without awaiting the result of the control procedure.

of the CFIUS review procedure is that no mandatory notification requirement exists. A CFIUS review begins either with a voluntary notice from a party to a planned transaction or on recommendation from a CFIUS member agency that believes that a transaction might affect US national security. In practice, parties tend to notify voluntarily, however, as in the absence of a notification they would remain indefinitely subject to the CFIUS review and potential remedial actions by the President. Any voluntary filing, on the other hand, will provide the parties with a regulatory safe harbour, immunizing them against subsequent reviews or actions except in cases where the parties have misrepresented their plans.

While the procedure itself is relatively formalized and transparent,[60] the political nature of the proceeding is apparent not only from the broad and open nature of the substantive test, but also from the composition of the CFIUS which brings together 12 branches of the administration, among them finance, justice, economy, defence. The Department of Treasury has remained the lead agency. The CFIUS enjoys broad discretion both in the identification of a risk and in the imposition of remedies: if national security interests are negatively affected, and laws other than Exon-Florio and the International Emergency Economic Powers Act[61] do not provide adequate and appropriate authority to protect national security, the acquisition can be prohibited, or mitigation measures may be imposed. FINSA empowers CFIUS to re-open a reviewed transaction if mitigation measures are materially breached. Upon completion of a review or investigation, CFIUS must provide written notice to Congress—in addition to a report which must be submitted annually.

In practice, foreign investment control has generally been handled cautiously in the US. During 2006 and 2007, for example, only 13 transactions were subjected to a 45-day investigation, and none was prohibited.[62] It is, however, widely believed that the CFIUS review has a further-reaching deterrent effect. Transactions which might become politically sensitive are abandoned before the CFIUS review kicks in.[63]

From a European perspective, the broad, open-ended nature of the review criteria and the political discretion in their interpretation and application is notable. A review regime of this kind may allow an effective response to any perceived act of 'imperialistic capitalism' or other threats to national security. But it runs the risk of becoming politicized and protectionist itself.[64] While over-inclusive in

[60] See in particular the Regulations Pertaining to Mergers, Acquisitions, and Takeovers by Foreign Persons, 31 CFR Part 800, which entered into force on 21 March 2008.

[61] This Act allows the President to declare a national emergency to deal with extraordinary threats to national security or the economy. 50 U.S.C. §§ 1701–1706.

[62] US Government Accountability Office (GAO), 'Foreign Investment: Laws and Policies Regulating Foreign Investment in 10 Countries' GAO-08-320, February 2008, 6. See also Georgiev (n 49) 129.

[63] See Prabhakar (n 49) 10.

[64] See Georgiev (n 49) 130 ff; Prabhakar (n 49) in particular 15: 'CFIUS' vulnerability to congressional pressure and lobbying is largely a function of its won statutory vagueness. …'.

some respects, the CFIUS review is under-inclusive in others: risks to national security which would result from a later shift of policy of a state controlling an SWF or SOE cannot be captured by a regime which is essentially a regime of *ex ante* control.

IV. The legal framework of EU law on Member States' involvement in economic activities

If the handling of the US regime of foreign investment control is thus prone to fall into the spiral of a politically popular protectionism,[65] the EU has reacted to similar dangers by replacing the logics of politics with the rule of law—at least as far as the relations between the Member States are concerned. Any national foreign investment entry control regime which potentially hinders cross-border investment from other Member States will be subject to review under the free movement rules, in particular the free movement of capital (Article 56 EC/Article 63 TFEU) and freedom of establishment (Article 43 EC/Article 49 TFEU). In light of the principle of neutrality vis-à-vis public or private ownership as derived from Article 295 EC (Article 345 TFEU), this is true irrespective of whether the foreign investor is privately owned or whether it is owned or controlled by another Member State. EU law subjects private and public undertakings to the same rules and constraints; in return they enjoy the same rights.

1. Do public undertakings really benefit from the protection of the free movement rules?

Recently, some doubts have been raised in this regard, albeit only implicitly. Among others, AG Maduro has suggested the existence of a fundamental difference in the conduct of private and public undertakings—a difference which could become legally relevant under the free movement rules. In his recent opinion in *Federconsumatori*, Maduro enquires whether the public ownership of shares itself can constitute a restriction of the free movement of capital, ie whether it is liable to dissuade investments from other Member States (para 23). Finding that '[t]he mere fact that a public body owns shares in a company does not reduce the attractiveness of cross-border investments in that company, as long as investors in other Member States can be sure that the public body concerned will, with a view to maximising its return on investment, respect the normal rules of operation of the market' (para 25), he simultaneously suggests that:

> [...] as public bodies are subject to local or national mechanisms of political accountability, they are naturally inclined to adjust their conduct in light of the interests of those

[65] See eg Prabhakar (n 49).

who are represented within the framework of those mechanisms. Therefore, when a public body holds shares which give it a privileged position in relation to other shareholders as regards its powers of control in the company concerned, there is a real risk that those powers will be used to grant selective and potentially discriminatory access to the national market (para 25).

The case did not require Maduro to take his theory to its logical limits. Taken seriously, Maduro's argument would call into question the EC Treaty's well-established principle of neutrality vis-à-vis public versus private ownership. If states are generally suspect to exercise their ownership rights based on a political rather than a market logic, general legal constraints imposed on cross-border investments by entities owned or controlled by another Member State might be justified. This view is reflected in a public opinion which—in a mix of legitimate fear of 'imperialist capitalism' and national protectionist sentiments—views cross-border ambitions of EDF, GDF, and similar state-owned firms with intense scepticism.

Irrespective of an empirical verification of the claim that public and private undertakings behave differently by their nature, EU law has refused to adopt this distinction which would have put into question the existence of public undertakings in and of itself. Instead, EU law subjects the interactions between Member States and public as well as private undertakings to a specific set of legal rules which shall ensure a level playing field. Such rules include, in particular, the state aid rules, the prohibition for Member States to enact or maintain in force any measure contrary to the competition rules in their relation to public undertakings and undertakings to which they have granted special or exclusive rights (Article 86(1) with Article 81, 82 EC/Article 106(1) with Article 101, 102 TFEU), the competition rules which apply equally to private and public market actors, and the public procurement rules. While these rules may not have erased the difference that exists in the fundamental motivations of private and public ownership, they have imposed a tight corset upon public undertakings, subjected them to the rules of the market and competition, and have largely contained the risks of a chain of 'imperialist capitalist' actions and protectionist responses. It is in this logic that EU Member States which implement a foreign investment entry control procedure have to justify the restrictions of the freedom of establishment and of the free movement of capital, irrespective of whether investors from other Member States are state-owned or state-controlled. Public undertakings, like private undertakings, benefit from the protection of the free movement rules.

2. Cross-border investments: freedom of establishment or free movement of capital?

In the EU, most Member States have abandoned foreign investment entry control for investments originating in other Member States. Only in a very narrow set of cases will investments from other Member States be subject to an authorization regime, namely where the acquisition of control or substantial shareholdings in companies is involved which produce military equipment, create cryptographic systems admitted for the transmission of governmental classified information, or deal with nuclear technologies. Since such transactions may compromise the vital security interests of a Member State, the restrictions implicit in an authorization regime are justified, regardless of whether they are assessed under the rules on freedom of establishment (Article 43 EC/Article 49 TFEU) or under the free movement of capital rules (Article 56 EC/Article 63 TFEU).

A few Member States have maintained broader regimes of foreign investment control vis-à-vis investments originating from other Member States. French law, for example, for a long time required prior authorization by the French Ministry of the Economy for every direct foreign investment which is 'such as to represent a threat to public policy [and] public security'. The Court of Justice reviewed this regime in *Eglise de Scientologie*[66] and found it to be incompatible with Article 56 EC (Article 63 TFEU). It accepted that, with a view to the difficulty in identifying and blocking capital once it has entered a Member State, a prior authorization scheme for foreign direct investment may in principle be justifiable, since a (less restrictive) prior declaration regime might be inadequate to counter a serious threat to public policy and public security. However, the French system was contrary to the principle of legal certainty: it failed to give any indication to investors as to the specific circumstances in which prior authorization would be required and in which a serious threat to public policy and public security might be found to exist (paras 19–23).

In *Eglise de Scientologie,*[67] the foreign investment control regime was assessed against the guarantee of free movement of capital (Article 56 EC/Article 63 TFEU). Freedom of establishment—the right to take up and pursue activities as self-employed persons and to set up and manage undertakings, in particular companies or firms, under the laws of the host Member State (Article 43(2) EC/Article 49(2) TFEU)—was not mentioned as a legal reference point. The approach chosen by the Court of Justice is explained by the structure of the French foreign investment control regime which was to be reviewed: it did not only address the acquisition of control or a stake conferring substantial influence in a French undertaking, ie such foreign investments which fall within the scope of Article 43 EC (Article 49 TFEU),[68] but it potentially extended to mere portfolio investments which are outside its scope. National investment control regimes which are more narrowly construed and apply only to such cross-border investments which 'serve to establish or maintain lasting and direct links between the persons providing the capital and the undertakings to which the capital is made available in order to carry out an economic activity', ie to the acquisition of control or a substantial stake below the level of control, will

[66] Case C-54/99 *Eglise de Scientologie* [2000] ECR I-1335.

[67] Ibid.

[68] Article 43 EC protects those cross-border investments which 'serve to establish or maintain lasting and direct links between the persons providing the capital and the undertakings to which the capital is made available in order to carry out an economic activity' (frequently called 'direct investment'). It does not protect mere portfolio investments.

potentially be assessed both under Article 43 EC (Article 49 TFEU) and under Article 56 EC (Article 63 TFEU).

V. Foreign states' involvement in economic activities within the EU: what rules do we have? What rules do we need?

1. Concerns regarding the involvement of foreign states in economic activities within the EU—the Commission's proposal for a 'common European approach to Sovereign Wealth Funds'

Compared to the densely-knit European legal framework regulating the Member States' interventions into markets such as to ensure a 'level playing field' whenever the Member States themselves engage in economic activities, the absence of rules binding foreign states engaged in economic activities within the EU is striking at first sight. Despite the absence of constraints imposed on the market activities of foreign states matching those to which the EU Member States are subject, Article 56(1) EC's (Article 63(1) TFEU's) scope of protection has been unconditionally extended to third-country investors, including entities owned or controlled by third-country states.

For some time, the EU Commission itself seemed to be divided on the question whether a specific European regime of entry control or behavioural control vis-à-vis third-country state-controlled investors would be needed in order to balance the absence of legal constraints on the interaction between these investors and their home states. The proposal to introduce an EU committee on foreign investment that should mirror the CFIUS review in the US was ultimately rejected, however, as was the proposal to introduce some kind of 'European golden share' mechanism to monitor 'suspicious' non-EU foreign investment.[69] In its communication on 'A common European approach to Sovereign Wealth Funds' of 2008,[70] the Commission rather adopted a non-interventionist soft law approach closely aligned with the approach favoured by the IMF[71] and the OECD.[72] SWFs are advised to base their investment decisions strictly on economic objectives and to compete on fair terms with private-sector investors.[73] Moreover, SWFs are requested to follow certain principles of 'good governance' and transparency

69 Commission (n 5) 8.

70 Commission (n 5).

71 See in particular the so-called 'Santiago principles'—the 'Generally Accepted Principles and Practices' on Sovereign Wealth Funds issued, in October 2008, by the International Working Group of Sovereign Wealth Funds in cooperation with the IMF. The 'Santiago Principles' are meant to serve as a voluntary code of conduct for SWFs and for their owners.

72 See OECD, 'Guidance on recipient country policies towards SWFs', adopted by OECD members on 8 October 2008.

73 Commission (n 5) 5.

in order to build confidence vis-à-vis recipient states. The principles of good governance shall include:[74]

- a clear allocation and separation of responsibilities in the internal governance structure of a SWF
- an investment policy that clearly defines the overall objectives to be pursued by the SWF
- operational autonomy for the SWF in achieving these objectives
- public disclosure of the general principles governing a SWF's relationship with the governmental authority
- the disclosure of the general principles of internal governance that provide assurances of integrity
- a fully developed risk-management policy.

In addition, SWFs should disclose investment positions and asset allocations annually, in particular investments for which there is majority ownership; they should disclose the exercise of ownership rights; the use of leverage and of the currency composition; the size and source of their resources; and their home country regulations and oversight.[75] Such transparency is meant to provide for an increased accountability and a disciplinary effect on the management of SWFs.[76] Finally, the Commission considers an extension of the 2001 IMF Guidelines for Foreign Exchange Reserve management[77] to SWFs.[78]

The Commission's approach must be valued for the political effort it makes to discourage protectionist responses to SWFs—or, for that matter, to SOEs—to maintain an open investment environment in Europe and to co-operate at an international level in the search for an adequate response. At the same time, the effectiveness of the measures proposed may be questioned—provided that the investment activities of SWFs and third-country SOEs do raise real concerns: The actual compliance with principles of 'good governance' will be almost impossible to monitor. Moreover, a commitment to a voluntary code of conduct may be abandoned by an SWF-owning country any time, with no legal consequences attached. Reliance on the self-enforcing character of such commitments due to the shared interests of all SWFs in the maintenance of an open international investment environment may underestimate the force of the political dynamics in some SWF-owning states. Commitments to transparency, on the other hand, would not address the real problem,[79] even if they were made binding. Transparency will tend to strengthen the self-enforcing character of codes of conduct as long as SWFs and their sponsoring countries feel committed to these codes generally. They will likely fail to hinder politically motivated investment

74 Commission (n 5) 10.

75 Commission (n 5) 11.

76 Commission (n 5) 10.

77 <http://www.imf.org/external/np/mae/ferm/eng/index.html> (last accessed 23 July 2010).

78 Commission (n 5) 10.

79 See also Gilson and Milhaupt (n 3) 19.

strategies by SWFs where the sponsoring countries would decide in favour of such a path.

In one area—namely in the energy sector—the Commission has opted for a significantly more restrictive approach. Both Article 11 of Directive 2009/72/EC concerning common rules for the internal market in electricity[80] and Article 11 of Directive 2009/73/EC concerning common rules for the internal market in natural gas[81] provide that, if a transmission system owner or operator which is controlled by a person or persons from a third country or third countries requests a certification as an approved and designated transmission system operator in one of the Member States, a special control procedure shall be conducted by the competent national regulatory authority in close co-operation with the EU Commission. The certification shall be refused if the applicant does not demonstrate that the unbundling requirements set out in Article 9 of the Directive are complied with, and that a certification would not put at risk the security of energy supply of the Member State and the Community. In taking its decision, the national regulatory authority shall take 'utmost account' of the opinion of the Commission which it is obliged to request before deciding itself. Interestingly, it is not for the national regulatory authority to prove that a risk to the security of energy supply positively exists; rather any remaining doubts will go against the third-country applicant.

The recitals accompanying both directives set out the rationale underlying these rules. They acknowledge that security of supply is essential for public security, for the competitiveness of the economy, and for the well-being of the EU citizens, and that it is inherently connected to the efficient functioning of the internal market in energy. Persons from third countries should therefore be allowed to control a transmission system or a transmission system operator only if they comply with the unbundling requirements that apply inside the EU. Moreover, the high importance of security of supply of energy to the Community would justify special measures to protect public order and public security. The case by case assessment which is to be performed shall take into account in particular the independence of network operation, the level of the Community's and individual Member States' dependence on energy supply from third countries, and the treatment of both domestic and foreign trade and investment in energy in a particular third country, but also the rights and obligations arising under international law, in particular the international agreements between the Community and the third country concerned.[82] In the area of energy, the EU rules thus appear to acknowledge that an important difference may exist between EU and non-EU investors, as both are not subject to the same set of rules. No special reference is made to the question whether a non-EU investor is privately owned or state controlled, but a potential link between this question and the assessment criteria to be applied is difficult to deny.

[80] Directive 2009/72/EC of 13 July 2009, [2009] OJ L211/55.

[81] Ibid.

[82] See recital 25 of Directive 2009/72/EC of 13 July 2009, [2009] OJ L211/55 and recital 22 of Directive 2009/73/EC of 13 July 2009, [2009] OJ L211/94.

2. Entry controls for foreign investment at the Member State level—a brief survey

The EU Commission's communication highlights that its proposals are meant to complement the Member States' prerogatives and existing powers to protect legitimate public policy objectives and interests.[83] In particular, it refers to the Member States' powers under Article 58 EC/Article 65 TFEU to restrain the free movement of capital to the extent necessary and proportionate to the Member States' legitimate public policy goals and national security interests. The Commission has refrained from taking a clear position on what national measures may be justified under Article 58 EC/Article 65 TFEU. The Member States' legal regimes put in place to address the risks associated with foreign investment differ significantly. Most Member States provide for a possibility of foreign investment entry control, but while some Member States limit such restrictive regimes to investments into the defence and military equipment industry and other directly security-relevant industries, others extend the control procedure beyond this core. Differences exist also with a view to how precisely the public interests to be protected are defined. Frequently, the reach of foreign investment control procedures is broad and the assessment criteria leave substantial room for political discretion.[84]

France, for example, is traditionally known for a relatively rigid foreign investment control. According to the French Monetary and Financial Code, financial dealings between France and foreign countries are in principle unrestricted (Article L151-1). However, the French Government may make certain foreign exchange transactions, including mergers, acquisitions, and other types of foreign investment, subject to a notification requirement and a prior approval by the French Government, not only if they concern companies engaged in research, production or sales of arms, munitions, powder, or explosive substances, but also if the target companies participate, even occasionally, in the exercise of public authority or if they are engaged in activities such as might endanger public order, public safety, or the interests of national defence (Article L151-2). In reaction to the Court's judgment in *Eglise de Scientologie*,[85] France issued the Decree No. 2005-1739 of 30 December 2005 which now specifies 11 'sensitive' sectors where foreign investment may raise such risks.[86] In some industries, a national security

[83] Commission (n 5) 11.

[84] The claim that common law systems generally tend to be less specific and less detailed than laws and policies of countries that operate under a civil law system (for this claim see GAO [n 62] 9) is not borne out by the evidence.

[85] Case C-54/99 *Eglise de Scientologie* [2000] ECR I-1335.

[86] The Decree No 2005-1739 now lists 11 sectors which are thought to be particularly sensitive with regard to national security. These sectors include (1) gambling and casinos; (2) private security; (3) research, development, or production of means to stem the unlawful use, in terrorist activities, of pathogens or toxins; (4) equipment designed to intercept correspondence and monitor conversations; (5) testing and certification of the security of information technology products and systems; (6) production of goods or supply of services to ensure the security of the information

review will be performed only if the acquirer is a non-EU investor, in other industries the review will extend to EU-based investors as well.[87] The control procedure, which will kick in in the case of an acquisition of control of a firm with its headquarters in France, the acquisition of a branch of a firm with corporate headquarters in France, or the acquisition of more than one-third of the capital or voting rights of a firm with its headquarters in France,[88] is led by the Ministry of Economy, Finance, and Employment, with additional input from other ministries, in particular the Ministry of Defence. If the Government finds that an investment jeopardizes public order, public safety, or national defence interests, it may prohibit the relevant transactions, or it may authorize them with conditions attached.[89] Particular attention is given to the preservation of industrial capacities (R&D, know-how, other IP assets or production capacity) on French territory, the assurance of continuity of supplies and compliance with existing contractual commitments (eg public procurement contracts). The fact that the investor is a foreign state-owned enterprise or an SWF can be considered during the review process, although no specific rules or guidelines exist in this regard. A specificity of the French regime is that the notification requirement and the prior authorization scheme kick in at various occasions: not only at the time when the initial investment is made, but also during any recapitalization, change in the shareholding, or upon a resale of the investment. A continuous oversight is thus ensured. Any negative decision can be appealed to the French administrative courts.

Germany, by contrast, has long had a reputation for a particularly liberal foreign investment regime. A specific foreign investment control for public security-related investments was introduced into the German Foreign Trade and Payments Act (*Außenwirtschaftsgesetz*—AWG) only in 2004 in reaction to concerns whether the German export control laws were sufficient to protect national security interests in case of a foreign acquisition of a directly security-relevant

systems; (7) dual-use items and technologies—a potentially broad category; (8) cryptology equipment and services; (9) activities carried out by firms entrusted with national defence secrets, in particular under the terms of national defence contracts or of security clauses; (10) research, production, or trade in weapons, ammunitions, powders, and explosives intended for military purposes or war materials; and (11) activities carried out by firms holding a contract for the design or supply of equipment for the Ministry of Defence, either directly or as subcontractors, to produce an item or supply a service for one of the sectors listed in No. 7–10.

[87] A limited number of exceptions exist to the notification and prior authorization requirement—eg creation of a branch; extension of an existing business, increases in participation if the investor already holds more than 66.65% etc.

[88] For the definition of the term 'control' see Article L233-3 of the French Commercial Code.

[89] In practice, conditions have been imposed on FDI transactions repeatedly. An example is the acquisition of the 'Saft' batteries business of the French company Alcatel by a pan-European group of investment funds in 2004. The French Government imposed stringent conditions on the grounds that certain batteries are used for defence purposes. Among the conditions was the requirement that the Saft headquarters remain in France, along with all research centres and production facilities serving French military purchasers.

German company. The possibility for intervention was, however, narrowly construed. The relevant parts of § 7 AWG read:

Protection of Security and External Interests:

(1) Legal transactions and acts in foreign trade and payments may be restricted in order to
  1. guarantee the vital security interests of the Federal Republic of Germany.
  2. prevent a disturbance of the peaceful coexistence between the nations, or
  3. prevent a major disruption of the foreign relations of the Federal Republic of Germany.

(2) According to paragraph 1 above, the following may be restricted in particular [...]
  4. legal transactions on the purchase of resident companies which produce or develop war weapons and other military equipment, or produce cryptographic systems admitted for the transmission of governmental classified information by the Federal Office for Information Security Technology with the company's approval, or legal transactions on the acquisition of shares in such companies, in order to guarantee the vital security interests of the Federal Republic of Germany; this applies in particular if the political and security interests of the Federal Republic of Germany or the military security precautions are jeopardized as a result of the purchase.

  [...]

For transactions of the kind covered by § 7 AWG, a mandatory notification scheme was introduced: Foreign acquisitions of a German firm active in the production of weapons and other military equipment or cryptographic systems, or acquisitions of stakes of 25 per cent of the voting rights or more, must be reported to the German Government. The notification will trigger a control procedure which must be completed within one month and ends with an approval or, alternatively, with a prohibition.

In reaction to a broad public debate on SWFs in Germany, this originally narrow foreign investment control regime has recently been extended. Based on a 2009 amendment of the AWG,[90] the Federal Minster of Economics and Technology is now empowered to subject any acquisition of a stake of 25 per cent or more of any listed or non-listed German firm[91] by a non-EU investor to a control procedure case by case (§ 53 AWG). The stated goal of such a control procedure is to enquire whether the acquisition will endanger the public order or security of the Republic of Germany. According to § 7(2) No. 6 AWG, the public order or security shall be considered in danger only if a real and sufficiently severe

[90] *Dreizehntes Gesetz zur Änderung des Außenwirtschaftsgesetzes und der Außenwirtschaftsverordnung*, [2009] Bundesgesetzblatt I 770. The new law entered into force on 24 April 2009.

[91] § 4 no 5 AWG uses the term 'Gebietsansässige'. In particular, this comprises corporations with their seat or headquarter in Germany, or branches of foreign firms managed from the German territory and with a separate accounting system.

danger can be identified which affects a fundamental interest of society.[92] The kind of threat that could lead to a prohibition of the investment or any other type of restraint is not specified. While the main aim of the amendment has been said to be the protection of the well-functioning of essential infrastructures and the continued provision of infrastructure services, eg in the area of telecommunications or energy, the AWG's regime of investment control is not limited to these sectors under the text of the law.

The amendment does not impose a mandatory notification regime upon non-EU investors, nor does it impose a prior authorization scheme. The responsibility to acquire the necessary information on mergers and acquisitions and to intervene in those cases where, according to its own assessment, a danger for the public order or security might exist, is with the Ministry for the Economy. A control procedure can only be initiated within three months after the conclusion of the relevant purchase contract. The Ministry then has another two months to decide whether a threat to the public order or public security exists. If so, it can—with the approval of the Government—impose conditions to remedy the threat[93] or prohibit the transaction. A prohibition of the acquisition of the firm, or of the shares of the corporation, shall have the effect of rendering the relevant contract null and void (*auflösende Bedingung*, § 31(3) AWG).

3. The review of national entry controls for foreign investment and the free movement of capital: the application of Article 56 EC (Article 63 TFEU) and its relationship with Article 43 EC (Article 49 TFEU)

These types of national foreign investment control regimes raise a number of questions: are they an adequate response to the perceived threats posed by SWFs or other foreign-state-controlled investments? And are they compatible with EU law, in particular where they are addressed against non-EU investors? The EU Commission has expressed concerns both with a view to the reformed French investment control regime[94] and with a view to the German reform of the AWG.[95] In the context of the discussions surrounding SWF investments, an important question is whether and to what extent Member States may be justified in imposing more stringent regimes of entry control on investments originating

[92] § 7(2) no 6 AWG: 'Die Gefährdung der öffentlichen Ordnung oder Sicherheit der Bundesrepublik Deutschland durch den Erwerb gebietsansässiger Unternehmen oder von Anteilen an solchen Unternehmen 'setzt voraus, dass eine tatsächliche und hinreichend schwere Gefährdung vorliegt, die ein Grundinteresse der Gesellschaft berührt'.

[93] Conditions can, inter alia, take the form a prohibition or limitation of the exercise of voting rights in the target company or the appointment of a trustee to reverse the transaction.

[94] In October 2006, the EU Commission formally requested France to amend its regulations—see IP/06/438 of 4 April 2006 and IP/06/1353 of 12 October 2006. France has presented some proposals to address the EU Commission's concerns in February 2008.

[95] The EU Commission has announced that it will review the AWG's compatibility with EU law.

in non-EU countries as compared to EU investors, and in particular on investments controlled by non-EU states. There is, however, a preliminary question whether Article 56 EC (Article 63 TFEU) applies at all to such national foreign investment control regimes which are addressed solely to those cross-border investments by which a third-country national acquires full ownership or control of an EU-based firm, or such a substantial stake that, in an intra-EU context, Article 43 EC (Article 49 TFEU) would apply.

(i) The scope of protection of Article 56 (Article 63 TFEU) with a view to third-country investments

Article 56(1) EC (Article 63(1) TFEU) prohibits 'all restrictions on the movement of capital between Member States and between Member States and third countries'. It is the only fundamental freedom which extends to non-EU nationals. The decision to broaden Article 56's scope of protection was taken with the Maastricht Treaty and accompanied the introduction of the second stage of the Economic and Monetary Union. It was to signal Europe's firm commitment to an open investment environment to the world and was based on the conviction that a free inflow of capital would benefit the EU even if granted unilaterally. With a view to the broad interpretation which Article 56 EC (Article 63 TFEU) has traditionally received, its extension to third-country investors has, however, created substantial conceptual difficulties.[96]

Prior to the entry into force of the Maastricht Treaty and thus to the extension of Article 56 EC (Article 63 TFEU) to third-country nationals, the Court of Justice had started to refer, in a consistent line of jurisprudence, to a nomenclature of capital movements annexed to Council Directive 88/361[97] in order to define the scope of protection of the free movement of capital. According to this non-exhaustive list, capital movements do not only include portfolio investments and investments in other instruments normally dealt in on the capital markets or money markets; operations in current and deposit accounts with financial institutions; loans; credits related to commercial transactions; and real estate, but they also comprise so-called direct investments which include the 'establishment and extension of branches or new undertakings belonging solely to the person providing the capital, and the acquisition in full of existing undertakings; participation in new or existing undertakings with a view

[96] See for a broader discussion: J A Usher, 'The Evolution of the Free Movement of Capital' (2008) 31 Fordham Intl L J 1533 ff; R Lyal, 'Free movement of capital and non-member countries—consequences for direct taxation', speech given at the CFE conference on 24 November 2006 (available at <http://www.cfe-eutax.org/sites/default/files/ac2006_lyal.pdf> (last accessed 23 July 2010); S Peers, 'Free Movement of Capital: Learning Lessons or Slipping on Spilt Milk?' in C Barnard and J Scott (eds), *The Law of the Single European Market* (Oxford: Hart Publishing, 2002) 333 ff.

[97] Council Directive 88/361/EEC of 24 June 1988 for the implementation of Article 67 of the Treaty, [1988] OJ L178/5.

to establishing or maintaining lasting economic links'.[98] From this reading of Article 56 EC (Article 63 TFEU), a broad overlap with the scope of protection of Article 43 EC (Article 49 TFEU) has resulted.[99] It thus seemed that, if this jurisprudence were upheld after the entry into force of the Maastricht Treaty, the extension of Article 56 EC (Article 63 TFEU) to third-country nationals would also extend a substantial portion of the privilege of the free movement of establishment to them—a fundamental freedom which, according to its wording, is reserved to EU nationals.

Despite concerns raised in this regard, the Court of Justice has not followed suggestions to construe the 'new' free movement of capital more narrowly than it had originally been construed, and to distinguish its scope of protection more clearly from that of Article 43 EC (Article 49 TFEU) by reducing it to 'passive' investments, while reserving the protection of 'active' investments for Article 43 EC (Article 49 TFEU).[100] Instead, the Court of Justice has continued to refer to the broad nomenclature of capital movements annexed to Council Directive 88/361.[101] Moreover, the Court of Justice has rejected propositions to interpret Article 56 EC (Article 63 TFEU) differently depending on whether it is applied in an intra-Community context or with a view to movements of capital with third countries. In *A*, the Court of Justice held:

> Even if the liberalisation of the movement of capital with third countries may pursue objectives other than that of establishing the internal market, such as, in particular, that of ensuring the credibility of the single Community currency on world financial markets and maintaining financial centres with a world-wide dimension within the Member States, it is clear that, when the principle of free movement of capital was extended pursuant to Article 56(1) to movement of capital between third countries and the Member

[98] See also Case C-463/00 *Commission v Spain* [2003] ECR I-4581 para 53: 'Points I and III in the nomenclature set out in Annex I to Directive 88/361, and the explanatory notes appearing in that annex, indicate that direct investment in the form of participation in an undertaking by means of a shareholding or the acquisition of securities on the capital market constitute capital movements for the purposes of Article 56 EC. The explanatory notes state that direct investment is characterised, in particular, by the possibility of participating effectively in the management of a company or in its control.'

[99] Article 43 EC allows all Community nationals 'to participate, on a stable and continuous basis, in the economic life of a Member State other than his State of origin and to profit therefrom, so contributing to economic and social interpenetration within the Community [...]' (Case C-55/94 *Gebhard* [1995] ECR I-4165 para 25). Among the forms of establishment protected by Article 43 EC are the ownership and control of firms in another Member State. While the mere acquisition of a portfolio investment with no influence on the management of the firm is outside the realm of Article 43 EC, so-called 'direct investments', ie investments which 'serve to establish or maintain lasting and direct links between the persons providing the capital and the undertakings to which the capital is made available in order to carry out an economic activity' are thus protected not only by Article 56 EC, but also by Article 43 EC.

[100] For a discussion of different proposals see Usher (n 96) 1544 ff; Lyal (n 96).

[101] See Case C-222/97 *Trummer and Mayer* [1999] ECR I-1661 para 21: '[...] the nomenclature in respect of movements of capital annexed to Directive 88/361 still has the same indicative value for the purposes of defining the notion of capital movements ...'. See also Case C-463/00 *Commission v Spain* [2003] ECR I-4581 para 52 f.

States, the latter chose to enshrine that principle in that Article and in the same terms for movement of capital taking place within the Community and those relating to relations with third countries.[102]

It thereby also rejected far-reaching propositions that third-country nationals relying on Article 56 EC (Article 63 TFEU) should be denied the benefit of a direct effect which was allegedly justified only by the specific and novel character of the legal order established by the EC Treaty.[103]

(ii) The interaction between the freedom of establishment and the free movement of capital: The ECJ's centre-of-gravity approach

While the Court of Justice has rejected a principled differentiation between the scopes of protection of Article 56, Article 49, and Article 43 EC (Article 63, 56, and 49 TFEU),[104] it has at times—and in particular in its tax-related cases—opted for what has been called a 'centre of gravity' approach: in the light of an overlap between the scope of protection of Article 56 EC (Article 63 TFEU) and the free movement or establishment or the freedom to provide services it may apply only that provision which it finds to be most directly affected if the other is thought to be 'entirely secondary'. *Fidium Finanz* has become the leading case in this regard.[105] The Court of Justice had to decide whether the granting of credit on a commercial basis constituted a provision of service and was thus protected by Article 49 EC (Article 56 TFEU), whether instead it fell within the scope of Article 56 EC (Article 63 TFEU), or whether both provisions applied in parallel. Despite the fact that Article 50 EC (Article 57 TFEU) appeared to designate Article 49 EC (Article 56 TFEU) as the 'residual' provision, which would have argued in favour of the application of Article 56 EC (Article 63 TFEU), the Court of Justice found that no order of priority should be assumed between the two fundamental freedoms at issue. Rather, they were designed to regulate different situations, each having their own field of application. Where a national measure relates to the freedom to provide services and the free movement of capital at the same time:

[...], it is necessary to consider to what extent the exercise of those fundamental liberties is affected and whether, in the circumstances of the main proceedings, one of those prevails over the other. The Court will in principle examine the measure in dispute in relation to only one of those two freedoms if it appears in the circumstances of the case that

[102] Case C-101/05 *A* [2007] ECR I-11531 para 31. See also Case 194/06 *Orange European Smallcap Fund NV* [2008] ECR I-3747 para 87.

[103] See AG Geelhoed, Opinion of 10 April 2003, in Case C-452/01 *Ospelt* [2003] ECR I-9743 paras 45–47.

[104] For an overview of the relevant case law see Usher (n 96) 1545 ff.

[105] Case C-452/04 *Fidium Finanz* [2006] ECR I-9521. Sometimes, Case C-251/98 *Baars* [2000] ECR I-2787 para 22 is also mentioned as a case in point. In *Baars,* the Court found that Article 43 EC (Article 49 TFEU) applies to fact patterns where a shareholder holds enough of a foreign company's shares to give him 'definite influence' and to 'determine its activities'. Since it found Article 43 EC to be infringed, it did not answer the second question posed by the national court which concerned Article 56 EC. However, it did not find that Article 56 EC would be, in principle, inapplicable.

one of them is entirely secondary in relation to the other and may be considered together with it (paragraph 34)

In the case at hand, the Court of Justice found that the restriction on free movement of capital was 'merely an unavoidable consequence of the restriction on the freedom to provide services' (paragraph 48). The national rules were therefore to be assessed under Article 49 EC (Article 56 TFEU) alone—a provision on which a company established in a non-member country could not rely (paragraph 50). Based on a similar line of argument, the Court of Justice held in *Lasertec*,[106] that 'national provisions relating to holdings giving the holder a definite influence on the decisions of the company concerned and allowing him to determine [the company's] activities come within the material scope of the Treaty provisions on freedom of establishment' (paragraph 20). Any restrictive effects on the free movement of capital would need to be seen as 'an unavoidable consequence of the restriction on freedom of establishment' and would not justify an examination of that measure in the light of Articles 56 to 58 EC (Article 63 to 65 TFEU) (paragraph 25).[107] Also in *Lasertec*, it followed that third-country nationals could not challenge the relevant national rules, as they did not come within the scope of protection of the freedom of establishment.

It seems that the Court's recent case law has firmly established the 'centre of gravity' approach in its jurisprudence on the interaction between the free movement of capital, the freedom of establishment, and the freedom to provide services. However, the scope of application of this new doctrine remains unclear. Apart from *Fidium Finanz*—a case about banking regulation—the 'centre of gravity' approach has mainly been used in tax cases so far. Both banking regulation and tax cases are special in many regards, and linked in particular ways to issues of territorial sovereignty. In other, non-tax cases, including more recent ones, the Court of Justice has continuously held that, in principle, Article 56 EC (Article 63 TFEU) and Article 43 EC (Article 49 TFEU) apply in parallel where their scopes of protection overlap.[108]

[106] Case C-492/04 *Lasertec* [2007] ECR I-3775.

[107] See also Case C-524/04 *Test Claimants in the Thin Cap Group Litigation* [2007] ECR I-2107 paras 26–35: in a case where the national legislation at issue was only targeted at relations within a group of companies and primarily affected freedom of establishment; the case should be analysed under the perspective of Article 43 EC alone (paras 33–35). And Case C-196/04 *Cadbury Schweppes* [2006] ECR I-7995 paras 31–33.

[108] See eg Case C-279/00 *Commission v Italy* [2002] ECR I-1425 paras 36 ff, an Italian requirement that undertakings engaged in the provision of temporary labour established in other Member States have to lodge a guarantee with a credit institution having its registered office in Italy breaches both Article 49 and of Article 56 EC. The Court did not give priority to either freedom in this case. In a number of other cases, the Court has, after finding an infringement of one of the free movement rules, found that it is not necessary to analyse the compatibility of a national measure with other free movement rules—see, for example, Case C-105/07 *NV Lammer & Van Cleeff v Belgium* [2008] ECR I-173 para 35: 'Since the Treaty provisions on freedom of establishment thus preclude national legislation such as that at issue in the main proceedings, it is not necessary to examine whether the Treaty provisions on the free movement of capital also preclude that legislation'; Case C-314/08 *Filipiak* [2009] ECR I-000 para 59.

If the 'centre of gravity' approach were indistinctively extended to EU-bound investments by SWFs, those national rules applying to all types of investments—passive or active, portfolio or controlling shares—would likely be analysed under Article 56 EC (Article 63 TFEU). In such cases, Article 56 EC would presumably be applied even if the specific case at hand were about an attempt to acquire control. At the same time, Member States would be free to restrict the acquisitions of *controlling stakes* by third-country investors at will, since Article 43 EC (Article 49 TFEU) alone would be applied to those national measures that relate to holdings giving the holder a definite influence on the decisions of a target company.[109]

A 'centre of gravity' approach, so broadly understood, would lack any consistent theoretical basis, however: if the scope of Article 56 EC (Article 63 TFEU) covers controlling stakes in principle, it is difficult to see a justification for denying third-country nationals its protection just because in an intra-EU context, the freedom of establishment would primarily apply.[110] From a purely practical perspective, it is doubtful whether the 'centre of gravity' approach would meet its apparent goal to protect the Member States' full political discretion to regulate third-country acquisitions of control, as third-country investors can gain the full protection of Article 43 EC (Article 49 TFEU) by establishing a subsidiary in any one of the Member States.[111]

Much argues in favour of a narrow construction of the Court's 'centre of gravity' approach, therefore, and to limit it to those cases where the territorial regulatory authority with regard to companies with their seat in a certain Member State is of the essence as is the case, in particular, in the area of tax.

4. The justification of restraints to the free movement of capital: A special regime for cross-border investments originating in non-EU states?

If it is doubtful whether an adequate balance between the protection of a generally beneficial freedom to invest vis-à-vis third countries and the right of the Member States to implement safeguards against associated risks can be achieved by curtailing the scope of protection of Article 56 EC (Article 63 TFEU) and differentiating it from the scope of protection of other free movement rules case by case, an alternative mechanism for balancing individual rights and regulatory limitations may be found at the justification level.[112] While it would involve a

[109] See Case C-492/04 *Lasertec* [2007] ECR I-3775 para 20 f.

[110] For a critical view see also M Martini, 'Staatsfonds als Herausforderung an das europäische und internationale Recht' [2008] Die Öffentliche Verwaltung 314, 318 ff; M P Weller, 'Ausländische Staatsfonds zwischen Fusionskontrolle, Außenwirtschaftsrecht und Grundfreiheiten' [2008] ZIP 857, 863 ff; M Schäfer and T Voland, 'Staatsfonds: Die Kontrolle ausländischer Investitionen auf dem Prüfstand des Verfassungs-, Europa- und Welthandelsrechts' [2008] EWS 166, 168 ff, 171.

[111] K Krolop, 'Stellungnahme zu dem Gesetzesentwurf der Bundesregierung für ein Dreizehntes Gesetz zur Änderung des Außenwirtschaftsgesetzes und der Außenwirtschaftsordnung' (Berlin, 22 January 2009) 24.

[112] See also Lyal (n 96).

greater measure of control of the actions of Member States through EU law, the resulting 'de-politicization' of the Member States' responses to perceived threats would help to avoid protectionist over-reactions. It would thus strengthen the EU's commitment to openness and legal certainty for third-country investors. The necessity to distinguish between intra-EU investments and third-country investments at the justification level has been repeatedly acknowledged by the Court of Justice.

(i) Justification of restrictions to the free movement of capital at the Member State level—the legal framework

According to Article 57(1) EC (Article 64 TFEU), Article 56 EC (Article 63 TFEU) is:

> [W]ithout prejudice to the application to third countries of any restrictions which exist on 31 December 1993 under national or Community law adopted in respect of the movement of capital to or from third countries involving direct investment—including in real estate—establishment, the provision of financial services or the admission of securities to capital markets.

This so-called 'grandfather clause' implies that foreign investment controls that were imposed on direct investments originating in third countries before 1994 are *per se* justified. National rules implemented later on in reaction to the perceived threats of government-controlled investments, including SWFs, like the French reform of 2004/2005 and the German reform of 2009, do not benefit from this privilege, and have to be justified on other grounds.

According to Article 58 EC (Article 65 TFEU), Article 56 (Article 63 TFEU) shall be without prejudice to the right of Member States to apply their relevant tax laws which distinguish, inter alia, based on the place of residence (Article 58(a) EC/Article 65(a) TFEU); or to '[...] take measures which are justified on grounds of public policy or public security' (Article 58(b) EC/Article 65(b) TFEU).[113] Such measures 'shall not constitute a means of arbitrary discrimination or a disguised restriction on the free movement of capital and payments as defined in Article 63' (Article 65(3) TFEU). The Court of Justice has interpreted Article 58 EC (Article 65 TFEU) in the light of its jurisprudence on restrictions to the free movement rules generally: national restrictions can be justified where they pursue a legitimate aim and are in compliance with the principle of proportionality.

[113] Article 58(b) EC reads in full: Article 56 shall be without prejudice to the right of Member States 'to take all requisite measures to prevent infringements of national law and regulations, in particular in the field of taxation and the prudential supervision of financial institutions, or to lay down procedures for the declaration of capital movements for purposes of administrative or statistical information, or to take measures which are justified on grounds of public policy or public security'.

In the intra-EU context, the Court of Justice has explored the limits of Article 58 EC (Article 65 TFEU) in its jurisprudence on 'golden shares'[114] which it has consistently treated like regulatory interventions, despite their formal design as property rights. According to the Court of Justice, 'golden shares' are justified only if their introduction is based on clearly defined policy objectives that are legitimate and proportionate under the free movement rules. Only a 'genuine and sufficiently serious threat' to the requirements of public policy or of public security affecting 'one of the fundamental interests of society'[115] will justify a restriction of the free movement of capital. Interests which the Court of Justice has recognized as sufficiently fundamental to potentially justify a restriction of the free movement of capital include the security of supply with essential services, like energy, telecommunications, water etc[116] and the essential security of infrastructure networks, including transportation routes or traffic infrastructure.[117] By contrast, pure economic grounds can never serve as justification for obstacles to the free movement of capital.[118] The threat to public policy or public security which a restrictive measure is meant to address must be clearly articulated, and the criteria for intervention must be specified in objective terms such that the preconditions for imposing the restriction are transparent and predictable and investors have a sufficient degree of legal certainty. The public authority which imposes the relevant restriction must not be endowed with an overly broad discretion,[119] and it must be subject to judicial control. Finally, the intervention must be proportionate to the identified threat to public policy or public security. While the Court of Justice has held in *Eglise de Scientologie v France* that a prior authorization regime may be justified with regard to foreign direct investments,[120] a prohibition of a given transaction will only be justified

[114] See, inter alia, Case C-367/98 *Commission v Portugal* [2002] ECR I-4731; Case C-98/01 *Commission v United Kingdom* [2003] ECR I-4641; Case C-483/99 *Commission v France* [2002] ECR I-4781; Case C-463/00 *Commission v Spain* [2003] ECR I-4581; Case C-503/99 *Commission v Belgium* [2002] ECR I-4809; C-174/04 *Commission v Italy* [2005] ECR I-4933; Case C-282/04; and 283/04 *Commission v Netherlands* [2006] ECR I-9141. See also Case C-112/05 *Commission v Germany (VW)* [2007] ECR I-8995. For a summary of the case law see also Commission, 'Staff Working Paper: Special rights in privatised companies in the enlarged Union—a decade full of developments' (22 July 2005). For comments in the academic literature see: H Fleischer, 'Case Note on the Golden Shares Cases', (2003) 20 Common Market L Rev 493; S Grundmann and F Möslein, 'Die Goldene Aktie—Staatskontrollrechte in Europarecht und wirtschaftspolitischer Bewertung' (2003) Zeitschrift für Unternehmens- und Gesellschaftsrecht (ZGR) 317; E Szyszczak, 'Golden Shares and Market Governance', (2002) 29 Legal Issues of Economic Integration 255.

[115] See Case C-30/77 *Regina v Bouchereau* [1977] ECR 1999 paras 33–35 (public policy); and Case C-463/00 *Commission v Spain* [2003] ECR I-4581 para 72 f (public security).

[116] See Case C-503/99 *Commission v Belgium* [2002] ECR I-4809 (veto right of the ministry against certain measures of a firm that would endanger the security of supply in energy); Case C-282/04 and 283/04 *Commission v Netherlands* [2006] ECR I-9141.

[117] Case C-98/01 *Commission v UK* [2003] ECR I-4641 (air traffic control).

[118] See eg Case C-54/99 *Eglise de Scientologie v France* [2000] ECR I-1335 para 17 with further references.

[119] Case C-463/00 *Commission v Spain* [2003] ECR I-4581.

[120] Case C-54/99 *Eglise de Scientologie v France* [2000] ECR I-1335 para 20.

if a specific risk is clearly discernible. A prohibition based on a purely speculative risk would likely be considered disproportionate.

(ii) The application of the legal framework to cross-border investments within the EU

According to these rules, restrictions on foreign investments will likely be justified where they are restricted to certain security-relevant industries, in particular the defence and military equipment industry, industries using nuclear materials, or industries involved in the production of cryptographic systems. The German rules on the control of acquisition of stakes in firms active in the defence industry or in 'cryptographic systems'[121] would thus be in line with EU law. Likewise, a substantial part of the industries listed in the French Decree No 2005-1739 of 30 December 2005 would indeed seem to be security-relevant—although the initial inclusion of gambling and casinos has likely overstretched the European concept of public security. In clearly security-relevant industries, control regimes may well extend to the acquisition of non-controlling stakes: privileged access to information may suffice to raise relevant security concerns. The thresholds set out in the German AWG (25 per cent) and in French law (one-third of the voting rights or control) hence don't raise concerns under EU law. Purely passive portfolio investments, on the other hand, would not seem to raise any significant risks,[122] and neither the French nor the German regime of foreign investment control extend their control regimes that far. Moreover, relatively stringent measures of control will likely be justified in security-relevant industries, including notification and prior authorization requirements. The review process should, however, be clearly structured and predictable, with clear time frames that take into account the time sensitivities of major capital market transactions. In particular, it should protect the legitimate confidentiality interests of the parties.[123] In case of a negative decision, the investor must be entitled to judicial review.

The legality of national investment control regimes becomes doubtful the more they extend beyond the scope of clearly security-relevant industries. As the Court of Justice's golden share jurisprudence shows, EU law will in principle recognize serious dangers for public policy and public security even outside the defence and military equipment industries. Beyond the pure protection of the borders of the state from military attack, the protection against terrorism and espionage, national security includes protecting the public from large-scale threats to its safety and vital interests more broadly understood. The protection of energy security and the protection of other critical infrastructures are examples in point.

[121] For example, the provision of the German AWG according to which the acquisition of stakes in firms active in the defence industry or 'crypto technology' of 25% of the votes or more must be notified to the German Government and according to which the Government can prohibit such acquisitions based on public security criteria should be considered as justified under Article 58(1)(b) EC.

[122] Kimmitt (n 16) 123.

[123] Kern (n 20) 30.

However, the Court of Justice has required a clear, objective, and predictable specification of the relevant risks in this regard which protects against any hidden forms of discrimination. The recent reform of the Foreign Trade and Payments Act in Germany which has extended the foreign investment control regime to potentially all sectors raises serious doubts in this regard: the Minister for the Economy shall be entitled to intervene whenever he perceives a serious threat to public policy or public security. The kinds of threats that could lead to a prohibition of the investment or conditions being imposed, ie the relevant assessment criteria, are not specified. Such a broad reach of the investment control regime, and the discretion it conveys on the Minister for the Economy, would seem to run counter to the requirement of predictability and legal certainty.

(iii) Restrictions on foreign investments by third-country investors, in particular SWFs and SOEs

One may, however, question whether the Court's jurisprudence on the handling of Article 58 EC (Article 65 TFEU) in an intra-Community context can be fully transferred to situations in which a justification of restrictions to the free movement of capital vis-à-vis third countries is at stake. Although Article 56 EC (Article 63 TFEU) defines the scope of protection in a uniform manner for both groups of investors, the threats they create for public policy and public security may objectively differ owing to the different institutional and legal context they are subject to in their home state. The Court of Justice has explicitly recognized the relevance of these differences for the breadth of potential justifications of restrictions in *A*.[124] In *Orange European Smallcap Fund NV* it confirmed that it may be that 'a Member State will be able to demonstrate that a restriction on the movement of capital to or from third countries is justified for a particular reason in circumstances where that reason would not constitute a valid justification for a restriction on capital movements between Member States'.[125] With a view to foreign state-controlled investments, the fact that the state-market relationship is not subject to comparable constraints in third countries as it is in the EU Member States and that reflexes of 'imperialist capitalism' have not been tamed to the same extent by the rule of law may justify more stringent regimes of control

[124] Case C-101/05 *A* [2007] ECR I-11531 para 60: the Court emphasizes that movements of capital to or from third countries take place in a 'different legal context' compared to intra-Community movements and that, therefore, 'case-law, which relates to restrictions on the exercise of freedom of movement within the Community, cannot be transposed in its entirety to movements of capital between Member States and third countries'. The Court refers, in particular, to EU legislation which 'established a framework for cooperation between the competent [tax] authorities of the Member States which does not exist between those authorities and the competent authorities of a third country where the latter has given no undertaking of mutual assistance' (para 61). For a similar reasoning see Case C-194/06 *Orange European Smallcap Fund NV* [2008] ECR I-3747 paras 89–90.

[125] Case C-194/06 *Orange European Smallcap Fund NV* [2008] ECR I-3747 para 90, with further references.

vis-à-vis third-country investors as compared to investors from other Member States.

(1) Entry controls to address the risk of dependency

As far as national entry control regimes are concerned, the approach adopted by the EU itself in its directives on the internal market in electricity[126] and in natural gas[127] (see above) provides important indications regarding the types of restrictions that can be justified. Three aspects of the EU legislation are of particular relevance:

(1) The EU directives impose restrictions on the acquisitions of control of energy networks by third-country investors—restrictions which will not apply to EU investors—in particular with a view to addressing risks of dependence vis-à-vis third countries. Within the EU, the risk of dependence is constrained by EU law and by the intense inter-dependence which both the institutional structure and the common market create. With regard to third countries, the risk may be more acute, however—albeit to different degrees, depending on the type of investment, the third country involved and the degree of economic, legal, and political interaction that exists. Generally, a risk of dependence will be created only by an acquisition of control; the acquisition of a minority stake would not appear to involve similar risks. The risk may be particularly acute in the case of *state-controlled* investments—the ownership structure may clearly be a relevant assessment criterion. But with a view to possible informal state influence, the line between openly state-controlled investments and apparently private investments can be blurred. National control regimes may therefore extend to private investments as well.

(2) Secondly, the EU energy directives reverse the burden of proof: whereas it is normally for the Member State that restricts free movement to prove the necessity and proportionality of the restrictions, the EU energy directives provide that it is for the applicant to demonstrate the absence of a risk to security of supply. As the types of threats that may justify restrictions remain relatively vague, this burden is a heavy one.

(3) Thirdly, and contrary to general principles of EU law, the EU energy directives allow for a 'piercing of the corporate veil': in determining whether the rules for intra-EU investment or the rules for third-country investment apply, it is ultimately not the nationality of the investing entity that matters. Rather, the directives look to the nationality of the controlling entity to identify the existence and seriousness of a threat.

[126] Article 11 of Directive 2009/72/EC of 13 July 2009, [2009] OJ L211/55.
[127] Article 11 of Directive 2009/73/EC of 13 July 2009, [2009] OJ L211/94.

It is likely that the Member States may rely on similar principles in designing entry control regimes for third-country investors as far as the acquisition of control of important infrastructures or natural resources is concerned or wherever a plausible threat of dependence can be identified. Arguably, the EU law requirements as regards the exact specification of the risk to public order or public security are somewhat lower vis-à-vis third-country investors. This will also weaken the proportionality analysis. Nonetheless, there will be little room for restrictive investment entry policies outside the realm of the most important infrastructure industries.[128] Foreign investments in most reasonably competitive industries will not have the potential to create dependence. Risks of harm to the interests of a target company and its shareholders, to the stability of financial markets, or risks of industrial espionage are difficult to address at the stage of a public entry control procedure, on the other hand, that is at a stage where they necessarily remain theoretical and speculative. Rather, such risks must be addressed as they arise. The increased relevance of third-country state-controlled investments thus requires a review whether the general rules of corporate law, capital market law, and competition law must be adjusted to address the specific risks such investments may raise.

(2) Modifications of general rules of corporate law, securities regulation and competition law?

General rules of corporate law and corporate governance An issue remains whether foreign investments by state-controlled third-country investors may justify (and from a national perspective possibly require) a modification of the general rules of corporate law, securities regulation, and competition law. Do such investments raise risks that cannot be adequately addressed within the framework of the general rules?

Conflicts of interest may be considered the most obvious risk resulting from third-country-controlled investments in national firms. They may arise where a third-country investor acquires a majority stake in the pursuit of interests which clearly diverge from the goal of shareholder value maximization, or where an important minority position is used to get access to, and misappropriate, important information, to block important strategic decisions etc.[129]

Conflicts of interests between majority and minority shareholders are not specific to foreign state-controlled investments, however. They are addressed by the general rules regulating the conduct of majority shareholders, and in some

[128] OECD, 'Building Trust and Confidence in International Investment' (March 2009) 10.

[129] For this type of concern see Gilson and Milhaupt (n 3) '... an SWF may have a strategic motive in addition to, or instead of, an investment motive. The SWF may wish to help domestic companies secure technology or other expertise from a portfolio company even if that transfer reduces the portfolio company's value—the loss to the portfolio company is shared by all owners, while the transfer for the benefit of the SWF's government accrues entirely to it'.

countries by the law on corporate groups. The misappropriation of information by a shareholder is likewise dealt with under the general rules of corporate law.

What remains is a potential 'systemic risk': where state-controlled third-country investors would acquire control of European firms on a broad scale and systemically replace the normal profit-maximization goal of firms with a regime of political goals, market processes could be seriously distorted.[130] It seems to be this concern that Gilson/Milhaupt intend to address with their far-reaching proposition to deprive SWFs or other foreign state-controlled investors of the voting rights attached to their shareholdings.[131] The idea is to separate investment value from control. Sovereign equity investors will be able to generate returns identical to those of other shareholders; but they will have no direct influence over management through voting. Within such a regulatory framework, sovereign investors with purely financial motives would invest, but sovereign investors seeking strategic benefits would likely find an investment unattractive and would withdraw. According to Gilson/Milhaupt, the integrity of the structure of capitalism could thus be ensured.

Contrary to their claim that this is a 'minimalist response to the new merchantilism', it is, however, a drastic one: the threat to which it responds has not materialized, nor does the available data suggest that it is imminent. Relatively rarely do SWFs acquire control of European companies, and even anecdotal evidence of a politicization of the management of European companies by third-country shareholders is absent so far. Instead, there is substantial empirical evidence that stock prices react positively to the announcement of an investment by SWFs.[132] At the same time, Gilson/Milhaupt's proposal breaks with fundamental principles of corporate governance: in recent years, attention has turned once again to the importance of shareholder activism in monitoring management. Disempowering investors with an important stake in a company and thus a real interest in effective control may be counterproductive in this regard. It will increase the power of management—and the management's interest in securing investments by SWFs.

Financial market regulation To date, there is no evidence that the conduct of SWFs or other foreign state-controlled investment poses specific risks to the stability of financial markets.[133] Rather, there is substantial evidence that SWFs, typically acting as long-term investor with mainly unleveraged positions, can have a stabilizing effect. They can sit out longer during market downturns or even trade against market trends.[134] Although they hold large and frequently

[130] For such a concern see eg Cox (n 3).

[131] According to Gilson/Milhaupt, the voting rights would be regained when the sovereign investor transfers its stake to a non-state owner. This mechanism shall ensure that the full value of the investment can be realized. See Gilson and Milhaupt (n 3) 10.

[132] Sun and Hesse (n 39).

[133] See, in particular, Beck and Fidora (n 16) 23 and 24.

[134] Sun and Hesse (n 39) 3.

opaque positions such that a sudden sale could potentially lead to market disturbances, it will be in the best own interest of SWFs to pursue portfolio reallocations gradually so as to limit adverse price effects.[135] As regards the potential systemic effects of SWF disinvestments, it has been observed that a withdrawal of foreign government investments from the equity market may be less of a strategic threat than if the investments had remained entirely in US government debt.[136]

Nonetheless, there is an intense debate whether new financial market regulation regarding, inter alia, investments by SWFs is needed. The debate mainly centres on transparency rules.[137] The former SEC Chairman Christopher Cox has argued that the opacity of the SWFs' investments creates a risk of market abuse and insider trading.[138] Others have claimed that increased transparency is needed to allow markets to anticipate the broad allocation and risk-preference trends of this investor class, thus avoiding inaccurate pricing and market volatility.[139] Finally, policy makers in host countries may need more data, and thus more disclosure, to assess the potential existence and size of systemic risks.[140] These issues are at least partly specific to SWFs. They cannot be equated with the general disclosure requirements to which all market participants are subject under the various regimes of financial market regulation. In the future, financial market regulators may thus develop specific disclosure regimes for SWFs.

But calls for regulation sometimes go further. For example, it is currently debated whether the EU Commission's proposal for a Directive on Alternative Investment Fund Managers,[141] if it were to enter into force, would apply also to SWFs. The proposed Directive strives to establish common regulatory and supervisory standards for hedge funds, private equity, and other systemically important market players in order to address a variety of risks associated with such investments, ranging from macro-prudential (systemic) risks to, inter alia, micro-prudential risks, risks regarding market efficiency and integrity. It requires managers of all alternative investment funds (AIFs) covered by the Directive to receive authorization by a regulatory authority for marketing their fund to professional investors. The authorization will be based on a demonstration that the manager is suitably qualified to provide AIF management services, and on detailed information on the planned activity of the fund. The Alternative Investment Fund Manager (AIFM) will be required to hold and retain a

[135] Ibid. [136] Gilson and Milhaupt (n 3).

[137] For a call for greater transparency see eg Commission (n 5) 10; former SEC chairman Cox (n 3). [138] Cox (n 3).

[139] For this argument see Sun and Hesse (n 39) 3; Cox (n 3).

[140] See M A Weiss, 'CRS Report for Congress: Sovereign Wealth Funds: Background and Policy Issues for Congress' (2008), 14 (available at <http://fpc.state.gov/documents/organization/110750.pdf>; last accessed 23 July 2010).

[141] Proposal for a Directive of the European Parliament and the Council on Alternative Investment Fund Managers and amending Directives 2004/39/EC and 2009/.../EC, COM (2009)207 final of 30 April 2009.

minimum level of capital. He must moreover satisfy the competent authority of the robustness of the risk management; the management and disclosure of conflicts of interest; the fair valuation of assets; and the security of depository/custodial arrangements. The proposed Directive sets out far-reaching disclosure requirements on various levels. A minimum level of service and information must be provided on an ongoing basis to the investors of the fund. In addition, the AIFM is required to report to the competent authority on a regular basis on the principal markets and instruments in which the fund trades, its principal exposures, performance data, and concentrations of risk. The acquisition of a controlling interest in a company must be reported to its shareholders and the representatives of employees. The EU Commission may, through comitology procedures, set leverage limits where this is required to ensure the stability and integrity of the financial system.

The primary targets of the Directive are hedge funds and private equity funds. SWFs are not easily subsumed under the definition of 'alternative investment funds' in Article 3(a) of the proposed Directive.[142] In fact, an application of the Directive to SWFs would be inappropriate at least in part. Hedge funds and private equity funds differ in their structure and in the concerns they raise. SWFs, however, differ from both. Investor protection is not an issue with regard to SWFs; nor are they known typically to engage in highly leveraged transactions. In light of the remarkable variety of investment policies pursued by SWFs—some acting more like pension funds, some more like strategic investors—it seems that any regulatory regime meant to capture SWFs that would reach beyond transparency requirements would need to start from a definition of specific risk scenarios. To this day, these risk scenarios have not been well defined.

Competition rules Finally, the risk of a distortion of competition which foreign state-controlled third-country investments might entail do not appear to be sufficiently concrete and severe to justify special restrictions for the investment of SWFs or third-country SOEs. Indeed, non-EU investors may be subject to a much more lenient competition law regime in their home states, and competitive advantages may result in particular for third-country SOEs. In some cases, they may cross-subsidize their EU activities with monopolistic profits gained elsewhere. SWFs and SOEs may have access to state resources which would be qualified as state aid, and hence be prohibited, in an EU context.[143] The positive ratings that SWFs have typically received, and thus their access to finance at particularly attractive terms, have so far been based on an implicit presumption

[142] In Article 3(a), 'alternative investment funds' are defined 'any collective investment undertaking, including investment compartments thereof whose object is the collective investment in assets and which does not require authorisation pursuant to Article 5 of Directive 2009/.../EC [the UCITS Directive]'. It is unclear whether SWFs are 'collective investment undertakings'.

[143] Based on the 'private market investor test'.

that large SWFs would be bailed out by the home states.[144] Foreign government-controlled and -financed market operators may thus not be subject to the full pressure of the market.[145] It is, however, relatively unlikely that SWFs and SOEs will enjoy privileges of such a scale that competition within European markets would be seriously distorted in the longer term. The incentives for foreign governments to subsidize the activities of their entities abroad—and thus to subsidize foreign consumers—will normally be limited. The great importance of state aid control within the EU is linked to an environment where the subsidizing state is omnipresent, and pursuing a broad scope of politically motivated interests in the economy. This is not equally true for a foreign state. A politically motivated intervention by a foreign state into the actions of an SOE or an SWF that runs counter to its own commercial interests should not be expected to be of systemic importance. It should rather be a relatively rare and isolated act.

A possible exception to this rule may exist in markets where competition is already weakened, and subsidies granted for a limited period may contribute to the creation or strengthening of dominance. Normally, this risk will be greater with vertically integrated state-owned enterprises than with SWFs.[146] If in a concrete setting such a risk can be identified, the relevant firm's conduct will be analysed under the EU and/or national competition rules. The EU state aid rules would not apply to subsidies granted by a third-country state; but a conduct based on privileged non-market driven access to finance could potentially be analysed under Article 82 EC/Article 102 TFEU. One shortcoming of the EU regime vis-à-vis s 2 Sherman Act might be that, based on its wording, it does not seem to apply to the creation of dominance, but presupposes the existence of dominance. The Court might opt to re-interpret Article 82 EC/Article 102 TFEU more widely, and along the lines of s 2 Sherman Act, however, were otherwise serious risks to the competitive order would result. Similarly, Article 82 EC/Article 102 TFEU could be applied to any attempts by foreign state-controlled dominant firms to inflict harm through boycotts, drastic increases of prices, or a systematic discrimination of certain firms.

(iv) European restrictions of the free movement of capital by third-country investors

Article 57(2) EC/Article 64 TFEU empowers the Council, acting by qualified majority and on a proposal by the Commission, to adopt measures on the

[144] This assumption has come under review, however, in the context of the crisis of Dubai World and Dubai's refusal to take rescue measures.

[145] See OECD, *Competition Law and Foreign-Government Controlled Investors* (January 2009) 3 ff.

[146] See also Truman (n 1) 15: 'The US-suggested principle that an SWF should commit to compete fairly with the private sector is more relevant to the activities of a government-owned or government-controlled financial or non-financial corporation than to an SWF except to the extent that the SWF acts to support another government-owned or government-controlled entity'.

movement of capital to or from third countries involving direct investment, establishment, the provision of financial services, or the admission of securities to capital markets. It reflects a decision that, with the European Monetary Union, the main competence for legislative measures concerning free movement of capital has shifted from the Member States to the EU. However, where a measure will restrain rather than liberalize the movement of capital to and from third countries, unanimity will be required. While this requirement underlines the EU's strong commitment to a liberal investment and capital movement regime on an international scale, it may be too narrowly construed to answer effectively the challenges that a broad construction of Article 56 EC/Article 63 TFEU poses. The overlaps between Article 56 EC (Article 63 TFEU) and Article 43 EC (Article 49 TFEU) and the relative ease by which third-country investors can gain the protection of the latter by establishing in any one Member State, thus circumventing other Member States' restrictions, show that national controls of foreign direct can easily become ineffective, even where they are justified under EU law. The possibility for Member States to establish controls that 'pierce the corporate veil' partly answers to this threat—but is an awkward instrument under EU law. Thus, much argues for a European response to the challenges raised by third-country investments generally, and by SWFs and other foreign-government-controlled investments in particular. These challenges may involve a need to impose tailored restrictions at the European level—restrictions which the EU should be empowered to implement acting by qualified majority.

VI. Conclusions

In the intra-EU context, the principle of neutrality vis-à-vis private or public ownership is deeply engrained in the structure of EU law (Article 345 TFEU). It is matched by intense legal constraints imposed on Member States' interventions into markets, including Article 106(1) TFEU and state aid rules. These rules have no equivalent at the international level nor, for the most part, at the national level of non-EU states. The principle of neutrality vis-à-vis private or public ownership can therefore not be transferred to non-EU investors: state control or ownership of investment vehicles can be an important aspect in defining and assessing risks to legitimate national interests resulting from third-country investments.

The main international concern with SWF cross-border investments and investments by other state-controlled entities is that the sponsoring states may use these investment entities as instruments of 'imperialistic capitalist' strategies, that is that they will use the influence or control they gain in other target companies not for the end to maximize returns, but to maximize the interest of the sponsoring state, eg by obtaining access to technology or expertise that will help the sponsoring state to pursue an aggressive industrial policy at the cost of the interest of other shareholders of the target companies and/or at the interests of the host states.[147]

According to some observers, some SWFs (as well as SOEs) have indeed pursued such strategies in developing countries. Taking advantage of the weak institutional and regulatory framework, they have acquired strategic stakes in those countries' natural resources, infrastructure, and defence sectors.[148] At the same time, SWFs have been careful not to act in such a fashion in Western industrialized countries so far—possibly in anticipation of an expected retaliatory response. Nonetheless, the risk as such cannot be completely dismissed.

Within the EU, a proportionate response to the remaining risk—a risk contained by the possibility to react ad hoc to a manifest abuse—should be based on the general European commitment to an open investment environment. The application of Article 63 TFEU is the most important instrument in this regard, as it subjects national responses to perceived risks to public security and public policy to the rule of law and thus helps to break the dangerous spiral of 'imperialistic capitalism' and protectionism. It does not call into question the Member States' ability to defend against real risks; but it requires the Member State to define clearly and plausibly the relevant risks, and it subjects national measures to judicial review by the Court of Justice. These beneficial effects will only materialize, however, if Article 63 TFEU is consistently applied. If the Court of Justice were to apply the 'centre of gravity' approach to the Member States' regulatory regimes and thus allow them to develop policies regarding controlling investments by third-country investors outside the realm of Article 63 TFEU, the rationalizing effect of EU law would be lost and the door for protectionist sentiments at national level re-opened. In the absence of the constraints of EU law, Member States have frequently tended towards discretionary frameworks of entry control.

In applying Article 63 TFEU to third-country investments, one must recognize that different risks may attach to them—and in particular foreign—state-controlled third-country investments—as compared to pure intra-EU cross-border investments. Broader restrictions of third-country investments may therefore be justified. Three different categories of risks associated with foreign state-controlled investments can be distinguished: public security risks resulting from investments in security-relevant industries (defence, military equipment, nuclear energy, etc); risks of dependence resulting from the acquisition of control of strategic infrastructures; and more general risks of an abuse of influence or control by the foreign investor within the target company, of a misappropriation of intellectual property or trade secrets, of a destabilizing effect on capital markets, of distortions of competition, etc.

[147] For this concern see eg Commission (n 5) 5.

[148] B J Balin, 'Sovereign Wealth Funds: A Critical Analysis' available at <http://ssrn.com/abstract=1477725> (last accessed 23 July 2010).

The first two categories of risk justify a regime of *ex ante* control—but must be limited to sensitive industries. Restrictions on investments into security-relevant industries, even on investments below the threshold of control, can be broadly justified. Risks of dependence from a foreign investor resulting from the acquisition of control of strategic infrastructures should be verified carefully case by case and will justify restrictions on cross-border investments only in a narrow set of cases where they are necessary to respond to clearly specified risks. The approach developed in Article 11 of Directive 2009/72/EC concerning common rules for the internal market in electricity[149] and in Article 11 of Directive 2009/73/EC concerning common rules for the internal market in natural gas[150] with regard to controlling investments in essential infrastructures is of special interest in this regard. This is true in particular with a view to the 'piercing of the corporate veil' it allows with a view to distinguish between intra-EU investments and foreign investments. But it is also true with a view to the consideration it gives to the political context and international legal commitments to which a third-country investor is subject; and with a view to the easing of the burden of proof regarding the existence and imminence of a risk. By contrast, the approach chosen by the German legislator in the course of its most recent reform of the German Foreign Trade and Payments Act—a generalized foreign investment entry control in cases which involve a 'serious threat to public policy or public security'—does not comply with the EU law requirements of predictability and legal certainty, since it does not specify the type of threat to be addressed and the conditions in which such threat becomes real.

The third category of risks should be addressed through the general laws of each host state (corporate law, capital market law, competition law, etc). Here, more work will be needed to specify the type of risks that may go along with SWF investments and to insert adequate regulatory responses into the general framework rules.

Developing a real 'common European approach' to SWFs beyond the merely complementary soft law approach that the EU Commission has outlined in its recent communication[151] remains a challenge to be met. A common European framework for national regulatory reactions to all three categories of risk outlined above would effectively contain the danger of protectionist overreactions at national level, and it could provide more effective rules on the entry of third-country investments into the EU (where they will then freely circulate).[152]

The EU law perspective on non-EU SWFs must be distinguished from its perspective on the establishment of SWFs by Member States. Recently, France—after having unsuccessfully lobbied for a European SWF to defend European strategic industries against foreign takeovers—has created its own *Fonds stratégique*

[149] Directive 2009/72/EC of 13 July 2009, [2009] OJ L211/55.

[150] Directive 2009/73/EC of 13 July 2009, [2009] OJ L211/94.

[151] Commission (n 5).

[152] Commission (n 5) 7–8.

d'investissement. The fund, capitalized with € 20 billion, will help French enterprises in need of stable investors to finance their projects. More specifically, the objectives of the French SWF include: the support of promising SMEs which have difficulties in accessing finance; safeguarding the capital of strategic enterprises; and providing temporary help to undertakings of strong potential to develop innovative, risky projects. In principle, the SWF will invest in profitable projects that generate revenue; it will only acquire a minority of the capital of the target companies; it will team up with private partners; and it will primarily engage in long-term investments. The creation of such an SWF and its investment activities must again be assessed within the framework of the free movement rules, and in particular of Article 63 TFEU—but also within the framework of the state aid rules. With a view to the applicability of Article 63 TFEU, the main challenge is to establish whether such an SWF can be said to act in a purely private capacity, or whether it is an instrument for the state to act in a regulatory capacity. Based on the general EU law principle of neutrality vis-à-vis public or private ownership, Article 63 would apply with full force only in the latter case. In any case, any discrimination based on nationality—for example selective interventions to protect French companies against foreign takeovers—would be outlawed. The goals pursued by the French SWF suggest that it must be assessed primarily against the state aid rules, however, in particular the Community Framework for State Aid for Research, Development and Innovation[153] and the Community Guidelines on state aid to promote risk capital investments in small and medium enterprises.[154] The Court of Justice has tended to treat the state aid rules as *lex specialis* vis-à-vis the free movement rules to the extent that the relevant effects of a measure on the internal market are fully captured by the state aid rules.[155] Only where a clear-cut infringement of the free movement rules could be easily established were the free movement rules applied in parallel.[156]

[153] [2006] OJ C323/1 [154] [2006] OJ C194/2

[155] See Case 74/76 *Iannelli/Meroni* [1977] ECR 557 paras 9–10. See also T-197/97 *Weyl Beef Products v Commission* [2001] ECR II-303 paras 77 ff.

[156] Case 21/88 *Du Pont de Nemours Italiana* [1990] ECR I-889 paras 10 ff and para 20.

13

Sovereign Wealth Funds: Neither Market Investors Nor 'Imperialist Capitalists'—A Response to Heike Schweitzer

Katharina Pistor

I. Introduction

In her contribution to this volume 'Sovereign Wealth Funds—Market Investors or "Imperialist Capitalists"', Professor Schweitzer develops a binary typology for analysing whether Sovereign Wealth Funds (SWFs) pose a threat to market economies, and whether the legal rules currently in place or in the process of being adopted should or could restrain investments by SWFs. The contrast between market investors and 'imperialist capitalists' was meant to be stark. The author is careful to point out that SWFs can be labelled only with great difficulty: their investment strategies and governance structures are too varied to allow for a simple classification scheme; this statement holds true not only for SWFs from different countries, but also for SWFs that originate within a single country. For example, Singapore's Temasek has traditionally held large stakes primarily in domestic companies and has only recently diversified internationally, whereas the Government of Singapore Investment Corporation (GIC) invests exclusively abroad and for the most part in a portfolio of well-diversified minority stakes. Similarly in China, the China Investment Corporation (CIC)'s role is that of indirect parent to the country's largest banks and holds substantial stakes in international financial intermediaries, such as Morgan Stanley or Blackstone, whereas the State Administration for Foreign Exchange invests in small stakes that largely escape detection by foreign regulatory or domestic monitors—and it is no understatement that these examples could be expanded.[1]

[1] For a comprehensive analysis of SWFs and their long-term investment strategies, see Monitor Group, 'Assessing the Risks: The Behaviors of Sovereign Wealth Funds in the Global Economy' (New York: Monitor Group, 2008). On SWF investments in globally operative financial intermediaries during the global financial crisis, see K Pistor, 'Global Network Finance' (2009) 37 J of Comparative Economics 552 and 'Sovereign Wealth Funds, Banks and Governments in the Global

In this commentary I argue that SWFs are neither market investors nor 'imperialist capitalists'. Moreover, I hope to convey that framing the inquiry or the legal responses in this fashion may miss the profound changes in global financial relations currently underway; this does not mean I disagree with Professor Schweitzer's analysis—to the contrary, I find her detailed legal analysis both illuminating and persuasive. Rather, I am suggesting that Weber's notion of imperialist capitalists just as the West's legal defence strategies for protecting its particular mode of capitalism are too close to home in the sense that they reflect well-known uses and abuses of the state and the law in the West, but for that very reason fall short of understanding SWFs from the Far or the Middle East. This also suggests that legal and political response strategies that are rooted in this framework may not achieve their aims, and in fact may be counterproductive, because they fail to recognize the extent to which the West has become dependent on SWFs and the countries that sponsor them.

In this brief commentary I limit myself to a few observations: First, the concept of control is not an absolute one, but its meaning and the means used to shape outcomes may vary across countries. Second, even if SWFs do not exercise the kind of control that may be associated with 'imperialist capitalist', this does not mean that they therefore are market investors. SWFs are likely to use their influence to advance their own interests or, more precisely, those of the ruling elite in their country of origin. I suggest here that those interests are rooted in domestic politics and concerns, but may nonetheless have a profound impact on global finance and geopolitics. Third, the well-meaning and well-thought-out constraints on state aid in the EU, as well as the political constraints attached to government bail outs, may—paradoxically—strengthen the role of SWFs in global finance: financial intermediaries who wish to avoid such constraints are likely to turn to SWFs rather than their home governments for help, and in many cases their home governments may well encourage this—thereby outsourcing, at least in part, the role of lender or investor of last resort. Fourthly, the same countries that sponsor the largest SWFs have evolved into the largest lenders of Western debtor countries. With China holding 20 percent of the US budget deficit the notion that CFIUS could control foreign influence on US soil by scrutinizing individual investment projects is somewhat curious. Similarly, the EU may well hope that China or the Gulf States show greater appetite for the debt of highly indebted Member States—such as Greece—to avoid having to bail them out itself. This makes efforts at the EU level or that of Member States to enhance transparency of or curtail investments by SWFs on European soil somewhat circumspect.

Crisis: Towards a New Governance of Global Finance?' (2009) 10 Eur Business Organization L Rev 333.

II. The concept of control

Numerous countries employ legal and political constraints on foreign capital or investment flows to ensure that they do not pose a threat to the existing economic and legal system. The key concept here is control: can the direct or indirect owner of the investment vehicle exert control in the domestic realm that might pose a threat to the system? Control is typically associated with ownership, ie the right to exercise the residual control rights over an asset. In the US, the possibility that a foreign entity might 'control' a US business is at the heart of the CFIUS review mechanism. Recently, the definition of control has been expanded to now explicitly include minority stakes as well as warrants or proxies. Still, even this broader definition is rooted in concepts of ownership as the means by which control is exercised. Foreign investors—whether private or state—are welcome to invest unless they seek control over firms that are deemed to be of particular importance to the US economy. And Member States of the European Union may impose restrictions on the free movement of capital flows, if and when important national interests are at stake—but otherwise have to respect market forces in the flow and allocation of capital whether from other Member States or third countries.[2]

While ownership of firms has long ceased to be associated with physical control over assets, in Western legal systems, ownership confers the key elements of control: the right to appoint and dismiss management and thereby influence the strategy of a firm and the right to vote on key issues: including changes in the certificate of incorporation, a company's capital, a future merger, or the company's liquidation at a time when it may still be viable. Ever since Berle's and Means' analysis of the changing control structure of publicly traded corporations we have, of course, been well aware of the 'separation of ownership and control'[3] in companies where dispersed shareholders are incapable of exerting effective control of their *de jure* rights over management, which exercises *de facto* control.

I submit that the separation of ownership and control can also take different forms and that these alternative modes of governing firms and even entire financial systems need to be scrutinized and understood if we are to make sense of the transformation of global relations that are under way. In China, for example, existing laws and corporate statutes mirror the close affinity between share ownership and control rights familiar to Western lawyers; yet in key sectors—finance being one of them—shareholders are not the ones who appoint or dismiss top management personnel. Instead, the Organizational Committee of China's

[2] See Article 63 TFEU and the detailed discussion of these provisions by Professor Schweitzer in ch 12 of this volume.

[3] A Berle and G Means, *The Modern Corporation and Private Property* (New York: Council for Research in the Social Sciences, Columbia University, 1932).

Communist Party (CCP) exercises these important control rights.[4] These control rights appear to be for the most part confined to sectors where state ownership remains prevalent, but goes well beyond entities that are wholly state owned. Neither is this an aberration from an otherwise well-marked path towards convergence on a Western model of market-based capitalism. In fact, the influence of the CCP over finance has increased rather than decreased as China has opened its financial system to the West.[5] Instead, I would argue that it constitutes a new form of the separation of ownership and control: owners can exercise all control rights that are not explicitly or implicitly reserved by the CCP, which encompass the most critical rights, namely the appointment and dismissal of key management personnel. Indeed, the entire management team of China Investment Corporation—the SWF that was formally established in September 2007—was appointed by the CCP's Organizational Committee. By contrast, it would be difficult to pin down exactly who 'owns' this new vehicle either directly or indirectly[6]: the State Council authorized it, the Ministry of Finance financed it—but with debt, not with equity—and the People's Bank of China sold to it foreign exchange reserves in exchange for domestic currency.[7] More generally, governance in China is as much about controlling the career of top 'cadres'[8] as it might be about controlling assets.[9] This system of control is deeply rooted in China's political and economic system. It implies that focusing on formal control rights associated with ownership may be highly misleading. Whether or not this particular governance regime is transferable beyond China's shores is questionable. However, evolving relations between CIC and some of the financial intermediaries in which CIC has invested reflects once more a strong emphasis on people, not assets. Thus, CIC invested in Blackstone just prior to the onset of, and in Morgan Stanley in the midst of the global crisis and now holds above 10 per cent in both entities. CIC does not occupy any board seats. In fact, like other SWFs it has strenuously avoided taking on such responsibility for fear of the costs

[4] S Heilmann, 'Regulatory Innovation by Leninist Means: Communist Party Supervision in China's Financial Industry' (2005) 181 The China Q 1 and K Pistor, 'The Governance of China's Finances' (2009) unpublished manuscript on file with author.

[5] See also Heilmann (n 4).

[6] As Professor Schweitzer points out, at least in the natural resource sector, the EU is willing to 'pierce the corporate veil' and inquire about the indirect owners of an investment vehicle. However, the capital structure of CIC—at least if taken at face value—may even defy this strategy.

[7] For details on CIC's formation and initial capitalization see M Martin, *China's Sovereign Wealth Fund* (Washington DC Congressional Research Service, 2008).

[8] Yashing Huang has made this point for explaining how China's central government has maintained control over the country's vast bureaucracy. See Y Huang, *Inflation and Investment Controls in China* (Cambridge: Cambridge University Press, 1996).

[9] Karl Marx, of course, has emphasized that control over assets also confers control rights over people thus enabling capitalists to exploit the masses even without imposing a system of slavery. Ironically, a very similar point has been made by leading proponents of the property rights theory of the firm, who have pointed out that the residual right of control is key to controlling employees, not only machinery. See S J Grossman and O D Hart. 'The Costs and Benefits of Ownership: A Theory of Vertical and Lateral Integration' (1986) 94 J of Political Economy 691.

and legal obligations that come with it.[10] CIC also incurred substantial losses on these investments. Nonetheless, they appear to have created the foundation for a mutually beneficial reciprocal relationship: China's SWF recently announced that Blackstone and Morgan Stanley were selected as asset managers and advisors for its global investment strategies. The *Wall Street Journal* captured this with the headline 'CIC turns to friends'.[11] Friendship is obviously not the same as controlling the appointment of financial cadres to key positions in government agencies or commercial banks. Yet, the means of control may not be entirely different. It is less about domination and more about reciprocity. The commitment thus is not to maximize the return on a given asset, but the value of the relationship in the long term.

III. Are SWFs market investors?

The previous discussion already holds the answer to the question whether instead SWFs are market investors. It has certainly been difficult for analysts to detect overt political investment strategies in the behaviour of SWFs in the long term.[12] Like market investors, SWFs seek financial returns. The very purpose of establishing SWFs in the Gulf States, for example, has been to transform oil wealth into financial wealth, and in the Far East, to recycle foreign currency reserves in order to secure the export-led growth strategy for countries of that region. However, this does not mean that financial return is the only objective that SWFs pursue. It is a means to an end, and if achieving the end sometimes requires alternative strategies, they too will be pursued. Thus, the largest SWF of the world, ADIA of Abu Dhabi, has invested US $7.5 billion into Citigroup when former US Secretary of the Treasury and then vice president of Citigroup, Paul Rubin, asked for help in December of 2007.[13] Western commentators have frequently portrayed the investments by SWFs into Western banks during the global crisis as naïve and foolish, especially after stock prices of these entities continued to fall. If the sole purpose of these investments were short-term financial gains, that assessment is correct, as SWFs made substantial losses on their investments. This view, however, underestimates the sophistication of asset managers at these funds many of whom were trained in or recruited from the West.[14] It may therefore be worthwhile exploring whether the different

[10] Interviews with board members of Temasek and CIC on file with the author.

[11] 31 July 2009, available at http://online.wsj.com/article/SB124896400764393841.html>.

[12] See Monitor Group (n 1).

[13] For a detailed account of investments by SWFs into ailing Western financial intermediaries during the global crisis, see Pistor (n 1).

[14] ADIA, for example, has long been managed by J P Villain from France; and Gao Xiqing, one of the top executives of CIC has a law degree from Duke University and can boast experience on Wall Street.

investment patterns we observe can be explained in ways that do not disparage them. Comparative research into the history of SWFs and their role within their home countries suggests such an explanation, namely that the major purpose of SWFs is to maximize the autonomy of the ruling elite in the SWFs' home countries and to keep both internal conflicts and external interferences at bay.[15] The oil-producing Gulf States are deeply intertwined with powers in the West as consumers of the oil produced, but also to protect their security interests. The first Iraq war was a vivid illustration of the willingness of the US to come to the rescue of a country that lacked the military power to protect itself against an Iraq invasion.[16] Critically, the exiled ruling elite retained control over the SWFs even as its control over the territory of Kuwait was challenged. Over 85 per cent of investments by the Kuwait Investment Authority (KIA) are invested in US assets[17]—and to a substantial amount in US treasury bonds.[18] Put differently, SWFs can be regarded simultaneously as an economic and political insurance device. They buy security for the region both in military and economic terms and they help provide financial stability that allows them to monetize their wealth, which has made them dependent on the stability of the US dollar. Viewed in this light, bailing out US banks during the financial crisis can be regarded as part of a complex geopolitical arrangement the key pillars of which consist of 'black gold' (oil), military security, and financial stability. Stabilizing Citigroup and other global financial intermediaries is less naïve or altruistic than it might appear, but was perceived to be vital for the interests of ADIA and the royal family of Abu Dhabi.

Neither Singapore nor China is an oil-producing country. Their wealth rests in manufacturing (China) and global trade in manufactured goods (both Singapore and China).[19] Export-led growth depends on the availability of reliable export markets. In theory, a strategy built on a growing imbalance between current and capital accounts should not be sustainable in the long term as excessive inflows of foreign currency should drive up the value of the domestic currency and thus make exported products less competitive on world markets.[20] This self-regulating feedback loop, however, can be side-stepped by sterilizing foreign currency

[15] K Pistor and K Hatton, 'Sovereign Wealth Funds as Autonomy Maximizers' (2010), unpublished working paper on file with the author. In this note I discuss only external threats.

[16] The reciprocal oil for security arrangements between the Gulf States and external powers has its roots in the role of the British Empire in the region prior to World War II. For details see Pistor and Hatton (n 15).

[17] Data available from Monitor Group (n 1).

[18] Exact breakdowns of the investment portfolio of KIA or other SWFs are not available. Neither do most countries receive the composition of their investors.

[19] On the importance of export-led growth for the rise of Asia after World War II, Asian Development Bank, *Emerging Asia: Changes and Challenges* (Manila: Asian Development Bank, 1997).

[20] For details, see B Eichengreen and Richard Baldwin (eds), *What G20 Leaders Must do to Stabilise our Economy and Fix the Financial System* (London: CEPR, 2008), available online at <http://www.voxeu.org/reports/G20_Summit.pdf>; and M Wolf, *Fixing Global Finance* (Baltimore: Johns Hopkins University Press, 2008).

inflows and by re-investing foreign currency on world markets. GIC of Singapore and SAFE and CIC of China do the latter. Temasek of Singapore played a critical role in nurturing key industries in Singapore, including shipbuilding, airlines, banking, and telecommunication.[21] However, beginning in the early 2000s Temasek retooled its investment strategy and is now heavily investing abroad, especially in greater Asia. The willingness of SWFs from the region to rescue financial intermediaries from the West thus was most likely motivated by concerns similar to those of SWFs from the Gulf Region: While military security is less of an issue, financial stability takes on greater importance. This is particularly true for Singapore, which is competing for the leading financial centre in the Far East. However, it also holds true for China, as it has invested most of its foreign currency reserves in dollar-denominated assets.

In sum, SWFs are market investors seeking the highest returns when it suits their overall objective of insuring the ruling elites in their home countries, however, they are willing to depart from this strategy if and when circumstances pose threats to the systems they serve. This does not make them advocates of misguided industrial policies nor does it induce them to invest continuously in losers just for the sake of controlling them. Indeed, SWFs have for the most part divested from global financial intermediaries once that proved feasible. ADIA has even gone as far as taking Citigroup to arbitration for fraudulent conduct in relation to their original investment agreement.[22] Indeed, there are strong signs that these funds have begun to diversify their foreign holdings in order to make them less dependent on the US dollar. The key point is that whatever their future strategies may be, they will ultimately reflect the fact that these countries view themselves as being deeply intertwined with Western powers—both politically and economically—and that their relative autonomy depends on arrangements that mitigate their dependence; SWFs are therefore likely to continue to play a role as insurers for the elite they serve.

IV. The West's increasing dependence on SWFs

As Professor Schweitzer points out in her contribution, the total amount of wealth accumulated and managed by SWFs dwarfs when compared with other financial intermediaries. Yet the crucial difference between them is that SWFs' actions prove they are willing to invest at times when private markets

[21] Critical information on the investment portfolio of Temasek is available in its annual reports. See <http://www.temasekholdings.com>. See also the discussion in C Milhaupt and K Pistor, *Law and Capitalism: What Corporate Crises Reveal about Legal Systems and Economic Development Around the World* (Chicago: Chicago University Press, 2008) ch 7, 125.

[22] F Guerrera and H Sender, 'Citigroups' Shares under Fire' *The Financial Times* (London, 16 December 2009) available at <http://www.ft.com>.

freeze up. When in 2007 and 2008 regulators of banks in the US, the UK, and Switzerland reprimanded them to raise fresh capital, private investors took flight. Even a reasonably well-off bank, such as Barclays—the number two globally before the crisis and one that had less toxic assets on its books than its main competitors—found that it was unable to sell sufficient numbers of shares to private investors in a public offering conducted in June of 2008. Instead, it had to place the unsold shares with SWFs that agreed to buy up any unsold shares from the public offering: The Qatar Investment Authority (QIA), Temasek, and China Development Bank.[23] Not surprisingly, in the autumn of 2008, Barclays switched to a private placement of shares with SWFs and individual investors from the Gulf States. It had to convince shareholders to forego their pre-emptive rights and agreed to rather stiff financing conditions. The major gain for Barclays from this deal was that it enabled the bank to decline government funding,[24] yet retain access to liquidity provisioning by the UK Government should occasion arise in the future. Credit Suisse of Switzerland implemented a similar recapitalization strategy also with QIA. From the perspective of the relevant governments this must have been a welcome move. It assured them that the relevant banks were stabilized without requiring government assistance. Indeed, regulators appear to have played a critical role in identifying SWFs as outside investors that could provide this service at a critical time.[25]

The implications of these arrangements may well be more far-reaching than appears at first glance: in the context of the global financial crisis they were arranged on an ad hoc basis and may therefore be easily relegated to one-shot rescue deals, however, they deliver the point that in times of crises there are only two reliable sources of last-resort investments: the home country governments of banks, and (foreign) SWFs—which has strengthened the hand of SWFs vis-à-vis foreign governments and their regulators. It is probably not a coincidence that CIC of China as well as its subsidiary Hui Jin corporation were exempted from bank holding status under US laws in the autumn of 2008—at a time when the US Government was desperately trying to shore up the capital base of commercial and investment banks—even though Hui Jin is the immediate parent and CIC the grandparent of Bank of China, China Construction Bank, and similar institutions in China that have opened branches and subsidiaries in the United States.[26] This has freed these entities from regulatory oversight and has saved

[23] The recapitalization of Barclays in June and October 2008 is recounted in detail in Pistor (n 1 a/b).

[24] The UK Government injected vast amounts of capital into other banks, including the Royal Bank of Scotland and Lloyds banking groups. The total costs are currently estimated at over £850 billion. See Andrew Grice, '£850bn: official cost of the bank bailout', *The Independent* (London, 4 December 2009) available at <http://www.independent.co.uk>.

[25] Conversation with regulators from one of the two countries; notes on file with the author.

[26] For details, Pistor (n 1 a/b) esp footnote 53 and accompanying text.

them substantial regulatory costs of reporting to, and complying with standards imposed by the Federal Reserve and relevant banking regulations. It also serves to illustrate the willingness of regulators of ailing banks to rely on and make concessions to foreign SWFs. Indeed, the growing dependence of Western governments on SWFs is likely to be reinforced by constraints on state aid imposed by the European Union. To the extent that home countries have to accept EU-imposed constraints on actions aimed at protecting their financial system, banks will instead have to rely on other sources—and where private investors may not be forthcoming, these may well be SWFs. Given the risk aversion demonstrated by the private sector in times of financial duress, the global financial crisis may not have been the last time that Western governments have come to rely on SWFs from the Middle and the Far East.

V. The future of SWF investments

In the past, most SWFs invested in a diversified portfolio of financial assets bearing moderate risk. A substantial amount of this portfolio consisted of, and to this day still consists of foreign government bonds. More recently, there have been signs that at least some SWFs have broadened their investment strategy and have begun to invest in assets that promise higher returns. CIC has just announced that it will be investing larger parts of its portfolio in private equity, not by setting up its own equity fund, but at least for the time being by using other financial intermediaries.[27] An important consideration for this move may well be the search for higher returns, especially for a SWF that is capitalized by debt and needs to ensure high returns on its own investments in order to fulfil its obligations.[28] In addition, it allows CIC and indirectly the Chinese Government to diversify away from financing the US budget deficit. Whereas in a stronger global economic climate deficit finance was a critical component of China's growth strategy—as cheap deficit financing by outside funders kept US interests rates low and fuelled economic growth despite increasing household and government leverage—the global financial crisis demonstrated that such a strategy is not without risk. Indeed, China has scaled back purchases in newly issued treasury bonds, bumping them back to second place behind Japan in the ranking of major creditors to the US Government.[29] China's political elite may well have concluded that the

[27] See A Or, 'CIC Hires Three Firms to Invest in Private Equity', *The Wall Street Journal* (New York, 19 February 2009), available at <http://online.wsj.com>. Total funds invested are US $1.5 billion so far, $500 m for each one of them.

[28] CIC was capitalized with the returns on bonds issued by the Ministry of Finance, which in turn imposed on CIC the obligation to pay the interests on the bonds. See Martin (n 7).

[29] M Zeng, 'As China's Treasury Purchases Slow, Others Step Up', *The Wall Street Journal* (New York, 18 February 2009) available at <http://online.wsj.com>.

best insurance in times of crisis is a diversified portfolio as well as close ties with prominent financial intermediaries.

Incidentally, the way in which this new investment is structured allows CIC CFIUS-style controls: Many of the anticipated investments may be well below the control threshold stipulated by these regulations anyway; even those that are within the vicinity of 'control' may avoid oversight as the immediate investors will be US-based financial intermediaries rather than a foreign SWF.[30] This serves to illustrate that the kind of control mechanisms the US—or Germany for that matter—have devised to ensure that foreign governments may not acquire control over private entities on their territories may be largely ineffective. In a world of mobile capital where the ultimate investor can be easily disguised by employing a host of other intermediaries, these mechanisms are largely toothless. Moreover—as has been argued above—in times of crisis they are likely to be set aside as the advantages of accommodating wealth and liquid intermediaries willing to serve as investors of last resort may well outweigh the potential costs associated with them.

It is my assertion that it may be time to reconsider the role of SWFs in the global economy and to adjust political and legal response strategies accordingly. To do so requires a better understanding of what motivates SWFs and whose interests they serve, and require closer inspection of the function of SWFs by their home regimes. If the argument made in this brief note is correct, the West should not fear control by most SWFs,[31] nor should it assure itself that SWFs are no different from private institutional investors. Instead, it may be more productive to recognize that SWFs pursue legitimate interests of their home government primarily to insure them against the fallout from future shocks and minimize their dependence on others. While one may want to object to the kind of regimes or elites SWFs serve—and indeed, it is noteworthy that most SWFs are housed in non-democratic regimes—it cannot be denied that the West has benefited from this insurance strategy as the recipient of cheap outside funding and bail out transactions throughout the financial crisis. Rather than seeking to control SWF investments in entities on their territory, the West needs to come to terms with the fact that the world has become both more diverse and interdependent. Diverse in the sense that convergence on a single model of Western capitalism appears to be much less likely after the global crisis than it appeared to commentators during the boom years[32]—which, as we now know, were unsustainable.

[30] Since CIC does not control any of the intermediaries it has selected, it can also avoid allegations of exerting control indirectly.

[31] This is not to say that some SWFs will not try to use their economic prowess to gain control—especially if they are sponsored by countries that have traditionally relied on control strategies for protecting their interests in the world.

[32] See, for example, H Hansmann and R Kraakman, 'The End of History for Corporate Law' (2001) 89 Georgetown L J 439, picking up on the theme first introduced by Francis Fukuyama in his *The End of History*, that the demise of socialism has confirmed the superiority of a single regime: the Anglo-Saxon model of capitalism.

And interdependent in the sense that the West has become highly dependent on other countries and their resources and can no longer dictate the terms of these mutually dependent relationships. SWFs are only one symptom of this growing interdependence. Fighting individual funds or specific investments they seek to make in domestic firms is unlikely to alter the more fundamental reconfiguration of global affairs.

PART IV

HOW TO OVERCOME ECONOMIC PROTECTIONISM?

14

The European Model Company Act (EMCA)—A New Way Forward

Paul Krüger Andersen

I. There is a need for alternative regulatory instruments

Despite the harmonization that has taken place in the field of company law by means of directives, etc, it is a fact that the state of law in this field is still substantially different across Member States. These differences are partly caused by different legal traditions in the Member States and partly because of different traditions and economic conditions in the national business environments. However, differences in regulation can also be used as a tool for economic protectionism.

The existing company law harmonization primarily concerns the regulation of public limited companies, while private limited companies are regulated nationally. Consequently, there are even larger differences among Member States' regulation in the latter area. Thus, some countries have implemented the EU directives on public limited companies also in the regulation of private limited companies. Other countries, eg the UK, have not. This situation has serious implications for cross-border issues.

Development and strengthening of the internal market and of an integrated European capital market depends on whether national company law can provide an efficient framework for business. This has become even more significant after the enlargement of the EU where modern and dynamic company law is essential if all the benefits of the enlargement are to be maximized. Therefore, an effective approach to regulation of companies will foster the efficiency and the competitiveness of European businesses.

In its 2003 Action Plan *Modernising Company Law and Enhancing Corporate Governance in the European Union—A Plan to Move Forward,*[1] the Commission raises questions concerning the overall aim for future priorities in relation to the regulation of companies as well as questions on the appropriate regulatory measures. These issues were addressed again in its 2006

[1] COM(2003) 284.

follow-up consultation.[2] Generally, the consultation process shows broad acceptance both of the Commission's reluctance to propose new legislation on an EU-level and of the plans on simplifying existing rules.[3] There is no doubt about the need to improve the Companies Acts of the Member States in order to make the most of the Internal Market and to ensure the competitiveness of European businesses. Consequently, alternative regulatory instruments are to be considered. The EMCA project aims at producing such an alternative approach.

II. The aims of the EMCA

The objective of the project is to bring about—on a solid scientific foundation—a new way forward for European company law. Therefore, inspired by the US Model Business Corporation Act, the aim of this project is to develop the European Model Company Act (EMCA). The EMCA will be designed as a free-standing general company statute that can be enacted substantially in its entirety by the Member States, or they may enact selected provisions of the Model Act. This approach differs from previous European company law initiatives as it is a general settlement of the debate on which of the two regulatory approaches is superior—regulatory competition or harmonization.

The EMCA will offer the Member States a harmonized company law, but leaves it to each Member State to decide whether it will offer its businesses the advantages given by harmonization. The major benefit from an integrated company law framework is that it establishes similar conditions for company shareholders and third parties all over the EU, thus facilitating cross-border investment and trading by ensuring shareholder rights and rebuilding investor confidence. However, at the same time the EMCA allows for special local considerations and for experimentation with new or different ideas, as Member States are free to opt out of parts of the Model Act in order to implement national company law innovations.

Allowing local considerations should not be seen as an opportunity for economic protection in Member States. Economic protection should not be considered best practice, neither according to EU law in general, nor in European company law. The EMCA is not a mandatory harmonization instrument, as the Member States are not bound to follow the Model Act. The EMCA can promote

[2] A Report summing up the findings of the consultation and the succeeding hearing can be found at <http://www.ec.europa.eu/internal_market/company/docs/consultation/final_report_en.pdf. >

[3] See the report from the Directorate General for Internal Market and Services: *Consultation on Future Priorities for the Action Plan on Modernising Company Law and Enhancing Corporate Governance in the European Union*. Eg 3 and 5.

regulatory competition,[4] but can also act as a tool for a harmonization of and convergence between the Member States' company law. Thus, the EMCA can be a tool for better regulation in the EU, as it will be a coherent, dynamic, and responsive European legislative framework. Member States can benefit from using the Model Act as a company law paradigm, as it will be a modern competitive Company Act. Moreover, it allows the Commission to take part in, or to support, a continuous modernization of the Model Act, without enforcing legislation on the Member States.

An EMCA, drafted and continuously further developed, may be able to respond more rapidly to the changing circumstances and market conditions that modern businesses face, such as the recent financial crisis. An EMCA may overcome some of the criticism of traditional law-making being inflexible, as it will offer a more informal and organic convergence of European company law.

III. The European Model Act Group

The implementation of the project is co-ordinated by the European Model Act Group, which was officially formed at a meeting at Aarhus School of Business, Aarhus University, which took place during September 2007. Since then more members have joined the Group and now it consists of prominent legal scholars from most of the Member States in the EU. The Group is independent of business organizations as well as Member States' governments and the European Commission. The EMCA does not have—nor is it intended to have—political authority. The impact depends on the quality of the EMCA. The European Commission has expressed its support for the project, and the Commission is invited to the meetings of the Group as observer and discussion partner. However, the Model Act will not be restricted by the present EU-regulation. Presently, the members of the group are:

- Professor Paul Krüger Andersen, Denmark
- Professor José Engrácia Antunes, Portugal
- Professor Theodor Baums, Germany
- Professor Blanaid Clarke, Ireland
- Professor Waltschin Daskalov, Bulgaria
- Professor Paul Davies, England
- Professor Guido Ferrarini, Italy
- Professor Susanne Kalss, Austria
- Professor András Kisfaludi, Hungary
- Professor Harm-Jan de Kluiver, The Netherlands

[4] See eg H Søndergaard Birkmose, *Konkurrence mellem retssystemer—Delaware-effekten i et europæisk selskabsretligt perspektiv* (Copenhagen: Thomson, 2004).

- Professor Isabelle Urbain-Parleani, France
- Professor Maria Patakyova, Slovakia
- Professor Evanghelos Perakis, Greece
- Professor Jarmila Porkoná, Czech Republic
- Professor André Prüm, Luxembourg
- Professor Juan Sanchez-Calero, Spain
- Professor Matti Sillanpää, Finland
- Professor Rolf Skog, Sweden
- Professor Stanislaw Soltysinski, Poland
- Professor Andres Vutt, Estonia
- Professor Hans de Wulf, Belgium

Associated company law experts:

- Professor Pierre-Henri Conac, Luxembourg
- Professor Ronald Gilson, USA
- Professor Isabelle Corbisier, Luxembourg
- Professor Rolf Doteval, Sweden
- Professor Joachin Hennrichs, Germany
- Professor Karsten Engsig Sørensen, Denmark.

Project researcher:

- Postdoc. Evelyne Beatrix Cleff, Denmark.

The members of the Group are recognized and experienced company law professors and at the same time have extensive experience in drafting company regulation at national level as well as at EU level. The work of the Group is co-ordinated by a chairman (Professor Paul Krüger Andersen from the Aarhus School of Business (ASB), University of Aarhus). ASB hosts the secretariat.[5]

IV. Theory and methodology

1. Legal theory on different legal tools for regulation

In its action plan, the European Commission calls for 'alternative tools for regulation', meaning alternatives to EU directives implemented in national Companies Acts. One alternative is soft law, such as corporate governance codes and other self-regulation measures. Usual Companies Acts and soft law are sources of law placed in the hierarchy of national sources of law.[6] Companies Acts as well as soft law are aimed at the authorities applying the law and at citizens (companies).

[5] Email: ebcl@asb.dk.

[6] See eg R Nielsen and C D Tvarnø, *Retskilder og Retsteorier* (2nd edn, Copenhagen: DJØF, 2008) 56.

Model acts are different. They may contain 'principles' in the way used in the DCFR,[7] meaning 'principles [...] intended to be applied as general rules (on contract law) in the European Union'. As such, principles can have a normative function in the Member States. The EMCA aims at containing basic principles of European company law, such as equal rights for shareholders, other rules on minority protection, principles on directors' duties of loyalty and care, and principles of creditor protection. Also a general principle about freedom of movement within Europe will be included. Further, the purpose and objects of the company will be defined.[8]

However, the EMCA also aims at containing a model for a full text Companies Act which could be used as a model for legislation in the Member States in the future. As said above, the aim is to save costs for the Member States and offer a tool for convergence of European company legislation and at the same time to show the way forward and how to deal with new developments in the economy, such as the recent financial crisis.

To clarify the theoretical basis and thereby the precise aim of the EMCA, a subproject will contain an elaboration on 'the European Model Company Act and the choice of regulatory method'.

2. Some fundamental problems and approaches

Analysing the company regulation in the Member States and developing the EMCA, some fundamental problems appear, and some approaches must be clearly defined. As a superior criterion for the choice of regulation method the project accepts that the EMCA shall improve the following elements, also accepted by the EU better regulation principles:[9]

- simplification of regulation
- flexibility of regulation
- reducing agency cost.

Dealing with national differences in company regulation and legal traditions, the analysis will take a functional approach, meaning that the starting point for the analysis is company problems regardless of whether, for example, a problem is dealt with in the national Companies Act or in the Insolvency Act.[10]

[7] Principles, Definitions and Model Rules of European Private Law, Draft Common Frame of Reference (DCFR), Interim Outline Edition, 2008, 8 f.

[8] Including the questions caused by the discussions on CRS—Corporate Social Responsibility—protection of the environment, etc. See for example the discussion in B Sjåfjell, *Towards a Sustainable European Company Law. A Normative Analysis of the Objective of EU Law, with the Takeover Directive as a Test Case* (Deventer: Kluwer, 2009).

[9] See COM(2006) 689.

[10] Take eg the directors' duty not to let a company continue business at a stage where it is foreseeable that the company cannot survive. In the UK this duty is regulated in the Insolvency Act s 214 (wrongful trading); in Denmark it is part of the Companies Act's Liability Rule.

In line with the principles on simplification, flexibility, and agency cost mentioned above, there are some necessary considerations on:

- the choice between mandatory and non-mandatory rules
- the use of disclosure rules versus substantive rules
- the choice between codes/self-regulation and substantive (Model Act) rules.

In general, the recent and general trend is that non-mandatory rules, disclosure rules, and codes/self-regulation are preferable, but it will be examined in detail in subprojects, how these general principles should be used in the EMCA. Among other things, it has to be taken into consideration in what way the recent financial crisis might alter the mentioned general view. For example, it has to be considered if the European Commission Recommendation on remuneration of directors of listed companies (2009/385/EC) should be implemented in Member States corporate governance codes or in the Companies Acts—and thus also in the EMCA.[11]

3. Use of comparative method

The most important method to be used in preparation of the EMCA is the comparative method. Since the members of the Model Act Group in practice have solid knowledge of the Companies Acts in every Member State, it is possible to use a combination of the *Länderbericht* method and the analytic method.[12]

The comparative process starts with questionnaires on each topic which will be summarized to give a general view of similarities, differences, new ways to deal with problems, and recent problems. At the same time, a collection of Companies Acts is established for specific analysis of problems and solutions. The analyses will be carried out by working groups representing more Member States (old/new Member States, common law/civil law countries, etc) together with ad hoc company law experts.

4. Use of law and economic theories

Over the last decade or two there has been a paradigm shift in European company law. In short form, the aim of company legislation/regulation has shifted from being exclusively creditor and shareholder protection to being economic

[11] See the Commission's Memo 09/213 on frequently asked questions. Among other things, the memo mentions that a recommendation allows Member States to take due account of national corporate governance traditions and practices and further that it is left to Member States, if they so wish, to extend all or some of the provisions introduced at national level to all or some categories of non-listed companies.

[12] See eg K Zweigert and H Kötz, *An introduction to comparative law* (3rd edn, Oxford: Oxford University Press, 1998) 32 and, in Danish, O Lando, *Kort indføring i komparativ ret* (3rd edn, Copenhagen: DJØF, 2008).

efficiency.[13] Use of economic theory and law and economy studies has been a natural part of the way to develop company regulation.[14] In particular, this applies to corporate governance, financing companies, and takeovers.

In a number of the areas regulated by the EMCA relevant economic theories as well as law and economy studies will be taken into account. For specific questions economic/law and economic experts will be invited to join the group as ad hoc experts. Furthermore, a subproject, carried out by a postdoc, will serve as the basis for the EMCA in that respect.

V. Comments on the Act

After each section, a description and explanation will be given of the content of the section. The existing EU regulation on each particular issue will be described, and where the Group agrees to deviate from the EU position, the rationale for doing so will be set out clearly in the Comments. The Comments will also identify and explain any differences in national rules among Member States.

VI. Expected impacts and output of the project

As said, we believe that the EMCA can be a tool for better regulation in the EU as it will prove to be a coherent, dynamic, and responsive European legislative framework. Member States can benefit from using the Model Act as a company law paradigm as it will be a modern and competitive Companies Act, and furthermore, it will be a low-cost, easy-to-use alternative to drafting national Companies Acts, not at least to the new Member States which can be brought up to a European standard. The individual Member States can also benefit from the comparative part of the project, because the project will make it possible for all Member States to take advantage of the experiences of the individual states and newest regulatory practices. The project will contribute to disseminating a standard of best practice throughout the Member States as well as fundamental principles of European company law.

An EMCA drafted and continuously developed by the European Model Company Act Group may be able to respond more rapidly to the changing circumstances and market conditions that modern businesses face. As mentioned above, the EMCA should consider the necessity of Companies Acts/company

[13] See eg P Krüger Andersen, *Aktie- og anpartsselskabsret* (10th edn, Copenhagen: DJØF, 2008) 37 f.

[14] See eg the Danish 'Debatoplæg om Aktivt Ejerskab' from 1999, drafted by the Ministry of Trade and Industry; and S Thomsen, *An Introduction to Corporate Governance* (Copenhagen: DJØF, 2008).

regulation in the light of the recent financial crisis. The drafts for each part of the EMCA will be published on a continuous basis on the website that has been established (and can be found at <http://www.asb.dk/EMCA>) and partly in leading international journals. Moreover, drafts will be sent to the EU Commission and to the governments of each Member State. An Article by Theodor Baums and Paul Krüger Andersen on the European Model Company Act Project, introducing the project to the international legal community, has been published in the ECGI working paper series as well as on SSRN.[15] The article has also been published in German (Theodor Baums/Paul Krüger Andersen, ILF Working Paper Series No. 78), in French (Theodor Baums, Revue des Sociétés, 2008), in Danish (Theodor Baums/Paul Krüger Andersen, NTS 2008:1), in Portuguese (José Antunes/Theodor Baums/Paul Krüger Andersen, O Direito 140 2008), in Greek (Evanghelos Perakis/Theodor Baums/Paul Krüger Andersen, ETOΣ 2008/12), in Polish (Stanislaw Soltysinski/Theodor Baums), and in Hungarian (András Kisfaludi/Theodor Baums). Further, the project has been and will be presented and discussed at more international conferences. Thus, the knowledge of the project is already widespread and discussions are going on among legal scholars.

Further comparative studies on special issues within the project—such as the study on the choice of regulatory method and on law and economic issues—will be published separately in internationally reviewed journals.

VII. Working plan and status

The project is expected to be carried out over a total period of five years (2007–2012) and will be concluded by the development of the first European Model Company Act. The project will be broken down into a number of subprojects based on the different areas of company law. Thus the project will cover all parts of company law, including issues pertaining to public as well as private companies (ie companies covered by the new Danish *Selskabsloven* from 2009 and similar company forms in other EU Member States). The first parts of the project focus on the following issues:

- general company law principles
- the formation of companies
- the duties of directors and the organization of companies (corporate governance issues).

The first drafts of these parts will be published in the autumn of 2010.

[15] ECGI Working Paper Series in Law 2008. The article was for a long period among the top ten downloaded articles and has at present been downloaded—in full or in part—more than 1,000 times which shows great international interest in the project.

After that follow subprojects on:

- shares
- shareholder meetings and protection (including minority protection)
- the financing of companies
- companies capital (capital protection)
- the re-organization of companies (mergers, divisions)
- liquidation, bankruptcy, etc
- liability of directors, shareholders, and others
- conflicts of law, cross-border issues
- employee representation
- groups of companies
- registrar and the registration process.

The approach to each subproject will be the same, and the result of the work of each subproject will be made public. Each subproject will open with an extensive comparative analysis of the existing company laws of the Member States in the given area. The comparative analysis will both consider the harmonization that has been carried out on EU level and include a study of how EU company law regulation has been implemented in each Member State. The analysis will also include studies on any special national legal and/or business conditions taking effect and which must be considered in particular.

Members of the Group will prepare national reports for the comparative study. The national reports will be summarized with a view to establishing trends and original solutions and establishing what EU law requires as a minimum standard in each area. The general report will serve as working material for the draft of (part of) the Model Act. Special working groups will be formed for drafting of parts of the Model Act. Postdocs and ad hoc company law experts will carry out research which supports the project. Furthermore, visiting professors at the ASB will carry out research which supports the project.

The Group meets biannually, and drafts will continuously be discussed and approved by the Group during these meetings. The progress of the Group will be published subsequent to the meetings. As stated above, the final aim of the process is a complete European Model Company Act covering all aspects of traditional company law. During the last year of the total project period, the Group will sum up the work on the subprojects, revise the published subresults and draw up the final Model Act.

During the drafting period it is our aim to generate research which discusses the different parts of the Model Act and some of the more fundamental issues such as the impact of model acts, the choice of regulatory methods, the law and economics of the suggested model acts, etc. For that purpose the Group will organize a number of international seminars and conferences. Once the first Model Act has been finalized, it is expected that the Group will continue as an organization to meet to review and offer proposed revisions to various parts of the Model Act.

VIII. The EMCA covers both private and public companies

The present EU regulation only covers some of the issues that are regulated in the Companies Acts of the Member States. Thus, for example, most of the problems related to company management structure and directors' duties are not covered by EU directives. The proposed Fifth Directive on company structure has been abandoned.[16] Like most of the other directives, the proposed Fifth Directive only dealt with public companies, and in general the EU harmonization directives leave the regulation of private companies to the Member States.

Some Member States, like Denmark, have decided to keep the regulation of private companies close to that of public companies. This especially applies to the mandatory rules that protect creditors and shareholders. In particular, as concerns the management structures of small and medium-sized companies (SMEs), there is a need for simple and flexible provisions. Such provisions can be freely implemented by the individual Member States. With its proposal for a Regulation on the Statute for a European private company (*Societas Privata Europaea*—SPE)[17] in 2008, the EU Commission has taken an initiative in the field of small and medium-sized companies. The SPE proposal creates a new European legal form which is intended to enhance the competitiveness of SMEs by facilitating their establishment and operation across the single market.

If the SPE Statute is adopted, the SPE will be an alternative to establishing and carrying on businesses by means of national companies. The proposals in the Statute are not limited by restrictions in the Company Law Directives. For example, the provisions on capital (minimum capital/distribution) do not need to follow the requirements in the Second Directive. The SPE Statute will thus put pressure on national lawmakers to establish company legislation that can match the SPE Statute. The recommendations of the EMCA are faced with the same challenge.

The Companies Acts of the EU Member States are divided into two categories—those governing public companies and those governing private companies (AG/GmbH/AS/ApS etc). The distinction is not based on the size of the company but on the fact that only in public companies shares can be offered to the public/be publicly traded.[18] Even though most small companies in fact choose the private company form, there are also some SMEs that are public companies.

[16] Proposal for a Fifth Directive on the coordination of safeguards which, for the protection of the interests of members and outsiders, are required by Member States of companies within the meaning of Article 59, second paragraph, with respect to company structure and to the power and responsibilities of company boards, (COM)1972 887 final. The proposal was officially withdrawn in 2001.

[17] COM(2008) 396 final.

[18] See the Danish Companies Act, para 5, Swedish Companies Act, Ch 12, para 7. The former Danish Act on private companies (*anpartsselskaber*) aimed at regulating companies with only a little capital and few members. The Danish White Paper on Modernising Company Law 1498:2008, 32 states that both the public company form and the private company form are used by small and

The EMCA will cover both private and public companies. Like the Companies Acts of the Member States, the EMCA will use the distinction referred to above between private and public companies. However, this will not exclude the possibility that in certain provisions the EMCA could apply the size of the company as a criterion. As for directors' duties, it seems to be possible to formulate provisions which can cover these duties in SMEs as well as in large companies.

IX. The EMCA uses a one-law model

1. Specific issues

The Model Law Group has started its work with these issues: 'general principles', 'formation of companies', and 'directors' duties'. The last is probably one of the most difficult issues as there is no EU regulation on fundamental questions and there are substantial differences and strong national traditions in the Member States. Compared to that the formation of companies is regulated by the First Directive (68/151/EC) amended by Directive 2003/58/EC.

All Member States have two company forms but the legislations differ. A number of Member States have a two-law system, like Germany which has implemented the *Aktiengesetz* and the *GmbH-Gesetz*. A growing number of Member States use a one-law model like the UK Companies Act. The Model Law Group has decided to use a one-law model. The EMCA will therefore contain regulation on three categories of companies:

(1) the private company;

(2) the public company; and

(3) the publicly traded company

Regarding publicly traded companies there is a borderline between securities regulation and company law. The EMCA will not deal with securities regulation in general, but since publicly traded companies are public companies, certain parts of the regulation are a natural part of Companies Acts. This is particularly the case concerning directors' duties and minority protection.

The structure of the EMCA follows a pyramidical concept. Thus, each chapter contains rules which are applicable to all companies. If certain rules only apply to private companies, this will be marked in each section of the EMCA. Rules which only apply to public traded companies will be stated as the last sections in each chapter.

medium-sized companies. The committee therefore decided not to use a distinction based on the criterion of size. See also the SPE proposal, Article 3(1)(d).

X. Formation of companies

Although management of the company is not regulated by EU directives, the First Company Directive (68/151/EEC amended by Directive 2003/58/EC) includes provisions on the protection of the interest of members and third parties that also apply to the formation of companies. The First Directive applies to both private and public companies. The Second Company Directive (77/91/EEC) co-ordinates provisions concerning the formation of public companies. The Directive has been amended by Directive 92/101/EEC and Directive 2006/68/EC. The latter deregulates the existing capital regime in different areas regarding the formation of companies. As mentioned above, the provisions stated in the Second Directive apply only to public companies. Thus, regarding private companies the EMCA is free to decide whether to adopt the provisions stated in the Second Directive. This is decided in each paragraph of the chapter on formation of companies.

This contribution only reports a few observations and recommendations from the first draft of the chapter on formation of companies of the EMCA. One major difference that can be found between the Member States concerns the registration process: the agency or person responsible for registration differs among Member States. In some Member States it is a judicial body whereas in other Member States it is a pure administrative procedure. In most Member States, however, there is a requirement to consult a notary. Where notaries or other independent experts are used, the EMCA recommends that there should not be a duplication of functions. For example, if there is a requirement in national law that a notary confirms a property valuation with real estate, the same requirement should not be imposed on the Registrar.

The amending First Company Directive (2003/58/EC) requires that tools must be available for online registration. Online registration is currently possible in the majority of Member States. In some Member States, such as Germany, Hungary, and Italy, this is a mandatory procedure. The EMCA recommends that online registration is mandatory but also recommends a system like the current Danish system where authorized persons, such as lawyers, auditors, or notaries are permitted to conduct online registrations.

Regarding companies' capital the EMCA follows the requirement to have a minimum capital. Section 18 of the draft chapter on formation of companies states that:

> Public companies and private companies must have a share capital. The share capital in public companies shall be at least €25,000 or the equivalent in any other currency (as stated in the Second Company Law Directive). Private companies decide about the amount of their share capital.

The international debate is characterized by critical views on the nominal value system. The majority of Member States allow companies the choice between nominal value of the shares and no-par value. The Model Law Group has agreed to adopt a system of real no-par-value shares, as implemented in Finland and which has been working well there since the Finnish company law reform in 2006.

XI. Directors' duties

The Model Law Group has not yet completed its work on directors' duties. Thus, this contribution only represents a personal view on the issues discussed. Further, this contribution only discusses some fundamental questions. Many problems, for example on directors' liability, have been left out until now. The first draft on directors' liability will be made in the autumn of 2010.

1. One-tier and two-tier systems—or something in between

It is a well-known fact that there are two main systems for board structures: the UK one-tier system, with a single management body consisting of the board of directors, and the German two-tier system with a management body (*Vorstand*) and a supervisory body (*Aufsichtsrat*). With respect to public companies, a number of EU Member States have German-inspired management structures, for example Austria, Poland, and Slovakia. The UK system is followed by Greece, Ireland, Luxembourg, and Spain.

A growing number of states have optional one- or two-tier systems for public companies. This is the case in Belgium, Bulgaria, Finland, France, Italy, Portugal and, lately, in Denmark.[19] In small companies (private companies etc) the majority of EU Member States follow the UK one-tier system, but some countries, including Austria, the Czech Republic, Denmark, Germany, Latvia, Lithuania, and Poland allow such companies to form a supervisory board. In a number of countries, such as Austria, Germany, Hungary, Italy, and Poland, a two-tier structure is mandatory under certain circumstances, for example with regard to the number of employees, share capital, or the number of shareholders.[20]

In the German two-tier system there is a sharp distinction between the functions of the management board and of the supervisory board. However, some countries, such as the Nordic countries, have systems which fall in between the one-tier and two-tier systems. For instance, the supervisory board in the traditional Danish system[21] must not only supervise the management board, but can also make day-to-day decisions if it sees fit.

[19] A new Danish Companies Act (which has not yet come into force) was passed by the Danish Parliament (*Folketinget*) on 29 May 2009.

[20] For instance, Danish private companies (*anpartsselskaber*) with employee representation must have a two-tier board structure pursuant to the Danish Companies Act, para 111(3).

[21] According to the new Danish Companies Act, para 111(1)(1)a *capital company* (the collective name for public companies and private companies) can still choose the traditional Danish system.

A picture is emerging showing a softening of the two main systems, with more and more countries giving freedom of choice between different management structures, recognizing that there is no empirical evidence that one system is better than the other.[22] The EMCA must respect these differences. We cannot make a model act with only one model for the management of a company. In the model act the provisions on directors' duties must deal with the systems that exist in the EU Member States.

The directors' duties must correspond to the legal basis of the corporate bodies. When, for instance, paragraphs 115-119 of the new Danish Companies Act describe the management duties of the supervisory board and the board respectively, this description of duties acts simultaneously as a basis for the evaluation and regulation of issues relating to directors' liability and conflicts of interest etc. So, according to the new Danish Companies Act, if a Danish company changes the board structure to a two-tier structure like the German model, this will change the evaluation of the liability of the supervisory board. Likewise, if the supervisory board is not involved in day-to-day business decisions, there will be fewer conflicts of interest at this level.

2. Division of work of managing directors and supervisory boards

As stated, there are some differences within two-tier systems:

Model 1: The management of the company lies exclusively with the management board. The supervisory board must (only) supervise the management of the company.

Model 2: The supervisory board can (also) give instructions to the management board on day-to-day management and decisions, and for certain important business transactions approval by the supervisory board is required.[23]

There is no evidence that requires the EMCA to prefer either model 1 or model 2. There are pros and cons for each model. There are two basic arguments. The traditional argument is about whether the supervisory board can exercise effective control of the management board. The second argument concerns corporate governance and the best management system. Both arguments lead towards a (degree of) separation of duties and a prohibition of overlap of personnel. Other views may also be relevant. If, for example, provisions on employee representation

A public company can also choose a two-tier structure (like the German model), ie a management board and a supervisory board with personal and functional separation. A private company can choose to be managed by a management board only.

[22] See Danish White Paper No 1498:2008, 291–4.

[23] See the Danish Companies Act, para 117, and the Swedish Companies Act, Ch 8, paras 4 and 29.

at supervisory board level are mandatory, which is the case in Denmark, Germany, and Sweden, the employees will have a different position, depending on whether they are on a supervisory board of the model 1 type (Germany) or of the model 2 type (Denmark and Sweden). For the moment, it is not possible to say how many Danish SMEs will choose model 1.

3. May the same person be a managing director and a member of the supervisory board?

A main purpose of the supervisory board is to control the management. An overlap of personnel between the management board and the supervisory board will undermine this control function. Some Member States have taken the full consequences of this and have completely banned overlapping personnel (Austria, Bulgaria, Finland, France, Germany, Italy, and Portugal among others). Other countries (Denmark and Sweden) only have partial bans.[24]

In a one-tier structure the problem of control can be solved by distinguishing between executive and non-executive directors. This is the case in Greece, in the UK, and in Ireland (in listed companies). A prerequisite for this, of course, is that the board must consist of more than one member, which need not always be the case, for example in Danish and Swedish private companies (see footnote 23). Nor does the proposal for the SPE Statute require this.

The reason for allowing small companies to have simpler board structures is the need for flexibility and for avoiding burdensome costs. One consequence of this, however, is the increased risk of conflicts of interest and minority problems. The EMCA should consider whether special provisions are needed to protect minorities in small companies in these areas.

In my opinion, the provisions for avoiding conflicts of interest and minority problems should be mandatory and should be included in the EMCA for SMEs as well as for larger companies.

[24] Danish Companies Act, para 111(1): The majority of the board members of public companies must be individuals who are not executive directors of the company. An executive director of a public company cannot be a chairman or a deputy chairman of the board of the public company. If the capital company chooses to be managed by a management board, the public company must have a supervisory board to supervise the management board. A member of the management board cannot be a member of the supervisory board; see para 111(2). A private company can choose to have only a single board with one or more members. According to the Swedish Companies Act, Ch 8, paras 1 and 50, there must be a two-tier management consisting of a board of directors and a managing director in public companies (*publika bolag*). In a public company, the chairman of the board of directors may not be the managing director of the company; see para 49. Swedish private companies (*privata bolag*) only need a single board with one or more members; see Companies Act, Ch 8, para 1.

4. Decision-making by the board

There are substantial differences between the Member States, both in terms of where to find the provisions on decisions by the management and in terms of the content of the provisions. In most countries the basic provisions are found in the relevant Companies Act. For instance, this is the case in Austria, Bulgaria, Denmark, Finland, France, Germany, Greece, Hungary, Poland, Portugal, and Sweden. Usually, supplementary provisions can be stipulated in the articles of association, in rules of conduct for the board,[25] or in similar internal rules of the company.[26] In the UK Companies Act, model articles set out a set of provisions for decision-making by the directors. These are not mandatory rules, however.

The proposal for the SPE Statute does not contain any specific provisions on how the management must make decisions. As mentioned above, the proposal offers a high degree of freedom in determining the internal organization of the SPE. Thus, the articles of association must determine the management structure, whether a single director or several directors, a one-tier or a two-tier board system, etc. Furthermore, the articles of association must regulate the composition and organization of the board and, if the SPE has a supervisory board, its composition, organization, and relationship with the management board.

The founders of an SPE will probably choose national rules as a starting point when working out the precise provisions on management bodies. If, for instance, a Danish company is transformed into an SPE, the provisions in paragraphs 122–126 of the Danish Companies Act on the election of the chairman and the holding of meetings by the management board or the supervisory board can be transferred to the articles of association of the SPE. Thus, the very different national provisions on management structure and decision-making may result in considerable structural differences between SPEs.

The European Model Companies Act will contribute to compensating for (the needless) differences between the national Companies Acts with regard to the structure of corporate bodies, among other things. However, some important differences will continue to exist in the Member States. By implementing what the Model Law Group considers best practice, the EMCA could also become a model for the provisions to be included in the articles of association of an SPE.

5. General duties of directors

The national Companies Acts contain a wide range of special duties to be discharged by the various management bodies. For instance, paragraphs 115–117

[25] See eg the Danish Companies Act, para 130 (Rules of conduct of the Board and the Supervisory Board).

[26] See the Swedish Companies Act, Ch 8, para 6 (Rules of procedure governing the work of the Board of Directors) and para 7 (Allocation of work between company organs).

of the new Danish Companies Act emphasize that the management board/ supervisory board or the management must ensure that the required procedures for risk management and internal controls exist. Until now, special rules on risk management have (only) been included in the Danish corporate governance code for companies listed on the stock exchange, but these have now been included in legislation—in the light of the current financial crisis and various business scandals. Also in the light of a previous business scandal (the *Nordisk Fjer case*), the Danish Companies Act (paragraphs 115–117) includes a special duty to ensure that a capital company always has adequate capital resources. The concept of capital resources refers to both liquidity and net capital.

Pursuant to the new Danish Act, these requirements apply to both public and private companies, but what is specifically required by the provisions will depend on the size and structure of the company.

The Swedish Companies Act, Chapter 8, paragraph 4, and the Finnish Companies Act, Chapter 6, paragraph 2, have retained only more general provisions on directors' duties. The Finnish provision—which is almost identical to the Swedish provision—states that 'the board of directors shall be responsible for the appropriate arrangement of the control of the company accounts and finances'. The explanatory notes on the Finnish provision are relevant for a model act which embraces both public and private companies (as do the Swedish and the Finnish Acts). Thus, the explanatory notes state that the circumstances may favour a general definition if there are large variations in companies and their areas of activity, which means that the duties of the directors cannot be defined precisely. Further to this, the duties of the management will change over time, which speaks in favour of a general definition.[27]

The Model Law Group will consider which specific duties should be included in the EMCA. Here it should be considered that a company can include specific provisions on how to deal with different matters in the rules of conduct for its board or in its articles of association, and supplementary provisions are continuously being developed in corporate governance codes. Modern company law thinking has focused much on corporate governance. Good corporate governance depends on the board structure as well as on how directors fulfil their duties. Modern Companies Acts are more flexible with regard to the board structure. It is more and more up to the company itself to choose the company's board structure, keeping the best balance between a simple board structure and boards with strictly separated functions and without an overlap of personnel. Thus, the EMCA should not favour one model—neither for SMEs nor for larger companies.

As for the duties of directors, two questions arise: one is whether provisions relating to corporate governance should be mandatory, and the other is which provisions should be included in the EMCA and which should be included in soft law regulations, such as corporate governance codes.

[27] RP 109/1005 rd, 80.

The answer to the first question should—in my opinion—be that the EMCA should include basic corporate governance provisions with some fundamental corporate governance principles. The aim of such principles would be to ensure that the directors run the company economically and efficiently. These principles should be mandatory and should ensure that the directors make well-informed decisions and that the directors focus on the most important business questions. To be sure that the directors are aware of their duties and, especially for SMEs, to help the directors, the EMCA could set up a list of mandatory provisions which should be included in the rules of conduct for the board.

The corporate governance codes include a number of provisions which should only be considered by the company as an incentive for good corporate governance. Also, corporate governance can spot critical areas that, at a later stage, should be regulated by company legislation. The new Danish provisions on risk management referred to above are an example of this.

In any event, the EMCA should include provisions on a series of fundamental issues, including those discussed in the following.

Duty of care/Duty of loyalty

In most EU Member States, the Companies Acts or general principles of company law (Austria, Denmark, Germany, Poland, and Sweden) contain general rules on the duty to demonstrate care with regard to the company and to act in the interests of the company (meaning a duty of loyalty/fiduciary duty, see below). Article 31(1) of the proposal for the SPE Statute phrases this in a way which will probably cover most countries. The proposal states as follows: 'A director shall have a duty to act in the best interest of the SPE. He shall act with the care and skill that can reasonably be required in the conduct of business.' Using the wording of the Finnish Companies Act, Chapter 1, paragraph 8, the EMCA could express it even more briefly: 'The Management of the company shall act with care and promote the interest of the company.' Alternatively, the duty of care principle should be based on the UK principle in the Companies Act, section 174, on the 'duty to exercise reasonable care, skill and diligence'.

The duty of loyalty means that the directors have a duty to act in the interest of the company. This principle is expressed both in the proposal for the SPE Statute and in the Finnish Companies Act quoted above. However, that leaves open to discussion what 'the interest of the company' is. If, like the proposal for the SPE Statute, the EMCA chooses this short wording, it will be up to each Member State to define what it means by 'the interest of the company'. The UK version of the duty of loyalty can be found in the Companies Act, section 172, 'Duty to promote the success of the company'. The UK version is an answer to the shareholder/stakeholder view discussion: the duty of loyalty is a duty to maximize the interests of the shareholders having regard to other considerations.

Different things have been taken into account in section 172—for example the impact of the operation of the company on the community and the environment (corporate social responsibility, CSR). CSR is a developing area of the law. The Model Law Group will consider whether CSR should be included in the EMCA or perhaps left for the national corporate governance codes to deal with. A shorter version of the UK rule could be:

> The directors of a company must act in the way they consider, in good faith, would be most likely to promote the success of the company for the benefit of its shareholders as a whole. In doing so, they should take into account the interest of creditors, suppliers, customers and employees.

In choosing this concept, the explanatory comments to the EMCA should give examples and explanations on the application of the provision.[28]

Duty to avoid conflicts of interest

The EMCA must include provisions to deal with conflicts of interest between the management and the company. A general provision on the duty of loyalty can be considered a sort of general clause that can—and must—be supplemented by provisions on typical cases of conflicts of interest. None of the Nordic countries have a general provision on how to handle conflicts of interest, but only a provision concerning disqualification in connection with certain decisions of the management.

In my opinion, the EMCA should include a general provision on conflicts of interest. The inspiration for such a provision can be found in section 175 of the UK Companies Act which, under the heading 'Duty to avoid conflicts of interest' stipulates: 'A director of a company must avoid a situation in which he has, or can have, a direct or indirect interest that conflicts, or possibly may conflict, with the interests of the company.' A largely identical provision is found in the proposal for the SPE Statute, Article 34(3).

As opposed to the UK provision, the proposal for the SPE Statute only includes this general statement. The UK provision is partly supplemented by a special ban on the exploitation of the corporate opportunities of the company (section 175(2)). The Model Law Group is considering whether a special provision on corporate opportunities should be included in the EMCA. The problem with corporate opportunities relates to the problem of a director competing with the company. The UK Companies Act does not have any specific provision for this. Nor can such a provision be found in the Companies Acts of the Nordic countries. An explicit provision prohibiting competition—without the permission of the general meeting—can be found in the Greek Companies Act, paragraph 23.

[28] Like the US Model Business Corporation Act, the provisions in the EMCA will be supplemented by comments and explanations on existing EU regulations, regulations in Companies Acts of the Member States, etc.

Similarly, the EMCA could state: 'A director cannot carry on a competing activity or be a manager or a director of a competing company without prior approval of the company.'

The regulation of conflicts of interest in the EMCA should build on a combination of openness (transparency) and consent from the board of directors/the general meeting. Thus, the UK Companies Act, section 177, contains a provision stipulating a 'duty to declare interest in proposed transaction or arrangement', and section 175 includes a provision on authorization by the directors.

The Nordic provisions on conflicts of interest only partly cover the conflicts that arise. First of all, they only describe exclusion from participation in decisions made by management bodies (management board or supervisory board). They only concern certain decisions; pursuant to the Danish Companies Act, paragraph 131, only agreements between the company and the person in question and lawsuits brought against that person are covered. The provisions do not ensure the required transparency with regard to whether there is a conflict of interest or not. The provisions of the EMCA should cover a wide range of issues and be more principle-based.

The UK Companies Act, section 177, deals with the subject of self-dealing transactions. According to section 177, a director must declare the nature and extent of his interest to the other directors. However, there are several deviations from this; section 188 ff mentions four situations, where a director must obtain shareholder approval. A procedure for the regulation of self-dealing transactions should be included in the EMCA. Four possible solutions can be discussed:

(1) disclosure to the board;
(2) approval by the shareholders;
(3) written agreement (as in the Twelfth Company Law Directive); and
(4) court approval.

As stated above, disclosure to the board should be the starting point in all self-dealing transactions. This should be the case for executive as well as non-executive directors and this could also work in a two-tier system. Further, it should be made clear which cases require approval from the shareholder(s). Thus, the four situations mentioned in the UK Companies Act, section 188 should be considered. These are:

(1) substantial property transactions;
(2) loans and quasi-loans to directors;
(3) directors' long-term service contracts; and
(4) credit transactions.

In cases where shareholder approval must be obtained, the interested party/parties should not be allowed to vote. This is contrary to the Danish Companies

Act, paragraph 86, on conflicts of interest at the general meeting. This provision only covers lawsuits. In Denmark other conflicts must be evaluated according to the provisions on minority protection. The EMCA should not contain a specific provision on court decisions in connection with conflicts of interest, but it should include general provisions to the effect that the decision of the general meeting can be questioned in the courts.

6. To whom are the duties owed?

An important question is to whom the directors' duties are owed. The questionnaire shows that there are substantial differences between the EU Member States as to where to find the answer, as to whom the duties are owed, and who can enforce the duties. As stated above, the question of enforcement is not dealt with in this contribution.

In many states, company law is considered to be part of general civil law. Thus, the duties in the Companies Acts may be supplemented by general civil law duties. For example, this is the case in Italy and Poland. A Danish example is the provisions on representation and signature in the Companies Act, paragraphs 135 and 136, which are supplemented by the provisions on representation in the Danish Contracts Act. Danish cases also show that the specific liability provisions of the Companies Act may be supplemented by principles from the law of tort.

The EMCA must carefully examine the areas in which civil law supplements the provisions in the existing Companies Acts. In most cases claims for damages under the law of contract or the law of tort will be the issue. How the EMCA should deal with this problem also depends on whether and how the EMCA chooses to have a special provision regarding to whom the duties are owed. The simplest solution would be a provision stipulating that 'the duties of directors shall be owed to the company'. The proposed SPE Statute, Article 31(2), has chosen this solution. Related to this provision, Article 31(4) of the Statute states that 'a director of the SPE shall be liable to the company for any act or omission in breach of his duties . . . which causes loss or damage to the SPE'. Further, Article 31(5) states that 'without prejudice to the provisions of this Regulation, the liability of directors shall be governed by the applicable national law'.

The SPE approach leaves a lot of questions open. Among them are, whether the duties are owed to the shareholders in general (which could be marked by adding the words 'as a whole') or also to individual shareholders. In some Member States a duty to the company does not mean a duty to individual members (for example Belgium). In the UK and Ireland, the fiduciary duties are owed to the company as a whole and not to individual shareholders, but in exceptional cases the courts have also recognized a duty directly to individual shareholders. Individual members are protected directly according to the Danish Companies Act, paragraph 376.

The greatest problem probably concerns duties towards creditors. According to the proposed SPE Statute, this is governed by national law. The EMCA cannot use this solution when giving recommendations to national legislators. In general, creditors only have a specific interest in the company in the event of insolvency or near insolvency. In the UK the wrongful trading provisions of the Insolvency Act 1986 make directors liable to the creditors in situations where the directors knew or ought to have known that there was no reasonable prospect that the company would avoid going into insolvent liquidation. The provision is consistent with the principle that duties are only owed to the company, since only the liquidator can enforce the wrongful trading provision. There is a very similar provision to the UK provision in Denmark, but it is based on the liability provisions of the Danish Companies Act. Thus, the creditors are directly protected by paragraph 376 of the Danish Companies Act.

The Model Law Group has agreed that the Model Act should take a functional approach. An analysis of directors' duties should take into account the existing duties in the various Member States and whether the duties are based on provisions in the national Companies Acts, Insolvency Acts or on civil liability rules. The Model Law Group will consider how the EMCA can best deal with this problem.

XII. Some preliminary conclusions

As stated, the first drafts of chapters of the EMCA concern general principles, formation of companies, and directors' duties. The chapter on general principles is not a final draft, but will be revised in the ongoing process of drafting the various chapters.

The chapter on formation follows in many details the provisions in the (amended) First and Second Directive and the current international discussions. However, the chapter also contains important new recommendations, for example on the function of the Registrar and on the registration process (online registration) as well as on the companies' capital (real no par value system).

The questionnaire on directors' duties in EU Member States shows that there are substantial differences, but—taking a functional approach—also many similarities. As said, our aim is to make a European Model Companies Act that expresses European best practice. The EMCA should learn from how the different Member States make their laws, for example how detailed the EMCA should be and how to manage the connection between the Companies Acts and the principles of civil law.

In contrast to other areas where there are mandatory EU directives, there are few EU limitations on the EMCA regarding directors' duties. A preliminary observation is that the sharp distinction between the one-tier system and the two-tier system is gradually disappearing. There is no empirical evidence that one system functions better than the other.[29] Still more countries are introducing freedom of choice between more systems of management or have systems that in one or several respects are distinct from the pure one-tier or two-tier system.

The EMCA should follow this trend. The EMCA should not unilaterally recommend a one-tier or a two-tier system. This means that the provisions of the EMCA on directors' duties must relate to how the company's board structure has been determined by the company itself or by national law. Irrespective of the management system chosen, a number of general provisions on directors' duties can be drawn up.

There seems to be widespread agreement that rules should apply to a director's duty of care. Most Member States also recognize that directors have a duty of loyalty, but the principle is not always expressed in the Companies Acts. It has not been decided yet, but in my opinion, the EMCA should confirm that directors have a duty of loyalty. The Model Law Group will decide whether the EMCA should add specific provisions to a general provision, for example about wrongful trading. The question of to whom these duties are owed is answered rather differently in the various Member States. This is also the case regarding the question of how to deal with conflicts of interest and some other provisions on directors' duties which are not mentioned in this article.

Compromise is necessary in negotiations aimed at drafting national legislation and in matters of EU regulation. Of course, this does not always lead to optimal solutions. Discussions and decisions of the Model Law Group aim at 'learning by experience' from the solutions of the Member States. The ambition is not to draft an EMCA compromise in such a way that everyone can agree to every detail. Using the expertise of the members of the Model Law Group, we also want to show the way forward.

[29] See eg the Danish White Paper on Modernising Company Law 1498:2008, 291–4.

15

The Role of European Regulation and Model Acts in Company Law

Jennifer Payne

I. Introduction

The European Model Company Act (EMCA) project described by Paul Krüger Andersen in his paper raises interesting issues about the nature and role of company law harmonization within Europe. To date, European regulation of company law has largely been in the form of mandatory harmonization measures via a series of company law directives. The EMCA project offers an alternative form of harmonization. The idea behind a Model Company Act is to provide a model set of company law provisions which Member States can then adopt. A Model Company Act functions to provide uniformity of the laws governing companies from state to state. The aim of the EMCA is to provide an 'integrated company law framework' which would establish 'similar conditions for company shareholders and third parties all over the EU, thus facilitating cross-border investment and trading by ensuring shareholder rights and rebuilding investor confidence'.[1] The idea is to offer Member States a harmonized company law, but to allow them opt out of some or all of the provisions of the EMCA.

In order to evaluate the EMCA project, it is first useful to consider the role that European regulation plays in company law generally. This role has been dominated by the EU to date and will be discussed in the next section. Although EU harmonization has been mandatory, and has largely been confined to publicly listed companies, and therefore is not on all fours with the EMCA project, a consideration of these issues nevertheless raises important considerations for that project. The nature and benefit of the EMCA project will then be discussed in Section III.

[1] See Paul Krüger Andersen's paper in ch 14 of this volume, p 304.

II. EU regulation of company law

Almost from its inception the European Community regarded mandatory harmonization of the company laws of the Member States as an important goal.[2] This was closely linked to the idea of freedom of establishment. The role of harmonization was to allow companies based in one Member State to penetrate more easily into the economies of other Member States without necessarily having to establish a subsidiary in those states. The EC Treaty and its replacement permits the Council of Ministers to adopt directives which aim to protect the interests of members and others (primarily creditors) by 'co-ordinating to the necessary extent the safeguards which ... are required by Member States of companies or firms ... with a view to making such safeguards equivalent throughout the Union'.[3] From the late 1960s to the late 1980s nine company law directives were adopted.[4] After this 'golden age' company law harmonization at EU level slowed down considerably. Indeed, during the 1990s there was little, if any, progress made in this context. In large part this was due to the difficulty of reaching agreement on some of the more controversial proposed harmonization measures. For example, the proposed Fifth Directive[5] was never adopted as a result of the difficulty of harmonizing board structure (should a one-tier or two-tier structure be adopted?) and the issue of whether employee representation on the board should be mandatory. However, some of this slowdown may also have been due to increasing concerns about the role of mandatory company law rules in this period.

Such was the level of uncertainty about the direction of EU company law harmonization by 2001 that the Commission appointed a High Level Group of Experts to provide recommendations for a modern European company law

[2] G Wolff, 'The Commission's Programme for Company Law Harmonisation' in M Andenas and S Kenyon-Slade (eds), *EC Financial Market Regulation and Company Law* (London: Sweet & Maxwell, 1993) 19.

[3] Article 50 TFEU (ex- Article 44(2)(g) EC). The Council of Ministers are permitted to adopt directives by qualified majority vote, on a proposal from the European Commission and under the joint decision-making procedure with the European Parliament: Article 251 EC/Article 294 TFEU.

[4] First Company Law Directive (safeguards for third parties) Council Directive 68/151, [1968] OJ L65/8; Second Company Law Directive (formation of public companies and the maintenance and alteration of capital) Council Directive 77/91, [1977] OJ L26/1; Third Company Law Directive (mergers of public companies) Council Directive 78/855 [1978] OJ L295/36; Fourth Company Law Directive (accounts) Council Directive 78/660, [1978] OJ L222/11; Sixth Company Law Directive (division of public companies) Council Directive 82/891, [1982] OJ L378/47; Seventh Company Law Directive (group accounts) Council Directive 83/349, [1983] OJ L193/1; Eighth Company Law Directive (audits) Council Directive 84/253, [1984] OJ L126/20; Eleventh Company Law Directive (branches) Council Directive 89/666, [1989] OJ L395/36; Twelfth Company Law Directive (single-member companies) Council Directive 89/667, [1989] OJ L395/40.

[5] (Draft) Fifth Company Law Directive [1972] OJ C13/49 (although this initial draft has been revised significantly subsequently).

framework. Following the Final Report of this Group,[6] the Commission put in place an Action Plan for company law.[7] This has effected a significant change of direction for the role of the EU in company law harmonization. Instead of the primary purpose of harmonization being the protection of members and creditors, the focus has shifted to providing 'a legal framework for those who wish to undertake business activities efficiently, in a way they consider best suited to attain success'.[8]

As a result, the EU's harmonization programme has moved away from a focus on domestic company law. The Commission has recently dropped its proposals for a mandatory 'one share/one vote' rule, following an empirical investigation which found that the case for reform was unclear.[9] In addition, it is possible that there will be a retreat from some of the company law directives that are already in place. There has already been a small retreat from the legal capital requirements of the Second Directive.[10] However, in a document published in July 2007 the Commission seems to contemplate more radical reform of a number of existing company law directives.[11] The Commission put forward two different possible models for how to proceed with a number of company law directives, one of which would involve a dismantling of those directives so that the remit of EU regulation in those areas 'should be reduced to those legal acts specifically dealing with cross-border problems'. As Charlie McCreevy, former European Commissioner for the Internal Market and Services has said:

> I know that not everyone in the EU agrees with the idea of repealing directives in the area of company law. However, if we want to be serious about making real progress, we cannot accept any taboos. In my view, we need to ask the question whether there is a need for Community rules on domestic mergers and domestic divisions, and whether the EU would not do better to focus on cross-border situations.... Even if the result of our considerations is that these directives still serve a legitimate purpose, I really wonder whether the EU needs to go into the level of detail that some of the company law

6 *Final Report of the High Level Group of Company Law Experts on a Modern Regulatory Framework of Company Law in Europe* (Brussels: 4 November 2002) ('Final Report').

7 Communication from the Commission to the Council and the European Parliament COM(2003) 284, 21 May 2003.

8 Final Report, Ch II.1.

9 Shearman and Sterling, *ISS and ECGI, Report of the Proportionality Principle in the European Union* (May 2007) (report commissioned by the European Commission). See WG Ringe, 'Deviations from Ownership-Control Proportionality—Economic Protectionism Revisited' ch 10 of this volume, p 209.

10 Directive 2006/68/EC of 6 September 2006 amending Council Directive 77/91/EEC as regards the formation of public limited liability companies and the maintenance and alteration of their capital. Adoption of the amendment of the Second Company Law Directive (July 2006) available at <http://ec.europa.eu/internal_market/company/capital/index_en.htm>. This followed on from a report of the High Level Group of Company Law Experts, *A Modern Regulatory Framework for Company Law in Europe* ('Winter Group, *Report*') ch IV.

11 Communication from the commission on a simplified business environment for companies in the areas of company law, accounting and auditing, COM(2007) 394 final, 10 July 2007.

directives currently contain In my view we must ensure the 'less is more' principle is applied in practice.[12]

The other approach put forward by the Commission is a move away from detailed directives for company law and towards more principles-based drafting, which would allow Member States more latitude in adapting those principles to their own national situation. Whichever model is adopted, the Commission seems to accept the need for a reduction of EU regulation of domestic company law issues. This is based on a consideration of the costs that company law harmonization measures currently entail[13] and an appreciation that a rigid, harmonized European framework might sometimes appear to be more of an impediment to innovation than a benefit for the Internal Market.[14] When dealing with sensitive issues of company law, such as board structure and directors' remuneration, the approach of the EU more recently has not been to engage in mandatory rule-making, via directives, but to make use of non-binding recommendations.[15]

However, the Commission has not backed away from harmonizing company law issues entirely. Instead, its focus has shifted to those areas of company law where it has a particular legislative advantage, principally in relation to cross-border corporate issues. The Cross Border Mergers Directive[16] and the Shareholder Rights Directive[17] are good examples of this development. The Commission has also shifted its attention to the harmonization of securities law, and to the creation of a single financial market for Europe.[18]

This is the correct approach. Regulation comes at a cost, to the companies themselves and to the EU generally if the regulation makes Europe uncompetitive in the global market. It therefore needs to be justified. Harmonized disclosure requirements for publicly listed companies, for example, can be justified

[12] Speech on 'Simplification of the business environment for companies at Public event on Better Regulation/Simplification of Company Law' with the Portuguese Ministry of Justice, Lisbon, 13 September 2007.

[13] The Commission has also started to measure the administrative burdens in company law throughout the EU: Commission Working Document of 14 November 2006 COM(2006) 690 final.

[14] Ibid.

[15] Eg Commission Recommendation of 15 February 2005 on the role of non-executive or supervisory directors of listed companies and on committees of the (supervisory) board, [2005] OJ L52/51; Commission Recommendation of 14 December 2004 fostering an appropriate regime for the remuneration of directors of listed companies, [2004] OJ L385/55. Recommendations have no binding force (Article 249 EC/Articles 288–292 and Section 2 TFEU).

[16] Directive 2005/56/EC, [2005] OJ L310/1.

[17] Directive 2007/36/EC, [2007] OJ L184/17. Although this Directive confers minimum rights on all shareholders, the aim of the Directive is to deal with the difficulties where a shareholder in Member State A wants to exercise his voting rights in a company incorporated in Member State B. The fact that the Directive is limited to companies with publicly traded shares is evidence of the cross-border focus of this Directive.

[18] See Financial Services, Implementing the framework for Financial Markets: Action Plan, COM(1999) 232, 11 May 1999. Following this Action Plan a large number of directives in the area of securities regulation have been introduced eg Takeover Directive 2004/25/EC; Market Abuse Directive 2003/6/EC; Prospectus Directive 2003/71/EC; Markets in Financial Instruments Directive (MiFID) Directive 2004/39/EC.

because of the strong investor protection they promote. There are also significant co-ordination and standardization advantages to mandatory harmonization in this area.

Mandatory harmonization of company law at European level does not seem to be a sensible or helpful way forward, unless there is a significant cross-border issue in place. In this regard the EMCA project is preferable, since the harmonization it proposes would not be mandatory for Member States. However, the retreat of the Commission from domestic company law issues also raises difficulties for the EMCA model. It has become clear that the Commission is not in principle better equipped to identify an appropriate system of company law than Member States, given that national contexts differ so substantially, unless there is a strong cross-border element. Equally, it is unclear why any other organization, such as the European Model Company Act Group, is in a better position than Member States to do so. Of course, it is open to Member States simply to ignore any EMCA that is produced, but if this is the outcome it will surely call into question the value of the project. One of the reasons for the EU moving away from the mandatory harmonization of company law during the 1990s was an increasing concern about the role of mandatory rules. This issue is not faced by the EMCA project. However, the other, and arguably the dominant, reason was the difficulty of reaching agreement on some of the more controversial harmonization measures, such as board structure, where Member States have very different views as to what is appropriate. The EMCA project will have to tackle just these same issues and will face just these same difficulties. This is discussed in the next section.

III. The role of Model Company Acts

When considering the potential role of the EMCA, it is instructive to compare it with its US equivalent, which provided inspiration for the EMCA project. What would later become the US Model Business Corporations Act (US MBCA) began in 1928 as a document entitled the 'Uniform Business Corporation Act'. This act was adopted by only three states and partially adopted by a fourth. The current US MBCA emerged in 1950 when the American Bar Association set out its version of a uniform business code.[19] This act has been constantly reviewed and revised, and has now been adopted in some form or another by more than 24 states. While more than half of the states in the US therefore use some version of the US MBCA, many states also use some form of the Delaware General Corporation Law, which can be seen as the major 'competitor' to the US MBCA.

[19] American Bar Association, Model Business Corporation Act, 4th edn (2008), adopted by the Committee on Corporate Laws of the Section of Business Law with support of the American Bar Foundation.

It is notable that the US MBCA was drafted at a relatively early stage in the development of corporate law in the USA. Model acts like the US MBCA are beneficial because they generally produce similar results in the way the law is applied to corporations in different states. This similarity in interpreting the law helps to build a body of law that can be interpreted the same way over and over again when similar facts and circumstances present themselves. This in turn means that the law becomes well settled and less apt to produce different results on the same facts and circumstances. Where model acts exist at an early stage in the development of a body of law, this can be very beneficial. However, within the EU, many Member States already have very well-developed company laws in place and are not likely to want to adjust their existing company law in line with this EMCA. Neither does there seem to be a pressing need for Member States to adjust their existing company law.[20] There does not appear to be any empirical evidence that shareholders and other stakeholders are currently suffering as a result of existing company law provisions within the EU. As a result it is not immediately clear that the EMCA project has a great deal to offer many of the established Member States.

Another possibility is that the primary market for this project might be to offer guidance to emerging Member States in helping them to develop their regimes. While this is a laudable aim, it is not obvious that creating a model set of laws will necessarily assist such jurisdictions. It is unclear how the needs of the emerging Member States would be assessed in order to provide them with the assistance they require. Neither is it clear that merely providing a set of model laws for them to adopt in whole or part will necessarily be helpful to such countries. There is literature to the effect that legal transplants and extensive legal reforms are not sufficient for the evolution of effective legal and market institutions in transition economies because of the significant role that legal institutions (rather than law on the books) play in this context.[21]

The EMCA aims to provide both general principles regarding company law (eg equal rights for shareholders) and a model for a full text Companies Act that 'could be used as a model for legislation in the Member States in the future'.[22] In order to determine the content of these provisions the EMCA project proposes to adopt a functional approach,[23] ie to analyse company law problems regardless of whether they are classified as company law problems by national law (or as some other issue, such as insolvency law) and to adopt a comparative approach.[24] As a starting point therefore the EMCA project will start with questionnaires on each topic which will amass information regarding the way in which each Member State deals with a particular issue. This is likely to produce a wealth of interesting information which will be a valuable

[20] See Paul Krüger Andersen's paper in ch 14 of this volume, p 304 on this point.

[21] Eg, K Pistor, M Raiser, and S Gelfer, 'Law and Finance in Transition Economies' (2000) 8 Economics of Transition 325.

[22] Paul Krüger Andersen (n 20), p 307.

[23] Ibid, 307–8.

[24] Ibid, 308.

resource for comparative company lawyers. However, actually moving from this stage to determining the content of the Model Act itself is not likely to be straightforward.

While it might be possible to reach agreement in some areas (eg on the number of days' notice that should ideally be given for shareholder meetings), other issues, such as how best to resolve the owner-manager problem in a way which is potentially appropriate to all Member States, will be much trickier. This is because agency issues and not economic efficiency are still the key issues underlying many of the matters facing policy makers. It is suggested that there has been a paradigm shift in European company law in the last decade or two from a focus on creditor and shareholder protection to a focus on economic efficiency, particularly in areas such as corporate governance, financing companies, and takeovers.[25] However, if takeovers are taken as an example, economic efficiency does not in fact seem to be the key driver in developing appropriate regulations of this issue, but rather the question of how to balance the interests and roles of the directors, shareholders, and other stakeholders.[26] The variation between Member States on the agency issues they face, and how they therefore choose to deal with them, does pose a very difficult hurdle for this project—and one which did not face the US MBCA project in quite the same way.

One example provided by Paul Krüger Andersen in his chapter illustrates the difficulty. In terms of directors' duties it is relatively easy to reach consensus on some general principles, such as that directors should make well-informed decisions and should focus on the most important business questions and that directors should have a duty to act in the interest of the company. However, difficulties arise when you attempt to put some detail on these general principles, for example what the interest of the company comprises in this context, and to whom these duties are owed. This goes to the heart of what the EMCA is trying to achieve. Is it just framing the issues and providing a high level, results-orientated set of general principles, and leaving the detail to be filled in by Member States, or does it also want to provide answers to these difficult questions? If the former, it is questionable what benefit is to be gained by the EMCA. If the latter, it will surely run into the same difficulties that led to the failure of the Fifth Company Law Directive. Would the EMCA seek to prescribe a one-tier or two-tier model, for example? Many of the same problems that have beset the EU company law harmonization programme, in terms of the difficulty of reaching a consensus on the content of the provisions, and doubts about the value that harmonization might bring, surely beset this project too.

25 Paul Krüger Andersen (n 20), 309.

26 For discussion see R Kraakman and others, *The Anatomy of Corporate Law* (2nd edn, Oxford: Oxford University Press, 2009), ch 8.

IV. Conclusion

Over the past decades, since the establishment of the European Community, there has been a shift away from providing mandatory rules for what are essentially domestic company law issues within the Member States. The Commission has, rightly, turned its attention to harmonizing securities law and to those company law matters which display a strong cross-border element. The recent approach of the Commission has been to provide much lighter touch regulation, in the form of non-binding recommendations rather than directives, where it has felt the need to regulate company law at all. To the extent that harmonization is felt to be helpful, Community forms of incorporation have been developed, in particular the European company (*Societas Europaea*)[27] and the planned new European Private company,[28] although the degree of harmonization achieved by these new corporate forms is undermined by the extent to which the national laws of individual Member States is still relevant to their operation. The approach adopted by the Commission in this regard is appropriate. Member States are generally best placed to identify an appropriate system of domestic company law for themselves, given that national contexts differ so substantially. This same problem besets the EMCA project, since it is not clear why the European Model Company Act Group is in a better position than Member States to resolve these issues either. While a statement of European best practice in company law is a laudable aim, and the non-mandatory nature of this project is clearly preferable to the early Community approach to company law harmonization, it is difficult to see how a meaningful model act could be drawn up that would provide benefit to all Member States.

[27] Council Regulation 2157/2001/EC and companion Directive 2001/86/EC which supplements the Regulation as regards the involvement of employees.

[28] Proposal for a Council Regulation on the Statute for a European Private Company COM(2008) 396/3.

16

How Does the Market React to the Societas Europaea?*

Horst Eidenmüller, Andreas Engert, and Lars Hornuf

When Council Regulation (EC) No 2157/2001 on the Statute for a European Company (*Societas Europaea*—SE) became effective on 8 October 2004, it offered existing publicly traded companies, for the first time, a choice between competing company laws, namely the national law of the company's home state and the law of the supranational SE. Using an event study methodology, we analyse a unique dataset of publicly traded firms that have announced to re-incorporate under the SE Regulation. Our findings offer insights into how the market accepts the new European legal form.

I. Introduction

When it came to company law, European firms used not to have much choice. In most Member States of the European Union (EU) as well as the European Economic Area (EEA), a legal rule known as the 'real seat doctrine' restricted companies from incorporating in a jurisdiction other than that where their corporate headquarters were located. The situation began to change fundamentally when in 1999 the Court of Justice of the EU ruled that applying the real seat doctrine to companies from other EU Member States violated the freedom of establishment under the Treaty.[1] The new case law effectively permitted company founders to

* Slightly modified reprint from European Business Organization Law Review 11 (2010), with kind permission of the publisher. This article is a thoroughly revised version of an earlier working paper circulated under the title 'The Societas Europaea: Good News for European Firms' (see n 7). We are indebted to Florian Heiss, Klaus Wohlrabe, and the participants in the Empirical Economics Research Workshop at the University of Munich. We also thank Jodie Kirshner, participants in Oxford University's conference on 'Company Law and Economic Protectionism' and an anonymous referee for their thoughtful comments.

[1] See Case C-212/97 *Centros Ltd v Erhvervs- og Selskabsstyrelsen* [1999] ECR I-1459; Case C-208/00 *Überseering BV v Nordic Construction Company Baumanagement GmbH* [2002] ECR I-9919; Case C-167/01 *Kamer van Koophandel en Fabrieken voor Amsterdam v Inspire Art Ltd* [2003] ECR I-10155.

choose a company law of their liking. It did not, however, provide the same freedom of choice to *existing* companies and their shareholders. There was no simple mechanism for 're-incorporating' a firm, that is, for transforming a company established in one jurisdiction into a company governed by the law of another jurisdiction.[2] Particularly for public companies with a large and dispersed shareholder base, it was virtually impossible to switch to another, more favourable company law. For them, the first choice to become available was between the national law of their respective home state and a new corporate form created by the EU: the European Company (*Societas Europaea*—SE). The European Company owes its existence not to the national laws of the Member States but to EU law itself. Council Regulation (EC) No 2157/2001 on the Statute for a European Company (SE Regulation) entered into force on 8 October 2004. As soon as Member States had adopted the required transposition measures, public companies organized under the laws of an EEA Member State were able to re-incorporate as an SE,[3] thereby choosing to be governed by the SE Regulation.[4]

Firms can use the newly established freedom to re-incorporate under European law to escape national protectionist practices. Mandatory worker co-determination provides an example in point. Under German law, only domestic employees elect labour representatives on the supervisory board. Quite naturally, it becomes considerably more difficult to transfer production facilities or management abroad. The co-determination regime, in this sense, is a subtle form of economic protectionism. In the Porsche/Volkswagen takeover, as originally intended, Porsche attempted to avoid this problem by establishing a holding structure under an SE. Choice of corporate law can thus contribute to diminish protectionism.

Since 2004, the new corporate form has been increasingly used by European firms (see Figure 16.1). While the number of SEs is still in the hundreds, it has so far shown exponential growth. Commentators have asserted potential advantages that the SE might offer to firms and their shareholders.[5] In prior work, we have studied the validity of some of these claims by examining the motives of SE

[2] Meanwhile, re-incorporations among the EEA Member States should be possible by means of a cross-border merger into a shell company of the target jurisdiction under the Cross-Border Merger Directive 2005/56/EC. Member States were required to transpose the Directive into national law by 15 December 2007.

[3] Re-incorporation can be accomplished by way of a merger between two or more public companies from different Member States (SE Regulation Article 2(1)) or, more directly, by converting a public company into an SE; the latter method presupposes that the company has a subsidiary that has been governed by the law of another Member State for at least two years (SE Regulation Article 2(4)).

[4] It should be noted, however, that the SE company law differs only in part from that of the company's home state because the SE Regulation frequently makes reference to the national law of the Member State where the registered office is located, see SE Regulation Article 9(1)(c)(i) and (ii).

[5] See eg L Enriques, 'Silence is Golden: The European Company Statute As a Catalyst for Company Law Arbitrage' (2004) 4 J of Corporate L Studies 77; J Reichert, 'Experience with the SE in Germany' (2008) 4 Utrecht L Rev 22.

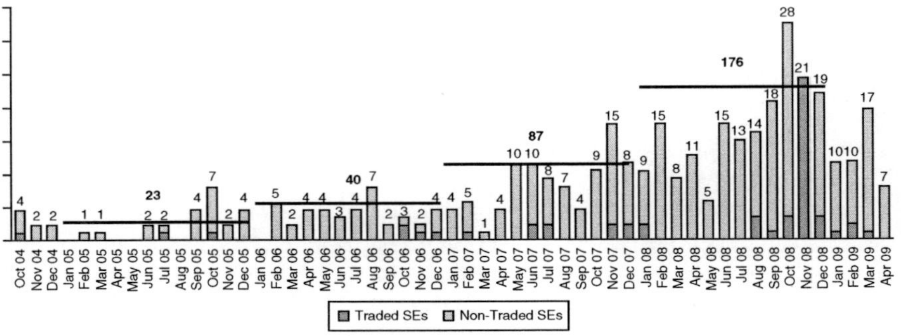

Figure 16.1 SE incorporations from October 2004 to April 2009

founders.[6] Yet we know only little about whether and to what extent the alleged benefits of the SE corporate form actually materialize. In this regard, stock prices offer a valuable opportunity. If markets are at least reasonably efficient, the stock price should reflect the quality of the corporate governance structure insofar as it has an effect on the position of shareholders in the firm.

Event studies are a proven research tool to exploit this source of information. They have been used extensively to evaluate re-incorporation decisions in the United States where firms have enjoyed free choice among the state company laws for much more than a century. With the emergence of the SE, the event study methodology can now be applied to charter competition in Europe. To the best of our knowledge, the working paper version of this article has been the first to do this.[7] Meanwhile, we have discovered eight more publicly traded firms that decided to re-incorporate as an SE.[8] Our results now build on 38 publicly traded firms, regarding which the intention to re-incorporate under the SE Regulation was publicized before 1 February 2009. Based on this new sample, our original finding of positive abnormal returns following the re-incorporation decision still holds but no longer comes out at conventional levels of significance. Besides documenting the present state of knowledge, the article comments on the methodological difficulties of an event study five years after the SE's introduction and offers an outlook for future research.

In the remainder of the paper, we briefly consider the relevant literature (Section II) before presenting our data (Section III) and the event study methodology relied on (Section IV). Section V contains the main results regarding the

[6] H Eidenmüller, A Engert, and L Hornuf, 'Incorporating Under European Law: The Societas Europaea as a Vehicle for Legal Arbitrage' (2009) 10 Eur Business Organization L Rev 1.

[7] H Eidenmüller, A Engert, and L Hornuf, *The Societas Europaea: Good News for European Firms*, Law Working Paper no 127 (European Corporate Governance Institute, 2009).

[8] We have learned of four new firms from the (almost concurrent) study by F Lamp, *The Costs of Different European Corporate Governance Legislation: Evidence from the New Legal Form—Societas Europaea*, Working Paper (2009), available at: <http://ssrn.com/abstract=1411793>.

abnormal returns on or around the re-incorporation decision. In Section VI, we discuss why we are no longer able to find significant results in our new sample. Section VII concludes.

II. Literature

We are concerned with the economic consequences of company law choice, particularly with regard to shareholders in public companies. Our research interest has important policy implications: which company law a firm elects may depend on substantive differences in legal rules between jurisdictions. Whoever is in control of the decision will opt for the jurisdiction that best serves his/her own interests. Therefore, it is not a trivial question whether firms should be free to choose the company law under which they are organized. If re-incorporating in another jurisdiction tends to harm certain stakeholders, the EU legislator may consider restricting firms' choices. For instance, additional requirements could be imposed to prevent harmful re-incorporations, such as exit rights for dissenting shareholders and creditors.[9] Learning about the consequences of company law choice can also inform policy-making at the national level. If Member States want to attract firms, or discourage firms from switching to another jurisdiction, they too should be interested in the effects of different legal rules on the various constituencies.

The USA has a long history of free company law choice. For more than a century, at least some states have actively engaged in what has come to be known as 'charter competition', ie competition among state jurisdictions to attract incorporations. Most of the time and until today, the tiny state of Delaware has dominated the market for incorporations. Its success has long been viewed with suspicion. The rival positions have originally been associated with Cary, who argued that states engaged in a 'race to the bottom',[10] and Winter, who took the opposite view that competition improved the quality of company law.[11] It is important to note that the discussion in the US focuses on the agency problem between managers and shareholders in public companies. Accordingly, the quality of Delaware's law—being the epitome of charter competition—was judged primarily by its impact on diversified shareholders. This common understanding and a growing confidence in market efficiency suggested a way to put the conflicting propositions to an empirical test: if re-incorporating in Delaware increased

[9] At present, the SE Regulation does not provide any such safeguards. If an SE is formed by way of a cross-border merger, Article 24 leaves it to the Member States to protect minority shareholders and creditors of the merging companies. Cross-Border Merger Directive Article 4(1)(b), (2) grants the Member States similar authority. To define its proper scope, the European Court of Justice should consider the impact of re-incorporations on the respective group.

[10] W Cary, 'Federalism and Corporate Law: Reflections upon Delaware' (1974) 83 Yale L J 663.

[11] R Winter, 'State Law, Shareholder Protection, and the Theory of the Corporation' (1977) 6 J of Legal Studies 251.

(decreased) stock market valuation, this would imply that charter competition benefited (hurt) shareholders.

Hyman was the first to take this cue and to conduct a (somewhat rough) analysis of stock returns of firms announcing their intention to re-incorporate in Delaware.[12] A survey by Bhagat and Romano counts a total of eight event studies on re-incorporations in Delaware alone, with none of them finding significantly negative returns on the announcement date and four documenting positive returns that are statistically significant.[13] More recently, the event study methodology has been complemented by another approach seeking to detect how the market evaluates Delaware law.[14] Daines[15] and Subramanian[16] examine whether Delaware companies generally enjoy a higher relative market valuation measured in terms of Tobin's Q[17] after controlling for a number of other factors. Again, the evidence seems to be slightly in favour of Delaware, with Daines finding a significantly higher valuation and the Subramanian analysis, using a refined methodology and a different sample, yielding no significant results.

As we pointed out in the introduction, choice of company law is a novel phenomenon in Europe. What little empirical research there is has mostly focused on the evolving use of foreign company law by start-ups since 1999.[18] For existing companies, the opportunity to opt out of the national company law under which they were established is an even more recent phenomenon. So far, re-incorporating as an SE under European Union law has been the only relevant alternative to the national company law of the firm's home jurisdiction.[19] We documented in prior work that the SE has gained some popularity among European firms.[20] In addition, we provided evidence on the reasons for choosing the SE form rather than incorporating under national company law.[21] While the German Helaba bank early on presented data on abnormal returns surrounding the decision to

[12] A Hyman, 'The Delaware Controversy—The Legal Debate' (1979) 4 Delaware J of Corporate L 368.

[13] S Bhagat and R Romano, 'Empirical Studies of Corporate Law' in S Shavell and M Polinsky (eds), *Handbook of Law and Economics* vol 2 (Elsevier: Amsterdam, 2007) 945.

[14] For a critical assessment of the event studies on Delaware law, see L Bebchuk, A Cohen, and A Ferrell, 'Does the Evidence Favor State Competition in Corporate Law?' (2002) 90 California L Rev 1775.

[15] R Daines, 'Does Delaware Law Improve Firm Value?' (2001) 62 J of Financial Economics 525.

[16] G Subramanian, 'The Disappearing Delaware Effect' (2004) 20 J of L, Economics & Organization 32.

[17] Tobin's Q is defined as the ratio of the market value and the replacement cost of the firm's (net) assets.

[18] See M Becht, C Mayer, and H Wagner, 'Where Do Firms Incorporate' (2008) 14 J of Corporate Finance 241; M Becht, L Enriques, and V Korom, 'Centros and the Cost of Branching' (2009) 9 J of Corporate L Studies 171.

[19] This will change gradually after the Cross-Border Merger Directive has been implemented in all Member States, see n 2.

[20] H Eidenmüller, A Engert, and L Hornuf, 'Die Societas Europaea: Empirische Bestand saufnahme und Entwicklungslinien einer neuen Rechtsform', (2008) 53 Die Aktiengesellschaft 721; Eidenmüller, Engert, and Hornuf (n 6).

[21] See Eidenmüller, Engert, and Hornuf (n 6).

re-incorporate as an SE,[22] our study and the almost concurrent one by Lamp are the first to analyse the stock price reaction based on a meaningful sample.[23]

III. Data

Our objective is to detect abnormal stock returns surrounding the decision of a listed firm to re-incorporate as a European Company. The first critical step is to identify the 'event day', ie the point in time when the re-incorporation decision was made public. We collected data on three events: the first public statement, by the firm itself or by a third party, on the firm's decision to re-incorporate, the shareholder meeting authorizing the re-incorporation, and finally, the registration of the SE in the company register. We relied on *Thomson Knowledge* and *LexisNexis* as primary sources to identify the event dates. For all firms, the intention to re-incorporate was publicly announced by the firm, included in the invitation to the shareholder meeting or otherwise mentioned in media reports before the respective shareholder meeting took place. We chose the earliest publication as the relevant event day in all cases because it was then that the market first learned of the re-incorporation plan. We obtained information on firms regarding which the intention to re-incorporate became known to the public by 1 February 2009,[24] even if these firms have not, or had not, yet been registered as SEs. For firms listed on German stock exchanges, we double-checked the dates against the inside information disclosure statements as recorded by the semi-official provider *Deutsche Gesellschaft für Ad-hoc-Publizität* (DGAP). Finally, we requested information from and clarified discrepancies with the investor relations departments of the respective firms.

As a result, we have generated a dataset of 42 publicly traded stock companies which announced to re-incorporate under the SE Regulation. Four firms were transformed into an SE just before or shortly after going public.[25] After dropping these four cases, our ultimate sample consists of 38 firms. We rely on daily stock prices and indices from *Thomson Reuters Datastream*. The information on the method of incorporation, a possible transfer of the registered office, the (new) board structure, the number of employees, and the industry branch of the firm were hand-collected from annual reports, special reports on the transfer of the registered office, and the website of the European Trade Union Institute.[26]

[22] S Rausch, *Die Europäische Aktiengesellschaft (SE) im Spiegel der Kapitalmärkte* (Helaba Volkswirtschaft Research, 2007).

[23] See Eidenmüller, Engert, and Hornuf (n 7) and Lamp (n 8).

[24] Since February 2009, at least two more firms (Nordex and Tipp24) announced to re-incorporate as SE. Other candidates that might soon announce to re-incorporate under the SE Regulation are M-Tech, Infineon, and EADS.

[25] The four firms are Artemis Global Capital, Equipotential, Wacker Neuson, and ENRO Energie.

[26] See 'About WP' at <http://www.worker-participation.eu> (last accessed 15 March 2010).

Table 16.1 Public companies regarding which an intention to re-incorporate as an SE was publicized by 1 February 2009

Name of company, state of registration	Reg. office transferred from	First public information of re-incorp. plan[1]	Shareholder meeting on re-incorp.	Date of registration as an SE	Board structure before re-incorp.	Board structure change	Industry[2]	Number of employees	Method of re-incorp.
Nordea, SE	-	19/06/2003	-	-	one-tier	-	K	32,000	-
Elcoteq, LU	FI	08/10/2004	27/09/2005	01/10/2005	one-tier	-	C	24,222	Conversion
Strabag Bauholding, AT	-	12/10/2004	12/10/2004	12/10/2004	two-tier	-	F	61,125	Conversion
Graphisoft, HU	LU	11/04/2005	10/05/2005	27/07/2005	one-tier	-	J	253	Conversion
Allianz, DE	-	11/09/2005	08/02/2006	13/10/2006	two-tier	-	K	177,000	Merger
Mensch und Maschine, DE	-	29/10/2005	30/05/2006	07/12/2006	two-tier	+	J	388	Conversion
Scor, FR	-	04/07/2006	24/05/2007	25/06/2007	one-tier	-	K	1,840	Conversion
Fresenius, DE	-	11/10/2006	04/12/2006	13/07/2007	two-tier	-	Q	114,000	Conversion
Surteco, DE	-	12/10/2006	31/08/2007	19/11/2007	two-tier	-	C	2,109	Conversion
HIT International Trading, DE	-	05/11/2006	24/09/2007	-	two-tier	+	G	5	Conversion
Prosafe, CY	NO	17/11/2006	22/12/2006	02/02/2007	one-tier	-	D	1,030	Conversion
BASF, DE	-	27/02/2007	26/04/2007	14/01/2008	two-tier	-	C	95,000	Conversion
Odfjell, NO	-	14/03/2007	03/05/2007	23/07/2007	one-tier	-	H	3,500	Conversion
Porsche Automobil Holding, DE	-	24/03/2007	26/06/2007	13/11/2007	two-tier	-	C	11,500	Conversion
Eurofins Scientific, FR	-	28/03/2007	02/05/2007	25/06/2007	one-tier	-	M	4,069	Conversion
Wiener Privatbank, AT	-	24/04/2007	31/05/2007	23/08/2008	two-tier	+	K	204	Conversion
Norddeutsche Affinerie, DE	-	24/06/2007	-	-	two-tier	-	C	4,700	-
I.M. Skaugen, NO	-	17/09/2007	18/10/2007	20/12/2007	one-tier	-	H	1,500	Merger
Klöckner & Co, DE	-	20/09/2007	20/06/2008	08/08/2008	two-tier	-	C	10,581	Conversion
Conwert Immobilien Invest, AT	-	22/09/2007	25/10/2007	14/12/2007	two-tier	+	L	436	Conversion
Interseroh, DE	-	26/09/2007	25/06/2008	24/09/2008	two-tier	-	D	1,729	Conversion
Catalis, NL	-	03/10/2007	03/01/2008	25/01/2008	one-tier	-	J	444	Conversion
SGL Carbon, DE	-	12/03/2008	25/04/2008	27/01/2009	two-tier	-	C	5,862	Conversion
Linde, DE	-	17/03/2008	-	-	two-tier	-	D	51,908	-

GfK, DE	-	31/03/2008	21/05/2008	04/02/2009	two-tier	-	M	10,000	Conversion
DVB Bank, DE	-	09/04/2008	11/06/2008	01/10/2008	two-tier	-	K	437	Merger
IMW Immobilien Invest, DE	-	11/04/2008	-	-	two-tier	+	L	88	Merger
Songa Offshore, NO	-	23/04/2008	26/05/2008	12/12/2008	one-tier	-	B	296	Merger
Betbull Holding, AT	UK	23/04/2008	17/11/2008	31/10/2008	one-tier	-	R	109	Conversion
Q-Cells, DE	-	14/05/2008	26/06/2008	23/10/2008	two-tier	-	C	2,300	Merger
Solon, DE	-	15/05/2008	24/06/2008	02/12/2008	two-tier	-	C	850	Merger
Fotex Holding, LU	HU	02/07/2008	04/08/2008	31/12/2008	one-tier	-	K	593	Conversion
Dexia, BE	-	03/07/2008	-	-	one-tier	-	K	35,200	-
MAN, DE	-	07/07/2008	03/04/2009	19/05/2009	two-tier	-	C	51,000	Conversion
SCA Hygiene Products, DE	-	18/11/2008	-	-	two-tier	-	C	8,000	Conversion
Colexon Energy, DE	-	27/11/2008	-	-	two-tier	-	C	93	Merger
Navigator Equity Solutions, NL	-	17/12/2008	12/02/2009	17/03/2009	two-tier	-	M	124	Conversion
Sword Group, FR	-	29/12/2008	30/01/2009	-	one-tier	-	J	2,018	-

[1] We report here the actual date of the first publication even if it was publicized after the market close or on a weekend or holiday.

[2] NACE Rev. 2 Statistical classification of economic activities in the European Community

B = Mining and quarrying
C = Manufacturing
D = Electricity, gas, steam and air conditioning supply
F = Construction
G = Wholesale and retail trade; repair of motor vehicles
H = Transportation and storage
J = Information and communication
K = Financial and insurance activities
L = Real estate activities
M = Professional, scientific and technical activities
Q = Human health and social work activities
R = Arts, entertainment and recreation

For six observations, the intention to re-incorporate was publicized on a weekend.[27] As securities were not traded over the weekend, we would not be able to calculate abnormal returns for the actual event and hence defined the event day as the following Monday. Furthermore, if we had knowledge that the information was revealed after the stock market had closed, we specified the following day as the true event day.[28]

IV. Methodology

In this section, we briefly outline our methodology for assessing the market response to the re-incorporation decision.[29] We take the following three steps: first, we predict the returns for each day of the event window that we would expect if no event had occurred. Second, we subtract the expected returns from the actual returns to obtain abnormal returns. In our third and final step, we test whether the abnormal returns are statistically different from zero.

There are different ways to calculate predicted returns.[30] The most widely used are the market model and the constant mean return model. The latter assumes that the mean return of a given security is constant over time and hence uses the security's mean return over a certain period of time as predicted return for the event window. By contrast, the market model presupposes a steady linear relationship between the returns of an individual security and the returns of the market. In so doing, the market model tends to reduce the variance in abnormal returns because it can capture the portion of the individual security's return that is related to the variation of the market return. We want to take advantage of this property and therefore adopt the market model. Since the predictive power of the market model depends primarily on how well the market index matches the market component in the returns of the security as measured by the R^2, we rely on different indices covering the various European stock markets and market segments. For instance, we choose from the DAX, MDAX, SDAX, and TecDAX for the subsample of German companies. If a firm is part of one of these indices, as is the case for Allianz and BASF with respect to the DAX, we use this index. In the remaining cases, we choose the index that best approximates the firm's size and industry. We estimate the predicted return parameters in a window from 230 to 30 days before the event date. To establish whether abnormal returns are

[27] The six firms are Allianz, Conwert Immobilien Invest, HIT International Trading, MAN, Mensch und Maschine, and Porsche Automobil Holding.

[28] This was the case for DVB Bank and Fotex Holding.

[29] For a more detailed account, see Eidenmüller, Engert, and Hornuf (n 7) 8–11.

[30] See S Brown and J Warner, 'Measuring Security Price Performance' (1980) 8 J of Financial Economics 205, 207–8; C MacKinlay, 'Event Studies in Economics and Finance', (1997) 35 J of Economic Literature 13, 17–19.

significantly different from zero we apply a t-test[31] and—as a robustness check—a non-parametric Wilcoxon rank-sum test.[32]

V. Empirical findings

Information is sometimes not disclosed to the market at one distinct point in time. It may leak out before and disseminate after the event day. Also, we are often not able to observe when exactly the decision to re-incorporate became known to the public for the first time. For instance, rumours spread some days before the official press release, or there may not even be a specific announcement by the firm that is clearly communicated to the market. To increase the chance of capturing the abnormal returns associated with a piece of information, it has become standard practice to consider event windows of more than one day around the event date and calculate cumulative abnormal returns (CARs) over those time frames.

We find both positive and negative abnormal returns for individual firms in our sample. The results for the event date (0), the day before (-1) and after (+1) the event date as well as for the time window from day -1 through day +1 are reported in the Appendix. Table 16.2 contains the *average* abnormal returns in our sample. The event date 0 yields a modest average abnormal return of 0.2 per cent, which falls far short of any significance level. The picture brightens somewhat when we cumulate average returns over broader time frames. Cumulative average abnormal returns (CAARs) rise to 0.9 per cent as we extend the event window from the event date 0 up to day +5. While these CAARs still fail to reach even the 10 per cent level of significance, the p-values decrease. This is the remnant of the result in an earlier version of this study, in which we did find significant positive CAARs for all time windows beginning on day 0 and ending at days 0 to 8. In the subsequent section we will examine why we fail to confirm this earlier finding with our larger sample. As Figure 16.2 depicts, the average stock market valuation of the firms in our sample increased around the event date. Given the behaviour of our test statistics on and after the event date, we still believe that 'something is going on'.[33]

In contrast to our results, the concurrent study by Lamp claims to find significantly positive CAARs.[34] However, this conclusion rests only on the time frames from -20 to +1 and -2 to 0. Other intermediate event windows in Lamp's analysis

[31] See S Brown and J Warner, 'Using Daily Stock Returns—The Case of Event Studies', (1985) 14 J of Financial Economics 3, 7–8.

[32] For non-parametric tests in the event study context, see MacKinlay (n 30) 32. The Wilcoxon rank sum test goes back to F Wilcoxon, 'Individual Comparisons by Ranking Methods' (1945) 1 Biometrics Bulletin 80.

[33] A difference-in-means test of the CAARs 30 days before and after the event day comes out at the 5 per cent level. This may be seen as a hint that the market valuation increases on or around the event day.

[34] Lamp (n 8).

Table 16.2 Cumulative average abnormal returns[35]

	$CAAR_t$	t-test		Wilcoxon rank-sum test	
window		t-value	p-value	z-value	p-value
−1 to +1	.006	1.09	28.1	.43	66.9
−2 to +2	.005	.77	44.4	.24	81.1
−3 to +3	.005	.60	55.5	.33	74.4
−4 to +4	.009	1.02	31.5	1.04	30.0
−5 to +5	.010	.91	37.0	1.34	18.0
−5 to −1	.000	.03	99.7	.53	79.7
−4 to −1	.002	.27	78.5	.44	65.8
−3 to −1	.000	−.07	94.7	.27	78.9
−2 to −1	−.001	−.24	81.0	−1.17	24.3
0	.002	.62	54.0	.07	94.8
0 to 1	.004	.96	34.3	.31	75.5
0 to 2	.006	1.23	22.6	.54	58.7
0 to 3	.005	1.04	30.5	.78	43.8
0 to 4	.007	1.37	17.8	1.20	23.2
0 to 5	.009	1.43	16.2	1.28	19.9

yield insignificant or significantly negative CAARs,[36] which is in line with the results reported in Table 16.2. While news of the re-incorporation decision may leak out before the information is published, we believe that at least some effect should occur on or after the event date. Unfortunately, Lamp does not report results for any post-event windows, making a direct comparison infeasible.

VI. Assessing the present findings

In the prior version of our analysis, we found significantly positive CAARs ranging from 1.2–3.0 per cent in a sample of 30 firms.[37] Why did we lose statistical significance when we moved to a larger sample consisting of 38 firms? One possible explanation, of course, is that re-incorporation does not affect market valuation and that our previous results were spurious. For instance, it may be that in our old sample other news was often disclosed simultaneously with the decision to re-incorporate. Although we cannot rule out this possibility, we do not believe that it was behind our old findings. As long as event days do not cluster, other news revealed on the event day can be positive as well as negative. Its effect should cancel out. To distort the results, concurrent information would have had to pull systematically in one direction.

35 We use robust standard errors to account for possible heteroskedasticity.
36 Lamp (n 8) 21.
37 Eidenmüller, Engert, and Hornuf (n 7) 15.

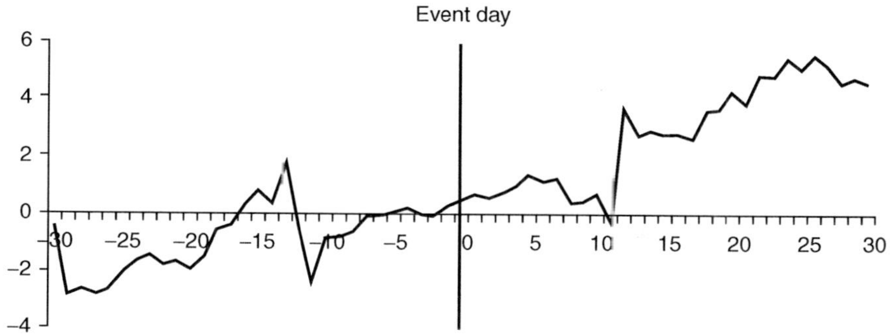

Figure 16.2 Cumulative average abnormal returns

In any event, adding eight firms to the sample (and correcting eight event days) made our CAARs drop to 0.4–0.9 per cent. While 38 observations can be a sufficiently large sample to conduct an event study, the power of the tests decreases rapidly as the magnitude of abnormal returns falls. For a sample size of 40, a Monte Carlo simulation by MacKinley reveals that the power of a t-test decreases from 100 to 35 per cent if abnormal returns fall from 2 per cent to 0.5 per cent, assuming that the standard deviation is 0.02.[38] Thus, CAARs of 1.2–3.0 per cent in our old sample of 30 firms gave the t-tests statistical power that is noticeably reduced for CAARs of 0.4–0.9 per cent in a somewhat larger sample of 38 firms.[39] The probability of committing a type II error—failing to reject a null hypothesis when it should have been rejected—rises considerably. It follows that our new result should not be read as evidence *against* the hypothesis that firms' decisions to re-incorporate as an SE leads to positive abnormal returns on average. Given the lack of statistical power, the loss of significance only implies that there is no valid evidence *in favour* of a positive stock market reaction.

The key question consequently is why CAARs in our larger sample are much smaller than in our original study. We attribute this to the greater problems in identifying the correct event day for re-incorporations of less prominent firms. It is often quite uncertain when news of the re-incorporation decision first hit the market. Even with an announcement by the firm, it was sometimes hard to determine the release date. In a number of cases, the earliest event date we could obtain was some type of media coverage, including reports from internet sources. We cannot be sure that we have actually spotted the first occurrence of the information. All of these difficulties increased as we discovered additional firms because they were typically smaller and less well known than the ones in our old sample. Missing the correct event day, and hence any abnormal returns associated with the decision to re-incorporate, is more of a risk for the new firms in our sample.

[38] MacKinlay (n 30).

[39] MacKinlay (n 30) 29.

Another, related point is that the market reaction is likely to differ depending on how the information on the possible re-incorporation is revealed. A posting on a market information website may amount to little more than a market rumour. Even a newspaper article can be misleading, as in the case of Siemens AG, where in April 2007 the weekly magazine *Euro am Sonntag* reported plans for a re-incorporation, which later turned out to be the result of a misunderstanding during an interview with a company representative. Because reports from third parties involve a greater degree of uncertainty, one would expect such information to be discounted by investors as compared to statements from the firms themselves. But even when firms announced their decision to re-incorporate as an SE, the communication was often far from clear-cut. Some announcements were only made orally during press conferences, others through a mere post on the company website, still others consisted of no more than an agenda item on the invitation to the shareholder meeting. In all these cases it may have taken a couple of days or even weeks for the information to spread. Its price impact on the event day should therefore be much weaker than its total effect over time. Again, the new firms that were added later are likely to suffer more from this problem because we had already combed news providers like Reuters and DGAP for our old sample. Our old dataset, therefore, covered most firms with a well-defined announcement that was publicized on a specific date.

VII. Concluding remarks

Our analysis of the market reactions to the decision to re-incorporate under European law has led to a sobering result: in contrast to the findings in a precursor to this article, the positive abnormal returns on and after the event day cease to be statistically significant in our new and extended sample. The available data as of 1 February 2009 do not yet allow a reliable conclusion as to whether the new European Company appeals not only to firms and their managers (which we know) but also to diversified shareholders of public companies. The loss of significance in our results can be attributed to the lower quality of the data for those firms that we learned of only after our working paper was published. Our original results may thus have been diluted by new bad data. Alternatively, they may have simply been wrong in the first place. At present, there is no way of distinguishing which of these two possibilities applies. We will have to wait until more publicly traded firms opt into the new legal form and, accordingly, provide us with a larger sample and more statistical power.

If significantly positive abnormal returns can be re-established, this would carry a general policy lesson: a broader range of company law choice for European firms may open up new opportunities and help to unlock hidden value. One implication would be that the EU should keep experimenting with enhancing company law choice as well as offering additional company types, such as the

European Private Company that is presently being contemplated.[40] A larger sample would also enable us to investigate the important follow-up question of what drives the market's appreciation—if any—of the SE. We have some evidence that avoiding or mitigating the effects of mandatory worker co-determination laws plays an important role in the choice of the SE corporate form.[41] However, firms for which this motive may have been relevant do not exhibit higher CAARs than others; rather, the converse is true.[42] If SE incorporations keep their pace, we will be able to study this and other important issues in a not-too-distant future.

Appendix

Table 16.3 Firm-level abnormal returns (based on author's own estimates)

Day (t)	–1	0	1	–1 to 1
Firm				
Allianz	–.0054	–.0292***	.0034	–.0312
Bauholding Strabag	–.0170	–.0039	.0108	–.0101
BASF	.0077	–.0028	–.0000	.0049
Betbull	.0004	–.0149	–.0014	.0016
Catalis	–.0158	–.0149	–.0188	–.0495***
Colexon Energy	.0246	.0762*	–.0376	.0632
Conwert Immobilien Invest	.0456***	–.0347***	–.0088	.0021
DVB Bank	–.0035	.0147	.0147	.0007
Elcoteq	.0139	–.0079	.0017	.0077
Dexia	.0088	.0264	.0016	.0368
Eurofins Scientific	.0057	.0021	–.0130	–.0052
Fotex Holding	.0325**	–.0320**	.0293*	.0298
Fresenius	–.0153	.0039	–.0106	–.0221
GfK	.0477**	.0076	.0173	.0726*
Graphisoft	.0022	.0027	.0131	.0179
HIT International Trading	.0026	.0010	.0027	.0063***
I.M. Skaugen	–.0181	.0061	–.0015	–.0135
IMW Immobilien	–.0030	–.0032	–.0031	–.0093***
Interseroh	.0086	–.0205	.0160	.0041
Klöckner & Co	.0152	–.0073	.0180	.0258
Linde	.0049	.0299**	.0185	.0533**
MAN	–.0058	–.0013	–.0087	–.0158**
Mensch und Maschine	–.0026	–.0008	.0011	–.0023
Navigator Equity Solutions	–.0056	–.0017	–.0079	–.0151***
Norddeutsche Affinerie	–.0086	–.0174	–.0159	–.0419***

(continued)

[40] See the recent Commission proposal for a Council Regulation on the Statute for a European Private Company, COM(2008) 396 final.

[41] Eidenmüller, Engert, and Hornuf (n 6) 26–7, 29–31.

[42] This point is elaborated for our old sample in Eidenmüller, Engert, and Hornuf (n 7) 20.

Table 16.3 (*Continued*)

Day (t)	−1	0	1	−1 to 1
Firm				
Nordea	−.0048	−.0032	−.0002	−.0082*
Odfjell	−.0010	−.0134	−.0056	−.0022
Porsche Automobil Holding	.0129	.0162	.0723***	.1015*
Prosafe	−.0254	−.0053	.0192	−.0115
Q–Cells	−.0132	.0447**	.0055	.0370
SCA Hygiene Products	.0042	−.0141	−.0374*	−.0473
Scor	.0025	.0226	.0374**	.0625**
SGL Carbon	−.0212	.0171	.0155	.0113
Solon	−.0289	.0059	−.0087	−.0316
Songa Offshore	.0035	−.0023	−.0023	−.0010
Surteco	−.0008	−.0019	−.0001	−.0028*
Sword Group	−.0006	.0170	−.0288	−.0123
Wiener Privatbank	.0000	−.0008	.0001	−.0006

*** indicate the 1 per cent, ** the 5 per cent and * the 10 per cent level of significance.

17

Empirical Notes on the Societas Europaea

Jodie A Kirshner

Eidenmüller's contribution is a thought-provoking study of the impact that the decision to reincorporate as a European Company, or 'SE', has on the share price of companies, and what benefits the SE thereby offers to corporate investors. The new legal form could develop into a tool for overcoming economic protectionism. Understanding its consequences for shareholders and other stakeholders forms an important step in assessing its significance.

I. The event study: Technique and contributions

While other articles have set out the goals of European policy makers in creating the SE and the opportunities that the SE legislation actually offers companies, Eidenmüller's research, co-authored with Engert and Hornuf, represents the first attempt to quantify how shareholders value the utilization of such opportunities. Theoretical studies, beginning with an article by Luca Enriques, have carefully documented the incentives for companies to convert to the SE and to engage in cross-border regulatory competition.[1] Empirical papers, including earlier research by Eidenmüller, Engert, and Hornuf, have suggested that companies may choose the SE over other national corporate forms, in order to mitigate the requirements of mandatory co-determination.[2] These articles have demonstrated that companies that adopt the SE form can reduce the cost of their transnational

[1] L Enriques, 'Silence is Golden: The European Company Statute as a Catalyst for Company Law Arbitrage', (2004) 4 J of Corporate L Studies 77. Further, see, eg, WG Ringe, 'The European Company Statute in the Context of Freedom of Establishment' (2007) 7 J of Corporate L Studies 185; M Bouloukos, 'The European Company (SE) as a Vehicle for Corporate Mobility within the EU: A Breakthrough in European Corporate Law' (2007) 18 Eur Business L Rev 535, 549; C D Stith, 'Federalism and Company Law: A "Race to the Bottom" in the European Community' (1991) 79 Georgetown L J 1581, 1611–12.

[2] H Eidenmüller, A Engert, and L Hornuf, 'Die Societas Europaea: Empirische Bestandsaufnahme und Entwicklungslinien einer neuen Rechtsform', (2008) 53 Die Aktiengesellschaft 721; H Eidenmüller, A Engert, and L Hornuf, 'Incorporating Under European Law: the *Societas Europaea* as a Vehicle for Legal Arbitrage' (2009) 10 Eur Business Organization L Rev 1; P L Davies, 'Workers on the Board of the European Company?' (2003) 32 Industrial L J 75.

operations. Eidenmüller's research supplements these studies by beginning to unravel the economic consequences of an SE transformation for shareholders.

The legal context in which European companies operate recently entered a period of unprecedented change. Whereas previously the real seat doctrine restricted most companies to incorporations within their home jurisdictions, case law emanating from the European Court of Justice over the last decade has liberalized the regime that start-up companies face.[3] With the inception of the SE, in 2004, established companies have been able to opt into the handful of European-level rules that the SE legislation offers, and also utilize the SE as a vehicle for re-incorporating under the laws of a different European Member State. These abilities represent a sea change in the European corporate law environment, and understanding their implications for shareholders has become crucial, as policy makers seek to regulate corporate behaviour. Eidenmüller's attempt to analyse the effects of corporate choice crucially informs the debate over how best to do this.

Eidenmüller's results remain tentative, as not much time has elapsed since the SE legislation took effect, and his study has had to navigate complications in the data surrounding its adoption. He emphasizes the limited sample size of publicly traded SE companies, which reduces the power of the event study particularly in regard to small abnormal returns, and the difficulties involved in identifying the precise date on which news of a decision to convert to the SE reaches the market. I would like to raise three additional concerns: First, the framework structure of the legislation has resulted in 30 different SE companies, one for each European Member State and one for each of the three countries in the European Economic Area. Should the event study treat every publicly traded SE company as equivalent? Second, publicly traded SEs account for only a small fraction of

[3] See, eg, Case C-212/97 *Centros Ltd v Erhvervs- og Selskabsstyrelsen* [1999] ECR I-459 (holding that Denmark could not refuse to register a branch of a company incorporated in the UK, despite the fact that its Danish owners did not intend to conduct operations there and had incorporated in the UK in order to evade Denmark's minimum capital requirements); Case C-208/00 *Überseering BV v NCC Nordic Construction Company Baumanagement GmbH* [2002] ECR I-9919 (holding that if a company incorporated in State A moves its centre of administration to State B, State B cannot deny the company the right to bring legal proceedings there); Case C-411/03 *SEVIC Systems Aktiengesellschaft v Amtsgericht Neuwied* [2005] ECR I-10805 (affirming the right of a German company to undertake commercial activities in another Member State, by way of a merger with a local company); Case C-196/04 *Cadbury Schweppes v Commissioners of the Inland Revenue* [2006] ECR I-7995 (upholding the right of Cadbury Schweppes plc, a UK company, to establish a subsidiary in Ireland so that certain profits would fall under the more favorable Irish tax regime); W H Roth, 'From Centros to Überseering: Free Movement of Companies, Private International Law, and Community Law' (2003) 52 Intl and Comparative L Q 177; K Baelz and T Baldwin, 'The End of the Real Seat Theory (Sitztheorie): The European Court of Justice Decision in Überseering of 5 November 2002 and its Impact on German and European Company Law' (2002) 3 German L J 12. But see Case C-210/06, *Cartesio Oktató és Szolgáltató BT* [2008] ECR I-9641 (denying a Hungarian company the right to remain subject to Hungarian law after moving its central headquarters to Italy).

total, registered SE companies.[4] Might it be important to explore the reasons for the disparity, in order to better place the event study in context? Third, in each Member State the number of companies eligible to transform to the SE varies widely, along with the number of companies that operate transnationally and for which conversion would be attractive. Is it therefore possible to draw accurate country-level comparisons? Eidenmüller's framing of the research question, however, elegantly bridges a significant degree of the ambiguity in the available data on SE companies by focusing on the current group of 38, active, publicly listed firms. This reduces statistical noise created by shelf companies and other unused or empty structures.[5]

Eidenmüller's study offers significant contributions to the understanding of potential trends in SE usage that may bear out for shareholders over time. In response, I would like to present four interrelated observations.

II. Observation 1: Direction of competition?

First, the research analogizes itself to similar event studies in the USA that have explored the effects of corporate re-incorporations in Delaware. The American context, however, involves purely horizontal competition among the 50 states. While the Federal government sometimes acts to legislate in the company law area, companies cannot incorporate at the federal level or adopt federal-level corporate law rules in place of state legislation. The SE, by contrast, appears to open avenues for regulatory competition in both the vertical and the horizontal directions. The SE offers a modest framework of European-level company law that converting companies substitute for national-level rules (vertical competition). The form has also introduced horizontal competition between Member States, as its references to national law combine with the ability of SE companies to re-incorporate, triggering Member States to compete to attract their business.

III. Observation 2: Interpreting co-determination results?

A key example of an opportunity for vertical competition that the SE presents relates to board structure. Companies that adopt the SE form may choose between a one-tier and a two-tier board structure. Those without co-determination, or limited co-determination, can freeze their status; those with full co-determination can renegotiate its formula, within specific parameters. While the study does not

[4] See Table 3 in ch 16.

[5] For a description of the prevalence of shelf SE companies and other empty structures, see J A Kirshner, 'An Ever Closer Union in Corporate Identity—A Transatlantic Perspective on the *Societas Europaea*' (2010) 84 St John's L Rev (forthcoming).

demonstrate positive abnormal returns to shareholders of companies that change their board structure or freeze their co-determination status, it does show positive abnormal returns to shareholders of large German companies that utilize the form to recalibrate the precise composition of workers on their boards. More information on who comprises the pool of investors in these companies would be useful in evaluating the findings. Does the population change in response to the SE conversion? If the investors are German, the returns likely reflect national attitudes toward German co-determination legislation. If the number of foreign investors increases, the data could show that foreign investors are wary of co-determination, and grow more comfortable investing in German companies as its burdens diminish. Or, do German and non-German investors actually evaluate co-determination in a similar manner? The positive abnormal returns could, of course, point to other conclusions entirely, such as a perception in the market that a company is actively re-evaluating its corporate structure or strategy.

IV. Observation 3: Effect of within-group restructurings?

Eidenmüller has tested several additional motivations for converting to the SE as potential drivers of positive abnormal returns and rejected each one. My own empirical research related to the SE, for which I conducted 75 extended interviews and spoke with representatives from half the active SE companies, revealed an additional motivation for companies that transformed: a desire to complete within-group restructurings, in order to submit to an integrated regulation at the level of the parent company.[6] Advantages of integrated regulation include the avoidance of conflicting requirements among multiple regulatory regimes and reductions in filing costs and other administrative expenses related to compliance. It would be interesting to learn whether such savings contributed to gains for shareholders. Did the leaders of these companies misjudge the valuation by the market of the structural changes that they pursued?

V. Observation 4: Additional stakeholders?

Finally, the attempt to quantify the implications of SE conversions for corporate shareholders is of great importance, and Eidenmüller and his co-researchers deserve considerable commendation for conceiving of the project. Other studies have convincingly demonstrated that the opportunity to reduce the cost of transnational operations motivates companies to adopt the SE form. The SE enables companies to complete legal cross-border mergers, re-incorporate under the more

[6] J A Kirshner, 'A Third Way: Regional Restructuring and the Societas Europaea', (2010) 7 Eur Company and Financial L Rev (forthcoming).

favourable legal regimes of other Member States, and reduce their regulatory burdens. Whether facilitating such operations conflicts with protecting the interests of other stakeholders, however, has not previously been documented. It would be useful to discover the results of an expanded study, encompassing additional stakeholders. Is the ability of workers to organize helped or harmed by the transformation of their company to an SE? What is the effect of re-organization on creditors, or on managers? Do SE companies increase systemic risk in the markets due to reduced regulation, or decrease it by adopting streamlined structures that are more easily monitored by company directors? In short, does furthering the development of the single European commercial market impose costs on other actors, and should the ability of companies to select and deselect the rules according to which they will operate be restricted?

Eidenmüller's research contributes to an extremely fruitful area of study.

Index